This book addresses the current "literacy crisis" alleged in professional journals and the popular press. Literacy is at once a contentious social and educational issue, a continuing concern of parents and teachers, and the focal point of a range of disciplinary inquiries. *Literacy, Society, and Schooling* draws together specially commissioned essays on the nature, history, and pedagogy of literacy by social historians, philosophers, literary scholars, linguists, educators, and psychologists. The editors have attempted to convey, in an accessible format, the range and diversity of the scholarly debate about literacy – theory, research, and practice. Students, teachers, and researchers will find this book an invaluable resource.

Literacy, society, and schooling

Literacy, society, and schooling

A reader

Edited by

SUZANNE DE CASTELL
Simon Fraser University

ALLAN LUKE
James Cook University of North Queensland

KIERAN EGAN
Simon Fraser University

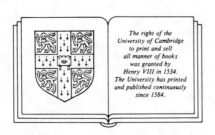

The right of the
University of Cambridge
to print and sell
all manner of books
was granted by
Henry VIII in 1534.
The University has printed
and published continuously
since 1584.

CAMBRIDGE UNIVERSITY PRESS
Cambridge
London   New York   New Rochelle
Melbourne   Sydney

Published by the Press Syndicate of the University of Cambridge
The Pitt Building, Trumpington Street, Cambridge CB2 1RP
32 East 57th Street, New York, NY 10022, USA
10 Stamford Road, Oakleigh, Melbourne 3166, Australia

First published 1986

Printed in the United States of America

Library of Congress Cataloging-in-Publication Data
Main entry under title:
Literacy, society, and schooling.
Chiefly revisions of papers originally presented at a
conference on the topic "Literacy: what is to be
done?", held at Simon Fraser University.
1. Literacy – Congresses. 2. Literacy – Social aspects
– Congresses. 3. Reading – Congresses. I. Castell, Suzanne de. II. Luke, Allan.
III. Egan, Kieran.
LC149.L514   1986   302.2   85–30948

British Library Cataloguing in Publication Data
Castell, Suzanne de
Literacy, society, and schooling : a reader
1. Literacy
I. Title
302.2   LC149

ISBN 0 521 30844 5 hard covers
ISBN 0 521 31340 6 paperback

Contents

v

Part III Matters empirical

Part IV Matters practical

Preface

It has long been assumed that literacy is a necessary part of socialization in industrial and postindustrial countries and that it is an unqualified educational good for all. Literacy, it is thought, has both utilitarian and aesthetic values: Being literate enables us to play productive roles in our own society, and it allows us contact with other minds in distant places and times. It is thus a key element in making individuals beneficial to the economy and to society in general, and in enlarging and enriching their experience and the pleasures they can derive from it. Given such assumptions, the realization that levels of literacy are in general far below what the literate elite considers desirable – or, in light of expenditures on schooling, excusable – we have the makings of a crisis. Frank Kermode, in *The Sense of An Ending*, has argued that references to "crisis" are endemic to modern consciousness; they are a means we use for ascribing significance to events. Our "literacy crisis" takes many forms, and the essays collected here address a variety of these forms. They address also the set of assumptions that led to the viewing of our current situation as one of crisis – a crisis, it is asked, for whom, and why?

The relatively new field of "literacy studies" has emerged, exploring the role of literacy in social development; the economic and cultural values of literacy; and the effects of literacy on cognitive processes. The particular concern of this collection is with the formal transmission of literacy in educational institutions. We are concerned with the varying conceptions of literacy that educators have traditionally valued, and with the research that aims to explain, justify, and prescribe educational practices intended to increase literacy. For the authors of this collection, at issue here is not just the conceptualization of literacy, but also the pressing need for an understanding of the social and educational values of literacy, and of the ways in which it can best be transmitted.

This volume serves as an introduction to the modern educational

vii

debate on literacy. As in the wider field of literacy studies, we find diverse approaches to the study of literacy in education, and we have tried to represent these in this collection. Historians, philosophers, sociologists, psychologists, literary critics, and linguists all tackle aspects of this so-called educational crisis from distinctive perspectives. We have tried to convey the range of theoretical and practical idioms in terms of which questions about literacy and education are currently being explored and discussed.

Part I is broadly concerned with the meaning of literacy. All four essays deal with contemporary definitions, functions, and values. de Castell, Luke, and MacLennan argue for a context-specific approach to definition, and suggest three frameworks within which any educational debate on literacy must be situated. The authors argue that existing operational definitions of literacy in educational settings are inadequate for addressing the range of concerns generally associated with declines in literacy. Literacy obviously entails more than grade-level attainment, but what more does it involve? Shirley Brice Heath's essay on the uses and functions of literacy attempts to answer this question empirically. Reporting on the actual contexts and uses of literacy in daily life, Heath identifies seven fundamental functions of literacy. She argues, however, that it is precisely these social uses of literacy that are neglected in school literacy instruction. She suggests that educators need to pay greater attention to the importance of out-of-school contexts in which literacy becomes "functional," and the ways in which literacy is acquired informally. In short, schools do not have a monopoly on either the definition or the transmission of "functional literacy."

Taking up the same theme from a philosophical standpoint, John Wilson writes on the properties, purposes, and promotion of literacy. Wilson discusses the conditions required for literacy to yield what he considers its proper educational values. In contrast to Heath, he focuses on that odd kind of community, the school, and argues for its potential to foster a literacy that transcends the merely functional and utilitarian. Wilson rejects the view that literacy instruction is merely the matter of transmitting the "skills" of reading and writing. His concern is with literacy as a cultural phenomenon, whose promotion is both the right and duty of teachers and schools.

We move to a somewhat unconventional explanation of why literacy matters, both to society and the individual. Literacy, in Robert Solomon's essay, is a means to the proper education of our emotions. Sharing emotions and understanding emotions are a part of what makes a culture and society cohere, and learning such emotions is one of the profoundest values of literacy. Solomon elaborates his argument in the context of a society which he views as having only minimal contact with those texts that can best provide the education of our emotions.

This first section, then, presents competing perspectives on the social and cultural value of literacy. Common to them, however, is a concern with the ongoing fragmentation of a profoundly cultural phenomenon into readily teachable and measurable skills of reading and writing.

Definitions of literacy, however – whether arrived at philosophically or empirically – are themselves constructed from within particular contexts. In Part II we are shown how the meanings ascribed to literacy – its presumed functions and purposes – are dependent on historically specific social conditions. Historian Harvey Graff puts our present concerns about declining literacy standards into a broad context which reduces much of the present-day obsession with declining standards and test scores to vacuousness. Reviewing the historical research on literacy, Graff argues that much of our conventional wisdom is based not on historical fact, but on broadly held social and cultural "myths" about literacy. His analysis of the changing social, economic, and political roles of literacy enables us to situate the present perceptions of crisis in the context of what he calls recurring "continuities" and "contradictions" in the history of literacy. In particular he emphasizes that, viewed historically, formal schooling has functioned not so much to expand literacy on a mass basis but to control literacy within given institutional contexts. Indeed, he cites cases in which literacy levels *decreased* as formal schooling assumed the functions of literacy instruction.

Suzanne de Castell and Allan Luke further this enlarging of contexts: They look in detail at the demands made on children in North American schools over the past century in the name of literacy. They show how these demands have changed in significant ways, and in charting these changes describe three major "paradigms" of literacy. Each of these different forms of literacy instruction is still with us, and claims that literacy is improving or declining are, they point out, wholly ambiguous unless they are viewed in the context of specific institutional definitions and practices.

As Graff and de Castell and Luke point out, the differential provision for types and levels of literacy has generally served purposes of social stratification and control. Michael Cole and Peg Griffin explore the circumstances that limit the acquisition of literacy in various subgroups within the population of elementary school children. They show how the basic structure of remedial reading instruction has been shaped by sociohistorical contexts, arguing that teaching reading must be viewed as an *activity* within a cultural organization of experience, and that a narrow focus on skills with little regard for their context can be pedagogically ineffective. They try to describe the conditions or contexts that can be most effective in re-mediating the acquisition of literacy, drawing on the sociohistorical school of psychology associated with Vygotsky, Luria, and Leont'ev.

Questions of pedagogy are intimately connected to questions of curriculum. Rowland Lorimer, extending this section's theme into a more public arena, provides case studies detailing the economic and administrative procedures whereby educational textbooks are authorized and prescribed for classroom use. Lorimer thereby reveals considerations of marketing and corporate expansion that determine the process of cultural selection. As a result, he states, the texts that children read often depict a "massified" or "generic" culture, suppressing any significant differences in the educational needs of children of differing class and ethnic backgrounds. Lorimer urges us to recognize that teachers of literacy, with the best of intentions, today labor under what has become a multimillion dollar technology of literacy instruction, embracing standardized reading series, standardized testing, quasi-medical schemes for diagnosis, and purportedly scientific programs for remediation.

Empirical research into the processes of literacy acquisition has been largely dominated by educational psychology. So far as teacher education is concerned, at least, educational psychology has exerted considerable influence over the theoretical bases of literacy instruction, curriculum, and evaluation. Teachers and administrators have looked to psychologically designed reading programs for curricula, to standardized tests for criteria of student excellence and pedagogical efficiency, and to a corps of university-trained "reading specialists" for diagnostic tools, methods of individualized remediation, and so forth. The work of reading researchers like E. B. Huey, E. L. Thorndike, and later Gray, Gates, Carroll, and others has had a significant impact on how teachers teach reading and the language arts.

Among educational psychologists of late, however, there has been a major reconsideration of behaviorist approaches to the study of the reading process. In recent years a widely acknowledged "paradigm shift," from behavioral to cognitive models, has occurred in the research community – a shift that, incidentally, confirms many of the fundamental insights of classical rhetoric and contemporary literary criticism. Largely through the work of W. Kintsch, T. Van Dijk, R. C. Anderson, D. Rumelhart, and a host of others, the "reading process" has undergone its first fundamental reconceptualization since Thorndike and Huey's time. Broadly speaking, the behaviorist model of reading as a perceptual, linear process has been supplanted by a cognitive, "global" model which posits an active reader participating in a constructive relationship with the text. The emerging consensus is that the text does not cause or fully constrain the reader's apprehension of meaning. Reading psychologists increasingly recognize that the reader to some degree reconstitutes the text to correspond to his or her background knowledge and social situation.

This work in the field of applied cognitive psychology has emphasized the relationship between oral and written language, and a renewed interest in questions of linguistic meaning and text comprehension. That is our concern in Part III. Drawing on the insights of linguistics, cognitive psychology, and speech act theory, David Olson's research focuses on the transition from oral to written language as a crucial step in cognitive development. His paper examines the relationship between "what is said" and "what is meant" as the linguistic expression of cognitive structures of intention and meaning. On the basis of his observation of schoolchildren, Olson concludes that literacy acquisition is contingent on the child's capacity to match his or her prior knowledge with the "possible world" within which the text can be seen as valid and meaningful.

Michael Herriman discusses the research basis for the claim that encouraging awareness of language structure and function contributes to children's becoming literate. Herriman presents an image of literacy which places it as a process crucially developed, not so much by oral mastery of language, but by the child's realization of language as an object in itself. This "metalinguistic awareness" is, Herriman argues, underutilized by teachers in attempts to advance children's literacy.

The concept of comprehension, Herriman points out, is problematic for teachers and researchers alike. Walter Kintsch offers a theoretical framework for constructing an adequate model of comprehension – adequate, that is, for the practical purposes of teaching literacy *with* comprehension. He describes a model which moves from the truism that some texts are easy for some people to understand and difficult for others, to a focus on the particular inferences that a reader must make in comprehending a text. Kintsch is thereby modeling the cognitive processes that enable the reader to make use of schematized background knowledge in making sense of narrative structures. It is only with such a cognitive model of comprehension, he argues, that we can identify students' difficulties with comprehension, select and construct readable texts, and come up with effective dialogue and questioning that will enhance rather than impede students' comprehension.

If the concept of comprehension has been unclear and ill-understood, it is to be expected that instruments for the assessment of comprehension will be equally unsatisfactory. And, we should note, it is the results of standardized reading assessments upon which much of the current debate centers. J. Jaap Tuinman reports that the array of criterion-referenced tests of comprehension are based on highly problematic theoretical assumptions. This state of affairs he attributes to "decades of cross validation of tests" and "conceptual in-breeding among researchers"; he traces current problems of definition to Thorndike's 1917 dictum that "reading is reasoning," questioning whether existing research and test instruments have come to a coherent understanding of the relationship of "recognition" and "reasoning" as coconstitutive factors in comprehension. Whether comprehension entails "reasoning" and/or "recognition" is largely contingent on the context of use: the goals and intentions of a particular reader given a particular reading task. We need to distinguish, he says, three formal categories of comprehension: the private, the communicative, and the formal.

One implication of Tuinman's discussion of current research is that the cognitive processes involved in reading comprehension are largely determined by variables of social context. How the reader perceives the task and whether the task is framed in terms of a particular goal will largely determine in what way and to what extent the reader "comprehends" the text. But what of the broader social and cultural conditions of literacy acquisition and use on a large scale? Empirical research takes a different turn with Heath's discussion of critical factors in literacy development from the standpoint of societal evolution. Reviewing literature on the social conditions and consequences of literacy, Heath sets out to identify critical elements of social organization that affect the acquisition and use of literacy. Reporting on her comparative study of literacy in two working-class communities in the southeastern United States, Heath shows how the cognitive and social processes by means of which literacy is acquired and reinforced are both culturally variable and significantly influenced by the specific institutional reinforcements for acquisition and use in particular communities. She thus draws our attention to the need for a closer analysis of the wider social contexts and conditions of literacy use which constrain and, to some extent, determine the effectiveness of literacy instruction in formal educational settings.

The concluding essays focus on matters of practical pedagogy, on the nurture of literacy. They prescribe various methods that begin, extend, and support competence with the printed word. Jana Mason's article should appeal particularly to parents and teachers of preschoolers who seek clear and practical direction in preparing children to achieve an early mastery of print. Her article is in many ways an extension of the concerns voiced by Olson and by Herriman. She makes the case for preschool literacy instruction, both formal and informal, that draws from and enhances the child's earliest experience with print. Notable is her call for discarding what she considers traditional views of "reading readiness" that relegate both child and parent to a passive role.

Sharing Mason's concern with levels of development of literacy, Kieran Egan focuses on the content of print materials, arguing for a development-sensitive selection of appropriate texts for literacy instruction. Framing his proposals in the idiom of "environments" for stimulating reading and writing, Egan distinguishes four schemata which engage the interest and understanding of children at successive stages of development. He speaks of these as "paradigms of understanding" and differentiates the mythic, romantic, philosophic, and ironic paradigms, showing how each can be embodied within "story form." The story form, he suggests, is a universal medium that serves both to engage the child's affective response and to fix the meaning of various incidents as these are differently ordered in different stages of educational development.

Surveys of reading achievement in North America (and elsewhere) have indicated a decline in advanced levels of reading comprehension and higher-order literacy skills. Walter and Ruth MacGinitie offer an explanation of this decline in higher-order abilities, contending that both curriculum and instruction in recent years have resulted in teaching students strategies for *avoiding* reading and writing. They argue that teachers must be given considerable training and practice in determining how children understand and misunderstand written texts, and in grasping the significant differences between teacher talk and textbook language. In particular, they stress the important difference between helping students understand the content of a text and helping students understand the text qua written word.

The educational debate over literacy standards has focused on reading, and indeed the selections in this volume reflect that trend. Recently, however, there has been a growing concern with falling standards and achievement in student *writing*; in particular, university English departments have attributed perceived declines to the teaching of writing in secondary schools. Richard Coe reviews the data base on writing achievement in secondary schools and universities, arguing that there is no statistical support for perceptions of decline. Coe finds major inadequacies, however, in existing models for the teaching of writing and offers a reconceptualization of writing and writing pedagogy as communicative processes. As an alternative, both Coe and Michael Flanigan propose a "process approach" to writing instruction. Flanigan, for his part, offers a model for "collaborative revision" in the classroom as an effective pedagogy. Flanigan sees peer collaboration as an effective support for young writers in the development of an authentic "persona" – a voice, he argues, that is suppressed in teacher-dominated and product-oriented instruction and evaluation.

This book grew out of a conference held at Simon Fraser University on the topic "Literacy: What is to be Done?" Most of the essays that follow began as lectures at that conference; they have been revised in light of discussions. In some cases the editors solicited papers from people who had not attended the conference but whose work we thought would well augment those essays we already had in hand; in this way we added the essays by Michael Cole and Peg Griffin, Walter Kintsch, Michael Herriman, and Shirley Brice Heath.

We tried in the conference and again in this book to bring together a statement of the best present understanding of the nature of literacy, an outline of promising research, and prescriptions for the proper nurture of literacy in children.

Part I

Matters of value

1   On defining literacy

Suzanne de Castell, Allan Luke, and David MacLennan

Any attempt to make the world intelligible begins with some form of definition. This definition, which on the most basic level involves the figure/ground distinctions of perceptual processes, has special relevance to the study of problem solving. Watzlawick, Weakland, and Fisch (1974) argue that failures to respond adequately to problems at all levels of human endeavor often stem from a failure to define or "frame" a problem properly. Only when habitual and unexamined definitions of a problem are made conscious and their inadequacies exposed can appropriate responses to the problem be substituted for inappropriate ones in a manner that allows positive change to take place.

This perspective on the dynamics of problem solving provides important guidelines for the study of literacy, a problem that has recently provoked much controversy about the effectiveness of our education programs.[1] With the Labour Canada report (1979) that 20% of our population is "functionally illiterate,"[2] and in the face of an increasingly vociferous "back to the basics" movement in education whose appeal is to the so-called literacy crisis and alleged "falling standards," claims of widespread illiteracy have become a focus of public, professional, and governmental concern. Despite massive economic investment – Canada having the highest percentage of its population engaged in full-time education of the 10 countries studied in the OECD Paris Report (1976) – approximately five million Canadians are reported to be functionally illiterate.

Just what is literacy? What are its functions and aims? It is only when we have the requisite theoretical understanding to respond to these questions that we can ascertain the extent and the significance of illiteracy and determine which methods and programs best facilitate literacy. The view of the basics movement, of course, is that as a result of "progressive" instructional methods and curricular content, public monies are increasingly being frittered away, with diminishing returns in terms of educational achievement.

3

In the face of this inflammatory situation, the primary question must be: What are the actual data on which the allegations of a literary crisis are based? Our preliminary investigations have revealed critical deficiencies in the educational literature concerned with providing data on and definitions of literacy. Concepts of literacy and thus criteria for its achievement have varied significantly over time, place, and populace (Resnick & Resnick, 1977; Graff; de Castell & Luke, in this volume), so that the charge of falling standards appears as yet impossible to substantiate. National assessments of literacy achievement in Canada have not been undertaken, and the sort of empirical research that might defensibly support a longitudinal study of literacy achievement appears not to exist. Nonetheless, all Canadian provinces and most American states have initiated major curricular reform and reintroduced mass-scale standardized testing programs.

Current responses to the so-called literacy crisis originate, we believe, in a failure to define or frame the problem appropriately. In what follows, we identify problems of methodology (operational frame), definition (conceptual frame), and application (contextual frame) that must be addressed in order to establish empirical research and instructional strategies on firm theoretical foundations.

Remarks on methodology

In response to the alleged literacy crisis, proponents of what might be termed the technocratic (educational technologists') approach have advocated the formation of strict instrumental goals with an eye toward increasing the institutional efficiency with which these kinds of goals can be reached. One of the consequences of this priority of instrumental ends via administratively efficient means has been a proliferation of research and development focused on standardized instructional systems and evaluation instruments. Because much contemporary educational decision making has been subsumed under a Tylerian view of curriculum development based on standardized evaluation and "scientific" stipulation of educational objectives (Tyler, 1949), rarely has current research been guided by anything more than a perfunctory definition of literacy. Indeed, with the overwhelming emphasis on immediate, empirically measureable objectives came a tendency to consider such short-term prespecified outcomes (behavioral objectives, skill acquisition, grade equivalency achievement) as conceptually adequate to guide research and development. The result has been an orientation among many reading researchers and curriculum developers toward behavioristic accounts of literate performance, reinforcing a view that literacy is merely the sum of a set of precisely specifiable subskills.

The early-20th-century reading experiments of Edward L. Thorndike (1917) set the tenor for subsequent modern reading and literacy research. Canadian and American reading researchers – from Peter Sandiford, Thorndike's graduate student and administrator of the first British Columbia province-wide standardized reading instruments (Putman & Weir, 1925), to modern researchers like John Bormuth (1978) – have adhered to Thorndike's postulate that the foundation of the reading process is textual stimulus and reader response. Sandiford, who from 1920 to 1940 significantly influenced standardized measurement of literacy in Canada, endorsed the suppositions of modern behaviorist psychology, and the language and concepts of stimulus and response were imported from physiology to education (Sandiford, 1926).

To be sure, such narrow definitions of performance have traditionally been opposed by those progressive educators who recognized the need for a more psychologically comprehensive and socially relevant definition of literacy. Since the advent of standardized instruction and evaluation of literacy, however, the broadly envisaged performance goals recommended by progressive educators have been reshaped by the increasing popularity of behaviorist instructional and evaluative methods. In British Columbia, for instance, as standardized evaluation and modern management methods came to dominate educational decision making, the Ministry of Education employed behaviorist formulae to derive efficient means for achieving purportedly "progressive" pedagogical ends (e.g., Conway, 1973). This was due in part to the fact that many educational progressives of the Dewey era articulated desirable performance goals in terms so lofty and universal as to be effectively devoid of meaning. Historically, the Programmes of Studies in British Columbia went from explicitly specified goals in the 1920s (British Columbia Department of Education, 1920, pp. 2-4) to educational aims framed in increasingly vague and often romanticized terms by the 1930s (British Columbia Department of Education, 1930, p.11). Contemporary progressive goals are equally vague: for instance, "to allow self-discovery and personal growth through creative language use."

It becomes apparent that despite the appearance of opposition between the technocrats and the progressives, both movements embody the same methodological defect; they both fail, whether through excessive particularity or excessive generality, to provide educationally useful criteria of literacy which take into account the subtleties and complexities of literate behavior.

The technocratic approach to education has come to dominate current educational practice and research. Following the war, local educational jurisdictions throughout North America implemented systems of standardized intelligence and literacy-related achievement tests. Providing teachers with an unprecedented volume of scientifically researched and documented guidelines for reading instruction and evaluation, provincial and state departments of education increasingly linked criteria for the attainment of educational literacy in public schools to the performance demands of standardized evaluation instruments. Such a move was related, in part, to the public's concern with getting value for its education dollar. Because the technocratic approach is concerned with the manageable transmission of readily measurable skills, a simple quantitative index of "effectiveness" can be presented as a central component of educational self-justification. However, this convenient administrative strategy – to reduce accountability to the results of mass testing – opened the public schools to facile, often unjustified criticism. Throughout the last 15 years, falling scores on standardized reading tests have repeatedly been used by critics of the educational system to substantiate claims of a modern literacy crisis (e.g., Copperman, 1978). The kinds of curriculum reform currently underway throughout the English-speaking world, focusing on behaviorally assessable "basic" knowledge and skills, represent a modern response to this alleged crisis.

Unfortunately, however, everyday life in the schools is now suffering under the influence of the well-meaning administrators and consultants whose unreflective enthusiasm for new and better instruments for assessing literacy achievement has been accompanied by a preoccupation with fine-tuning and standardizing the exacting processes whereby literacy is thought to be acquired. Empirically based technocratic literacy instruction, such as SRA, Distar, CRP, Ginn 720, and other commoditized and packaged curricula generate uniformity; and measurability of student response and teacher behavior. However, the pedagogical efficiency that is evaluated by the testing devices which accompany or complement these curricula may be more indicative of internally stipulated levels of "skill acquisition" than of the achievement of an authentic literacy in use. In other words, the quality control that these packages facilitate has come to depend on internal criteria of adequacy (the student's level of performance on a standardized test) to measure for what is assumed to be an externally sufficient ability (developing the kind of literacy which is of daily practical use). The result is a significant discrepancy between what counts as literacy in the school, and the actual kinds of literate competence useful in community and occupational activities.[3]

These exigencies of educational policy and practice reinforce the tendency of researchers to control *against* the influence of variable contextual factors (e.g., social and linguistic background, situational appropriateness, pragmatic function) and to substitute for these, internally stipulated criteria of validity and (frequently statistical) significance. In consequence, researchers are condemned to address the symptoms of an alleged literacy "crisis" without the valuable insights into the acquisition and use of literacy that a comprehensive historical, social, linguistic, and psychological overview would provide.

Remarks on definition

It is generally recognized that the demands of work and citizenship in modern society require some degree of literacy in a large proportion of the population; in a democratic society the need, elevated to the level of principle, is for a high degree of literacy for all. The classical definition of literacy as embracing the domain of high culture fails to address our situation, and we no longer accept its implicit associations linking literacy with an esoteric lettered class. Significant in such rejected definitions are notions of aesthetic appreciation and the intrinsic worth of the written word. As against classical definitions, and in recognition of changing societal requirements, new definitions of literacy have emerged. Attempts have been directed toward articulating a concept of literacy that is relevant to the more practical aspects of everyday life for society as a whole. The term currently used to express this instrumental perspective is "functional literacy."

The term "functional literacy" was coined by the United States Army during World War II to indicate "the capability to understand written instructions necessary for conducting basic military functions and tasks ... a fifth grade reading level" (Sharon, 1973, p.148). Now, some 40 years later, the term remains a principal referent in Canadian as well as American testing of vocationally related literacy (e.g., B.C.'s 1977 and 1980 Provincial Reading Assessments; Florida's 1978 Minimum Performance Standards).

While terms such as "survival literacy" and "basic literacy" have evolved from this definition, our vocabulary for dealing with literacy as an educational and vocational goal has been limited. For example, Bormuth comments that "literacy may be broadly defined as being able to respond appropriately to written language; in this sense it is one of man's most valued skills" (1977, p.125). The ostensibly neutral terms of "appropriate response" and "valued skills" belie a fundamental unwillingness to examine covertly normative principles underlying any socially sanctioned conception of literacy.

The term "functional literacy" has been used widely in Canada (Cairns, 1977; Thomas, 1976; Verner, 1964; Gravès & Kinsley, 1983). The apparent neutrality of the concept and the vagueness of its formulation, in conjunction with its pragmatic, utilitarian appeal, attract extensive approval. Unfortunately, however, there have been few attempts to define the term rigorously. The Canadian Association of Adult Education (CAAE), for example, has defined functional literacy in terms of the completion of nine years of formal schooling (Cairns, 1977); this definition remains normative for the analysis of census data in Canada.

Explaining the CAAE position, J.C. Cairns points out that "literacy and illiteracy are relative terms, and the concept of functional literacy is difficult to discuss with precision" (p. 43). He cites the definition of the 1971 UNESCO Committee for the Standardization of Educational Statistics, which states: "A person is literate when he has acquired the essential knowledge and skills which enable him to engage in all those activities in which literacy is required for effective functioning in his group or community" (p. 44). Cairns adopts the definition of the CAAE rather than that of UNESCO because he feels UNESCO's definition is expressed in terms too general to be utilized in empirical studies. At the same time, however, he cautions that the CAAE's definition of functional literacy in terms of number of years of schooling "does not take into account individual differences in literacy needs or use of literacy skills; nor does it consider the informal and non-informal learning acquired throughout life" (p. 44).

American researchers Kirsch and Guthrie (1977) stress that no useful measurement of literacy achievement can take place before the concept is formulated adequately. Thus, they distinguish literacy in its most general sense, which includes traditional, aesthetically oriented literacy, from functional literacy. Functional literacy, they suggest, "refers to how well a person can read materials associated with 'survival activities'" (p. 505). They further distinguish functional literacy from "functional competence" (which refers to the ability to perform adequately in a given situation). The error of conflating the two is evidenced in Sticht's 1975 study on Job Reading Task Tests (JRTT): He found "low correlations between reading scores and practice on-the-job performance tasks, and essentially no relationship between these measures and supervisors' ratings of individuals performing at a given job" (p. 504). Kirsch and Guthrie conclude that in questions of functional literacy it is necessary to specify precisely what levels and kind of reading abilities one wishes to measure.

Because of the limitations of existing research, this task of identifying the precise components of different literacy competences must be high on our list of priorities. But it has become increasingly clear that basing a definition of literacy on ever more accurate evaluation techniques is not enough. There also exists a need to rethink the problem in general terms – for questions of survival and performance are always contingent on contextual and historical factors.

Consider, for example, the three specific goals of Kirsch and Guthrie's approach to the conceptualization of functional literacy: to specify minimal reading performance levels for various jobs; to measure precisely the performance of individuals; and to make inferences from an individual's performance to his competence to fulfill the reading requirements of a given job. Kirsch and Guthrie also mention that concepts of functional literacy should be formulated in a manner that precisely specifies different kinds of job-related reading abilities – for instance, the different kinds of reading competences required of a cook and an editor. As a general rationale for formulating the concept of functional literacy in this manner, they refer to the need for a concept "that includes sound measurement principles and a set of purposes useful to decision makers in education" (p. 505).

We do not dispute the fact that measurement principles that may be very attractive to decision makers can be attained through a systematic carving up of the universe of literate behavior into ever more specific kinds of competences. But we do question whether such a stance will provide a theoretical understanding of and practical strategies for the development of literacy. Absent, for example, from the kind of conceptual framework proposed by Kirsch and Guthrie is a sensitivity to the underlying principles that enable an individual to select, modify, and apply an existing reading competence to a new reading task. Such metatextual "second-order competences" are necessary to enable individuals to apply the information-processing strategies used in reading to other information coding and decoding processes, such as writing, speaking, and nonverbal communication.

Also absent from this kind of perspective is the significance of the social and pragmatic contexts within which linguistic interaction occurs. The contextual nature of linguistic interaction influences both the acquisition and use of literacy. We are thinking first of the social conditions for the acquisition of various competences – such as the relationship between the learner's cultural background and the specific context of the school environment – and further, of the kinds of second-order competence that enable the individual to achieve desired goals in contexts other than those of the school.

Though little attention has been paid to this contextual aspect of literate behavior, three important sources of information suggest themselves. First, the ability to exercise competence consistently with the variables of social context has been identified by Pierre Bourdieu (1977) as "expanded competence":

> Language is a praxis: it is made for saying, i.e. for use in strategies which are invested with all possible functions and not only communication functions. It is made to be spoken appropriately. Chomsky's notion of competence is an abstraction that does not include the competence that enables adequate use of competence (when to speak, keep silent, speak in this or that style, etc.). What is problematic is not the possibility of producing an infinite number of grammatically coherent sentences, but the possibility of using an infinite number of sentences in an infinite number of situations, coherently and pertinently. [p. 646]

Bourdieu's notion of "expanded competence" may be difficult to operationalize. But it does lend itself to the kind of ethnographic research into language acquisition and use which literacy studies in modern industrialized societies have largely neglected.

The second source is historical. Classical studies of discourse, for example, speak not only of explicit rules of grammar (which correspond to notions of precisely defined skills), but also of when and how to apply rules (as in the notions of "appropriateness" that are examined by contemporary sociolinguists and rhetoricians).[4] The richness and complexity of classical rhetoric, long overlooked by educational researchers, offers much that may be helpful in specifying the subtle but distinct functions and forms of literate behavior.

A third source of insight on the importance of context in literacy comes from communications theory. Watzlawick, Beavin, and Jackson (1967), for example, provide a conceptual framework that includes much more than just the grammatical and semantic components of human speech. Drawing from a variety of sources (information theory, cybernetics, systems theory), they attempt to elucidate the pragmatic aspects of human speech and linguistic behavior in general – that is, the uses, functions, and effects of human literate behavior as these vary across contexts. The central guideline of this research is instructive: "A phenomenon remains unexplainable as long as the range of observation is not wide enough to include the context in which the phenomenon occurs" (p. 21). Educational research into the development and use of reading and writing still has much to learn from an exploration of both traditional and modern work of this kind. Our understanding of the possibilities and limitations of transcontextual skill application, as well as our understanding of the kind of literacy transmitted and tested in schools and its relationship to actual performance outside the classroom, could be substantially advanced by casting our nets beyond the theoretically impoverished foundations of most empirical studies of literacy achievement.

Application

Thus, if our concern is the remediation of functional illiteracy in the Canadian context, it is clear that any useful definition of this problem must consider factors specific to the Canadian context, among them level of economic development, social and technological change, schooling policy and practice, geographic and social mobility, cultural character, and form of political organization. Tuinman's (1978) thesis that literacy is necessarily "situational" means that operational definitions of functional literacy and criteria for its assessment are always culturally and historically specific. We cannot, then, merely adopt and apply concepts and criteria of functional literacy developed elsewhere and expect to advance national educational policy and practice. Yet the (minimal) theoretical research on functional literacy which informs Canadian educational research has been imported from U.S. and British sources.

Kirsch and Guthrie's definition of functional literacy, representative of the current state of the art, appears inadequate for Canadian educational research on at least two counts. First, it is too specific. "Functional literacy" is defined exclusively in terms of the literacy demands of one's particular occupation. The implicit conservatism of a definition that fails to consider or provide for social and economic mobility is both inconsistent with and inadequate for the promotion of the particular egalitarian political, social, and economic ideals of Canadian society. Second, with respect specifically to the responsibilities and obligations of members of a democratic community, it is too narrow. Participation in the political process entails not only sufficient functional literacy to operate effectively *within* existing social and economic systems, but also the ability to make "second-order" rational and informed judgments concerning the desirability of social rule systems themselves. "Functional literacy" has, therefore, to embrace not merely knowledge of rules and the ability to follow rules, but also the capacity to think, reason, and judge *beyond* existing social rules. For where the citizen has rights and duties with respect to social, political, and economic organization, the intelligent exercise of such rights and duties necessarily presupposes competency above and

beyond the ability to carry out limited interpersonal and specific occupational responsibilities.

In the particular context of Canadian education, it is evident that these
issues are of pressing concern. Studies of the structure of Canadian industry have revealed what might be termed a branch plant economy (Clement, 1977; Marchak, 1978): an economy dominated by large non-
Canadian corporations. Correspondingly, sociologists and psychologists
have argued that forms of a particularly Canadian identity may be
molded along lines of a passive branch-plant mentality (Friedenberg,
1978; Travis, 1979; Wilden, 1980). In the preface to their anthology,
Socialization and Values in Canadian Society, Zureik and Pike (1975) have
remarked that students of Canadian social structure are "frequently confronted with a vision of the maintenance of consensus through coercion.
By coercion we mean the utilization by dominant groups of manipulative
socialization in order to foster internalization of particular perceptions of
social reality to the exclusion of alternative viewpoints" (p. x). Surely then,
we ought to be particularly wary in Canada of importing and uncritically
applying conceptions of literacy that legitimate cognitive, social, and
political passivity and acquiescence by construing "functional literacy" in
terms of narrowly defined occupational or consumer "skills." As Freire
and others involved in mass literacy campaigns insist, the intent of
literacy instruction must not be the creation of a readily manipulable populace, characterized by passive acceptance of information and prescribed
behavior. Yet currently conventional definitions of functional literacy fail
to lead us beyond that level of literacy competence.

A contextually adequate definition of functional literacy, therefore,
must consider not only the limited literacy demands of interpersonal and
vocational practice, but also the broader literacy needs for social and
political practice, as determined by the demands of any truly participatory
democracy.

Functional literacy: the research agenda

The intent of these preliminary critical remarks has been to indicate areas
of deficiency in existing definitions of functional literacy as these preclude
any significant use being made of empirical data on literacy achievement,
and any significant improvements effected in literacy instruction. A correlative task has been to identify specific areas of theoretical concern in
proposing a practicable redefinition of the concept. Our intent then must
be to formulate a conception of functional literacy that (a) makes explicit
the normative presupposition of a concept of functional literacy situated

within particular sociocultural contexts; (b) entails a recognition and critique of the particular requirements of those contexts; (c) when implemented, enables acquisition of the transcontextual literate competence required for social and occupational mobility; and (d) accommodates a linguistic theory that includes pragmatic as well as semantic and syntactic elements.

Notes

1. In this essay we rely largely on Canadian data and illustrations because this is the context within which we ourselves are working; an earlier version of the paper appeared in the *Canadian Journal of Education, 6*(3), 1981 (reprinted by permission). The analysis proposed here, however, accommodates parallel data from American and British contexts. See for example, Richard Coe's and Walter and Ruth MacGinitie's contributions to this volume.
2. This figure is matched in the 1981 census, which reports 20% of Canadian adults as having less than nine years of schooling.
3. Heath's ethnographic studies (1983, chap. 2) of social uses and functions of literacy suggest that much in the stated curriculum for the teaching of reading and writing remains largely irrelevant to what occurs in "contexts of use." For a further comparison of "contexts of transmission and acquisition" with "contexts of use," see de Castell and Luke (1986).
4. Much of the renaissance in writing pedagogy has its basis in a rediscovery of the principles of classical rhetoric. Coe (see this volume), for example, sees writing as a rhetorical, thereby "communicative" process. This kind of conceptualization enables a profound rethinking of traditional teaching and evaluation.

References

Bernstein, B. (1971). *Class, codes and control* (3 vols.). London: Routledge and Kegan Paul.
Bourdieu, P. (1977). The economics of linguistic exchange. *Social Science Information, 6,* 645–668.
Bormuth, J. (1978). Value and volume of literacy. *Visible Language, 7,* 118–161.
British Columbia Department of Education (1920). *Courses of studies for the public, high, and normal schools of British Columbia.* Victoria, B.C.: King's Printer.
British Columbia Department of Education (1930). *Programme of studies for the high and technical schools of British Columbia.* Victoria, B.C.: King's Printer.
Cairns, J. C. (1977). Adult functional literacy in Canada. *Convergence, 10,* 43–52.
Clement, W. (1977). *Continental corporate power: Economic elite linkages between Canada and the U.S.* Toronto: McClelland & Stewart.
Coe, R. (1981). *Form and content: An advance rhetoric.* Toronto: John Wiley and Co.
Conway, C. B. (1973, June). *Report of a provincial survey of language arts* (Research and Standards Branch Tech. Rep.). Victoria: Ministry of Education.
Copperman, P. (1978). *The literacy hoax.* New York: William Morrow & Co.
de Castell, S. C., & Freeman, H. (1978). Education as a socio-practical field: The theory/practice question reformulated. *Journal of Philosophy of Education, 12,* 13–28.
de Castell, S. C., & Luke, A. (1986). Literacy instruction: Technology and technique. *American Journal of Education,* forthcoming.

Freire, P. (1973). *Pedagogy of the oppressed*. New York: Seabury Press.

Friedenberg, E. Z. (1978). Education for passivity in a branch plant society. In R. W. Nelson & D. Nock (Eds.), *Reading, writing, and riches: Education and the socio-economic order in North America*. Toronto: Between the Lines Press.

Graff, H. F. (Ed.) (1982). *Literacy and social development in the West: A reader*. Cambridge: Cambridge University Press.

Graves, F., & Kinsley, B. (1983). Functional and elective illiteracy in Canada. *Canadian Journal of Education, 8*(4), 315–331.

Heath, S. B. (1983). *Ways with words: Language, life, and work in communities and classrooms*. Cambridge: Cambridge University Press.

Kirsch, I., & Guthrie, J. T. (1977). The concept and measurement of functional literacy. *Reading Research Quarterly, 4*, 484–507.

Labour Canada (1979). *Education and working Canadians*. Ottawa: Ministry of Labour.

OECD (1976). *Review of national policies of education: Canada*. Paris: OECD.

Marchak, P. (1978). *In whose interests*. Toronto: McClelland & Stewart.

Putman, J. H., & Weir, G. M. (1925). *Survey of the school system*. Victoria, B. C.: King's Printer.

Resnick, D., & Resnick, L. (1977). The nature of literacy: An historical exploration. *Harvard Educational Review, 47*, 370–386.

Sandiford, P. (1926). Contributions to the laws of learning. In D. A. Lawr & R. Gidney (Eds.), *Educating Canadians: A documentary history of Canadian education*. Toronto: Van Nostrand Reinhold, 1973. (Reprinted from *Teachers' College Record, 27*.)

Sharon, A. T. (1973). What do adults read? *Reading Research Quarterly, 9*, 148–169.

Sticht, T. G. (Ed.). (1975). *Reading for working: A functional literacy anthology*. Alexandria, Va.: Human Resources Research Organization.

Thomas, A. (1976). *Adult basic education and literacy activities in Canada, 1975–76*. Toronto: World Literacy of Canada.

Thorndike, E. L. (1917). Reading as reasoning: A study of mistakes in paragraph reading. *Journal of Educational Psychology, 8*, 323–332.

Thorndyke, P. (1977). Cognitive structures in comprehension and memory of narrative discourse. *Cognitive Psychology, 9*, 77–110.

Travis, L. D. (1979). Hinterland schooling and branch-plant psychology: Educational psychology in Canada today. *Canadian Journal of Education, 4*(4), 24–42.

Tuinman, J. J. (1978). Literacy of the future. *The Journal, 19*(1), 13–15.

Tyler, R. W. (1949). *Basic principles of curriculum and instruction*. Chicago: University of Chicago Press.

Verner, C. (1964). Adult illiteracy in B.C. *Journal of the Faculty of Education of the University of British Columbia, 10*, 99–109.

Watzlawick, P., Beavin, J. H., & Jackson, D. D. (1967). *Pragmatics of human communication: A study of interactional patterns, anthologies, and paradoxes*. New York: Norton.

Watzlawick, P., Weakland, J. H., & Fisch, R. (1974). *Change: Principles of problem formation and problem resolution*. New York: Norton.

Wilden, A. (1980). *The imaginary Canadian*. Vancouver, B.C.: Pulp Press.

Zureik, E., & Pike, R. M. (Eds.). (1975). *Socialization and values in Canadian society* (2 vols.). Toronto: McClelland & Stewart.

2 The functions and uses of literacy

Shirley Brice Heath

Since the initiation of the public school system in the United States, national leaders have periodically issued statements of a "literacy crisis" and have launched reform programs designed to eliminate illiteracy and to ensure that the schools produce functional literates. But the concept of literacy covers a multiplicity of meanings, and definitions of literacy carry implicit but generally unrecognized views of its functions (what literacy can do for individuals) and its uses (what individuals can do with literacy skills).

Current definitions of literacy held by policy-making groups are widely varied, and they differ markedly in the relationship they bear to the purposes and goals of reading and writing in the lives of individuals. Public schools (and the widespread minimum competency movement) see literacy as an individual accomplishment measured by psychometric scales of reading ability. A survey conducted for the National Reading Council defined literacy as "the ability to respond to practical tasks of daily life" (Harris & Associates, 1970). A compilation of surveys of employer attitudes toward the preparation of youth for work defined literacy as the integration of mathematical and linguistic skills necessary for filling out a job application, filing, conducting routine correspondence, monitoring inventories, and expressing oneself clearly in writing (Research for Better Schools, 1978). The Adult Performance Level Project defined the standard for literacy as the performance of people at given conjoint levels of low income, low job status, and few years of schooling (Northcutt, 1975). The National Census defines a literate individual as one who has completed six or more grades of school and has the "ability to read and write a simple message in any language." In the past decade, however, those studying literacy in societies throughout the world have challenged these definitions, primarily on the basis that the generally assumed functions and uses of literacy which underlie them do not correspond to the social

15

meanings of reading and writing across either time periods, cultures, or contexts of use.

A number of historians (Davis, 1975; Eisenstein, 1979; and see Graff, this volume) have asked of social groups in certain places and times: What does it matter whether or not a person can read? What social consequences does literacy have for the group? What responses have societies made to the introduction of writing systems or print? Some unexpected patterns have emerged from the attempts to answer these questions. For example, knowledge of the possibility of written language (or the possibilities of print) does not in itself ensure that writing systems will be adopted. Furthermore, even in societies in which writing systems and/or print have been accepted, the uses of literacy have often been very much circumscribed, because only a small elite or particular craftsmen have had access to literacy. Finally, a restricted literate class can increase the range of functions of written language without increasing the size of the literate population.

In a study of the impact of printing on the unlettered masses of 17th-century France, Davis (1975) found a major paradox in the functions of literacy. Printing destroyed traditional monopolies on knowledge, and widely disseminated both information and works of imagination. But printing also made possible new kinds of control over the people. Until the appearance of the printing press, oral culture and popular, community-based social organizations seemed strong enough to resist standardization and thrusts for uniformity; but when the printing press appeared, people began to measure themselves against a widespread norm and to doubt their own worth. In today's American society, similar reasons are behind the desire of some American Indians who do not want their languages written (Walker, 1981), and of some religious groups, such as the Amish, who do not wish their children to move beyond certain levels of schooling.

The frequent assertion that literacy leads to improved economic status and participation in benevolent causes has been challenged by a number of studies. In 17th- and 18th-century New England, according to Lockridge (1974), distinction in occupational status was neither created nor reinforced by substantial differences in literacy. In addition, rising literacy in the general population erased former associations between wealth and literacy for individuals. Among the working classes of 19th-century England and Scotland, reading was learned in many situations outside formal education, and its purposes and consequences were varied (Webb, 1950, 1954). Economic laws of supply and demand with respect to job opportunities in 18th-century England dictated levels of literacy and secondary education that were set as ideals, but there was no direct relationship between skills achieved in secondary education and job success.

The equating of reading evaluation in the United States with an emphasis on oral reading style and correct responses to standardized performance seems to stem from late-19th-century teaching rationales (de Castell & Luke, this volume). Reading for comprehension and transferring the ability to the outside world were less readily assessed and were discounted in the general society. Soltow and Stevens (1977, 1981) point out the extent to which these standardized measures were lauded by parents of the late 19th century and suggest that such performance convinced parents that their children would be able to achieve occupational mobility. Whether or not the schools taught children to read at skill levels that made a difference in their chances for upward occupational mobility is not at all clear. Nevertheless, if students acquired the moral values, social norms, and general rational and cultural behaviors of literate citizens (even though their skills of comprehension were questionable), occupational mobility often resulted. These and other studies of the effects of printing and learning to read and write throw considerable doubt on time-honored beliefs regarding the consequences of literacy and formal schooling for individual social mobility.

Traditionally, the functions and uses of literacy have been examined at the level of the society. Kroeber (1948) traced the invention and diffusion of writing systems. Goody and Watt (1968) and Havelock (1963, 1976) suggested that the advent of alphabetic writing systems and the spread of literacy changed forms of social and individual memory of past events and useful information. Others (Goody, 1977; Olson, 1975, 1977) have proposed that societies also developed certain logical operations that led them to be able to classify and categorize the world about them in new ways.

However, studies of single societies (Goody, Cole, & Scribner, 1977; Scribner & Cole, 1981) or communities (Scollon & Scollon, 1979; Heath, 1983) have found that the functions of literacy suggested by Goody, Havelock, and others cannot be universally attributed, and that the methods of learning literacy skills, as well as their consequences, vary considerably across societies. For example, literacy may decline if it becomes nonfunctional in a society, or if the goals it has been thought to accomplish are not achieved. For example, in cargo cults, the millenarian movements that grew up in New Guinea and Melanesia at various times during the 20th century, members were initially anxious to have their young and old learn to read for the economic and religious benefits promised by missionaries. However, when the population recognized that they remained poor despite their sons' learning to read and write, they withdrew from literacy and maintained it only for select purposes in religious ceremonies (Meggitt, 1968).

Societies also differ with respect to the perceived benefits and functions of literacy. The Tuareg society in the Sahara has a centuries-old writing system, the *tifinagh*, which is adequate for representing their Berber language, and many members of the group are literate in the script. However, they use it only rarely – for graffiti on rocks in the desert, for certain kinds of talismans, and for brief love notes (Cohen, 1958). Among some American Indian groups who have developed and maintained a native literacy, it serves a variety of purposes: the practice of religion, the conduct of business, the recording of native medical practices, correspondence with relatives in distant places. In some cases, the proportion of literates within the group has actually decreased in the 20th century, although literacy is still highly valued even among those who do not read. Take the Cherokee as a good example. The Cherokee do not expect all members of their community to become literate; instead, certain individuals who play specific roles become literate, so that virtually every household has access to someone who can read and write (Walker, 1981). They do not insist that literacy be learned formally among the young; nor do they withhold literacy instruction from those who did not acquire literacy while they were young, or regard these people as failures. Those who become literate as adults do so by watching literates read and write and practicing by themselves for some time before trying it out before others. There is a long period of pre-learning, integrated into natural routines of home, church, and extended family, before one is expected to exercise the skill. Attempts to use formal educational methods at home may be viewed as coercive, and children do not learn from them. Later, however, as adults, they may remember and reactivate these early experiences.

Literacy without schooling was also studied by Scribner and Cole (1981) among the Vai of northwestern Liberia. Their work suggested that literacy is a culturally organized system of skills and values learned in specific settings. Moreover, generalizations about oral and literate modes of thought and their causative links to abilities in hypothetical reasoning, abstract thinking, or logical organization of ideas have not been borne out in cross-cultural studies of literacy. Literacy acquisition is often a function of society-specific tasks, which are sometimes far removed from those of formal schooling, and are not conceived of as resulting from effort expended by "teacher" and "learners." Indeed, the historically conditioned instructional strategies and social values and norms for literacy may not be related to those promoted today by some sectors of the population (see Coe; de Castell & Luke, this volume). Thus, much more must be known about the psychological and social consequences of both illiteracy and nonschooled literacy before pushing ahead with goals such as UNESCO's mission to eradicate illiteracy in the world before the year 2000 (San Francisco Chronicle, October 24, 1979).

Since reading varies in its functions and uses across history and cultures, it must also vary across contexts of use as defined by particular communities. For example, the highly publicized "Black English" court decision in the case of *Martin Luther King, Jr., Elementary School Children* v. *Ann Arbor School District Board* held that the school should provide appropriate models for students to follow in developing images of themselves as readers. The school's responsibility was seen as particularly important for those students whose parents and/or siblings did not read at home and did not view reading as having a positive effect on their lives. The expert witnesses and the court decision assumed here that children who were not successful readers by school standards were not exposed to types of reading and writing at home that could be transferred to their school experience (Labov, 1982). However, we know very little about the actual types, functions, or uses of literacy in the homes of these children, or in "constant television" homes, or, in general, in the homes of unskilled or semiskilled workers.

Numerous surveys have characterized the kinds of reading promoted in the homes of successful, academically oriented families and industrialized, urbanized populations (e.g., Hall & Carlton, 1977; Staiger, 1979; U.S. National Commission for UNESCO, 1978), but even these surveys provide only a limited picture of reading habits. In particular we expect surveys by questionnaire to tell us little about the actual reading and writing of lower-class or working-class families. Recently, ethnographers of education (Szwed, 1981; Spindler, 1982; Heath, 1983, 1984; Taylor, 1983) have suggested that participation in and observation of the lives of social groups can provide a more comprehensive picture of the uses of literacy and its component skills.

To find out who reads and writes, for what purposes, and in what circumstances, we observed reading and writing behavior in one community between 1969 and 1978 (Heath, 1983). We participated in the ongoing daily life of an all-black working-class community in the Southeastern United States and recorded the literacy behaviors of approximately 90 individuals in community, work, school, and home settings. Most households in the community had one or more members between the ages of 21 and 45 who worked at jobs providing salaries equal to or above those of beginning public school teachers in the area. Jobs were semiskilled, many residents being employed in the local textile mill, and many of the residents gardened, repaired homes, or worked on cars in their spare time.

Of particular importance in the study of reading and writing behaviors in the context of community life were questions related to how the adults participated in preschoolers' experience with print. Preschoolers were able to read many types of information available in their environment. Yet the adults did not read to the children, or consciously model or demonstrate reading and writing behaviors for them. Instead, the adults let the children find their own reading and writing tasks (defined, e.g., in terms of the trade names of bicycles or cars, house numbers and license plates, and the content of television messages), and they made their instructions fit the requirements of the tasks. Sometimes they helped with hard items, corrected errors of fact, and pointed out features of certain sounds (especially rhyming sounds). But in general, they kept their distance and let the children do what they could within their capabilities. Thus the children read to learn information they judged necessary in their lives. They watched others reading and writing for a variety of purposes, cooperated and participated in the process with older children and adults, and finally read, and often wrote, independently at very young ages.

Adults did not provide reading tasks unless children either wanted or needed to know something; nor did adults encourage older children to provide younger ones with graded tasks. While fulfilling responsibilities shared with older siblings, the children found reading tasks in their environment (reading the names of railroad lines on passing trains, reciting ads for taxi companies, noting changing prices of items in the store, etc.). On occasion, older siblings tried to provide school-like tasks for younger brothers and sisters, but these were rejected except when put in special frameworks, such as games. Thus the children did not necessarily require verbal reinforcement from parents or older siblings, and they needed neither teaching by overt demonstration nor talk about the reading process.

In effect, these children achieved some mastery of environmental print without being taught. They learned names of cereals or the meanings of railroad names, not because these were pointed out each time or because their letters were sounded out, but because of their juxtaposition with a spoken word or an action that carried meaning. The relevant context or set of circumstances of the material was often recalled by the children when the word later appeared in a different context. For these children, comprehension was the context rather than the outcome of learning to read.

They acquired the skill without formal instruction or reading-readiness activities generally used by school-oriented parents with their pre-schoolers (cf. Harste, Woodward, & Burke, 1984).

These children's methods of dealing with print were different from those encouraged by parents whose reading goals for their children were oriented to school success (cf. Heath, 1982). Similarly, adults in this community used literacy in ways that differed from those of academically motivated parents. Among these adults, reading was social activity, involving more than the individual reader. Solitary reading, in fact, was often interpreted as an indication that one had not succeeded socially; thus, women who read "romance" magazines or men who read "girlie" magazines were charged with having to read to meet social needs they could not handle in real life. Written materials were often used in connection with oral explanation, narratives, and jokes about what the written materials meant or did not mean. The authority of the materials was established through social negotiation by the readers (see Heath, this volume).

From the uses of reading in the community, we could describe seven uses of literacy:

1. Instrumental. Literacy provided information about practical problems of daily life (price tags, checks, bills, advertisements, street signs, traffic signs, house numbers).
2. Social interactional. Literacy provided information pertinent to social relationships (greeting cards, cartoons, bumper stickers, posters, letters, recipes).
3. News related. Literacy provided information about third parties or distant events (newspaper items, political flyers, messages from local city offices about incidents of vandalism, etc.).
4. Memory-supportive. Literacy served as a memory aid (messages written on calendars and in address and telephone books; inoculation records).
5. Substitutes for oral messages. Literacy was used when direct oral communication was not possible or would prove embarrassing (messages left by parent for child coming home after parent left for work, notes explaining tardiness to school).
6. Provision of permanent record. Literacy was used when legal records were necessary or required by other institutions (birth certificates, loan notes, tax forms).
7. Confirmation. Literacy provided support for attitudes or ideas already held, as in settling disagreements or for one's own reassurance (advertising brochures on cars, directions for putting items together, the Bible).

It is significant that these types do not include those uses – critical, aesthetic, organizational, and recreational (e.g., Staiger, 1979) – usually highlighted in school-oriented discussions of literacy uses.

Within each of these community uses, reading was highly contextualized. For example, a price tag on a roll of plastic tape might contain ten separate pieces of information, but community residents would scan the tag for the critical cue – the decimal point – and then read the price of the item. Similarly, only specific parts of soup cans, detergent boxes, brochures on automobiles, etc., were read, not because the individuals were incapable of reading the other information, but because it served no evident purpose for them to do so. They searched each item for only those messages they judged meaningful. For example, boys who modified their bicycles for sometimes unique effects selectively read portions of brochures on bicycles and instructions for using tool sets.

Reading of the local paper was selective and generally followed the sequence of obituaries first, followed by employment listings, ads for grocery and department store sales, captions beneath pictures, and headlines. Because the television was on most of the time in these households, family members tended to hear national news stories repeated frequently and to learn of news about the metropolitan center from which the local television shows originated. News from their small town, however, rarely was reported on these programs. Individuals therefore found it useful to read local news stories, but not national or metropolitan stories.

On the job, community members were not often called on to read. The employment officer wrote in the necessary information. Employees were "walked through" their new tasks with oral explanations. Bulletin boards contained general information about insurance, new regulations related to production, and occasionally news clippings from local newspapers – especially features about textile mill employees. However, most of the information on these boards was given to employees in oral as well as in written form, and employees thus did not find it necessary to read the bulletin board notices. Briefings were held with foremen and other senior employees when new production strategies were initiated; these employees, in turn, explained changes to employees on the line. Time charts and safety records were routinely filled out by employees without apparent difficulties.

The point of gathering this information on actual reading and writing practices is not to make judgments about how these uses of literacy compare with those of the school-oriented segments of society. It is to recognize that the extent to which physiologically normal individuals learn to read and write depends greatly on the role literacy plays in their families, communities, and jobs. Research from this study, as well as from historical and other social science studies, suggests that all normal individuals can learn to read and write, provided they have a setting or context in which there is a need to be literate, they are exposed to literacy, and they get some help from those who are already literate. This help, however, need not be formal instruction, nor must it necessarily follow what are frequently believed to be the basic tenets of reading instruction in school: graded tasks, isolated skill hierarchies, and a tight, linear order of instruction in sets and subsets of skills. Within this system of instruction, a student's success is measured by a sequenced move through a hierarchy of skills, and it is believed that acquiring these skills – that is, *learning to read*, is necessary before a student is *reading to learn*.

Typically, in order to help students improve their reading performance in school (that is, read school materials successfully and perform reading-related school tasks acceptably), standard reading programs are slowed down and broken into smaller and smaller fragments of skills, and high-interest, low-level reading materials are used along with numerous reading resources. When parents and community groups are asked to aid in this process, they are expected to continue and to reinforce the classroom practices, often being instructed in an explicit pedagogy. In many cases, the result of imposing this formal structure on parents is that the experience is fraught with feelings of inadequacy and frustration, and little measurable academic gain is realized by their children.

This process need not be the only way to teach reading. In a class of first-graders from the community reported here, a teacher built her reading program on the following philosophy, presented in various ways to her students throughout the year:

Reading and writing are things you do all the time – at home, on the bus, riding your bike, at the barber shop. You can read, and you do every day before you ever come to school. You can also play baseball. Reading and writing are like baseball or football. You play baseball and football at home, at the park, wherever you want to, but when you come to school or go to a summer program at the Neighborhood Center, you get help on techniques, the gloves to buy, the way to throw, and the way to slide. School does that for reading and writing. We all read and write a lot of the time, lots of places. School isn't much different except that here we work on techniques, and we practice a lot – under a coach. I'm the coach.

This teacher's views of literacy, its uses and functions, were obviously very different from those implicit in the standardized tests which had judged these students to be lacking in reading-readiness skills and having little potential for success in the first grade. Throughout the year, traditional

teaching methods (basal readers, phonics lessons, work sheets) emphasized *learning to read*, but equal stress was given to *reading to learn*.
Store advertisements, price tags, movie titles, instructions for new toys and
games, and classroom notices were used. The teacher's approach to reading enabled these students to define themselves as readers and writers by
their community norms, and to grow with confidence into being readers
by school criteria.

The challenge posed to a uniform definition of functional literacy, and
to universal patterns of functions and uses, may alter not only methods
and goals of reading instruction, but also assessments of the accountability of schools in meeting society's needs. For example, the dramatic
societal and cultural shifts caused by the mechanization and automation
of production have turned reading and writing into social events and instrumental actions for many segments of the population. The current state
of literacy research suggests, therefore, expanding the definitions,
measures, methods, and materials behind literacy teaching to incorporate
not only school-based skills, uses, and functions of literacy, but also the
counterparts and modifications of these in out-of-school contexts.

Furthermore, those literacy skills taught and reinforced in the college-
bound or general track of public schools are often not valued by potential
employers, an increasing number of whom do not see school-rewarded
reading and writing skills as marketable. Instead, as indicated in a recent
survey of employer attitudes toward potential employees, employers want
an integration of mathematical and linguistic skills, displays of the
capability of learning "on one's own," and listening and speaking skills required to understand and give instructions and describe problems
(Research for Better Schools, 1978).

Both research findings and community/business needs, therefore, suggest several conclusions about literacy skills and needs. First, reading and
writing need not be taught exclusively in the schools. In fact, a strict
adherence to formal methods of teaching and evaluating literacy may
limit potential opportunities for literacy learning and maintenance in
homes and communities, by alienating parents and creating feelings of inadequacy about their own competencies. Second, literacy acquisition does
not require a tight, linear order of instruction that breaks down small sets
and subsets of skills into isolated, sequential hierarchies. Third, learners
frequently possess and display in out-of-school contexts skills relevant to
using literacy that are not effectively exploited in school learning environments. Finally, for a large percentage of the population, learning and sustaining reading and writing skills are not primarily motivated by a faith in

their academic utility. For many families and communities, the major benefits of reading and writing may not include such traditionally assigned rewards as social mobility, job preparation, intellectual creativity, critical reasoning, and public information access. In short, literacy has different meanings for members of different groups, with a corresponding variety of acquisition modes, functions, and uses; these differences have yet to be taken into account by policy-makers.

Note

An earlier version of this paper appeared in the *Journal of Communication, 30*:1, 1980 (reprinted with permission).

References

Cohen, M. (1958). *La grande invention de l'escriture et son evolution*. Paris: Imprimerie Nationale.

Davis, N. (1975). *Society and culture in early modern France*. Stanford, CA.: Stanford University Press.

Eisenstein, E. L. (1979). *The printing press as an agent of change* (2 vols.). Cambridge: Cambridge University Press.

Goody, J. (1977). *Domestication of the savage mind*. Cambridge: Cambridge University Press.

Goody, J., & Watt, I. (1968). The consequences of literacy. In J. Goody (Ed.), *Literacy in traditional societies*. Cambridge: Cambridge University Press.

Goody, J., Cole, M., & Scribner, S. (1977). Writing and formal operations: A case study among the Vai. *Africa, 47*, 289–304.

Hall, D., & Carlton, R. (1977). *Basic skills at school and work*. Toronto: Ontario Economic Council.

Harste, J. C., Woodward, V. A., & Burke, C. L. (1984). *Language stories and literacy lessons*. Portsmouth, N.H.: Heinemann Educational Books.

Harris, Louis & Associates (1970). *Survival literacy study*. New York: Louis Harris & Associates.

Havelock, E. (1963). *Preface to Plato*. Cambridge, Ma.: Harvard University Press.

Havelock, E. (1976). *Origins of Western literacy*. Toronto: Ontario Institute for Studies in Education.

Heath, S. B. (1982). What no bedtime story means: Narrative skills at home and school. *Language in Society, 11*, 49–76.

Heath, S. B. (1983). *Ways with words: Language, life, and work in communities and classrooms*. Cambridge: Cambridge University Press.

Heath, S. B. (1984). Oral and literate traditions. *International Social Science Journal, 99*, 41–58.

Kroeber, A. (1948). *Anthropology*. New York: Harcourt, Brace.

Labov, W. (1982). Objectivity and commitment in linguistic science: The case of the Black English trial in Ann Arbor. *Language in Society, 11*, 165–202.

Lockridge, K. (1974). *Literacy in colonial New England*. New York: Norton.

Meggitt, M. (1968). Uses of literacy in New Guinea and Melanesia. In J. Goody (Ed.), *Literacy in traditional societies*. Cambridge: Cambridge University Press.

Northcutt, N. (1975). *Adult performance level project: Adult functional competency: A report to the Office of Education dissemination review panel*. Austin, Tex.: University of Texas, Division of Extension.

Olson, D. (1975). Review of *Toward a literate society*, ed. J. B. Carroll & J. S. Chall. In *Proceedings of the National Academy of Education, 2*, 109–178.

Olson, D. (1977). From utterance to text: The bias of language in speech and writing. *Harvard Educational Review, 47*, 257–281.

Research for Better Schools (1978). *Employer attitudes toward the preparation of youth for work*. Philadelphia, Pa.: Research for Better Schools.

Scollon, R., & Scollon, B. K. (1979). *Linguistic convergence: An ethnography of speaking at Fort Chipewyan, Alberta*. New York: Academic Press.

Scribner, S., & Cole, M. (1981). *The psychology of literacy*. Cambridge, Ma.: Harvard University Press.

Soltow, L., & Stevens, E. (1977). Economic aspects of school participation in mid-nineteenth century United States. *Journal of Interdisciplinary History, 8*, 221–243.

Soltow, L., & Stevens, E. (1981). The rise of literacy and the common school in the United States: A socioeconomic analysis to 1870. Chicago: University of Chicago Press.

Spindler, G. (1982) (Ed.) *Doing the ethnography of schooling: Educational anthropology in action*. New York: Holt, Rinehart & Winston.

Staiger, R. (1979). Motivation for reading: An international bibliography. In R. C. Staiger (Ed.), *Roads to Reading*. Paris: UNESCO.

Szwed, J. (1981). The ethnography of literacy. In M. F. Whiteman (Ed.), *Variations in writing: Functional and linguistic-cultural differences*. Baltimore, Ma.: Lawrence Erlbaum Associates.

Taylor, D. (1983). *Family literacy: Young children learning to read and write*. Exeter, N.H.: Heinemann Educational Books.

United States National Commission for UNESCO (1978). *A reason to read: A report on an international symposium on the promotion of the reading habit*. New York: UNESCO.

Walker, W. (1981). Native American writing systems. In C. A. Ferguson & S. B. Heath (Eds.), *Language in the USA*. Cambridge: Cambridge University Press.

Webb, R. K. (1950). Working class readers in early Victorian England. *English Historical Review, 65*, 333–351.

Webb, R. K. (1954). Literacy among the working classes in ninteenth-century Scotland. *Scottish Historical Review, 33*, 110–114.

3 The Properties, Purposes, and Promotion of Literacy

John Wilson

If in education some new or controversial or in any way uncertain area comes up for discussion and action, how should we proceed? We bump into such terms as "literacy," "value education," "environmental studies," "women's studies," and many others. These take on a life of their own, particularly if they are politically or otherwise fashionable, or if they appeal to our prejudices or neurotic weaknesses. They come to be uncritically accepted or rejected before we know, literally, what we are talking about.

The sane person (and I stress the "sane" rather than the clever person, or – worse – the person equipped with a doctorate, or – worse still – the person who is well-read in educational theory) would presumably want to get clearer about three things. First, he would want to know quite simply what these terms and titles *meant*: what counted as "value education" or "literacy" or whatever. Second, he would want to sketch out some of the main interests or *purposes* that might be served by engaging in such teaching: the point or points of being morally educated, or literate. And third, though a long way third (because the first two obviously have logical priority), he might try to find out something about practical methods and techniques, about how value education or literacy – knowing (1) that we know what we mean by these phrases and (2) what purposes education in these things may serve – might, "in practice," be promoted or improved.

All this seems to be boringly obvious; the interesting thing is that such clarification rarely happens. I do not know how many others have either addressed these questions, or assumed that the answers to the first two of them are clear. Do people in general think that we *do* know (1) what "literacy" should mean, and/or (2) what purposes we may categorize as being served by it? I suspect that they do not think that; but neither do they think that we do not know, for then some serious attempt would be made to get clear. All too often, we do not think at all in this mode. Rather, we often think – as of course it is much easier and more fashionable to think –

about ways of assessing literacy, practical techniques for implementing it in this or that situation, the practical value of literacy for social or political purposes, and so on. This manner of proceeding (a very common, indeed almost universal, state of affairs in education) neglects all the hard and important questions, and may well lead to serious trouble. I am reminded of the Nazi who said that to him "moral education" meant obedience to the Fuehrer. Asked whether it might not be worth discussing whether that was an appropriate meaning for the phrase, and what possible purposes moral education might have, he replied that as a practical man he would leave such questions to philosophers; he himself would get on with educating his children in Nazi-controlled schools.

It is, then, very important – of great practical importance – that concepts and purposes should be clearly set out and analyzed. That point of method is much more important than anything else I am likely to say. Which is just as well – because, of course, I cannot hope to deal with any of these three vast topics adequately. I shall aim simply at elucidating some of the questions that arise in all of them, whilst also attempting to make one or two rather more substantive if unfashionable suggestions.

Properties of literacy

People often speak of "literacy" as if it were some nonrational feature, like having red hair or a healthy skin, or at best as if it were – to use a disastrously infectious word – a "skill," like being able to ride a bicycle or swim. I doubt whether any elements in reading and writing involve much skill, in the strict sense, but in any case, the major elements certainly involve *understanding*, not just *doing* something. Computers can, in some sense, be programmed to read and write; but how thin this sense is – how much is missing from what we hope human beings do in their reading and writing – is, in general terms, clear enough. We want our children not just, like machines, to form strokes and letters, or to enunciate the syllables represented by "the cat is on the mat," but to express their thoughts and feelings in writing, and to understand those of others in reading. Literacy, so far from being a single skill or even a set of skills, is inextricably bound up with understanding, with choice of words, with grasp of syntax, grammar, and diction, and – what is all too often omitted – with a certain attitude toward the whole business.

At least three major questions, therefore, confront those interested in literacy. First, are we satisfied with the mere *ability* to read and write, even if that ability is never or rarely used – even if any motivation or desire to read and write is wholly lacking? Or are we concerned not just with whether our pupils can, but also with whether they want to, read and write? The answer to this is presumably not unclear: It is the latter. The desire, or at least the willingness, to read and write is obviously essential if literacy is to have any practical value; still more so if it is to have any more fully educational value, such as might be thought to be gained from the study of literature. But that now raises a host of questions about how attitudes toward literacy, or rather toward what can be read and written, are engendered, along with the prior questions about what attitudes we want. Do we, for instance, want our pupils to regard the written word with the kind of awe once felt for ancient ruins? Is their attitude toward writing going to be purely instrumental – as if, say, a personal letter could be replaced without loss by a taped oral message (as indeed some people do nowadays)? What do we actually think *is* the value of the written word and its various forms? Only by answering that can we clarify what attitudes we wish our pupils to adopt toward it.

The second question, closely connected with the first, is: If reading is to involve understanding what the person reads, as clearly it must, then what sort of writing do we expect the pupil to understand, and for what reasons? Similarly, if writing is to involve more than the mere formation of letters (and no doubt some machine will shortly be invented, if it has not already been, to do this for pupils without their bothering to hold the pen), then just what do we expect pupils to write? Are we concerned, for instance, with their ability to read road signs, or income tax forms (if indeed anyone has a chance of understanding these), or love letters, or political propaganda, or what? Are they to write crisp notes to their employers, or passionate declarations to their lovers, or witty remarks to the newspapers?

That these are (as they say) "real" and "practical" questions is clear enough: Obviously the whole strategy of teaching literacy will turn on how they are answered, since the very texts and materials will differ according to what one expects pupils to comprehend or express. A bit less obvious, perhaps, is the importance of a third question: How far are we concerned with the pupil's own natural language, on the one hand, and, on the other, with his general attitude toward and understanding of reading and writing? This is like the question which modern linguists and others face: How far is the teacher solely to be concerned with the pupil's ability to speak French, for instance, and how far with his interest in and general understanding of languages in general, or modern languages, or Romance languages, or linguistics? I do not suggest that there is a determinate solution to this question: I say only that one's concept of literacy, and therefore one's practical moves, will largely turn on it.

Purposes of literacy

It is not hard to see how certain views about the properties or nature of literacy lead, fairly directly or at least temptingly, to the serving of certain purposes. Indeed, often the purposes are (consciously or unconsciously) established first, and the properties or concept of literacy tailored accordingly. Purposes are multifarious, but it is possible to draw a fairly clear distinction between (1) society-oriented or utilitarian purposes and (2) purposes benefiting the individual human being as such, not as a role filler in a particular society at a particular time. Thus (1) to be able to fill in an income tax form in modern society is a useful and (I suppose) socially desirable ability; whereas (2) to be able to appreciate Shakespeare or write an amusing limerick has a value that we would not normally interpret in social terms, or in utilitarian terms – such things have no *use*, but much *value*.

Unsurprisingly – as education is always under improper pressure from politicians and from "society" in general, in liberal countries as much as in totalitarian ones – "literacy" is normally construed in utilitarian terms, and there will be a lot of talk about literacy as helping the individual to play a proper part in society, to be employable, to establish his self-esteem and identity, and so forth. I do not sneer at these or other social and utilitarian aims; though it is worth remembering that technological advances may make such education obsolete. Thus, if our *only* reason for the study of, say, French and German is a utilitarian one – to communicate with French and German speakers – then the arrival of an instantaneous translating machine would at a blow obviate any educational efforts in these fields. Only if one believes that there is a nonutilitarian value in studying French and German (and not only in their literatures) could education in them be properly defended. So, too, if literacy is seen primarily as a social tool, then it may become obsolete as an educational goal. Perhaps a machine will turn the oral into the written, and vice versa; why then – if we are utilitarian in our thinking – should anyone bother about literacy? It is in this sense that social and utilitarian ends in education are fragile, always liable to obsolescence; and educators sell their souls and their raison d'etre if they construe their job primarily as rendering a service to society. They ought to cooperate, if possible, with society; but they will need also, sometimes, to keep it at bay.

This is not the place to enlarge on the nonutilitarian benefits of literacy. It is obvious enough that without the ability to grasp and ponder on the written word – on the whole range of philosophy, history, and literature; without the effort at self-expression that comes not only in high-powered novels but in the lowliest love letter or the humblest attempt to describe the writer's feelings, or his job, or what his day has been like, or where he lives; without the ability to furnish the world with all those concepts and distinctions that a written language with its enormous vocabulary and tradition alone can supply; without all these (and I have omitted plenty), clearly we cannot begin to rise all that much above the animal level. It is precisely by language that we are human at all; and it is by the written and semipermanent language that we become reflecting, as opposed to day-to-day, unreflecting, unrecording, time-bound, humans. Language is central to education as, for all their importance, numbers and objects (the worlds of mathematics and science) are not – because language is central, logically central, to our being human.

That is an absurdly brief and slightly pompous attempt to remind us of what, in our better (less political and utilitarian) moments, we should know already; but it shows how very important it is that literacy – reading and writing is a better title, just because "literacy" does, as I have said, imply some single skill – be presented to children (and adults) as a transcendental, transcultural, time-free source of richness and pleasure: a vast human heritage, not a skill to be exploited. It is not, repeat *not*, something that we can without shame use either for purely utilitarian purposes, as if we needed better programming to be efficient robots; nor something that we must take up because our self-respect or identity need boosting, either as individuals or because we are black or Inuit (Eskimo) or female or disabled or whatever. No serious learner is concerned with such criteria: To be a serious learner precisely means to be able and willing to step outside these political and social categories into the worlds of literature, philosophy, art, and many other activities to which they are just irrelevant. But that will happen only if those in the education business resist the application of political criteria of this sort – something of which, to be frank, I see little evidence either in North America or in the U. K. (or, for that matter, anywhere else).

Promotion of literacy

The promotion of literacy, let me boldly say, seems to me to depend on the right sort of school community, not upon the (largely time-wasting) research usually conducted. The school as a community has been of interest to educationalists chiefly from two points of view: (1) internally, with reference to pastoral care and the development of certain very general qualities in the pupils; and (2) externally, with reference to the local community and to social class, social mobility, and other matters of orthodox sociological concern. Not much attention has been paid to the school community as a background to or agent of curricular or subject learning, despite talk of the "hidden curriculum" (a phrase in which "curriculum" has departed very far from its normal meaning of a structured course of study). I want here to make at least some inroad on two sets of questions that must be of interest in any education. First, what subjects are more naturally learned or picked up in a community than in a classroom? Second, what kind of community is required for this purpose, and what kind of moves have to be made in education if we are to improve matters?

It is important to note, but not to be bogged down by, questions about what is to count as "a subject" or "a community." Some might wish to say that anything to be learned can constitute a subject (not only mathematics, but also morality or even creativity), and that any group of people can constitute a community (not only a closely-knit family but also a classroom or even a conurbation). But that is to reject any kind of distinctions and hence to throttle our questions at birth. We can and should distinguish (1) between objects of learning that are circumscribed and have some kind of structured content – that is, subjects like English or mathematics or music – and objects which do not, as in learning to be self-confident or imaginative; and (2) between groups of people having some kind of corporate identity and life together that attracts a fair degree of emotional investment on the part of individual members (as in a family), and groups that are constructed ad hoc for certain purposes that are severely limited (as with a football team or a classroom). The differences here are admittedly of degree rather than of kind, but should be clear enough for our purposes.

The most obvious example, and one that may also help to sharpen up the distinctions, is in the field of language. There is a clear difference between learning to speak and understand English in an English family or factory or hotel, on the one hand, and in a classroom period labeled "English," on the other; so too with foreign languages. It is also clear that the former is a more natural and efficient method, not just because the learner is more fully immersed, but because he has an investment in the corporate background against which the language is used – the family or factory or hotel is a community that has other interests besides the use of language, that use being a kind of spin-off from those interests. This element will be absent from any program of "language across the curriculum," because it is not itself a curricular element but rather a function of the existence of a community.

It might be said that so far we are not talking about a structured curricular subject – but any merit there might be in that point disappears if we put a little pressure on the example. Within such a community one learns not just the motor skills and behavior patterns necessary for speaking and understanding, but also (a) the refinements of vocabulary, expression, grammar, syntax, and other things commonly taught under the heading of "language," and (b) assuming the community to be of a certain kind, familiarity with and appreciation of what is normally taught as "literature." We know well enough (though it is not often said) that someone brought up in a family in which people read a lot, do crosswords and play word games, argue, write limericks, swap quotations, and so forth becomes thereby very well educated in "English" – not only in oral communication, but in whatever higher reaches of language and literature we care to value.

Other examples are equally obvious. Children do not, generally speaking, learn to like good music by attending classes in musical appreciation, but by being in an environment where good music is constantly played. So too with all the arts and crafts and, if more obliquely, with science, mathematics, history, and all other subjects. Children become initiated into the forms of thought by being initiated into the forms of life that generate them: They learn what it is like to behave and think as a scientist, or a craftsman, or whatever. It would be surprising if this were not, at least characteristically, the case (of course, some children may react against prevailing forms of life), for most communities, like the family, deploy too many weapons for the child to resist. Quite apart from the force of example and the pressures of authority-figures (parents or others), the child is insensibly acclimatized to certain rule-governed systems in such a way that he regards them as fixtures. It even seems inappropriate here to talk of "motivation": In a musical family, music is part of the air one breathes.

That is perhaps truistic enough, but it raises rather sharply the question of just what – if the natural habitat for such learning is the community – the classroom is for. Extremists might want to abolish classrooms, or try to turn them into genuine communities. But the question has an answer. Just because in communities subjects and forms of thought are closely interwoven with forms of life, there is inevitably a certain lack of distance, objectivity, and "abstractness" about the learning. We need courses on English literature and woodwork, however well read or craftsmanlike our family background may be, because that background is not sufficiently public or objective: The family will follow its own personal tastes (however admirable) in books or in the making of some wooden objects rather than others. The child gets an all-important taste, perhaps a deep-draught, of the subject – but he does not get a balanced and overall view of it. The classroom, together with the lecture hall, the examination system, and other apparatuses of learning, is there to formalize his interest and give it perspective.

The distinction we need to make, then, is not between curricular subjects that can best be learned in the community and those that can best be learned in the classroom, but rather between those aspects of all subjects which the community most naturally promulgates and those which require a more formal setting. This is not to deny that there may be different proportions of such aspects in the case of different subjects: Thus, most of what we mean when we talk of learning language is essentially a communal matter, whereas most of what we mean by learning mathematics may require a more formal context. But all subjects require both contexts, and both are equally important. Thus it might be thought that the community can play little part in mathematics, but we have only to think of families that play with figures and shapes to see our mistake. That sort of background gives an impetus vital to subsequent sophistication and formalization. Conversely, many people still believe that moral education is entirely a matter of establishing a good moral tradition or background in the community, but clearly there is a very great deal of formal work and hard conceptual thinking appropriate to this department of life, for which the classroom is a more natural context.

Most schools are not potent enough to provide an adequate background of this kind: I mean, roughly, that the pupils do not invest enough emotion and loyalty in them for them to function as a natural habitat for learning. In particular, they are less potent than the norms of the local environment, or the mass media, or whatever "youth culture" may prevail. The honorable (or dishonorable, according to one's values) exceptions are all cases based on some overt or covert ideology: the ideology, for instance, of Arnold's Rugby or Neill's Summerhill or Hitler's youth camps. It is as if, or perhaps it is simply that, we do not feel capable of establishing a potent community without the benefit of some sectarian or partisan set of values to act as a unifying force: a strange lack of nerve, since the values inherent in the notion of education – that is, essentially, those that go along with the notion of learning – are quite enough to be going on with.

This lack of nerve is itself closely connected with certain relativist and egalitarian fantasies that are most obviously corrupting in relation to curricular subjects. We could reasonably argue, as indeed psychologists do argue, about how closely the members of families should be involved with each other – about how powerful, in this sense, the family should be –

but we could not reasonably maintain that the parents ought not to initiate their children into *some* kinds of worthwhile activities and studies. If
the parents had doubts about whether to speak good English or play good
music in the child's presence, on the grounds that this involved some sort
of cultural indoctrination or the imposition of an ideology, we in turn
would have doubts about their sanity. A fortiori, schools are there to put
before the pupils things that are better (by what or whose criteria is not
here relevant) than the things they would otherwise run across. If they lose
their nerve in this respect, becoming uncertain about (say) whether pop
music is in fact worse than classical or whether, more generally, any music
is better than any other, they cannot educate at all; indeed, they can hardly
engage in any intentional action, since in intending one goal rather
than another they necessarily take that goal to be more desirable.

It is surely this fantasy that lies behind our failures to replace disman-
tled traditions and other supports for the school community by satisfactory alternatives. To take an obvious, if humble, example: The tradition of
Christian worship in U. K. school assemblies and elsewhere immersed
pupils in certain worthwhile experiences – the language and literature of
the Bible, the hymns and the liturgy in general, the music, perhaps the
aesthetics and atmosphere of church buildings, and so on. In throwing out
the ideological bathwater of all this we have thrown out the nonideologi-
cal baby: not only the particular worthwhile accompaniments of this
ideology, but the existence of a corporate and binding activity in its own
right. Briefly: So long as we are unable to conceive of the idea of a potent
school without a partisan ideology to support it (though goodness knows
we ought to be able to conceive of a potent school without such ideology
easily enough – we say that its members are bound together by love and
other shared things, not by all being paid-up Moonies or Party members),
for just so long will we fail to generate or sustain schools that can actually
educate our children. For education – and literacy is only one part of this
– logically requires that the whole person should be dealt with, not just
that people should be taught a few scraps of knowledge and skills, and
made employable. Education demands giving much more power to
educators: something that members of a liberal society are, for various
psychological and other reasons, very fearful of trusting anyone with. Unfortunately, education cannot proceed without such powers – and it is
useless to complain of illiteracy, or a decline in morality, or anything of
that kind, unless we are at the same time prepared to give educators the
powers to improve matters.

I am very conscious of having only scratched the surface of these problems, but I am comforted by the fact, as I see it, that it is much more important for teachers and others to confront these questions themselves than to have them answered by me or anyone else. Teachers are an oppressed and powerless class, at the mercy of bureaucrats and others who are not adept at the (admittedly hard) task of thinking one's way through the philosophy of educational problems. A brief essay may help teachers to do this for themselves, as they should, more effectively than could a long-minded and pseudoscholarly (also pseudoauthoritarian) thesis. That, at least, is my hope.

4 Literacy and the education of the emotions

Robert C. Solomon

Only ten years ago, Marshall McLuhan and other media prophets were circulating the message (in books) that books were on their way out, the print medium moribund. Book publishers started emphasizing "multi" and "audiovisual" media, hedging their bets. But the revolution never took off. Computers may have become familiar household items, but book sales have been unaffected. PAC-MAN may have replaced Junior High School and drugs, but those who bought books still buy books, and they read them as they always did (Evelyn Wood notwithstanding), one line at a time, page after page.

And yet, we hear continually of a "crisis" in the book world, a crisis of illiteracy. Not long ago, an Op-Ed essay by Daniel Boorstin, the Librarian of Congress, appeared in the *New York Times*, identifying a "nation of readers" as nothing less than the prerequisite for a "free people" and expressing his fear that we are rapidly losing that prerequisite. About the same time, the *Boston Globe* and a number of other newspapers reprinted an address by Elisabeth Sifton, editor-in-chief at Viking Press, lamenting the decline in readers of "serious books." But why should this matter?

The theme of this collection, to be more immediate, involves a paradoxical disagreement about the importance of literacy. On the one hand, everyone agrees that literacy in some minimal form is essential to "getting ahead" in contemporary bureaucratic society, though there is considerable disagreement over the desirability either of that kind of society or of "getting ahead" in it. On the other hand, there is an unusually keen awareness, based on some startling and some profound recent research, that the importance of literacy, not only in education but in the formation of culture, has been overestimated. (See Harvey Graff's essay in this volume.) It is in response to the second concern, and with minimal reference to the first, that, as a philosopher, I want to address my essay.

What is the crisis? Literacy, first of all, obviously involves something more than the basic ability to read and write. (I will discuss different senses of "illiteracy" in a subsequent section.) In this sense, the fact is that there has always been a tiny readership for what Ms. Sifton calls "good books." Joyce Carol Oates has delved into the best-seller lists and book reviews of the last century to show that, before television and mass market advertising, the sales figures and the tastes of the reading public were not significantly different from today's. On the other hand, there is something undeniably shocking in those figures and tastes, given the supposed improvements in our educational system and in cultural awareness in general.

Even a best-selling (whether or not "good") book in this country might reach 5% of the population. In a country of nearly 200 million readers, a "serious" general-interest magazine such as the *Atlantic Monthly* or (worse) *Harper's* struggles to keep afloat with a readership of considerably less than a quarter of a million (.1%). A book written for that audience would be exceedingly successful if it sold 100,000 copies (.05%). If reading is still our primary access to detailed information and argument, then this does indeed bode ill according to Boorstin's appeal for a nation of readers. But books are not just the stuff of democracy; in an important sense, they are the stuff of life.

This is an embarrassingly self-serving statement from a person who lives by reading and writing books. I cannot deny that much of my own concern for the literate life of America is in fact a concern for my own livelihood, and I am just as sure that such self-serving market concerns lie behind Mr. Boorstin's prescription for a "free people" (he is also a best-selling author on the history of that free people) and Ms. Sifton's own market-oriented position. But self-interest is not the whole of the argument, nor even a very large part of it. We writers could make a much less neurotic living in nine-to-five jobs, and at least some of the publishing pundits I know would be just as happy in the breakfast food business.

So, why books? The arguments I hear these days, from some very literate and book-loving theorists, make it sound as if the love of books is nothing but self-serving, not just for writers and publishers but for the "elite" who maintain their political superiority via the pretensions of "culture." Literacy is a capitalist device to separate out the advantaged, some Marxists say (on the basis of very wide reading). Literacy is the ploy of a white, English-speaking elite to render "illiterate" people from a different culture, with a different language and a different history, say some very learned educators. And, indeed, there is something very right about these arguments: Whatever our clumsy attempts at democratic education, there remains a drastic difference in class and racial mobility, a difference that is easily and often measured in precisely those tidbits of knowledge that come from a literary education. Much of what is called "literacy" is indeed cultural pretension, and it is not hard to argue that, in a nation with a non-white unemployment rate of well over 20%, literature is a luxury that is practically, if not culturally, restricted to the relatively leisured upper middle class.

Against such arguments, what can be said in favor of books? There are nonliterate cultures, of course, and they are very much alive. But it is worth asking what they have instead of books, or rather, what it is that makes books so important to us.

The response I want to defend here is this: Books, not television, remain the primary vehicle of our culture, and not just as the source of our concepts and our ideals and our heroes. What is more difficult to show, but just as important, is that books are an important source of shared emotions as well as a means of understanding emotions in other people and of providing a safe and central vehicle for *having* emotions. In other societies, there are other vehicles, and, one might argue, some of them are superior. ("For what?" needless to say, remains the crucial question.) But for us, literacy-deprived life is often (not always) an emotionally deprived life, too, for substitutes are hard to find.

A second part of this answer is that the activity of reading books, again as opposed to watching television or any number of intellectually more passive entertainments, requires an exercise of the imagination and the use of a critical faculty that is forcibly suspended through the continuous onslaught of T.V. programming. Or, for that matter, through the continuous onslaught of words and images from almost any source – lectures and films, for example – that forces our attention rather than invites our critical, imaginative participation. Emotions are not just reactions; they are social, imaginative constructions. Here is the key to a "free people" – a "nation of readers" who know how to enjoy the privacy of a book, in which the wheels of their imaginations can spin at will and their private conversations and commentary can be perfected silently with or against the greatest minds of our history. But here, too, is an often unappreciated key to a rich and meaningful emotional life, for emotions, as I shall be arguing, are part and parcel of the imagination and are both exercisable and educatable through reading as well.

Three kinds of literacy

What if you haven't read *War and Peace*; what have you missed? What have you missed if you haven't read Dickens, or Camus, or Borges? Or, for that matter, Galbraith, Marx, Mill, or Einstein? One might respond that you've missed a certain pleasure in life, or an evening's entertainment, or in the case of *War and Peace*, a couple of weeks of engrossing involvement. There are the more practical replies – "You may have missed some important information" – or, perhaps, there is the possibility of blowing a job interview or a cocktail party conversation. And then there are the political answers, rarely presented as such: Not reading certain books excludes you from a literary elite, which also happens to be the power elite, with all of the opportunities and status thereof.

I find all of these answers inadequate. Some are self-congratulatory, some are vulgarly pragmatic; most are, in fact, false, and some are just resentful. And yet, the literature on literacy does not always make clear just what a good answer to such a question might be.

Spokespeople for the humanities, full of self-congratulation, often give lectures, invariably reprinted in alumni bulletins if not also in local newspapers, insisting that the liberal and literary arts will make a person a better human being, solve the world's problems, and enlighten "developing" countries about the wonders of western life. Indeed, one gets the impression that a student who reads becomes something of a saint in this day of television, movies, video games, and drive-in blood-and-gore horror films. And if such notions prove to be without foundation (Nero, Mussolini, and the Borgias were all well read), then the same spokespeople will retreat to the contradictory idea that reading is good in itself and "its own reward." (I have philosophical doubts about anything being "good in itself," but let's let that pass.) In any case, the whole idea behind such pronouncements is self-congratulation; they are not defenses of literacy.

On the other hand, there is a clearly practical problem of literacy in our public schools, which has little to do with the self-congratulatory advantages of a liberal education. Some students with high school diplomas can't read or write a coherent sentence. In the best schools, many students haven't heard of the Oedipus complex or read the classics, or even Classic comic books. Christopher Lasch writes in his *The Culture of Narcissism* of students who can't date the Russian revolution within a decade or so, and in a survey I carried out for the *Los Angeles Times* (August 4, 1980) I found that a majority of honors college students didn't know the names of Faulkner, Goethe, Debussy, or Virginia Woolf (though almost everyone knew the phrase "Who's afraid of . . . ," but didn't know where it came from). They didn't know who Trotsky was, or Niels Bohr, or Spinoza or Kafka. A small but frightening percentage didn't really know who Hitler was.

So, on the one hand we have self-congratulatory speeches about the liberal arts; on the other we have an apparently desperate educational situation. Between them, we can see the battle developing between "the basics" and the call for "elitist" education, with the inevitable consequence that the question of literacy becomes a political problem; literacy becomes status and "the basics" become the focus of an education that is conscientiously devoid of anything more than the "basic" ability to read and write.

If we are to cut through such problems, it is important, I would argue, to begin by distinguishing three kinds of literacy. The first is the ability to read and write, the nuts-and-bolts part of literacy – the skills that everyone in this society must learn if they are to have any possible chance at decent jobs and fair treatment and protection. This is "functional" literacy. It has to do with being able to read a simple contract (despite the fact that most of the contracts that we sign are unreadable, anyway). It has to do with being able to write a letter of application, or read a warning label or advertisement. Its practical importance is unquestionable and therefore, usually unquestioned.

Second, there is "literacy" in the snobbish sense, meaning "well read." This is the sense defended by liberal arts college presidents, for this is the commodity they sell. It is the sort of literacy that is paraded across the pages of *The New York Review of Books* and is displayed by readers thereof. It involves having read not only *Moby Dick* but also *Typee*, having Nietzsche and Eliot quotes at the tip of one's tongue, and being able to recite lines of Chaucer or Shakespeare without pausing even a moment in one's conversation. Such literacy is unabashedly elitist, often competitive (if not intrinsically so), and a mark of social superiority (which is not, I hasten to add, an argument against it). But between the "functional" and the highfalutin is a third kind of literacy, which is what concerns me here.

This third kind of literacy is really what one might call the "knowledgeable," except that the word smacks too much of mere information and know-how and too little of the affective and the experiential, which are what is crucial to it. It is a type of literacy that is concentrated in but not exclusive to books, and which today also involves film and the other arts. It can come from conversations on the street, lectures, and political rallies, but for a variety of reasons, it revolves around the printed word. It has to do with participating in certain basic or even essential experiences – knowing, if only vicariously, a form of life that touches on our own. In this sense, reading *The Iliad* is not just an exercise in reading (which is what it too often becomes in high school), and it is not a matter of being able to say you've read it or occasionally drop learned allusions. There is a sense in which living through the Trojan War is a part of all of us, and expected of us, if only in the safe and bloodless form of ever-newly translated Homeric verses. Reading Einstein or Darwin is not just acquiring knowledge; it is sharing an intellectual adventure that lies at the heart of our civilization. In this sense, literacy is a kind of love, not an ability or an accomplishment. It is participation, education in the classical sense – being brought up to be part of something, not just to be successful in a career.

Discussions of literacy shift among the three senses with disconcerting ease. Sometimes literacy is contrasted with utter illiteracy, the inability to even write one's name. Sometimes illiteracy is ignorance, sometimes social incompetence. Sometimes literacy is compared in a scholarly way with what is called the "oral" tradition in literature, and accused of imperialism in the demeaning thereof. But, of course, what one says about literacy and what one compares it with depends entirely on what one means by it.

The third kind of literacy is often confused with a kind of escapism or merely "vicarious" involvement in life. The experiences one gains from books are not "real" experiences, it is said, but purely formal ones – detached, and isolated from life rather than a part of it. I think that this is basically wrong, but to show this, I will have to turn to my concern for the emotions in literature. The question of what is a "real" experience and what is not is not nearly so simple as the critics of "vicarious" reading experience make it out to be.

The education – and the importance – of emotions

Literature, I want to insist, is vital to the education of the emotions. One very difficult question concerns what is to count as literature – just *Moby Dick* or *Treasure Island*, too? And for that matter, what about "Mork and Mindy" and "Kojak"? But an equally difficult question, if literature is said to serve the emotions, is just how emotions – which are generally considered to be unlearned, instinctual, visceral responses – can be educated at all. Perhaps, one might argue, literature can serve to provide models of self-restraint and control of the emotions – but this hardly counts as the education of the emotions. Perhaps, in the modern version of an ancient debate between Plato and Aristotle, it can be argued that literature provides an "outlet" for emotions, which might otherwise have their dangerous expression in real life. But as we know from the endless debates about violence and pornography, it is not at all clear from the evidence (and the evidence seems to be one of the lesser considerations) that such literature does not motivate and inspire such behavior instead of sublimating or defusing it. Whether inspiration or sublimation, however, the obvious effect of literature on the emotions is hardly evidence of education. One might argue that some literature stultifies and numbs the emotions, but this hardly helps make our case for literature and the emotions, either.

What we need, first of all, is a new and better conception of emotion. If an emotion is a physiological response, no matter how complex, then it will not do to talk of education, though we might talk in some limited way of cause and effect. William James, who wrote a classic treatise on the nature of emotions and came back to the theme many times in his career, defined an emotion as the sensation of visceral change, prompted by some unsettling perception. But as James unfolded his global vision of the human mind and its abilities, this physiological view of emotions tended to be weakened, watered down, and, finally, ignored. In his brilliant discussion of religious experience – a complex emotional experience if there ever is one – James all but completely ignores his physiological theory of emotion and focuses instead on the imaginative and creative aspects of faith as an emotion. Indeed, in his less transcendental discussions of curiosity and knowledge, the education of emotions is very much in evidence, and even in his writings on emotion as such, there is much discussion about *changing* one's emotions by way of changing one's behavior, one's thoughts, and one's outlook – in other words, by educating them.

James's retreat from the physiological view of emotions to a view both more flattering and more pragmatic led him and leads us to a realization that is not readily forthcoming so long as one thinks (as James did in his essays) of an emotion as an emergency secretion of adrenalin, as in panic, sudden anger, or "love at first sight." Such emotions are indeed blatantly physiological (though this is surely not all that they are) and difficult to control, much less advise intelligently, given the urgent nature of the circumstances. But the emotions that mean most to us are not those transient moments of fear, fury, and infatuation; they are such enduring passions as lifelong love and righteous indignation, which are clearly learned and cultivated with experience and which prompt and inspire us to actions far more significant and considered than a start of panic, an "outburst" of anger, or the first and often embarrassing first flush of love. Here too we can appreciate the importance of emotions and their education. It is not mere "control" that concerns us; it is cultivation, development, refinement. True love is not "natural"; it is taught, and learned. Moral indignation is nothing less than the end result of a moral education. Indeed, even fear – the most primitive of emotions – is more often learned than not, and the supposedly obvious examples of "inborn fear" do not make the general education of this emotion any less essential to life.

The most significant emotions are those that play the largest roles in the structuring of our lives. Philosophers sometimes talk as if reason can and should do this, but no novelist or poet could or would try to define a theme or a character through reason alone. The structures of literature as of life are infused with such grand emotions as love, patriotism, indignation, a sense of duty or honor or justice, and the less admirable passions of jealousy, envy, and resentment. One might try to teach such emotions and establish such structures through general principles or slogans ("love thy neighbor" or "*ecrase l'enfame*"), but one is much more assured of success when teaching by example, or better, through experience itself. And where direct experience is not available – as it often is not and is not desired – so-called "vicarious" experience will do the job. Thus the heart of literature is and has always been *stories*, narratives that provide not only examples of virtue and vice but also the opportunity to enter into a shared and established emotional world. There is and always will be considerable debate about the place of "morality" in literature, but it is hard to see how there could be that much debate about the place of emotion in literature. Literature is, whatever else it may be, the communication of emotion. But this need not depend on plot or narrative; it can be conveyed through form as well. Indeed, one is tempted to suggest that there may be as much emotion in the formalism of William Gass as in the moralizing of John Gardner.

What is an emotion, that it can be educated? If I may summarize a theory and three books in a phrase, I would say that emotions are essentially a species of *judgment*. They are learned and intelligent, even if they are not always articulate. They contain essential insights – often more accurate and more useful, even more "true," than the much-deliberated truths of reason that contradict them. (If reason tells us that our petty loves and desires are of no importance while our emotions proclaim them magnificent, it might well be foolish to be reasonable.) "Every passion," wrote Nietzsche, "has its own quantum of reason." Indeed, more than a quantum; it is its own reason. "The heart has its reasons," insisted Pascal, "that reason does not fathom." Every emotion is a way of constructing the world. It is a measure of place and importance by which we and all things of significance acquire that significance. Love creates its love, as anger indicts the accused. To enter into an emotion is not to "enter into someone else's brain." It is to participate in a way of being in the world, a way in which things matter, a way charged with shared understandings and obsessions.

To educate the emotions is nothing like the stimulation of a physiological state, though to be sure that can and sometimes does follow hard on certain emotional experiences. To educate a person is to provide him or her with an opportunity to have that emotion, to learn when it is appropriate and when inappropriate, to learn its vicissitudes and, if the term isn't too jarring, its *logic*. To learn to love is to learn to see another person in virtually infinite perspective, but it is also to learn the dangers of love: the disappointments, the foolishness, and the failures. Some of this one learns firsthand, but it would be a tragic love life indeed that had to go through the dozens of stories of love, lust, and betrayal in the first person illiterate. Not to mention the various wounds and greater injuries that one would have to suffer to learn even a chapter of *War and Peace* firsthand.

In a rather different context, Israel Scheffler has discussed the breach between emotions and reason as utterly destructive of education (Scheffler, 1977). He caricatures the standard view of emotion as "commotion – an unruly inner disturbance." The "hostile opposition of cognition and emotion," he says, "distorts everything it touches: mechanizing science, it sentimentalizes art, while portraying ethics and religion as twin swamps of feeling and unreasoned commitment." Education, he goes on to say, "is split into two grotesque parts – unfeeling knowledge and mindless arousal."

And emotion, we might add, gets lost, for it is neither unfeeling nor mindless, though it is both knowledge and arousal. It is knowledgeable arousal, one might say, educated through experiences in some sense not one's own, through shared stories, through literature.

Literature and the emotions

The influences of literature on the emotions can be cataloged into four groups – over and above the brute stimulation of passions, which while dramatic and often effective, should not really count as education. A well-wrought example or story may well inspire feelings of the strongest sort – of sympathy or compassion, of anger or indignation – but education means learning something, not just repeating a familiar feeling on the basis of an equally familiar stimulus.

1. Literature tells us what other people feel. The great significance of the increasing availability of foreign literature, for instance, is that such material can (if read) inform English readers about the circumstances

and expressions of passion in people unlike ourselves: the sense of shame in Indian family life; the sense of honor in Samurai Japan. In one sense, such information does not educate *our* emotions at all, but rather allows us to get some glimmer of understanding about the emotions of other people. But if emotions are judgments about the world, they are also influenced – and partially constituted – by knowledge about those judgments and their context. It is of no small value to our own emotional perspective to learn that romantic love is very much a "Western" emotion, for instance, or that other societies have conceptions of family intimacy and attachment far stronger than our own.

2. Literature not only lets us know *that* other people have such and such emotions; it also tells us *how* they feel. It lets us imagine "how we would feel if...." Sometimes the circumstances are recognizable but there is good reason not to know about them firsthand. The descriptions of the battles of Borodino in Tolstoy's *War and Peace* and of Waterloo in Stendhal's *Charterhouse of Parma* give us powerful portraits of "how it feels" to be on one of the great battlefields of the 19th century, but these are experiences most of us would gladly accept "secondhand." Few of us would want to actually suffer the remorse of Emma Bovary or Anna Karenina, but it is of no small importance to our emotional education that we have, at a safe distance, understood "what it would feel like if...."

3. Literature allows an actual re-creation of an emotion. This may not be true of the descriptions of Borodino or Waterloo or, for that matter, of Emma's and Anna's final, despairing moments. But tales of injustice – such as *Les Misérables* – do something more than inform us "what it feels like when...." Our sense of outrage and injustice is a genuine feeling of outrage, not just an understanding or reflection of it. The Northern sense of moral indignation on reading Stowe's *Uncle Tom's Cabin* was not a vicarious emotion but, in every sense, the real thing. Emotions are not isolated feelings but worldviews, and worlds, unlike sensations, require structure, plot, and details. Literature provides the structure, plot, and details, and once we have been submerged in them, the emotion is already with us; it does not follow as a mere effect.

4. Literature helps us articulate emotions we already have. Zola's descriptions of a harsh reality give us a language in which we can express our own sense of discontent, and examples for comparison. Marx is, whatever else, a powerful writer, who gives any sympathetic reader an enormous range of metaphors, as well as facts and theories, to bolster a large sense of dissatisfaction and give it expression. So, too, Rousseau. Literature gives us examples, models, metaphors, new words, and carefully crafted descriptions as well as whole structures in which and through which we can understand and express our own feelings. The education of the emotions is, in part, learning how to articulate them, learning what to expect from them, and learning how to use them.

It should be clear from the above four categories of "influences" that the education of the emotions involves learning to appreciate other people's passions at least as much as molding one's own emotions. This seems odd – or merely "empathetic" – only so long as we cling to the idea that emotions are our own "inner" occurrences, the private domain of each individual and exclusively his or hers, not to be shared (rather, at most expressed or confessed) with anyone else. But emotions are *public* occurrences. Not only are the expressions and the context of emotion evident to a sensitive observer; the structures and values of emotion are also an essential part of the culture. One feels this most dramatically in a mob at a political rally or in a large crowd at a sports event. The emotion is not just "in the heads" of the thousands or tens of thousands of people present; it is literally "in the air," with an existence of its own, in which the people participate. But much the same is true of more modest emotional gatherings. One sits around with one's own family and feels a complex of loving, defensive, and competitive passions fill the room. Or, one sits around while visiting with someone else's family, sensing the passion in the air but feeling quite "out of it." Visiting a strange culture gives one the sometimes overpowering sense of being present in the midst of emotions that one not only fails to share but fails to understand. Accompanying a visitor to one's own society who feels similarly throws into perspective our own emotional atmosphere, which, like the (unpolluted) air, is so familiar and so essential to us that we take it for granted and do not notice it at all.

Emotions are public in the sense that they are shared views, infused with shared values and based on shared judgments. Such judgments depend, to an extend rarely appreciated, on the particular language of the culture. A culture without an emotion word is not likely to experience that emotion. Certain Eskimo cultures lack a word for anger, for example, and it can be persuasively argued that they do not get angry. One might say that the lack of a word indicates a lack of interest, just as a multiplicity of words suggests an emotional obsession. The French, as we all know, have a multiplicity of words (and distinctions) for romantic love; the Russians have numerous words for suffering; Yiddish abounds in words for despair. American English, it is worth noting, has a high proportion of its emotion vocabulary dedicated to the identification of different kinds of anger, while Oxonian English has a remarkably flexible vocabulary for contempt. Cultural generalizations may always be suspect, but it is worth noting the distribution of emotion words in peoples' own languages. Not coincidentally, the language circumscribes values and judgments, and these in turn determine a distinctive outlook on the world.

How does one learn to participate in an emotional culture? In a word, by becoming literate. Not necessarily in the nuts-and-bolts/sign your name/read a contract sense, perhaps, although it cannot be denied that much of our emotional culture is defined and communicated by the written word – in newspapers, street-corner pamphlets, and subway and highway advertisements as well as in best sellers. And not necessarily by becoming part of that elite literary culture that proclaims itself the bearer of the better emotions. To participate in the emotions of a culture is to speak its language, share its value judgments, and partake in its stories, its history, and its heritage. To have an emotion – even the most exquisitely private and personal emotion – is to be part of an emotional culture. A teenager in love fervently believes that he or she alone feels a passion all but unknown in the history of the world – and shares this feeling with a million other teenagers (and post-teenagers). They are all part of the world of romantic love, a world promulgated and advertised with a ferocity unprecedented in the history of emotional propaganda. Orwell tried to be terrifying by imagining a society brainwashed by "the Anti-Sex League." Far more terrifying may be the present reality of an entire society awash in love-and-sex sentimentality and so comfortable with it that it even seems "natural."

Romantic love is but one example of an emotion that, no matter how private and personal, must nevertheless be understood as a public, cultural phenomenon. Love is something learned – from every movie and toothpaste advertisement, from a hundred romances, from street-corner gossip, and from our whole cultural apparatus of chance meetings, dating, and unarranged (not to say inappropriate) marriages. But learning love in general is not knowing how to love. Love can be vulgar (mere possessiveness, for example) or it can be exquisite – and the latter, like the former, is something learned. It is one thing to love someone; that in itself is learned in a society where (romantic) love is considered essential – more important, for example, than established family or community ties and obligations, more important than duty and honor (though not necessarily incompatible with them). But how one loves is something more, and this too is learned. What literacy does to love is nothing less than to make it possible. Love – every love – is a narrative that follows an embarrassingly small number of plots, but they are and must be well-known plots, for they define the emotion. A young couple need not share the tragic consequences of young Montague and Capulet to recognize in their own situation – feuding families, necessarily clandestine love – a story that is a classic of the genre, and a set of emotions that defines so much of our social structure. (Just suppose that we did not consider love to be legitimate unless it were sanctioned and encouraged by one's parents.) Learning the desperation of clandestine love, and the sense of heroism that goes with it, is one of the lessons of literature. (Learning the legitimacy and the heroism of *unrequited* love is also one of the classic and more curious dimensions of our emotional cultural life.)

Learning that love can be tender is obviously one of the more essential lessons of literature. A moment's thought should establish that such tenderness is by no means "natural" and requires a social emotional structure of considerable strength to maintain. Learning that love can be tragic is of no small importance, but perhaps most important is simply the lesson that love is important, even the most important thing in life (a sentiment that is by no means obvious in the state of nature). By the same token, one learns jealousy along with love – the strength of that emotion depending on corresponding lessons in possessiveness, betrayal, and the illusions of exclusivity. It is worth commenting, in this regard, that the prototype of our literature about jealousy – and the model for our emotion – is *Othello*, in which jealousy is a tragic emotion, inspired by trickery and maintained by a kind of stupidity, and most important (it turns out), unwarranted and unnecessary. Our lesson in envy from the same source, however, turns out to be much more mixed; Iago may not be a hero, but he does succeed in his envious designs. Our literature encourages love and discourages jealousy, but our vision of envy is not so clear. It would be a study of no small importance and enormous scope: the place of envy in American literature – and American life.

The kind of argument that is merely suggested here – the ways in which literature defines and teaches emotion – could and should be developed for a spectrum of emotions and a wide body of international literature. But the connection between emotions and literature inspires or illustrates emotions and provides us with examples of them. Literature – taken broadly as the shared perspectives and narratives of a culture – actually defines emotions and brings them into being. To teach literature *is* to educate the emotions, although, as with any teaching, this can be done consciously or unconsciously, competently or incompetently. To teach literature is to teach how other people feel, and how we would feel if. . . . It is to teach us *to* feel certain emotions, and to articulate and understand the emotions we do have. Literacy is not just good for or food for the emotions; it is, ultimately, what the emotions are all about.

Literature and the vicarious emotions

It is one of the oldest debates in both philosophy and social criticism: Do the emotions we experience "vicariously" through literature (including drama and film) have a healthy or a deleterious effect on us? Plato fought Aristotle on the desirability of "catharsis" in the theater, and long and varied traditions of moral psychologists throughout the history of Christian theology have argued the acceptability of vicarious experiences of the more sinful emotions as opposed to the actual sins. (Vicarious faith and Platonic love presented very different issues.) Greek comedies presented deception, cowardice, and foolishness; but the question was, did these encourage or discourage these vices in their audience? Medieval morality plays had as their unquestioned intention the discouragement of lust, envy, gluttony, anger, pride, etc., but it was a burning question then as now whether the portrayal of such passions, even unsympathetically, would nevertheless stimulate precisely the sins depicted. Today, the argument revolves around pornography and violence on television. The question remains whether such "vicarious" experiences, even if presented or intended in a discouraging light, have a positive or negative effect on the emotions.

The distinction between vicarious and genuine emotions, however, is not at all so clear as the proponents of the various traditional moral arguments would suggest. So, too, the charge that people who read books have thereby only vicarious emotions, not real experiences, does not hold up to examination. Of course, there is an obvious difference that can be granted right from the start: Readers of a terrifying or bloody novel (*Frankenstein, All Quiet on the Western Front*) or viewers of a horrifying movie (*Jaws, King Kong*) have the luxury of fear, terror, and horror without the real risk of harm. The "willing suspension of disbelief" explains how they have such experiences. What is by no means so evident is why they choose to have them. Whether they are real experiences of fear or not, they are certainly real emotions – real as such – of some kind, and this needs to be explained. In this regard it might also be wise to distinguish – as is too rarely done – between the emotions of fear and terror on the one hand and horror on the other. What gets experienced while reading frightening books and viewing "horror movies" is properly horror, not terror. Terror, one might say, is real fear; it believes in the danger of its object. No "willing suspension" there. Horror, on the other hand, tends to be horror regarding an idea, one step removed. One is horrified by the very thought of a war, or the very idea of child abuse, or the idea of invasion by creatures from other worlds. One does not experience genuine terror reading or viewing a "thriller," but one may well feel genuine horror on reading or viewing a horror tale. Vicarious horror, in other words, is real horror, whether or not vicarious terror is real fear. Both terror and horror should be distinguished, we might add, from mere grossness (a vivid description of an abortion, a close-up of the effects of a gunshot), which grade B writers and filmmakers now tend to employ instead of the more artful skills of suspense and true horror.

Discussions of vicarious emotions (and many discussions of genuine emotion) tend to focus much too heavily on the emotion of fear. A reader of Stendhal, we may readily admit, does not really fear the sudden impact of a bullet in his or her back, and it is also extremely debatable that he or she can literally be said to fear for the fictional hero. But we already mentioned that the emotion of moral indignation one experiences while reading *Uncle Tom's Cabin* is the genuine emotion. Indeed, moral indignation, even in "real life" (and in what sense was *Uncle Tom's Cabin* not "real life?") is an emotion that observes and judges rather than participates. The result of moral indignation may be real action, but the emotion itself is quite real regardless of the possibilities for action. Indeed, *Uncle Tom's Cabin* inspired very real action, even if the events depicted in the book were fictional.

What we just said about moral indignation holds for a great many important emotions. Certainly grief, sadness, amusement, compassion, and pity are real enough whether or not the persons and events on the pages or on the screen are real. So, too, the powerful experience of romantic love experienced by the reader or viewer of a novel or movie. Who would deny that love is often experienced at a distance, directed at persons whom we may know much less than we know a fictional character with whom we have briefly shared a vicarious adventure? And who would deny that the persons with whom we fall in love are often fictional, creations of our own imaginations or Freudian "phantasms" left over from more primal love experiences? What is true of love is also true of hate, and a dozen other passions besides. Indeed, once we start examining the list, it begins to look as if everything we experience while reading is real – except, that is, the story and its characters.

A proper analysis of vicarious emotions would take us far beyond the limited claims of this essay, but the essence of a theory can be sketched very briefly. It is typically argued that an emotion is vicarious and therefore not a real emotion because its object – what it is about – is not real. Now in this sense very few emotions are "real," since almost all emotions – love, hate, anger, or simple compassion – involve a certain subjective reshaping of their objects. The attention of every emotion is selective (we look for virtues in love, vices in hate). Most emotions involve a certain distance from their object, even when it seems that we have never been closer to them. Every emotion constitutes its own object, as the particular, perhaps peculiar, object of that emotion, even if that same object and emotion are shared by hundreds or millions of people – as the great books may be, and the emotions contained therein. To say that the object of an emotion is fictional (and known to be so) is therefore not necessarily to say that the emotion is not real. To insist on this absurdity would be either to limit the range of "real" emotions to a pathetic and extremely timid group of realistic attitudes, or to virtually deny the reality of emotions altogether. The reality of an emotion may have very little to do with the reality (or lack of it) of its object.

What is critical to the reality of an emotion is the position of its subject, the person who actually feels the emotion. In the case of reading (seeing films, etc.) this has a triple edge. It means, first, that to a certain extent the characters or situations in the book (film) already have a certain amount of emotion in them – a frightening situation, a lovable character, a vicious, envy-filled villain. Second, there must be some sense of inference to the emotions of the author, not by way of the infamous "pathetic fallacy" ("Dostoevski must have been really depressed when he wrote this"); but, rather, it is of no small importance that a story has been composed, or retained, by someone, perhaps an entire community. In oral traditions the importance of the emotion in the storyteller (perhaps the entire culture) is self-evident. In modern literature, this link is none too evident, and has often been under attack. But my interest here is not the method of literary criticism; it is the role of emotions in literature. In this connection, it is difficult to deny that the ordinary, nonformalist reader is well aware that behind the pages is another human being. The easy separation of text and author is no evidence against this.

Third, and most important, the reader (or viewer) has emotions, and these are the passions that concern us. The emotions of the personalities in the pages are more or less given to us, and the emotions of the author(s) are for most purposes irrelevant to us. But the emotions of the reader are determined in part by the text, in part by the reader him or herself. Here, perhaps, is the most important advantage of books over film (and other more determinate media): The reader of a book is free to visualize, no matter how precise the description of a character, his or her own version of that character. Not surprisingly, the envisioned figure almost always bears a striking resemblance (whether recognized or not) to persons of importance to the reader. (Such recognition is usually rare; as so many critics have so often said, much of what Freud said about dreams is certainly true of the literary imagination, but in the reader as well as the author.) The reader can "act out" a drama in much more personal terms than the movie viewer, and this same activity of the imagination, whereby one learns how to enact (and reenact) emotions, is, more than anything, the education of the imagination: learning to engage oneself in a variety of emotional roles, in a variety of situations that may never have been encountered in real life – at least, not yet.

What is critical to the education of emotions is precisely the fact that the emotions experienced while reading are not merely vicarious, not unreal, even if the situations and characters of the story may be wholly invented. It is not the reality of the emotion's object that is critical, but rather the reality of the emotion's subject, the reader. But it would be folly of a different kind to think that the reader simply creates his or her emotional experiences, that the emotions in the novel – including the form and structure of the novel as a whole – do not determine and teach emotions to the reader. That is the very importance of the great masterpieces of our literary tradition; they teach those emotions that, for better or worse, our collective culture has chosen as defining the temperament of our age.

Deconstruction and reader response: a polemical difference

My thesis here is that one of the functions of literacy and literature is to educate the emotions. This requires a renewed emphasis on the importance of the reader as subject, but it also requires a somewhat conservative respect for a literary tradition, as defined by its masterpieces and its greatest authors. These two requirements find themselves in uneasy company, however, with both traditional and some contemporary theories of literary criticism. It has long been argued that the text is everything, that the reader just reads, supplying nothing but, one hopes, literacy and comprehension, and perhaps some structural analysis. Today, this nonsense is being overcorrected by "reader response" theory; the reader supplies almost everything, the book and the author are all but incidental. So, too, it has long been argued that literacy demands an uncritical respect if not awe for one's own literary tradition. Today, this view has been violently challenged by some of the Derridian Deconstructionists, who rightly point out some insidious cultural biases in our literary tradition but also nonsensically deny the very existence of authors and masterpieces. Moreover, they reject (or "deconstruct") the very idea of the subject, of author, and of reader, creating an impossible dilemma. But however enticing the logical paradoxes and perplexities of such a position may be, our concern here is literacy and the emotions, and from that perspective, we may simply say that never has there been so inopportune or unfortunate a meeting of literary theory and the fate of literature.

"It would be considered an act of war," warned the National Commission for Excellence in Education (1983), "if some foreign power had done to our educational system what we have done ourselves." The Commission did not have nuts-and-bolts literacy in mind. What is also at stake is our sense of ourselves as a culture and the emotions that give our lives meaning.

It is in the context of this crisis, rather than in my usual spirit of philosophical irritation, that I suggest looking at some of the latest fashions in literary criticism. One might be all too tempted to simply dismiss such teapot tempests if it were not for the fact that they impinge so directly on the current catastrophe.

If anything that I have been saying about literature and the education of emotions is plausible, then it follows that reading and taking literature seriously is essential. Literary theory is not detached from literature (nor will it ever replace it, as a few pundits have recently declared). Literary theory guides reading – and the teaching of reading. An emotionally detached theory – or one that encourages emotional detachment – dictates reading and teaching reading, without emotion, or without taking the emotions seriously. Of course, the literary critic may have his or her own emotions – pride and vanity seem to be most in vogue these days – but they are not drawn from, and are typically antagonistic to, the emotions dictated by the text in question. Such critics teach reading to college students, many of whom go on in turn to teach reading. And contemporary literary theory, even when not the subject of discussion in the classroom, nevertheless circumscribes a manner, an approach to literature.

It is an approach defined, first of all, by the denigration of masterpieces. These are the books that carry our culture. They are also the books that students won't read. ("They are too long . . . they are too hard . . . they are boring.") How do the new theories encourage these resisting readers? These "smug iconoclasms" (so called by critic Jonathan Culler, who defends some of them) entreat students not to admire great books but rather to "deconstruct" them.

"Deconstruction" is the new weapon of high-level anti-intellectualism in America. It is also a devastating technique for undermining emotional involvement. It originated in the intentionally obscure style of French philosopher Jacques Derrida, but it has now infected probably half of the literature departments in our universities.

Deconstruction is, stripped of its self-promotion and paradoxes, a way of not taking texts seriously, not entering into them but undermining them, "reducing" their emotional context to petty subjectivity and thereby not taking it seriously – which is to say, not allowing oneself to feel what the book insists we ought to feel. Deconstruction is, in one sense, just criticism – but it is criticism of a particularly nasty variety. It goes after weaknesses rather than strengths, searching the margins of the text instead of trying to comprehend the whole. Of particular interest to the deconstructionists are political and cultural biases and inconsistencies and, especially, sexual hang-ups. And this is not Norman Mailer they are deconstructing, but Melville and Emily Dickenson.

Consequently, the geniuses of literature are no longer to be admired. Their texts are no longer there to be venerated but rather to be undermined. Their role as vehicles of culture is destroyed, and their power to inspire emotion – any emotion except perhaps contempt or pity – is extinguished. The resisting reader cannot help responding, "Why, then, read them at all?"

The power and the importance of literature in educating the emotions lies in literature's ability to submerge the student in a context (and perhaps a culture) quite different from his or her own. Teachers sometimes talk sympathetically about "tapping into the student's emotional experience," but in fact, this is getting it backward. Literature does not "tap into" so much as it informs and ultimately forms students' emotional experiences. It is essential that a book (or film, etc.) provides the student with something that he or she does not already have – a situation, at least. The core of the emotional experience is in the book (film, etc.), and the student enters into it. It is thus with particular alarm that we should look at those new theories of criticism that as a genus have attracted the title "reader response theories," of which deconstruction is one marginal example.

According to reader response theory, the new heroes of literature – replacing authors and masterpieces – are the barely literate readers and, of course, their English professors. It was Geoffrey Hartmann of Yale who notoriously proclaimed that the creative baton has passed from the author to the literary critic – which, given the readability and intelligibility of current criticism, philosopher John Searle rightly calls the reductio ad absurdum of the movement. But from an emotional point of view, one can only dimly imagine what our passions might be like if we depended upon literary theories to inform them.

Consider, for example, this recent comment from one of the more distinguished professors of literary criticism in America:

No longer is the critic the humble servant of texts whose glories exist independently of anything he might do; it is what he does, within the constraints of the literary institution [i.e., tenured English professors], that brings texts into being and makes them available for analysis and appreciation. [Fish, 1980]

In other words, *Moby Dick* is not the masterpiece. Indeed, Melville's masterpiece would not even exist if it were not being taught and written about by English professors. In fact, we now learn, Melville actually contributed very little; the true creator of the work is the student: "The reader . . . supplies everything" (Fish, 1981).

In other words, any emotions involved in literature are simply supplied by the reader. He or she does not learn. The reader simply supplies an emotion – any emotion, presumably, without regard for the text. If one wants to be amused by Anna's suicide or giggle through *Cry, The Beloved Country*, the text has lost its authority to insist otherwise. (Any relation to a society where teenagers occasionally gun down a stranger "for fun"?)

Literature, I have argued, also teaches us to articulate our emotions. What practical advice do the new theories have to offer today's student, trying to express an emotion in a proper sentence with at best insecure command of English vocabulary and grammar?

"Deprived of a scenario," opines O. B. Hardison, Jr., in the summer 1983 *Sewanee Review,* "students are left with a page on which it is impossible to write an incorrect sentence." (The author calls this "freedom.") The same professor of literature goes on to say,

Since language can no longer produce meanings that allow us to think about contemporary experience, we have to look elsewhere – to mathematics, or abstract art or superrealism, or movies, or, perhaps, new languages created by random selection of words.

One need not denigrate mathematics to doubt its ability to express emotion. And one would not have to look further than some student papers to find such a "random selection of words," but it is not at all clear that what is expressed thereby is "contemporary experience" – or any emotion whatever.

And finally, what could be more detrimental in the current situation than to give in to the worst form of student resentment – perhaps the least honorable of all emotions – and the fact that they despise their (unread) texts just because they are required. And they blame the author for this injustice. But consider a well-known Marxist literary critic who, whatever his political views, is also employed to teach students to admire and enjoy literature. This one celebrates "the revolt of the reader," who has been "brutally proletarianized by the authorial class." He encourages "an all-out putsch to topple the text altogether and install the victorious reading class in its place." It seems not to bother him that the class of readers is quickly becoming a null class. "We don't need the authors," he insists, leaving open the question whether we need any readers, either. And against the tyranny of literature, he encourages "political intervention," "if necessary by hermeneutical violence" (by which he means deliberate misreadings of books – another timely bit of advice for students who don't know how to read carefully in the first place) (Eagleton, 1982).

Now it might be objected that education is not just ingesting books and forming emotions; it is also learning to criticize them. Heroes are to be scrutinized. Emotions are to be evaluated.

But there is a difference between criticism with respect and criticism that undermines the very possibility of enlightened understanding and emotion. It is one thing to question a book or a passion as an ideal; it is something quite different to reject all ideals.

It might also be objected that it is important to encourage individual interpretations and the application of one's own emotional experience to the text. There is no doubt that a 19th-century New England reader of *The Scarlet Letter* inevitably interpreted that book very differently than a contemporary student in Los Angeles. But it is quite different to claim, as is now claimed with a bravado appropriate to its absurdity, that "there is no text," that there are only readers' individual interpretations and emotions. Hawthorne certainly has something to do with our feelings about Hester, and it is not very likely that her experience has already been duplicated by a typical Beverly Hills sophomore.

It might also be objected that most of our "masterpieces" and consequently most of our emotions are "ethnocentric," the product and property of a very narrow segment of the world's population. Deconstruction and its allies deflate this pretension. But the answer to this objection is to broaden the curriculum, to add more books from Africa, Asia, and South America. It is not to eliminate the best works of "Western" literature and pretend that they are of only negative value. To appreciate the emotions of others – including negative emotions caused by one's own society – is extremely important, but it does not necessitate disclaiming or demeaning one's own emotional experience.

Emile Durkheim wrote a century ago that education is primarily concerned not with careers and techniques but with passing along a culture and, we may add, the emotions that are deemed proper to it. Literature is a primary vehicle of that culture and those emotions, and theories of literature are tools to service that vehicle. They help teachers to focus and to criticize, to interpret, and to make literature accessible and exciting to students. Inevitably, they will also provoke an entertainment of their own – featuring battles between warring factions of faculty that make the sectarian disputes in Lebanon seem civilized by comparison. But when fashions and fury among the faculty undermine the very purpose of education, literary theory ought to teach and learn a new emotion – humility. If literature teaches us anything about the emotions, it is that whatever we learn to feel, it's all been felt before.

References

Eagleton, T. (1982). "The revolt of the reader." *New Literary History, 13*:3, pp. 449–52.

Fish, S. (1980). *Is there a text in this class?* Cambridge, Mass.: Harvard University Press.

Fish, S. (1981). "Why no one's afraid of Wolfgang Iser." *Diacritics, 11*:1 pp. 2–13.

Hardison Jr., O. B. (1983). "The de-meaning of meaning." *Sewanee Review, 91*, summer, pp. 397–405.

James, W. (1884). "What is an emotion?" *Mind*, pp. 188–205.

Lasch, C. (1978). *The culture of narcissism.* New York: Norton & Co.

National Commission on Excellence in Education (1983). *A nation at risk: The imperative for educational reform.* Washington, D.C.: U.S. Department of Education.

Scheffler, I. (1977). "In praise of the cognitive emotions." *Columbia Educational Review, 79*:2.

Part II

Matters historical and social

5   The legacies of literacy: continuities and contradictions in western society and culture

Harvey J. Graff

Let us set the stage. Consider these statements, from a variety of disciplinary and ideological perspectives, to assist us in preparing our minds for a reconsideration and reconceptualization of literacy:

> Since popular literacy as earlier noted depends not alone on the alphabet but on instruction in the alphabet given at the elementary level of child development, and since this is a political factor which varies from country to country, the alphabetized cultures are not all socially literate.... For whereas historians who have touched upon literacy as a historical phenomenon have commonly measured its progress in terms of the history of writing, the actual conditions of literacy depend upon the history not of writing but reading. [Havelock, 1976, pp. 83,18,19]

> Not long ago anthropologists equated civilization with literacy. Many archaeologists working in the Near East still believe that writing is highly likely to develop as a data storage technique when a given level of complexity is reached. This seems to be supported, for example, by the apparently extensive use of writing for bureaucratic purposes in ancient Egypt.... Yet, the evidence from Africa and the New World reveals that complex societies can exist without fully developed (initially logosyllabic) writing systems and that those early civilizations that lacked writing were of comparable complexity to those that had it.... [Trigger, 1976, p. 39]

> Literacy is for the most part an enabling rather than a causal factor, making possible the development of complex political structures, syllogistic reasoning, scientific enquiry, linear conceptions of reality, scholarly specialization, artistic elaboration, and perhaps certain kinds of individualism and of alienation. Whether, and to what extent, these will in fact develop depends apparently on concomitant factors of ecology, intersocietal relations, and internal ideological and social structural responses to these. [Gough, 1968, p.153]

> For certain uses of language, literacy is not only irrelevant, but is a positive hindrance. [Ong, 1970, p. 21]

These statements may seem too sweeping, too vast, for some, but they are, I believe, important examples of the correctives and revisions only now beginning with respect to our understanding of the presumed impact and consequences of literacy. For until quite recently, scholarly and popular conceptions of the value of reading or writing skills have almost universally followed normative assumptions and expectations of the abstract but powerful concomitants of and effects of changes in the diffusion of literacy. Furthermore, they have been for the last two centuries inextricably and inseparably linked with post-Enlightenment, "liberal" social theories as well as with contemporary expectations of the role of literacy and schooling in socioeconomic development, social order, and individual progress. This set of conjectures in theory, thought, perception, and expectation constitute what I have come to call "the literacy myth."

Along with other tenets of a worldview dominant in the West for the greatest part of the past two centuries, the "literacy myth" no longer suffices as a satisfactory explanation for the place of literacy in society, polity, culture, or economy. Nevertheless, given the massive contradictions that complicate and confuse our understanding of the world, it is hardly surprising that a perceived "crisis" and "decline of literacy" rank among the fears of our day. Because our comprehension of this crisis and decline is no more firm than that of the historical relevance of literacy, now is the time to ask new, if challenging and difficult, questions about literacy and its place, for the (presumed) roles of literacy and schooling are not sacrosanct. Such an awareness – especially in tandem with the advantages only a historical perspective can yield – can be tremendously liberating; and that, I think, is what is required. For, "if we have learned anything from modern European sociology, it is that historical and social interest, not systems of logic, determine what shall count as knowledge." (Martines, 1979, p. 201)

From this perspective, let us turn to an historical understanding of literacy, both for what it may teach us anew about that important past itself, and also for the illumination that it sheds upon pressing questions of the present. The observations and arguments that follow are based upon my work in progress, an interpretive and synthetic history of literacy in the Western world from the invention of writing, circa 3100 B.C., to the present.

Social reality and the literacy myth

Literacy is profoundly misunderstood. This is one natural consequence of the long-standing tyranny of the "literacy myth," which, along with other social and cultural myths, has of course had sufficient grounding in social reality to ensure its wide dissemination and acceptance.

Discussions about literacy are surprisingly facile, whether they come from the pen of a Marshall McLuhan or a contemporary social and educational critic like Paul Copperman, author of *The Literacy Hoax*. Virtually all such discussions, regardless of purpose or intent, flounder because they slight any effort to formulate a consistent and realistic definition of literacy: They have no appreciation of the conceptual complications that the subject of literacy presents, and ignore – often grossly – the vital role of sociohistorical context. The results of such failures surround us; they preclude our knowing even the dimensions of qualitative changes in the people's ability to employ usefully or functionally the skills of reading and writing. Expectations and assumptions with respect to the primacy and priority of literacy and print, for society and individual; the necessity of "functional" skills (whatever they might be) for survival; and the condition of mass literacy as an index of the condition of civilization – all stand unsatisfactorily and inadequately as substitutes for a deeper, more grounded understanding. This ought not be surprising, for it is itself the result of an important historical development: the ideological origins of our own world and society.

Such has often been recognized more cogently by nonhistorians than by those of us who ought to know better. David Olson, for example, an educational psychologist, has observed that

such an overwhelming concern with literacy can only increase one's suspicions that the significance of a universal high degree of literacy is grossly misrepresented. It is overvalued partly because literate people, such as educators, knowing the value of their own work, fail to recognize the value of anyone else's. More importantly, literacy is overvalued because of the very structure of formal schooling – schooling that, in Bruner's words, involves learning "out of the context of action, by means that are primarily symbolic." The currency of schools is words – words, as we saw earlier, that are shaped up for the requirements of literacy. We may have a distorted view of both the child and of social realities if we expect that the values and pleasures of literacy are so great that everyone, whether it is easy or difficult for him, or whether it leads to wealth or power ... or not, is willing to invest the energy and time required to reach a high level of literacy. [Olson, 1975–76, pp. 149, 170]

Reading psychologists Nan Elsasser and Vera John-Steiner also comment:

In spite of the belief, widely held in America, that education in and of itself can transform both people's sense of power and the existing social and economic hierarchies, educational intervention without actual social change is, in fact, ineffective. [Elsasser and John-Steiner, 1977, pp. 361–62]

We are, I think, quite familiar with these notions; the extent to which we permit them consciously and systematically to reorient our thinking about the roles and relevances of literacy and schooling, past and present, all too often remains a separate and distinct issue.

The first point to consider is definitional. This is at once insolubly complex and deceptively simple. It is depressing but instructive to note how rarely debates and discussions about literacy levels pause to consider what is meant by "literacy." A concomitant of the inattention to context, this failure, on the one hand, invalidates most discussions at the outset and, on the other, permits commentators to use the evidence of changes in such measures as Scholastic Aptitude Test and Armed Forces Qualifying Test results, performance on undergraduate composition examinations, and the like to be taken as appropriate representations of literacy. Whereas I am not claiming that the evidence of such measures should be ignored (although I urge a greater caution in their interpretation), I must emphasize that whatever these indicators reveal, it is typically little or nothing about the skills of literacy: the basic abilities to read and write.

To study and interpret literacy requires three tasks. The first is a consistent definition that will serve comparatively over time and across space. Basic or primary levels of reading and writing constitute the only flexible and reasonable indications that meet this essential criterion; a number of historical and contemporary sources, while not wholly satisfactory in themselves, may be employed (see Table 5–1). Included here are measures ranging from the evidence of written documents, sources that reveal proportions of signatures and marks, the evidence of self-reporting (surprisingly reliable, in fact), responses to surveys and questionnaires, test results, and the like. (see Graff, 1979; Schofield, 1968; Lockridge, 1974; Clanchy, 1979; Furet and Ozouf, 1977; Cressy, 1980; Johansson, 1977.) Only such basic but systematic and direct indications meet the canons of accuracy, utility, and comparability that we must consistently apply. Some may question the quality of such data; others argue that tests of basic skills are too low a standard to employ.

To counter such common objections requires moving to the second task in defining literacy. This is to stress, indeed to underscore, the fact that literacy is above all a technology or set of techniques for communications and for decoding and reproducing written or printed materials; it cannot be taken as any more or any less. Similarly, the protestations of recent scholarship to the contrary, printing is also a technique or tool, a mechanical innovation. Neither writing nor printing alone are "agents of change"; their impacts are determined by the manner in which human agency exploits them. Literacy, moreover, is an acquired skill, in a way in which oral ability or nonverbal, nonliterate communicative modes are not. And, as I will explain later, we need to be wary of drawing strict dichotomies between the oral and the literate. (See McLuhan, 1962, 1964; Eisenstein, 1979; Cremin, 1970; Inkeles and Smith, 1974.)

Writings about the imputed "consequences," "implications," or "concomitants" of literacy have assigned to literacy's acquisition a truly daunting number of cognitive, affective, behavioral, and attitudinal effects, ranging from empathy, innovativeness, achievement orientation, "cosmopolitism," information acquisition and media awareness, national identification, technological acceptance, rationality, commitment to democracy or to opportunism, linearity of thought and behavior, or urban residence! Literacy is sometimes conceived as a skill, but more often as symbolic or representative of attitudes and mentalities. On other levels, literacy "thresholds" are seen as requirements for economic development, "modernization," political development and stability, fertility control, and so on and on. The number of asserted consequences and ecological correlations is literally massive; large volumes could easily be filled with them. The evidence, however, does not support the expectations and presumptions, as a review of the literature quickly reveals. One major contradiction in the literacy-as-a-path-to-development argument (or should we say "industry"?) is the disparity between theoretical assumptions and the results of empirical investigations. Schuman, Inkeles, and Smith's effort to account for this (1967, p. 7) is revealing:

Rather than finding literacy to be a factor which completely pervades and shapes a man's entire view of the world, we find it limited to those spheres where vicarious and abstract experience is essentially meaningful. The more practical part of a man's outlook, however, is determined by his daily experiences in significant roles.

Literacy in the abstract, then, can at most be viewed as a technique or set of techniques, a foundation in skills that can be developed, lost, or stagnated; at worst, literacy in the abstract is meaningless.

Hence, understanding literacy requires a third, large step – into precise, historically specific material and cultural contexts. As the psychologist M.M. Lewis (1953, p.16) recognized, "The only literacy that matters is the literacy that is in use. Potential literacy is empty, a void." Our first two points are thus preparatory to the main effort, enabling us to clear the air of so much noise and unfounded generalization. The major problem becomes one of reconstructing the contexts of reading and writing: how, when, where, why, and to whom literacy was transmitted; the meanings that were assigned to it; the uses to which it was put; the demands placed on literate abilities and the degrees to which they were met; the changing extent of social restrictedness in the distribution and diffusion of literacy; and the real and symbolic differences that emanated from such distribution.

Table 5-1. *Sources for the historical study of literacy in North America and Europe*

Source	Measure of literacy	Population
Census	Questions: read and write, read/write	Entire "adult" population (in theory): ages variable, e.g., over 20 years, 15 years, 10 years
Wills	Signature/mark	20–50 percent of adult males dying; 2–5 percent of adult females dying
Deeds	Signature/mark	5–85 percent of living, landowning adult males; 1 percent or less of females
Inventories	Book ownership	25–60 percent of adult males dying; 3–10 percent of adult females dying
Depositions	Signature/mark	Uncertain: potentially more select than wills, potentially wider Women sometimes included
Marriage records	Signature/mark	Nearly all (80 percent +) young men and women marrying (in England)
Catechetical examination records	Reading, memorization, comprehension, writing examinations	Unclear, but seems very wide
Petitions	Signature/mark	Uncertain, potentially very select, males only in most cases
Military recruit records	Signature/mark or question on reading and writing	Conscripts or recruits (males only)
Criminal records	Questions: read, read well, etc.	All arrested
Business records	Signature/mark	1. All employees 2. Customers
Library/mechanics institute records	Books borrowed	Members or borrowers
Applications (land, job pensions, etc.)	Signature/mark	All applicants
Aggregate data source[a]	Questions or direct tests	Varies greatly

Source: Graff, 1979, Appendix A, pp. 325–27. This is a modified and greatly expanded version of Table A in Lockridge, 1974.

Country of availability	Years of availability	Additional variables
Canada, United States	Manuscripts: 19th century	Age, sex, occupation, birthplace, religion, marital status, family size and structure, residence, economic data
Canada, United States, England, France, etc.	Canada, 18th century on; U.S., 1660 on; others from 16th–17th century on	Occupation, charity, family size, residence, estate, sex
Canada, United States	18th century on	Occupation, residence, value of land, type of sale
Canada, United States, England, France, etc.	17th–18th century on (quantity varies by country and date)	Same as wills
Canada, United States, England, Europe	17th–18th century on (use and survival varies)	Potentially: age, occupation, sex, birthplace, residence
England, France, North America	From 1754 in England; 1650 in France	Occupation, age, sex, parents' name and occupation, residence (religion–North America)
Sweden, Finland	After 1620	Occupation, age, tax status, residence, parents' name and status, family size, migration, periodic improvement
Canada, United States, England, Europe	18th century on	Occupation or status, sex, residence, political or social views
Europe, esp. France	19th century	Occupation, health, age, residence, education
Canada, United States, England	19th century	Occupation, age, sex, religion, birthplace, residence, marital status, moral habits, criminal data
Canada, United States, England	19th, 20th centuries	1. Occupation, wages 2. Consumption level, residence, credit
Canada, United States, England	Late 18th–early 19th century	Names of volumes borrowed, society membership
Canada, United States, England, Europe	19th–20th century	Occupation, residence, family, career history, etc.
Canada, United States, England, Europe	19th–20th century	Any or all of the above

ᵃCensuses, educational surveys, statistical society reports, social surveys, government commissions, prison and jail records, etc.

To be sure, answers to these kinds of questions are never easy to construct; nevertheless, the point remains that an awareness of their overriding methodological and interpretive importance is only now beginning to appear in research. The meaning and contribution of literacy, therefore, can not be presumed; they must themselves be a distinct focus of research.

Let me point to several specific examples of such research orientations. The context in which literacy is taught or acquired is one significant area. The seminal work of cross-cultural cognitive psychologists Sylvia Scribner and Michael Cole with the Vai people in Liberia and elsewhere points to the enormously suggestive conclusion that the environment in which students acquire their literacy has a major impact on the cognitive consequences of their possession of the skill and the uses to which it can be put. Children who were formally educated in schools designed for that purpose acquired a rather different set of skills as part of their training than those who learned more informally. Scribner and Cole (1978, p. 449) point toward an interpretation that contradicts the usual view "that literacy leads inevitably to higher forms of thought." "Rather," they argue, "we advocate an approach to literacy that moves beyond generalities to a consideration of the organization and use of literacy in different social contexts" (p. 458). Whereas previous empirical studies did not test literacy itself, confounding it with schooling, Scribner and Cole attempt to distinguish the roles and contributions of the two. In contrast with other researchers, they conclude from their data

that the tendency of schooled populations to generalize across a wide range of problems occurred because schooling provides people with a great deal of practice in treating individual learning problems as instances of general classes of problems. Moreover, we did not assume that the skills promoted by schooling would necessarily be applied in contexts unrelated to school experience. As in previous research, improved performance was associated with years of formal schooling, but literacy in the Vai script did not substitute for schooling. Vai literates were not significantly different from non-literates on any of these cognitive measures, including the sorting and reasoning tasks that had been suggested as especially sensitive to experience with a written language. [Scribner & Cole, 1978, pp. 452–453]

Some psychological consequences were in fact associated with personal engagement in reading and writing, but they were both limited and highly specific to activities with the Vai script. These findings on the restricted impacts of literacy have wide implications; they can usefully enrich historical and contemporary analyses of literacy, especially regarding the time and place in which literacy is acquired and transmitted in circumstances outside the environment of the schoolroom and formal in-

stitutional settings. Such research must also limit the assumptions and expectations that researchers carry to studies of literacy – such as presuppos-
ing literacy to be "liberating" or "revolutionary" in its consequences. There
are, I suggest, better reasons to expect the opposite.

A second example involves the tyranny of conceptual dichotomies in
the study and interpretation of literacy. Few research areas suffer from the
obstruction to informed understanding which rigid dichotomization encourages as much as literacy studies. Consider the common distinctions:
literate and illiterate, written and oral, print and script, and so on. None of
these opposites usefully describes actual circumstances; all of them, in
fact, preclude contextual understanding. The oral/literate dichotomy is
the best example; for despite decades of scholars proclaiming a decline in
the pervasiveness and power of the "traditional" oral culture, from the
time of the initial advent of movable typographic printing henceforth, it
has remained equally possible and significant to locate the persisting
power of oral modes of communication. The work of Eric Havelock on
classical Greek literacy or that of Michael Clanchy on medieval English
literacy illustrates the workings of cultural and communicative processes
especially richly. Clanchy (1979) reveals the struggle that writing and written documents waged for their acceptance from the 11th through the 13th
centuries – a time of rising lay literacy. Early written documents, impelled
by the state and the interests of private property, faithfully reproduced the
"words" of oral ceremonies and the rituals that traditionally had accompanied formal agreements; they were also adorned with the traditional
badges of sealed bargains.

Oversimplifying a complicated and sophisticated sociocultural process
of interchange and interaction, we may say that Western literacy, from its
"invention" in the Greek alphabet and first popular diffusion in the city-
states of classical times, was formed, shaped, and conditioned by the oral
world which it penetrated. In earliest times, literacy was highly restricted
and a relatively unprestigious craft; it carried relatively little of the
association with wealth, power, status, and knowledge that it was later to
acquire. Literacy was a tool, useful primarily for serving the needs of state
and bureaucracy, church, and trade. This triumvirate, although reshaped
with the passage of time, has remained incredibly resilient in its cultural
and political hegemony over the social functions of literacy and schooling. And its hegemony was established and continued in a world in which
communications were comprised of the oral and the aural. As reading and
writing began to spread, irregularly and inconsistently, among the population (especially the free males), their links with the larger cultural world of
speech and hearing (and seeing too) were articulated ever more el-

aborately. Writing was used to set down the results of speech; it was also used – perhaps seminally by Plato, if Havelock's speculations are accurate – to facilitate patterns of thought and logic that were exceedingly difficult to understand without the services that its technology could supply. So even with the encroachment of literacy, the ancient world remained an oral world, whether on street corners or in marketplaces, assemblies, theaters, villas, or intellectual gatherings. The word as spoken was most common, and most powerful. This tradition continued from the classical era through the 1,000 years of the Middle Ages and beyond; it is not dead today and may well have been reinforced by the impact of electronic media.

The oral and the literate, then, like the written and the printed, need not be opposed as simple choices. Human history did not proceed in that way; rather, it allowed a deep and rich process of reciprocal interaction and conditioning to occur as literacy gradually spread and gained in acceptance and influence. The poetic and dramatic work of the ancients was supplanted, if not replaced, by a new word: a religion of Jesus rooted in the Gospels, yes, but propagated primarily by oral preaching and teaching. Analogously, classical and other forms of education long remained oral activities; any contradictions within the transmission of literacy by oral instruction are modern misconstruals of traditional ways that apparently succeeded as well as any we know now. They are no more "necessary" as contradictions than the many others that punctuate the historical or contemporary understanding of literacy. The written and then printed word were spread to many semiliterates and illiterates via oral processes; information, news, literature, and religion were thereupon spread far more widely than purely literate means could have allowed. For many centuries, reading itself was an oral, often collective, activity and not the private, silent one we now consider it to be.

Literacy, in the form based on the Western alphabet, therefore, was first shaped by a powerful oral culture; similarly and analogously, writing and written literature were so conditioned, as was printing, by the traditions of both the oral and the manuscript cultures. On the other side, it can not be ignored that reading, writing, and printing have had their impacts upon traditional and oral cultural modes, media, and processes. To search out the interactions and evaluate the nature and impact of the resulting patterns is the task of the student of culture and society.

Another point of special significance should be raised at this juncture. This involves a question of chronology: the comparatively late invention of literacy and the striking recency of the invention of moveable typographic printing, despite the sanctity with which we hold them. First, as Eric Havelock reminds us (1976, p.12):

The biological-historical fact is that *homo sapiens* is a species which uses oral speech, manufactured by the mouth, to communicate. This is his definition. He is not, by definition, a writer or reader. His use of speech, I repeat, has been acquired by processes of natural selection operating over a million years. The habit of using written symbols to represent such speech is just a useful trick which has existed over too short a time to have been built into our genes, whether or not this may happen half a million years hence. It follows that any language can be trans-literated into any system of written symbols that the user of the language may choose without affecting the basic structure of the language. In short, reading man, as opposed to speaking man, is not biologically determined. He wears the ap-pearance of a recent historical accident. . . .

The chronology is a devastatingly simple one: *Homo sapiens* as a species is about one million years old; writing dates from approximately 3,000 B.C. and so is about 5,000 years old (or .5% of humanity's existence); Western literacy dates from about 600 B.C., making it roughly 2,600 years old (.26%); and printing, dating from the 1450s, is now a mere 430 years old. The numerical exercise may appear frivolous; yet I contend that a reflection upon this time sequence and its implications can be both liberating – from the constraints of the present moment or the recent past – and stimulating to new points of view. It assists us in placing literacy and the primacy with which we hold it in a wider, historical context.

Reconceptualizing the history of literacy

On this note, let us return to the issues central to the necessary reconcep-tualization of literacy and its history. As we all are aware, the history of literacy is typically conceived, and always written, in terms of change – usually major kinds of changes in individuals, societies, or states. That is, the epistemological underpinnings governing most thought about literacy are evolutionary ones; the assumption is that literacy, development, growth, and progress are inseparably linked, especially in the modern period. Literacy becomes one of the key elements in the larger parcel of characteristics and processes that remade a traditional, premodern world into the modern West. It has not sufficed to model the history of the West itself in this way; social scientists during the past three decades have argued that the development of the underdeveloped areas must (or, nor-matively, should) recapitulate that of the West, and sometimes have at-tempted to put that vision into practice. This is clearly the moving spirit of the major works by such scholars as McLuhan, Elizabeth Eisenstein,

Lawrence Stone, Jack Goody and Ian Watt, and Carlo Cipolla, although we need not erase their differences in emphasis or interpretation nor their contributions to make the point. Thus, it is not surprising that the history of literacy is also commonly a truncated one: Most studies ignore, as irrelevant or inaccessible, the first 2,000 years of Western literacy – the ages before the so-called advent of printing – despite the major insights that historical experience provides.

This perspective is, I submit, an unduly limiting and distorting one. Its simplicity and linearity obstruct our understanding. We require instead a perspective which emphasizes *continuities* and *contradictions* in the history of Western society and culture, especially with respect to the place of literacy – one which considers the extent of change and discontinuity within that framework. On the one hand, this is a corrective to the long-standing interpretation that slights the role of continuities and traditions, the legacies of literacy. On the other, it constitutes a mode of analysis and a set of theoretical assumptions that seem to explain literacy's complex history more fully and effectively than the former approach has done. (See Graff, 1979, 1986.)

Continuity, as a historical concept, has a surprisingly broad meaning and applicability, despite historians' traditional abhorrence of this aspect of change and development. Among the insidious dichotomies that confuse more than they instruct, that of change versus continuity surely ranks highly. To focus on continuities, however, does not require any neglect of changes or discontinuities. As the economic historian Alexander Gerschenkron (1968, p.13) points out,

It does not require long semantic expeditions through the current uses of the term "continuity" to discover that it denotes a good deal more than stability. Confused and inconsistent as that usage is, unmistakably it refers time and again to the nature of change rather than its absence. Hence the phrase "continuous change" is by no means a contradiction in terms; by the same token, the phrase "discontinuous change" need not be pleonastic at all. It is precisely because continuity and discontinuity can relate to a certain kind of change that the two concepts may be expected to prove useful in historical research.

Thus, concepts of continuity involve comparisons over time as well as awareness of the need to determine the relationship between elements of change operating in any historical moment or situation. Nevertheless, it is useful to employ the language of continuity when describing circumstances in which development and change tend to be more gradual than rapid. This is certainly the case with respect to the history of literacy, especially when that history includes a chronology more inclusive than one beginning in the 15th or 16th centuries.

Table 5-2. *Key points in the history of literacy in the West*

ca. 3100 B.C.	Invention of writing
3100–1500 B.C.	Development of writing systems
650–550 B.C.	"Invention" of Greek alphabet
500–400 B.C.	First school developments, Greek city-states, tradition of literacy for civic purposes
200 B.C.–200 A.D.	Roman public schools
0–1200	Origins and spread of Christianity
800–900	Carolingian language, writing, and bureaucratic developments
1200 and onward	Commercial, urban "revolutions," expanded administration and other uses of literacy and especially writing, development of lay education, rise of vernaculars, "practical" literacy, Protestant heresies
1300 and onward	Rediscovery of classical legacies
1450s	Advent of printing, consolidation of states, Christian humanism
1500s	Reformation, spread of printing, growth of vernacular literatures, expanded schooling (mass literacy in radical Protestant areas)
1600s	Swedish literacy campaign
1700s	Enlightenment and its consolidation of traditions, "liberal" legacies
1800s	School developments, institutionalization, mass literacy, "mass" print media, education for social and economic development – public and compulsory
1900s	Nonprint, electronic media
late 1900s	Crisis of literacy

Particularly impressive within literacy's full history – from the classical Greek civilizations onward – is the role of traditions and legacies. The use of elementary schooling and learning one's letters, for example, for political and civic functions such as moral conduct, respect for social order, and participant citizenship, begins in the Greek city-states during the 5th century B.C. and constitutes a classical legacy regularly rediscovered in the West: during the late Middle Ages, the Renaissance, the Reformation, the Enlightenment, and again during the great institutional reform movements of the 19th century. (For a summary of key points in the history of literacy, see Table 5–2). This series of continuities, or legacies of literacy, is not reductive; rather, it allows us to consider the similarities and differences in rates of literacy, and the like that accompany renewed recognition of the value of expanded popular literacy within differing social or economic contexts. As Gerschenkron (1968, p.38) expresses it, "At all times and in all cases, continuity must be regarded as a tool forged by the historian rather than as something inherently and invariantly contained in the historical matter. To say continuity means to formulate a question or a set of questions and to address it to the material. In other words, this conceptualization provides an appropriate model with which to approach and reinterpret the history of literacy in culture and society.

To take another case, we may return briefly to the issue of the oral and the literate in Western culture. We may now observe that the exaggerated emphasis on change and discontinuity, in addition to the workings of radical dichotomization, were principally responsible for the neglect of the important contribution of oral communications and traditions in receiving, conditioning, shaping, and even accepting the penetration of reading and writing – from the time of the Greeks on to the present.

Finally, we need also consider the equally impressive power of the "trinity" of literacy's primary uses: for reasons of state and administration, theology and faith, and trade and commerce. The priority of these demands for and uses of literacy has remained regardless of the degree of social restrictiveness that regulated the supply curve of popular diffusion. They also have played vital roles in determining the very degree of restriction, the opening and closing of opportunities for the transmission and acquisition of the skills of reading and writing. Commerce and its social and geographical organization, for example, stimulated rising levels of literacy from the 12th century onwards in advanced regions of the West.

The significant link between literacy and religion forms a most vital, if conservative, legacy. Indeed, this critical connection is perhaps the best example of the intricate role of continuities and contradictions in nearly three millenia of Western literacy. The 16th-century Reformations, both Protestant and Catholic, are of course the most striking cases of this phenomenon. But the religious impulse for reading for the propagation of piety and faith long predates that time. Its history is closely tied to the history of Western Christianity, and the contradictions within one are often those of the other. Within the religious tradition, as well, the dialectic between the oral and the written has played a major part, with different balances being struck in different periods, places, and sects. Literacy served to record for time immemorial the Word, but its influence and diffusion came, for centuries, overwhelmingly through oral means of teaching and preaching. Still, many who never themselves came to take the cloth or the collar learned their letters through the agencies of the universal medieval Christian church, using them for the service of state, commerce, letters, or selves. This need not have been a conservative end. The Reformation, however, constituted the first great literacy campaign in the history of the West, with its social legacy of individual literacy as a powerful social and moral force and its pedagogical tradition of compulsory instruction in public institutions specially created for the purposes of the in-

doctrination of the young for explicitly social ends. One of the great innovations of the German or Lutheran Reformation was the recognition
that literacy, a potentially dangerous or subversive skill, could be employed (if controlled) as a medium for popular schooling and training on
a truly unprecedented scale. The great reform was hardly an unambiguous success in its time, but it may well have contributed more to the
cause of popular literacy than to that of piety and religious practice.

We might just add, a bit blithely perhaps, that Luther had a dream,
which depended on universal literacy and schooling for its success; that
the 18th-century Enlightenment prophets of progress and institutional
solutions found the means for its realization; and that the 19th-century
builders of mass institutions and promoters of schools and schooling put
them into practice! The 20th century, we might then conclude, lives with
these legacies.

We see the workings of contradictions in social and cultural development at the core of the progresses that shaped the historical movement of
literacy in the West; they are clearly revealed in the examples presented
here. Conceptually, this orientation requires a sensitivity to and awareness of the fact that the social order produced in a process of social construction contains contradictions, ruptures, inconsistencies, and incom-
patibilities in the fabric of the social life. Some contradictions are
order-threatening or destructive; others are embedded within the ongoing
processes of development. They are present regardless of the extent of
change or continuity, although the outcomes certainly differ. As so-
ciologist Kenneth Benson (1977, pp. 4,5) usefully summarizes, this perspective is a dialectical conceptualization which

differs from conventional strategies in treating these orderly patterns as created,
produced arrangements with latent possibilities which can be transformed. The
dialectical vision of the future (or past, for that matter) is not one of continuous,
predictable development through an extension or consolidation of the present
order; rather the future (or past) has many possibilities and the final determination depends upon human action or praxis.
Contradictions grow out of social production in two ways. First, there is in any
social setting a contradiction between ongoing production and the previously established social formation. . . . Second, the production process is carried out in different social contexts producing multiple and incompatible social forms.

I think it is indisputable that the history of Western literacy is a story of
contradictions and that an explicit recognition of this is a prerequisite to
a full understanding of that history. Even the relatively recent historical
conjuncture between the deep faith we place in the efficacy and utility of
literacy and schooling and the fragile evidence of the power of literacy's
own contribution is explicable only in this perspective. So too are the ap-

parent limits to literacy, and the dimensions of a crisis rooted in perceptions of its presumed decline.

Other examples are revealing. They exist on a number of social and cultural levels, ranging from the disjunctures between the promoted uses of literacy and the social purposes that propel its widest diffusion; the functional and nonfunctional uses of literacy; the self-activating potentials of literacy and the realities of its most common contributions and typical uses; the social theories and experiential realities; the liberating potentials and the integrating, homogenizing, controlling uses. To understand literacy, therefore, means that contradictions – oppositions, negations, countervailing factors, or dialectical synthesis – must be expected to result from the ongoing processes and developments along with culture, polity, economy, and society. These processes and developments are neither ironic nor paradoxical, as some call them, but fundamentally historical.

Literacy's relationship with the processes of economic development, from the Middle Ages through the 19th century, provides one of the most striking examples of the pattern of contradictions. Contrary to popular and scholarly wisdom, major steps forward in trade, commerce, and even industry took place in some periods and places with remarkably low levels of literacy; conversely, higher levels of literacy have not proved to be stimulants or springboards for "modern" economic developments. More important than high rates or "threshold levels" of literacy, such as those postulated by Anderson and Bowman or E. G. West, have been the educational levels and power relations of key persons rather than those of the many; the roles of capital accumulation, cultural capital, and technological innovations and the ability to put them into practice; or the consumer demands and distribution – marketing – transportation – communication linkages. Major "takeoffs," from the commercial revolution of the Middle Ages to 18th-century protoindustrialization in rural areas and even factory industry in towns and cities, owed relatively and perhaps surprisingly little to popular literacy abilities or schooling. Early industrialization, as the evidence from a number of studies agrees, owed little to literacy or the school; its demands upon the labor force were rarely intellectual or cognitive in nature. In fact, industrialization often reduced opportunities for schooling – and, consequently, rates of literacy fell as it took its toll on the "human capital" on which it fed. In much of Europe, and certainly in England – the paradigmatic case – industrial development (the "First Industrial Revolution") was neither built on the shoulders of a literate society nor served to increase popular levels of literacy, at least in the short run. In other places (typically later in time, however), the fact of higher levels of popular education prior to the advent of factory capitalism may well have made the process a different one, with different needs and results. The presence of a literate *and* formally schooled population may have contributed to a rapid but smoother, less violent and conflict-ridden, transition to the factory; the sequence of earlier school development serving to prepare the future work force for the conduct, habits, behavior, rhythms, and discipline required by the factory. Or so it currently seems. Literacy, by the 19th century, became vital in the process of "training in being trained." Finally, it may also be the case that the "literacy" required for the technological inventiveness and innovations that made the process possible was not a literacy of the alphabetic sort at all, but rather a more visual, experimental one.

In conclusion, let us turn to several additional aspects of the history of literacy in the Western world. Our goal here is twofold. On the one hand, we may learn a bit more about the emerging results of recent literacy studies; on the other hand, and equally importantly, we may also note some of the lessons of the past. For the proper study of the historical experience of literacy has more than antiquarian interest; it has much to tell us that is, I believe, relevant to policy analysis and policy making in the world in which we live today.

Consider first the idea of multiple paths to the making of literate societies and states. The history of literacy clearly shows that there is no one route to universal literacy, that there is no one path destined to succeed in the achievement of mass literacy. In the history of the Western world, one may distinguish the roles of private and public schooling in the attainment of high rates of popular literacy, as well as those of informal and formal, and of voluntary and compulsory, education. Mass literacy was achieved in Sweden, for example, without formal schooling or instruction in writing. High rates of literacy have followed from all of these approaches in different cases and contexts. The developmental consequences are equally varied. Yet,

perhaps the most striking feature of UNESCO discussions on literacy since 1965, when a campaign to wipe out world illiteracy got going, is that it is remarkably little based on either experiment or historical precedents. Rather, in spite of Adam Curle's careful warnings in 1964, action seems as much based on self-evident axioms and hope as on anything else. UNESCO assumes that literacy is a good thing – more latterly, functional literacy. Furthermore, in no clearly defined or understood way poverty, disease, and general backwardness are believed connected with illiteracy; progress, health, and economic well-being are equally self-evidently connected with literacy. UNESCO is committed to what amounts to a modernization theory to the effect that economic progress follows upon a change in man from illiterate to literate, preferably in one generation, and, even better, in the very same man. It is presupposed that such a change will lead, if not immediately then inevitably, to such changes and values in a society that economic progress – and in its train good health, longevity, and, perhaps, peace – is possible. [Winchester, 1978, 1980, p.1]

The past, not surprisingly, provides a different set of experiences than those assumed by UNESCO expectations. Although neither all the research nor the balance sheet of historical interpretations is in, we may safely argue that historical experiences furnish a more appropriate and accurate guide to such critical questions as how and to what degree basic literacy contributes to the economic and individual well-being of persons in different socioeconomic contexts, and under what circumstances universal literacy can be achieved. The costs and benefits of alternative paths can be discerned, too. Thus, the connections and disconnections between literacy and commercial development – a favorable relationship – and literacy and industrial development – often an unfavorable linkage, at least in the short run of decades and half-centuries, offer important case studies and analogs for analysis. If nothing else, the data of the past strongly suggest that a simple, linear, modernization model in which literacy is a prerequisite for development and development a stimulant to increased levels of schooling, will not suffice. Too many periods of lags, backward linkages, setbacks, and contradictions have existed to permit such cavalier theorizing to continue without serious challenge and criticism.

The example of Sweden is perhaps the most important in this respect. This case provides the most richly documented illustration of a transition to mass literacy in the Western world, and has much to teach us. As revealed in the pioneering researches of Egil Johansson, near-universal levels of literacy were achieved rapidly and permanently in Sweden in the wake of the Reformation. Under the joint efforts of the Lutheran Church and the state, reading literacy was required for all persons by law, from the 17th century. Within a century, remarkably high levels of literacy among the population existed, without any concomitant development of formal schooling, or economic or cultural development that demanded functional or practical employment of literacy, and in a manner that led to a literacy defined by reading and not by writing. Urbanization, commercialization, and industrialization had nothing to do with the process of making the Swedish people perhaps the most literate in the West before the 18th century. Contrary to the paths of literacy taken elsewhere, this campaign, begun by King Charles XI, was sponsored by the state church. By legal requirement and vigilant supervision that included regular personal examination by parish clergy, the church stood above a system rooted in home education. The rationale of this literacy campaign, one of the most successful in Western history before the last two decades, was conservative: piety, civility, orderliness, and military preparedness were its major goals. The former was as important as the other reasons, and in the end it was the decisive one. Ian Winchester succinctly summarizes the conclusions of Swedish scholarship:

A Protestant in order to receive the sacraments or to marry must be able to read God's word directly. With the enactment of laws restricting marriage to the literate, a direct incentive upon which the parish priests could act was in the hands of the Swedish church. The net effect was that the custodians of reading became the parish priests and their instruments the families in the Swedish farming villages. From the time of Charles XI onward the priests, with increasing rigour, made annual tours of every household, testing the reading and understanding level of every Swede with respect to Luther's Little Catechism (the Swedish translation of the Bible was a little delayed). The annual testing program was standardized early and the results survive in manuscript form for the bulk of the population. [Winchester, 1978, 1980, P.4; see also Johansson, 1977]

Significantly, the home and church education model fashioned by the Swedes not only succeeded in training a literate population, but it also placed a special priority on the literacy of women and mothers. This led to Sweden's anomalous achievement of female literacy rates as high or higher than male rates, a very rare result in Western transitions to mass literacy. Sweden also marched to its impressive levels of reading diffusion without writing; it was not until the mid-19th century and the erection of a state-supported public school system in Sweden that writing, in addition to reading, became a part of popular literacy and a concern of teachers. Finally, we note that the only other areas so fully and quickly achieving near-universal levels of literacy before the end of the 18th century were places of intensely pious religion, usually but not always Protestant: Scotland, New England, Huguenot French centers, and places within Germany and Switzerland.

From the classical period henceforth, leaders of polities and churches, reformers as well as conservers, have recognized the uses of literacy and schooling. Often they have perceived unbridled, untempered literacy as potentially dangerous: a threat to social order, political integration, economic productivity, and patterns of authority. But increasingly they also concluded that literacy, if taught in carefully controlled formal institutions created expressly for the purposes of education and supervised closely, could be a powerful and useful force. Precedents long predated the first systematic efforts to put this conception of literacy into practice – in Rome, for example, and in the visionary proposals of the 15th- and 16th-century Christian humanists. But for our purposes the Reformations of the 16th century represented the first great educational campaigns. As the Swedish case reminds us, they were hardly homogeneous efforts, either in design or in degree of success. Nonetheless, they were precedent-setting and epochal in their significance for the future of Western social and educational development. In their own times, many of wealth and power still doubted the efficacy of schooling the masses.

With the Enlightenment and its heritage came the final ideological underpinnings for the "modern" and "liberal" reforms of popular schooling and institution-building that established the network of educational, social, political, and economic relationships central to the dominant ideologies and their social theoretical expressions for the past century and a half. Prussia, revealingly, took the lead, and provided a laboratory that United States, Canadian, English, French, and Scandinavian school promoters and reformers regularly came to study. North Americans and Swedes followed, and in time and in their own ways, so did the English, French, and Italians.

We must not slight other important uses of literacy, such as for personal advancement, entertainment, or collective action in cultural, political, or economic terms. Although these crucial topics are not within my main focus in this essay, the significance of literacy to individuals and groups throughout history is undoubted. There is already a large if uneven body of studies with this emphasis, highlighting the value of literacy to individual success, the acquisition of opportunities and knowledge, and collective consciousness and action. The writings of Robert K. Webb, Richard Altick, Thomas Laqueur, and Michael Clanchy, among many others, make this case with force and evidence. The role of class and group-specific demands for literacy's skills, the impact of motivation, and the growing perception of its values and benefits are among the major factors that explain the historical contours of changing rates of popular literacy. Any complete understanding and appreciation of literacy's history must incorporate the large, if sometimes exaggerated and decontextualized, role of demand (in dialectical relationship to supply) and the very real benefits that literacy may bring. Literacy's limits must also be appreciated.

It remains, nevertheless, important to stress the integrating and hegemony-creating functions of literacy provision through formal schooling. Especially with the transition from preindustrial social orders based on rank and deference to the class societies of commercial and then factory capitalism, schooling became an increasingly vital aspect of the maintenance of social stability, particularly during periods of massive, but often poorly understood, social and economic change. Many persons, most prominently social and economic leaders and social reformers, grasped the uses of schooling and saw literacy as a vehicle for the promotion of the values, attitudes, and habits considered essential to the maintenance of social order and the persistence of integration and cohesion.

The acceptance by the "masses" of literacy's import forms the other dimension of this history. A final aspect focuses on the question of the quality, as opposed to quantity, of literacy. Because of the nature of the evidence, virtually all historical studies have concentrated on the measurement of the extent and distribution of reading and writing; issues involving the level of the skills themselves and the abilities to use those skills have not attracted a great deal of attention. What research has been conducted, however, arrives at the common conclusion that qualitative abilities can not be inferred simply or directly from the quantitative levels of literacy's diffusion. Studies of early modern England, 18th- and 19th-century Sweden, and urban areas in the 19th century all suggest that there is a significant disparity between high levels of the possession of literacy and the usefulness of those skills. In Sweden, for example, where systematic evidence exists, a great many persons who had attained high levels of oral reading skill did not have comparable abilities with respect to comprehension of what they read. Other data lean toward similar interpretations for other places.

Such findings mean that the measurement of the distribution of literacy in a population may in fact reveal relatively little about the uses to which such skills could be put and the degree to which different demands on personal literacy could be satisfied with the skills commonly held. Thus, it is possible that with increasing rates of popular literacy did not come ever-rising qualitative abilities. Finally, and potentially most important today, such evidence places the often-asserted contemporary decline of literacy in a fresher and historically informed perspective: that is, the possiblity that mass levels of ability to *use* literacy may have, over the long term, typically lagged behind the near universality of literacy rates. The recent decline, so often proclaimed but so ineffectively measured and so little understood, may be much less of a major decline than we are told. Perhaps we should pay more attention to longer-term trends than those encompassing a decade or two. Perhaps we should look more to changes in popular communicative abilities among students than to "competency examinations" and SAT test scores.

Having begun with quotations, I should like to conclude in like manner. First, we need to understand that:

The old gray mare was never what she used to be. Very few people read many books in this or any other country, and I think that a source of delusion is that many of us who think a lot about these things grew up in book-oriented homes and had book-orientated childhoods, and, hence, tend to project our childhood experiences back in the recollection of that era. I think this is certainly true of a lot of what we perceive as a dramatic new problem of marginal literacy, or illiteracy, in the core city populations of our country. We forget that this marginal literacy or illiteracy was there all along. It was just invisible in the plantations in Mississippi or Puerto Rico, and it's become very visible when you moved it up to a large city and into occupations where reading became a necessary function. [Lacy, 1978, pp. 82–83]

And then we can consider:

What would happen if the whole world became literate? Answer: Not so very much, for the world is by and large structured in such a way that it is capable of absorbing the impact. But if the world consisted of literate, autonomous, critical, constructive people, capable of translating ideas into action, individually or collectively – the world would change. [Galtung, 1976, p.93]

Literacy is neither the major problem, nor is it the main solution.

Note

This essay represents an interim statement of the interpretations presented in my book of the same title. Due to be published in 1986, this is a lengthy, interpretive survey history of literacy in Western society and culture spanning the five millenia from the invention of writing to the "future." For assistance, I wish to acknowledge the important contributions of the American Council of Learned Societies, the Spencer Foundation, the Newberry Library, and the National Endowment for the Humanities. The essay and most of the first draft of the book on which it is based were written while I was an NEH Fellow at the Newberry Library; the support of both of these important scholarly agencies has made my progress more rapid, satisfying, and enjoyable than it might otherwise have been. Those individuals who have aided me in one way or another are too many to list here; I hope they know my gratitude.

Preliminary versions of this paper or its major ideas were presented to audiences at the Social Science History Association in November, 1979; the University of Toronto and Ontario Institute for Studies in Education in January, 1980; the University of Delaware in February, 1980; the Seminar on the History of Literacy in Post-Reformation Europe, University of Leicester, England, in March, 1980; the Newberry Library Fellows' Seminar and the University of Pennsylvania Communications Colloquium in April, 1980; the University of Chicago History of Education Workshop in June, 1980; and the Summer Institute for Teacher Education, Simon Fraser University, in July, 1981.

A penultimate draft was presented to the Conference on the History of Literacy, sponsored by the Library of Congress Center for the Book and the National Institute of Education in July, 1980. My ideas were challenged, tested, and sharpened by encounters with all these groups. To them also go my thanks.

References

Anderson, C. A. (1965). Literacy and schooling on the development threshold. In C. A. Anderson and M. J. Bowman (Eds.), *Education and economic development*, pp. 247–263. Chicago: Aldine.

Aston, M. (1977). Lollardy and literacy. *History, 62*, 347-371.

Bataille, L. (Ed.) (1976). *A turning point for literacy*. New York and Oxford: Pergamon Press.

Benson, K. (1977). Organizations: A dialectical view. *Administrative Science Quarterly, 22*.

Blaug, M. (1966). Literacy and economic development. *School Review, 74*, 393-417.

Bowman, M. J., and Anderson, C. A. (1963). Concerning the role of education in development. In Clifford C. Geertz (Ed.), *Old societies and new states*, pp.247-279. New York: Free Press.

Bowman, M. J., and Anderson, C. A. (1976). Education and economic modernization in historical perspective. In Lawrence Stone (Ed.), *Schooling and society*, pp. 3-19. Baltimore: Johns Hopkins University Press.

Bruneau, W. A. (1973). Literacy, urbanization, and education in three ancient cultures. *Journal of Education* (British Columbia), *19*, 9-22.

Burke, P. (1978). *Popular culture in early modern Europe*. New York: Harper and Row.

Cipolla, C. (1969). *Literacy and development in the West*. Harmondsworth: Penguin.

Clanchy, M. T. (1979). *From memory to written record: England, 1066-1307*. Cambridge, Ma.: Harvard University Press.

Cremin, L. (1970). *American education: The colonial experience*. New York: Harper and Row.

Cressy, D. (1980). *Literacy and the social order*. Cambridge: Cambridge University Press.

Davis, N. Z. (1975). Printing and the people. In *Society and culture in early modern France*, pp. 189-226. Stanford, Ca.: Stanford University Press.

Douglas, G. H. (1977). Is literacy really declining? *Educational Records, 57*, 140-148.

Eisenstein, E. L. (1979). *The printing press as an agent of change*. Cambridge: Cambridge University Press.

Farr, R., Fay, L., and Negley, H. H. (1974). *Then and now: Reading achievement in the U. S.* Bloomington: University of Indiana School of Education.

Farr, R., Fay, L., & Negley, H. H. (1978). *Then and now: Reading achievement in Indiana (1944-45 and 1976)*. Bloomington: University of Indiana School of Education.

Ferguson, E. (1977). The mind's eye: Nonverbal thought in technology. *Science, 197*, 827-36.

Field, A. J. (1974). *Educational reform and manufacturing development in mid-nineteenth-century Massachusetts*. Unpublished Ph.D. Dissertation, University of California, Berkeley.

Field, A. J. (1976) Educational expansion in mid-nineteenth-century Massachusetts. *Harvard Educational Review, 46*, 521-552.

Field, A. J. (1979). Economic and demographic determinants of educational commitment: Massachusetts, 1855. *Journal of Economic History, 39*, 439-459.

Field, A. J. (1979). Occupational structure, dissent, and educational commitment: Lancashire, 1841. *Research in Economic History, 4*, 235-287.

Flora, P. (1973). Historical processes of social mobilization. In S. Eisenstadt and S. Rokkan (Eds.), *Building states and nations* (Vol. 1), pp. 213-258. Beverly Hills, Ca.: Sage.

Furet, F. and Ozouf, J. (1976). Literacy and industrialization. *Journal of Economic European History, 5*, 5-44.

Furet, F. and Ozouf, J. (1977). *Lire et ecrire* (2 vols.) Paris: Les editions de Minuit. (English translation of Vol. 1 published in 1983 by Cambridge University Press as *Reading and Writing*).

Galtung, J. (1976). Literacy, education, and schooling - for what? In Leon Bataille (Ed.), *A turning point for literacy*, pp. 93-105. New York and Oxford: Pergamon Press.

Gerhardsson, B. (1961). *Memory and manuscript: Oral tradition and written transmission in Rabbinic Judaism and early Christianity*. Uppsala, Lund, and Copenhagen: Acta Seminarii Neotestamentici Upsaliensis, XII.

Gerschenkron, A. (1968). *Continuity in history and other essays*. Cambridge, Ma.: Harvard University Press.

Goody, J. (1977). *The domestication of the savage mind*. Cambridge: Cambridge University Press.

Goody, J. (Ed.) (1968). *Literacy in traditional societies*. Cambridge: Cambridge University Press.

Goody, J., Cole, M., and Scribner, S. (1977). Writing and formal operations: A case study among the Vai. *Africa, 47*, 289–304.

Goody, J. and Watt, I. (1968). The consequences of literacy. in Jack Goody (Ed.), *Literacy in traditional societies*. Cambridge: Cambridge University Press.

Gough, K. (1968). Literacy in Kerala. In Goody (Ed.) (1968).

Graff, H. (1976, 1979). *Literacy in history: An interdisciplinary research bibliography*. Chicago: The Newberry Library; rev. ed., New York: Garland Press, 1981.

Graff, H. (1978). Literacy past and present: Critical approaches to the literacy-society relationship. *Interchange, 9*, 1–21.

Graff, H. (1979). *The literacy myth: Literacy and social structure in the nineteenth-century city*. New York and London: Academic Press.

Graff, H. (1986). *The legacies of literacy: Continuities and contradictions in Western society and culture*. Bloomington, Ind.: Indiana University Press.

Graff, H. (Ed.) (1982). *Literacy and social development in the West*. Cambridge: Cambridge University Press.

Havelock, E. (1963). *Preface to Plato*. Cambridge, Ma.: Harvard University Press.

Havelock, E. (1976). *Origins of Western literacy*. Toronto: Ontario Institute for Studies in Education.

Havelock, E. (1977). The preliteracy of the Greeks. *New Literary History, 8*, 369–392.

Inkeles, A., and Smith, D. H (1974). *Becoming modern*. Cambridge, Ma.: Harvard University Press.

Irvins, W. M., Jr. (1953). *Prints and visual communications*. Cambridge, Ma.: MIT Press.

Johansson, E. (1977). The history of literacy in Sweden, in comparison with some other countries. *Educational Reports*, No. 12. Umea. Sweden: Umea University and School of Education.

Johansson, E. (1979). The postliteracy problem – illusion or reality in modern Sweden? In Jan Sundin and Erik Soderlund (Eds.), *Time, space, and man*, pp. 199–212. Stockholm: Almqvist and Wiksell.

Johnson, R. (1976). Notes on the schooling of the English working class, 1780–1850. In R. Dale, G. Esland, and M. MacDonald (Eds.), *Schooling and capitalism*, pp. 44–54. London: Routledge and Kegan Paul.

Kaestle, C. (1976). "Between the scylla of brutal ignorance and the charybdis of a literary education": Elite attitudes toward mass schooling in early industrial England and America. In Lawrence Stone (Ed.), *Schooling and society*, pp. 177–191. Baltimore: Johns Hopkins University Press.

Kaestle, C., and Vinovskis, M. (1980). *Education and social change in nineteenth-century Massachusetts*. Cambridge: Cambridge University Press.

Katz, M. B. (1976) The origins of public education: A reassessment. *History of Education Quarterly, 14*, 381–407.

Katz, M. B. (1976). The origins of public education: A reassessment. *History of Education*

Kerber, L. K. (1974). Daughters of Columbia: Educating women for the republic. In Stanley M. Elkins and Eric L. McKitrick (Eds.), *The Hofstadter aegis*, pp. 36–60. New York: Knopf.

Lacy, D. (1978). The view from the world of publishing. In Library of Congress, Center for the Book, *Television, the book, and the classroom*. Washington, D.C.: Library of Congress.

Laqueur, T. (1974). Critique of Sanderson's "Literacy and social mobility in the industrial revolution." *Past and Present, 64,* 96–108.

Laqueur, T. (1976a). The cultural origins of popular literacy in England, 1500–1800. *Oxford Review of Education, 2,* 255–275.

Laqueur, T. (1976b). *Religion and respectability.* New Haven: Yale University Press.

Laqueur, T. (1976c). Working-class demand and the growth of English elementary education, 1750–1850. In Lawrence Stone (Ed.), *Schooling and society,* pp. 192–205. Baltimore: Johns Hopkins University Press.

Leith, J. A. (1973). Modernisation, mass education, and social mobility in French thought, 1750–1789. In R. F. Brissenden (Ed.), *Studies in the eighteenth century* (Vol. 2), pp. 223–238. Canberra: Australian National University Press.

Leith, J. A. (Ed.) (1977). *Facets of education in the eighteenth century.* Studies on Voltaire and the eighteenth century, 167.

LeRoy Ladurie, E. (1975). *Montaillou, the peasants of Lanquedoc.* Urbana: University of Illinois Press.

LeRoy Ladurie, E. (1978). *Montaillou: Promised land of error.* New York: Braziller.

Levine, D. (1977). *Family formation in an age of nascent capitalism.* New York and London: Academic Press.

Levine, D. (1979). Education and family life in early industrial England. *Journal of Family History, 4,* 368–380.

Lewis, M. M. (1953). *The importance of literacy.* London: Harrap.

Lockridge, K. A. (1974). *Literacy in colonial New England.* New York: Norton.

Lockridge, K. A. (1977). L'alphabetisation en Amerique. *Annales; e,s,c,30,* 503–518.

McClelland, D. C. (1966). Does education accelerate economic growth? *Economic Development and Cultural Change, 14,* 257–278.

McLuhan, M. (1962). *The Gutenberg galaxy.* Toronto: University of Toronto Press.

McLuhan, M. (1964). *Understanding media.* New York: McGraw-Hill.

Martin, H. J. (1975). Culture ecrite et culture orale, culture savante et culture populaire dans la France d'Ancien Regime. *Journale des Savants,* 225–282.

Martines, L. (1979). *Power and imagination: City-states in Renaissance Italy.* New York: Knopf.

Maynes, M. J. (1977). *Schooling the masses.* Unpublished Ph.D. Dissertation, University of Michigan.

Maynes, M. J. (1979). The virtues of anachronism: The political economy of schooling in Europe, 1750–1850. *Comparative Studies in Society and History, 21,* 611–625.

Mortier, R. (1968). The "philosophies" and public education. *Yale French Studies, 40,* 62–76.

Nipperdey, T. (1977). Mass education and modernization – the case of Germany. *Transactions,* Royal Historical Society, *27* 155–172.

Olson, D. (1975–76). Review: *Toward a literate society. Proceedings,* National Academy of Education, 109–178.

Olson, D. (1977). From utterance to text: The bias of language in speech and writing. *Harvard Educational Review, 47,* 257–86.

Ong, W. (1970). *The presence of the word.* New York: Simon and Schuster.

Ong, W. (1971). *Interfaces of the word.* Ithaca, N. Y.: Cornell University Press.

Ong, W. (1971). *Rhetoric, romance, and technology.* Ithaca, N. Y.: Cornell University Press.

Pollard, S. (1968). *The genesis of modern management.* Harmondsworth: Penguin.

Resnick, D. P., and Resnick, L. B. (1977). The nature of literacy: An historical exploration. *Harvard Educational Review, 47,* 370–85.

Sanderson, M. (1967). Education and the factory in industrial Lancashire. *Economic History Review, 20,* 266–79.

Sanderson, M. (1968). Social change and elementary education in industrial Lancashire. *Northern History*, 3, 131–54.

Sanderson, M. (1972). Literacy and social mobility in the industrial revolution. *Past and Present*, 56, 75–105; reply to Laqueur, 1974, 64, 109–12.

Schleunnes, K. A. (1977). The French Revolution and the schooling of European society. *Proceedings*, Consortium on Revolutionary Europe, 140–50.

Schofield, R. S. (1968). The measurement of literacy in pre-industrial England. In J. Goody (Ed.), *Literacy in Traditional Societies*, pp. 311–25. Cambridge: Cambridge University Press.

Schofield, R. S. (1973). The dimensions of illiteracy in England, 1750–1850. *Explorations in Economic History*, 10, 437–54.

Schuman, H.; Inkeles, A.; and Smith, D. (1967). Some social psychological effects and non-effects of literacy in a new nation. *Economic Development and Cultural Change*, 16.

Scribner, S., and Cole, M. (1973). Cognitive consequences of formal and informal education. *Science*, 182, 553–59.

Scribner, S., and Cole, M. (1976). *Studying cognitive consequences of literacy*. Unpublished manuscript.

Scribner, S. and Cole, M. (1978). Literacy without schooling: Testing for intellectual effects. *Harvard Educational Review*, 48, 448–61.

Scribner, S., and Cole. M. (1981). *The psychology of literacy*. Cambridge, Ma.: Harvard University Press.

Spufford, M. (1974). *Contrasting communities*. Cambridge: Cambridge University Press.

Spufford, M. (1979). First steps in literacy: The reading and writing experience of the humblest seventeenth-century spiritual autobiographers. *Social History*, 4, 407–35.

Stephens, W. B. (1977). Illiteracy and schooling in the provincial towns, 1640–1870. In David Reeder (Ed.), *Urban education in the 19th century*, pp. 27–48. London: Taylor and Francis.

Strauss, G. (1975). *Luther's house of learning*. Baltimore: Johns Hopkins University Press.

Thompson, E. P. (1967). Time, work-discipline, and industrial capitalism. *Past and Present*, 38, 56–97.

Trigger, B. G. (1976). Inequality and communication in early civilizations. *Anthropologica*, 18.

Verne, E. (1976). Literacy and industrialization – The dispossession of speech. In Leon Bataille (Ed.), *A turning point for literacy*, pp. 211–28. New York and Oxford: Pergamon Press.

Vinovskis, M. (1970). Horace Mann on the economic productivity of education. *New England Quarterly*, 43, 550–71.

Vovelle, M. (1972). Maggiolo en Provences. Collogue sur le XVIIIeme siecle et l'education. *Revue de Marseille*, 88, 55–62.

Vovelle, M. (1975). Y a-t-il une revolution culturelle au XVIIIe siecle? *Revue d'histoire moderne et contemporaine*, 22, 89–141.

Wallace, A. F. C. (1978). *Rockdale*. New York: Knopf.

Webb, R. K. (1955). *The British working class reader*. London: Allen and Unwin.

West, E. G. (1964). The role of education in 19th century doctrines of political economy. *British Journal of Educational Studies*, 12, 161–74.

West, E. G. (1975). *Education and the industrial revolution*. London: Batsford.

West, E. G. (1977). Literacy and the industrial revolution. *Economic History Review*, 31, 369–83.

Winchester, I. *How many ways to universal literacy?* Unpublished manuscript presented to the Ninth World Congress of Sociology, Uppsala, 1978, and the University of Leicester Seminar on the History of Literacy in Post-Reformation Europe, 1980.

6   Models of literacy in North American schools: social and historical conditions and consequences

Suzanne de Castell and Allan Luke

North American educators have come to view literacy as a set of context-neutral, value-free skills that can be imparted to children with near-scientific precision. Conventional research on literacy instruction in schools draws teachers' attention to the psychological processes whereby children acquire and use the skills of reading and writing. So seen, literacy is a value-neutral competence, and literacy instruction is an enterprise allegedly divorced from any particular ideology. Yet, historically, literacy instruction has always been embedded within a normative context. Each educational epoch has framed literacy instruction in terms of principles, norms, values, and beliefs considered to be worth reading and writing about. In order to situate modern instruction historically, we identify three paradigms of literacy in North American schools: the classical, the progressive, and the technocratic.

The late-19th-century classicist aim of a literacy of high culture subserved the goals of an aristocratic social structure. The progressive shift of focus to the pragmatics of interpersonal communication reflected the early-20th-century enthusiasm for the democratization of culture and society, and for the institutional provision of skilled industrial labor. The technocratic approach to literacy developed in concert with increasing centralization of schooling and led to an emphasis on more standardized and universally verifiable forms of literate behavior. Over the last 30 years, the concern with managerial efficiency and the quantification of educational output has led to a "deconstruction" of literacy – which, in its previous historical forms, constituted a communicational whole – into discrete and measurable subskills.

The prominence of scientifically based instruction, standardized testing, and corporate (multinational) control of school texts is evidence of the widespread acceptance of this most recent redefinition of literacy. We shall argue that the need in both developed and developing nations is for a less standardized and mechanized literacy model: – one that reintegrates the pragmatic and ethical dimensions of communication implicit in any and all literacy instruction. This requires that researchers and educators look beyond psychological explanations of literacy acquisition and use which purport to be exhaustive, universal, and ideologically neutral. Rather, the substantive context of personal, social, and political values must be explicitly addressed, since it is this basis that now, as in the past, determines what is to count as literacy.

Being "literate" has always referred to having mastery over the processes by means of which culturally significant information is coded. The criterion of significance has varied historically with changes in the kind of information from which power and authority could be derived. Educational attempts to redefine literacy, however, have not always faithfully reflected this fact. Studies of literacy in the more distant past (Hoggart, 1958; Havelock, 1976; Graff, 1979) have emphasized the relationship of literacy to evolving modes of social and political organization, yet contemporary educators and researchers have been reluctant to analyze literacy in terms of explicitly normative or ideological conditions. The redefinition of the processes of literacy instruction by educational psychologists in recent years has effectively concealed the necessity for addressing both the subjective and the social dimensions of literacy development. This encourages a view of literacy as a context-neutral, content-free, skill-specific competence that can be imparted to children with almost scientific precision. Literacy so seen bypasses controversial claims about what curriculum is worthwhile – what moral, social, and personal principles should operate within the educational context. This perception of literacy, as we can see historically, has never been accurate.

Literacy instruction has always taken place within a substantive context of values (Graff, 1982). In the European Protestant educational tradition on which the public schools of the New World were first based, commonality of religious belief was central to literacy instruction. The "criss-cross row" – the first line of the earliest 17th-century English reader, the Horn Book – was a graphic representation of the Cross, invoked to speed and guide the beginner's progress through the text. The expansion of literacy in Europe was initially inseparable from the rise of Protestantism, and the erosion of the Church's monopoly over the printed word (Eisenstein, 1979; p.431; Chaytor, 1966). The intent of the 16th- and 17th-century educational reformers was that "whosoever will" should have access to the word of God. It was believed that individual access to the Word, even though it might involve uncomprehending repetition, would improve the soul of the reader without the necessity of authoritative mediation by a cleric. This explains, in part, the importance ascribed in European schools to repetition and recitation of texts which children could not have been expected to "comprehend" – a religious and pedagogical tradition inherited by North American education in its earliest days. Aspects of that same tradition carried over into 19th-century three R's and classical literacy instruction, which augmented religious texts with venerable children's tales and literature. During the period of progressive reform, from 1900 to just after World War II, literacy instruction attempted to address the "practical" speech codes of everyday life. "Child-centered" curricula usurped the classics, and the normative stress moved from moral and cultural edification to socialization and civic ethics. After a neo-classical revival in the 1950s, the technocratic paradigm emerged, with a bias toward "functional skills" and the universal attainment of "minimum competence." As the touchstone of educational excellence moved from text to interaction to evaluation, what counted as literacy was systematically redefined (see Table 6–1.)

Classical and three Rs instruction

Long before the public schools movement in the 1960s, North American children received instruction in the three Rs (reading, writing, and arithmetic) in private and community schools. For the "common" child, literacy instruction took place in the home, at church, in the local shops, and in the few charity schools. Most communities had one-room schools where a teacher would provide the three Rs along with moral and religious instruction to those children of various ages whose labor was not required by the family. In the elite private and preparatory schools of the mid–19th century, like Boston's Roxbury Latin School, children of the wealthy and influential studied "Latin for six years, French for five, German for four, and Greek for three" (Joncich, 1968; p.48). Despite this differential provision of linguistic competence and cultural knowledge according to class status and geographic location, the blend of formal and informal schooling, family and religious education, and apprenticeship was nevertheless largely successful in creating a literate populus. In Upper Canada, this loosely organized system "produced a basic literacy for a majority of students" (Prentice, 1977; p.17). Of the mid-century United States, Bowles and Gintis (1977, p.198) note that

it is particularly difficult to make the case that the objective of early school reform movements was mass literacy. In the U.S., literacy was already high (about 90% of adult whites) prior to the "common school revival."

Whether there was a pressing economic need for a literate populus at the time is problematic. Graff (1979) notes that most mid-19th-century

Table 6-1.

	Classical	Progressive	Technocratic
Philosophy	Education as cultivation of the "civilized" person with the "instincts of a gentleman"	Education as "growth"–the natural "unfolding" of the child	Education as effective performance, behavior modification
Psychology	Plato: Faculty psychology: reason, will, emotion. Learning by imitation. Reason must subdue the passions	Dewey: The mind as unfolding organism, social theory of mind (organism/ environment transaction)	Thorndike: Empiricism, testing. Skinner: The mind as mechanism, learning through reinforcement (behavior modification)
Sociology	Aristocracy	Democracy	Individualism/pluralism
Conception of literacy	Literacy as literature, detailed analysis of exemplary texts, specification of precise rules and principles, explicit attention to rhetorical appropriateness	Literacy as self-expression, communication as social interaction	Functional literacy, "survival skills," minimum competence
Attitude to education	Intrinsic worth	Subjective/social significance	Instrumental value
Curriculum	Exemplary texts: (1) the Bible; (2) the Classics; (3) the English literature "greats"; (4) North American "classics," grammar texts, handwriting, spelling, pronunciation	"Adventure" stories; civics; self-generated text; idiom of "ordinary language"	Decontextualized subskills of literate competence. Systematic programmed instruction guided by behavioral objectives

Pedagogy	Rote learning: oral recitation; copying; imitation of "correct speech and writing"; direct instruction	Projects: "experiential" education; teacher/pupil interaction; teacher as "guide", "discovery" method. Socialized instruction	Streaming; "mastery learning" of common set of objectives. Learning "packages" with teacher as (preprogrammed) facilitator. Programmed instruction
			Vocational education
Evaluation	Connoisseurship model: oration; oral reading; direct questioning	Local, classroom tests; written tests stressed over oration; products (of "projects"); social skills stressed	Meeting behavioral objectives. Objective standardized testing (mass-scale)
Outcome	Domestication	Socialization	Individualism/commoditization

occupations required minimal competence with print; far from requiring universal literacy, communities typically featured a division of literate labor.

Whatever the concrete practical demands for literacy, the popular association of illiteracy with crime, poverty, and immorality fueled public enthusiasm for a universal free public education system. Ontario educator Archibald McCallum's comments (1875, pp. 17–77) reflected the popular conception of the consequences of illiteracy:

Over seven percent of New England's population over ten years of age can neither read nor write; yet 80 percent of the crime in these states was committed by this small minority; in other words, an uneducated person commits fifty-six times as many crimes as one with education.

The debate over illiteracy in 19th-century North America, then, was intimately connected with religious, ethical, and ultimately ideological questions. We find evidence of this in the theory and practice of three Rs and classical instruction, largely borrowed from existing European and British methods and texts. An overriding instructional emphasis on mental and physical discipline perfectly complemented mid-century educational goals: the domestication of a "barbarous" population, whose inclinations toward "materialism" and "ignorance" threatened cultural continuity, political order, and Protestant morality.

Universal free public school systems had been established in the majority of states and in Upper Canada by 1860. In the United States, over half of the nation's children were receiving formal education, and more students than ever before now had access to levels of schooling previously restricted to an elite few (Cremin, 1961; p.16). In Canada, under the direction of Egerton Ryerson, the Ontario Schools Act of 1841 had subsidized the existing common school system; by 1872, British Columbia had legislated a public school system modeled on that of Ontario.

Late-19th-century literacy instruction in Canada differed in one crucial respect from its American counterpart. For whereas Canadian schools imported curricula from England, teachers in America were by this time provided with locally developed textbooks, in the tradition of the McGuffey readers. Noah Webster's *American Spelling Book* (1873), the most widely used textbook in United States history, not only promoted American history, geography, and morals, but was itself a model for an indigenous vocabulary and spelling. Textbooks and dictionaries of this period attempted to engender a national literacy and literature free of European "folly, corruption and tyranny," in Webster's words. In Canada, by contrast, classrooms featured the icons of colonialism: British flags and pictures of royalty adorned the walls, younger students were initiated to print via the Irish readers, and literature texts opened with Wordsworth's and Tennyson's panegyrics to the Crown. In Canada, the reduction in pauperism and crime associated with illiteracy was seen as requiring the preservation of British culture and a colonial sensibility; in the United States, "custodians of culture" (May, 1959; p.30) sought to assure economic independence and political participation. The match between these differing societal and educational ideologies and the "civilizing" effects of traditional three Rs and classical education was near-perfect.

The model for this classical education was found in the philosophy, psychology, and social theory of Plato's educational treatise *The Republic*. Platonic faculty psychology subdivided the mind into three faculties: reason, will, and emotion. The child, a "barbarian at the gates of civilization" (Peters, 1965; p.197) was regarded as a bundle of unruly impulses needing to be brought under the control of the faculty of "right reason" – that is, morally informed rational judgment. Paraphrasing a speech of Ryerson's, the *Journal of Education* declared in 1860 that "a sensual man is a mere animal. Sensuality is the greatest enemy of all human progress" (in Prentice, 1977; p.29). To that end, rigid discipline and rigorous mental training characterized classical instruction.

Adopting Plato's stress on mimesis and imitation as the basis for the development of mind, classical pedagogy stressed rote learning, repetition, drill, copying, and memorization of lengthy passages of poetry and prose. Mental, moral, and spiritual edification were to be had through exposure to, in the words of Matthew Arnold (1864), the "best that has been thought and said in the world." Accordingly, the intermediate and secondary grades adopted a "great books" literacy curriculum which featured the Bible, Greek and Roman classics, and after some debate, acknowledged works of English and American literature; "far more time [was] spent . . . on ancient history and dead languages than upon the affairs of the present or even recent past" (Joncich, 1968; p.48). In the United States, public high schools retained a modified classical curriculum, sans Greek, as a "uniform program." This universal implementation of a classical curriculum in secondary schools forced practical studies of law, bookkeeping, and vocational skills outside the public system. In Canada, it was left to industry to initiate vocational education (Johnson, 1964, p. 65).

Curricular material did not vary from grade to grade according to controlled level of difficulty. In practice, this meant that the same literary texts, particularly the Bible, would be studied in greater and greater detail and depth; underlying "truths" were explicated in terms of grammatical rules, rhetorical strategies, moral content, and aesthetic worth. In the elementary grades, students copied passages for "finger style" penmanship exercise, in preparation for advanced composition study. Thus, stylistic imitation and repetition, guided by explicit rules, dominated writing instruction; students at all levels undertook précis and recitation of exemplary texts.

Following the European model, reading took the form of oral performance to an audience. Individual reading time was limited, and all students progressed at a fixed rate through the text. Both in grade and secondary schools, each student, in turn, would read passages aloud; those not reading were expected to listen attentively to the reader, since the intent of oral reading instruction was not merely to ascertain the reader's ability to decode the text, but to develop powers of effective public oration. Pronunciation, modulation, and clarity of diction were stressed. In the 19th-century classroom, reading was neither a private nor reflective act, but a rule-bound public performance.

Although texts were meticulously dissected and analyzed, and block parsing was a daily routine, the emphasis was not on mere grammatical correctness. In theory, analysis and repetition subserved the development of sensitivity to the aesthetic and didactic features of the text. Thus, the student's encounter with the text, whether fairy tales or Shakespeare, was to be both aesthetically pleasing and morally instructive – in accordance with the Horatian edict that literature should be "dulce et utile."

In the same way, vocabulary study subserved the ends of moral and literary education. Spelling lists often featured poetic language and Biblical and literary terminology. Precision of meaning and rhetorical effectiveness were to be achieved through the apt selection of words from this cultural lexicon – the range of vocabulary legitimated by "literati" as appropriate for each generic form of literate expression. The overriding sense of conformity and decorum was reflected in the rules that constrained classroom discourse and behavior. Corresponding to each literate act was a correct bodily "habitus" (see Bourdieu, 1977); reading, writing, and speaking were performed in prescribed physical postures. Moreover, "provincial" speech codes were frowned upon as evidence of rudeness or ignorance; textbooks of this period advised students to cultivate the friendship of children of higher station, so that they might assimilate more cultured and aristocratic speech habits.

At the secondary and college levels, unreflective and mechanical imitation was despised as the mark of an ill-bred social climber. Oration was the epitome of classical literate expression, for in its performance all of the diverse rules governing textual analysis and production could be organically unified and expressed. The truly successful high school student displayed a knowledge not only of rule following but of skilled and effective rule breaking, which may have been, in the final analysis, what elevated rhetorical performance from mere technique to the level of art. Implicit was an 18th-century ideal of "wit," following Addison's observation that there is sometimes a greater judgment shown in deviating from the rules of art than in adhering to them.

But if technical correctness was not a sufficient criterion of educational success beyond the grade school level, how could the attainment of classical literacy be evaluated? Evaluation in the three Rs or classical classroom was carried out on a "connoisseurship" model. Under the oratorical model of formal examination, the examiner embodied, however tacitly, standards of cultural and disciplinary excellence and applied these unstated criteria to laud or correct the performance, often undertaken in the presence of trustees, clergy, and parents. This system of assessment vested total control over evaluative criteria and procedures with the teacher or examiners, who retained the authoritative and final word in literacy instruction.

A neo-Platonic ontology underpinned an historically and culturally specific conception of knowledge: the idealist conviction that knowledge was immutable, and that forms of beauty, truth, and morality were embodied, so far as they could be realized in the phenomenal world at all, in those authoritative texts passed down by each generation of elite literati. The experience of becoming literate was to be an initiation into an ongoing cultural conversation with exemplary texts and human models.

The principal intent of 19th-century literacy instruction, then, was inextricably bound to the transmission of a national ideology and culture. In practice, this translated into a regimen of "benumbing" (Putman & Weir, 1925) drill, repetition, and physical constraint. This mode of literacy instruction was meant to provide a universal sense of physical, legal, and moral discipline to a growing, diverse, and increasingly mobile populus while ensuring that neo-British "high-culture" would be preserved in North America well into the next century. For late-19th- and early-20th-century students – even those 80 to 90 percent who left school by age 13 – it would have been impossible to conceive of reading and writing as entities, or "skills," distinct from codes of conduct, social values, and cultural knowledge.

Socializing the recitation

Between 1900 and 1914, the number of public high schools in America doubled, and the student population increased by 150 percent. With increasing immigration and regional migration to urban centers, the provision and enforcement of compulsory education expanded; educational costs spiraled and per capita expenditure in the United States went from $24 in 1910 to $90 in 1930 (Callahan, 1962). With the largest part of these costs shouldered by local taxpayers, the fact that in the early 1900s only about 15 percent of students continued beyond elementary school led to public complaints that schools were elitist, authoritarian, outmoded, and inefficient. E. P. Cubberly, Stanford University's advocate of modern management, noted in 1913 that Portland schools had become a "rigidly prescribed mechanical system, poorly adapted to the needs of the children of the community" (Tyack, 1967; p. 457).

Like their private school predecessors, late-19th- and early-20th-century public high schools continued to exclude those students unwilling or unable to demonstrate excellence at the "civilizing" activities of recitation and literary study. But of what use were these competences, anyway? The legitimation potential of classical literacy in a developing industrial democracy was rapidly eroded as the public was nurtured on scientific ideals and evolutionary theory by intellectuals of the day, and on scientific management and cost accounting by its leading businessmen. And although these two influential groups expressed divergent views about what should be done, they united in opposition to three Rs and classical instruction.

The material stimulus for reform came from the application of business methods to schools. Educational administrators were called upon to produce results consistent in the public mind with the increasing tax burdens they were compelled to shoulder. The stage was set by the application of F. W. Taylor's (1911), and later J. F. Bobbitt's (1918), work on "cost-efficient scientific management" to school administration, curriculum, and instruction. Accordingly, measures of costs per minute of instruction in each subject area were used to adjudicate educational value. Finding that 5.0 recitations in Greek were equivalent to 23.8 recitations in French, Superintendent of Schools F. Spaulding declared that

greater wisdom in these assignments will come, not by reference to any supposedly fixed and inherent values in these subjects, but from a study of local conditions and needs. I know of nothing of absolute value of recitations in Greek . . . the price must go down, or we shall invest in something else. [Callahan, 1962, p.73]

Extensive building programs were initiated, curricula were standardized, class size was increased, teaching hours were extended; testing of teacher, pupil, and administrator was introduced, and records and documents were collected to evaluate everything and anything pertaining to schools.

With a supply and demand mentality, and a cost–benefit analysis, schools were seen as "factories in which raw materials are to be shaped and fashioned into products to meet the various demands of life" (Cubberly, in Callahan, 1962, p. 152).

But the fact that it was traditional pupil recitations that "educational experts" were quantifying illustrates the impoverishment of their ideas on instructional reform. Beyond the belief that schools were maintained by and for business and public interests, administrative efficiency experts had little of substance to offer teachers. With the failure of platoon schools in the late 1920s, unmanageably large classes, and organized teacher resistance to industrialization, the stage was set for a new educational philosophy, one that would accommodate both scientific management and democratic individualism.

What Plato was for the classicists, John Dewey was for the progressives. Dewey articulated a philosophy of education which drew from experimental science, child psychology, evolutionary theory, and the moral aspects of American pragmatism. Adopting William James's (1899) critique of innatism, and his call for early training in an optimal environment, Dewey saw educational reform as the principal means of American social evolution. Deweyian progressivism, therefore, originated as a self-conscious attempt to make schooling socially responsive – oriented toward a social future rather than a cultural past. Its goal was to provide the skills, knowledge, and social attitudes required for urbanized commercial and industrial society.

Progressives derived their definition of literacy from the social psychology of James and of G. H. Mead. Language, for Mead, was created and sustained by the pragmatics of intersubjective communication – communicative "acts" involving "symbolic interaction" with a "generalized social other." Within the pragmatists' expanded theory of communication, linguistic development and socialization were deemed inseparable. Hence, the classroom was to be a microcosm of the ideal social community, one which fostered the development of equality and social exchange rather than authority and imitation. Teachers of the 1920s and 1930s were trained to view their classrooms as "learning environments"; within these democratic communities, children could "act out" the skills required for social and vocational life. Said Dewey (1915, p.315):

The key to the present educational situation lies in the gradual reconstruction of school materials and methods so as to utilize various forms of occupation typifying social callings, and to bring out their intellectual and moral content. This reconstruction must relegate purely literary methods – including textbooks – and dialectical methods to the position of necessary auxiliary tools in cumulative activities.

The "integrated curriculum," "learning by discovery," and the "project method" were to enable the natural unfolding of the child in accordance with his or her developing interests.

Rote recitation of literature was eliminated in this reconstructed environment. Dewey (1929) noted that conventional reading instruction "may develop book worms, children who read omnivorously, but at the expense of development of social and executive abilities and skills." Thus, whereas classical literacy was grounded in the exemplary text, progressives focused on questions of instructional method and social use.

Nonetheless, the progressive mandate that education be socially useful, that training "transfer" across contexts (Thorndike, 1917), made the content of literacy texts a crucial matter, albeit secondary to instructional concerns. Beginning in the 1910s and 1920s, American prescribed and authorized readers, also used in Canada, reflected the dominant values and popular culture of commercial and industrial life. Stories of "adventure" and "friendship" featured vignettes of family life, work, and play, and encouraged community service and individual achievement. Dick and Jane usurped Arthurian heroes; by the 1930s discussions of the latest "moving pictures" and radio programs coexisted in secondary classrooms with the study of Shakespeare. Literacy texts portrayed a vision of a harmonious American social community, blessed with the gifts of technological advancement and material prosperity.

Progressive speaking and writing instruction placed an emphasis on practicality and expressiveness rather than propriety. Students were encouraged to talk about their daily "experiences" and to discuss emotional and contentious matters; colloquialism and regional dialects were more readily accepted, and practical "plain speaking" encouraged. In creative writing instruction, students were expected to express their own ideas and experiences, rather than to reproduce literary style. Courses in Business English and journalism were introduced, and grammar study became "functional" rather than "formal." Students learned library techniques and book reviewing, how to record the minutes of a meeting, and how to write lab reports.

This stress on the cultivation of practical linguistic expression was matched by a virtual reinvention of reading. Dewey's call for a more scientific method of instruction was answered by the developments in educational psychology. Influential studies by E.B. Huey (1909), E. L. Thorndike (1917), and W. S. Gray (1925) indicated that oral reading instruction was inefficient and counterproductive. Thorndike (p. 24) proposed that

in school practice it appears likely that exercises in silent reading to find answers to given questions, or to give a summary of the matter read, or to list the questions which it answers, should in large measure replace oral reading.

Reading, then, was a form of "reasoning"; the psychologists convincingly argued that oral decoding and memorization did not engender an understanding or "comprehension" of textual meaning.

Accordingly, classroom reading instruction was reformulated; students read silently and responded to "objective" comprehension questions. This was called training for "work-type reading." Within this new system, the teacher would be freer to attend to individual remediation, small group projects, grading, and classroom management, while each student progressed through the text at an "individualized" rate. However, many teachers were burdened with far larger classes, as pedagogical reforms remained subservient to industrial reorganization. A "child-centered" instruction which attended to "individual differences" was more often a theoretical rationale than a practical reality.

Throughout North America, school and public libraries flourished under both government and corporate financing; as a result, the classical school master's monopoly over the selection and use of texts was diminished. Students were encouraged to undertake reading popular and technical works "outside of what is conventionally termed good reading matter" (Dewey, 1929; p.549): "dime store" novels, magazines and newspapers, "how to" books, and biographies of contemporary sports and political heroes. The curricular provision for "recreational" and "work reading" instruction was a sign of the attempt to integrate schooled literacy with all aspects of home and work life.

Oral examinations of reading were replaced with standardized, and hence, allegedly equitable, instruments of student assessment and teacher accountability. Standardized tests, like the Thorndike-McCall Silent Reading Test, were efficient and time-saving pedagogical devices and moreover, provided valuable data that could be used (often in conjunction with IQ tests) to determine instructional efficiency and individual progress. It is significant that these first psychometric measures of literacy – early reading and language achievement tests – were welcomed by educators as objective and neutral devices that would end the nepotistic and arbitrary evaluative criteria of the connoisseurship model (Goodenough, 1949; Smith, 1965).

Spelling instruction, as well, was modernized. Systematized pre- and posttest spelling instruction, for which students maintained their own progress charts, superceded the traditional spelling "bee." The lexicon of school literacy instruction changed noticeably; literary and religious terms were replaced by the language of democratic social life, the names of institutions and occupations, and the terminology of business transactions and the industrial workplace.

Thus, evolutionary social reform and industrial development provided the value framework pervading early- and mid-20th-century literacy instruction. Literacy was seen as a vehicle for expression, social communication, and vocational competence, rather than for improvement of the soul. But its moral imperatives were no less strongly instilled. It was not until well after World War II that the neutrality of scientific pedagogy came to be seen as absolving teachers of their traditional moral and spiritual leadership roles. For the progressives, scientific intervention meant only the more equitable and efficient realization of stated normative and political goals, not their elimination from the educational field. In Dewey's words, education was both an art and a science; science enabled the optimal development of the art of education.

But the attempt to reconcile apparent contradictions and conflicts within social praxis, to totalize personal, social, and empirical natures – Dewey's intellectual inheritance from Hegel – was, finally, the undoing of progressivism. For it was the very ambiguity of progressive rhetoric and sloganism in its attempt to dialectically resolve contradictions (between self and society, individual and institution, science and art, education and socialization) that led to the transformation of progressive ideals into industrial practices. The popular rhetoric of individualization of instruction, for example, was employed by both progressives and industrialists, but to very different ends. Throughout the progressive era, apparently harmonious but actually divergent goals and practices caused education in general, and literacy instruction in particular, to vacillate between the extremes of socialized education and an industrial socialization.

The technology of literacy instruction

By the end of World War II, social and political conditions were set for a major shift in literacy instruction. Assessing the postwar era, historian H. M. Covell (1961, p. 14–15) explained,

The shocking discovery that many of the young men in military service could not read adequately, and the impetus given the study of science by the discovery of nuclear energy and the space race have combined to result in a greater emphasis on the need for continuing instruction ... in the specific skills needed in reading.

The term "functional literacy" was coined by the United States Army to indicate "the capability to understand instructions necessary for conducting basic military functions and tasks ... fifth grade reading level" (Sharon, 1976, p.148). While our inheritance from the Army testing of the First World War was the concept of "IQ" as a measure of ability (Gould, 1981), the educational legacy of World War II may have been functional literacy as a measure of vocational and social competence. Throughout the 30-year development of the technocratic model, functional literacy remained a goal of North American schools, leading ultimately to the Competency Based Education movement of the 1970s.

After World War II, progressive education was besieged by public and media criticism. In his nefarious search for Communist influences, Senator Joseph McCarthy singled out progressivism as overly permissive and anti-American. Scientists and industrialists indicted American schools for failing to keep pace with the Russians in the production of technical expertise. In *So Little for the Mind* (1953), classicist educator Hilda Neatby argued that the "amorality" of progressive education had spawned "an age without standards" (p. 3). Out of the by then unruly weave of "child-centered" instruction and industrial management, a "neutral" and efficient system of instruction emerged: the technocratic model, a refinement of the scientific strand of progressivism.

To educators of the Atomic Age, then, it must have seemed eminently reasonable that schooling, along with other institutions, should become more scientific in order to promote universal literacy. Educational science would provide both the means and the ends of education: a body of universally applicable skills of reading and writing, transferable to a variety of social and vocational contexts. The psychological research that had dovetailed so neatly with the industrial reforms of the progressive era now established the direction of technological literacy instruction. Throughout the 1950s and 1960s, evaluation-oriented reading research stipulated to an ever greater extent the instructional form and curricular content of North American literacy instruction (cf. Smith, 1965). Following Thorndike, literacy was conceived of according to a behaviorist stimulus – response model. The linguistic and ideational features of the text, the stimulus, could be structured and manipulated to evoke the desired skill-related responses, ranging from rudimentary "decoding" to more advanced skills of "comprehension." Student response could then be measured to determine the student's level of language development.

Literacy was thus scientifically dissected into individually teachable and testable subskill units. Educational publishers and, later, multinationals developed total packaged reading "systems," based as much on exacting marketing research as on the insights of reading psychology. Beginning in the 1950s, teachers were introduced to the first in a series of "foolproof" methods for developing the "skills" of literacy (SRA and, later, DISTAR and CRP). Among the inbuilt incentives of packaged programs were promises of decreased planning and grading time, diagnostic tests, glossy audio-visual aids, precise directions for effective "teacher behavior," and the assurance of scientific exactitude and modernity.

One widely used reading series, *Ginn 720* (1980), a Xerox product revised for different countries to enable international distribution, defines its approach to literacy instruction:

> By using a management system the teacher can select specific objectives to be taught, monitor pupils' learning progress continuously, and diagnose the source of individual learning problems, prescribe additional instruction and meet pupils' needs and make sure the pupils have achieved proficiency in skill objectives. [T-26, Teachers' edition]

As a "professional," the technocratic teacher is encouraged to see the educational process in medical and managerial metaphors (cf. de Castell & Luke, 1983). Students are diagnosed, prescribed for, treated, and checked before proceeding to the next level of instruction, which corresponds to a theoretical level of advanced literate competence. The *Ginn 720* student, for instance, is processed through 14 such skill levels from ages 6 to 14.

A strong selling point of these programs is their capacity to "individualize" instruction, based on the students' needs as assessed by accompanying diagnostic tests. Students with the same "needs" are grouped together, and each reading group is assigned a basal reader, with adjunct worksheets and exercise books. Then, instructional "treatment" begins. Typically, teachers will monitor oral reading, review stories, and conduct discussions with one group, while other groups work at their desks, completing worksheets according to "fill in the blanks" and multiple-choice formats. Composition and literature study are not undertaken intensively until the second grades, when it is assumed (and verified through the near-universal administration of reading achievement tests) that the student will have acquired the basic "skills" of literacy.

Because the dominant view since World War II has been to equate functional literacy with basic reading skills, it is only recently that a correlative systematization of writing instruction has begun. Elementary writing instruction remains a highly variable blend of progressive "creative writing" and "language experience" with skill-based exercises; most secondary writing instruction is undertaken in the context of literature study. This is partially the result of the continuing influence of university English literature departments on conventional approaches to writing and criticism. However, in light of increasing complaints about high school graduates' inability to write in both essay and business formats, writing instruction is likely to follow a similar "research and development" process toward increased standardization.

How are speaking and listening skills defined within technocratic literacy instruction? The progressive acceptance of the child's own dialect and speech has carried over into today's schools, having been sustained by the progressive revival of the late 1960s. But relatively little attention is paid to oral language instruction in intermediate and secondary classrooms, apart from discussions of highly variable quality. As for listening skills, "management instructions" and "comprehension questions" delimit teachers' verbal behavior. Student listening becomes first and foremost listening to instructions and questions, rather than to substantive explanations of curricular content.

Every attempt is made within technocratic literacy instruction to specify its "behavioral objectives" in value-neutral terminology. Consequently, explicit ideological content is absent, overridden by the instructional format and skills orientation of the literacy text. The "skills" to be taught are thus ideologically neutralized; lessons aim to improve students' ability to grasp "word meaning," "context clues," and "decoding skills." In the teacher's overview chart of the Ginn program, literature study – the focal point of moral and social instruction in previous eras – is reduced to a body of neutral skills (e.g.: "Note the poet's use of animal symbolism," "Use alliteration"). These guidelines clearly indicate to teachers that they need not consider literacy instruction a matter of moral or social edification, but should simply "facilitate" the program as professionally as possible.

But such goals and practices are not value-neutral. How is it possible to "infer character motivation," for instance, without calling into play personal and social values? Similarly, we must ask how a student can determine "structures of cause and effect" in a textual narrative without invoking normative rules of social context and action? As Wittgenstein (1953) observed, every question and statement embodies a normative assumption; skills and concepts are not learned in isolation, but in the context of judgments.

The kind of research that focuses on the manner in which school readers instill social attitudes through the portrayal of particular roles, personality structures, and orientations to action (Pratt, 1975; Repo, 1974; Fitzgerald; 1980, Taxel, 1981) yields little beyond a surface level of understanding of the cumulative effects of technocratic texts. Instructional systems – however non-sexually stereotyping, nonracist, and nonsectarian in content – communicate not only a synthetic worldview, but a particular attitude toward literacy: Literacy is conceived of as a set of neutral behaviors within an attendant fabricated worldview, in which little of cultural or social significance ever occurs. What is conveyed to the teacher, correspondingly, is a reductive view of literacy instruction as the scientific management of skills transmission.

This claim to "neutrality" and cross-contextual validity places literacy instruction in line with the dominant belief that North American schools should assume no particular moral or political bias; there is an explicit avoidance of any story content or language that might appear to discriminate against or exclude any subcultural viewpoint. The result is an inherent blandness, superficiality, and conservatism in the texts children read. What standardized readers communicate to children is "endlessly repeated words passed off as stories" (Bettelheim and Zelan, 1981). In order to capture the multinational market, publishers and editors must create a product that will pass as culturally significant knowledge in diverse social contexts, without offending the sensibilities of local parents, teachers, special interest groups, politicians, and, of course, administrators who decide purchases. The result is a watering down of the content for marketing purposes. As mass-marketed commodities, then, children's readers follow a pattern identified by Raymond Williams (1976): The larger the audience of a given communications medium, the more homogeneous becomes the message and the experience for its consumers. Technocratic literacy systems posit an imaginary "everystudent" much as television networks seek to identify and communicate with "the average viewer."

Ironically, by attempting to address everyone, such literacy texts succeed in communicating with no one. As a result, this literacy model actively militates against the development of full communicative competence. In the attempt to design behaviorally infallible instructional systems, curriculum developers exclude all but the most trivial levels of individual and cultural difference. As a result, the dramaturgical aspect of teaching, the acquired moral convictions and lived cultural experience of students and teachers – key to both progressive and classical instruction – become "variables" which potentially interfere with the smooth operation of systematized pedagogy.

In secondary schools, the linear, information-processing model of technocratic instruction (stimulus – response, input – output) has led to an increase in "functional" exercises, such as reading classified advertisements, filling out job and credit applications, and so on. To enable ease and consistency of assessment, however, such tasks often encourage the learning of linear modes of functioning which exclude contextual factors. Several studies (e.g., Kirsch and Guthrie, 1977; de Castell, Luke, and MacLennan, Chapter 1) have questioned the validity of functional literacy assessment and the success of instruction in producing vocational competence. Often, the pursuit of an explicitly "functional" literacy presents as legitimate educational knowledge information that is artificially simplified, linear, mechanistic, and essentially powerless.

Classicism was condemned for imposing a colonized, aristocratic worldview on every student. Progressivism was criticized for its subversive and "left-wing" ideology. But technocratic education imposes only the surface features, the "skills" of a worldview, and a predominantly "middle-class" one at that. We argue that where technocratic instruction dominates in classrooms and in teacher training institutions, the literacy of students will remain culturally and intellectually insignificant. And, given the informational content and cognitive simplicity of the texts and methods used, and the mechanistic character of the interactions prescribed, we have good reason for concern about the students who *succeed* in such programs.

Literacy instruction: derived or imposed?

By way of conclusion, we have little to offer beyond the observation that cries of falling standards and widespread "illiteracy" among today's graduates appear vacuous given the noncomparability of the various definitions of "literacy" by the public education system since its inception. What we wish to consider in closing, however, are implications of this analysis for contemporary problems of pedagogy and research.

As the number and variety of students in public schools have increased, literacy curriculum, instruction, and evaluation have become more and more standardized. With the relinquishing of family and community control over education to centralized government agencies came the expectation of universal mechanisms of accountability. The rise of standardized testing culminated in the recent move throughout North America toward universal functional literacy testing. The popular ethic of functional literacy, however, begs crucial questions: Functional at what? In what context? To what ends? And is it in the interests of the literate individual to become "functional" within any and every economic and political circumstance?

Political participation within liberal democratic societies demands more than the ability to follow rules; it entails also the ability to understand and to evaluate the sociopolitical rule system itself. This necessitates a kind of "second-order" competence which cannot be accommodated within the dominant idiom of "functional" literacy. The glory of techno-cratic education – its neutralization of personal, social, and political sanctions; indeed, its independence from any substantive context and, therefore, content – produces students who follow instructions simply because they are there, as the designated and assessed conditions of pro-ceeding to the next level. In disregarding the social and ethical dimen-sions of communicative competence, technocratic education nurtures the literally superficially, uncommittedly, but "functionally" literate.

The tendency among both national and international development agencies has been to assume that increasing the percentage of a populace that can read and write – as measured by years of schooling or standar-dized tests – is essential to furthering a nation's political interests and so-cial participation. The rush to modernize schooling in developing coun-tries and to cut educational costs in developed countries serves to increase the appeal of cost-efficient and scientifically based "state of the art" literacy programs.

Yet, models of literacy instruction have always been derived from con-crete historical circumstances. Each has aimed to create a particular kind of individual, in a particular social order. In the United States, the sub-stance of literacy instruction, its ideological functions and roles not-withstanding (Soltow and Stevens, 1981), was derived from distinctively American language, culture, and economic life. In Canada, on the other hand, each era involved the importation of a model of literacy instruction, first from Britain, and subsequently from the U.S. Schoolchildren recited Tennyson's "Power should make from land to land, the name of Britain trebly great," evoked en masse God's salvation of their majesties in morn-ing song, and learned to read and write, in the end, "for Queen and coun-try." The question "Whose country?" was never asked. Later, in residential schools, Indian children were beaten for speaking their native tongue, and were taught to read "See, Jane, see! Jane helps mother in the kitchen." In effect, an imposed literacy model was reimposed to eradicate an in-digenous native culture. As A. Wilden (1981) notes, the colonized sen-sibility is convinced of the inauthenticity of its own cultural messages. What are the social, cultural, and political consequences of a national literacy that is based on imposed, rather than derived, culturally signifi-cant information?

Today in Canada and other English-speaking countries, locally adapted literacy curricula are purchased from U.S.-based multinational publishers. These corporations are able to absorb research and marketing costs, taking what are called "loss leaders" in the certainty of dominating the international educational market. Crucial in the success of this enterprise are two beliefs: first, that there is no necessary relationship between the processes of literacy acquisition and the literate product; and second, that it is possible to transmit literacy per se, as a value-free, context-neutral set of communicational skills. Both beliefs are false. Unless the instructional process itself is educational, the product cannot be an educated individual. Furthermore, the context within which we acquire language significantly mediates meaning and understanding in any subsequent context of use. Our analysis has indicated that the processes and materials of literacy instruction have historically been based on the ideological codes and material constraints of the society from which they are derived. We argue that the wholesale importation of a literacy model, imposed and not locally derived, into both developed and developing "colonies" counts as cultural imperialism. We cannot look at reading and writing per se. We have to ask, instead, what kind of child will take readily to and profit from a given model? What is the nature of motive formation that an instructional model depends on and develops? And, most importantly, what kind of individual and social identity will the program engender?

It is within this set of questions that educators have defined what will count as literacy in a given era. A literacy curriculum that is imposed, whether on individuals or entire cultures, cannot serve the same ends as one that is derived. We confront today two practical problems: solution of the alleged "literacy crisis" in developed countries, and the advancement of mass literacy in developing nations. The intention of this historical reconstruction has been to refocus debate on these problems, and to broaden the context of that debate beyond the disciplinary constraints of educational psychology and commerce, within which it has largely been confined for the last 30 years.

Note

The authors would like to thank Kieran Egan, Carmen Luke, Linda Ruedrich, and David MacLennan for their criticism and suggestions. An earlier version of this paper was read at the X World Congress of Sociology, August, 1982, Mexico City, and appeared in the *Journal of Curriculum Studies, 15*, 4, 1983 (reprinted with permission).

References

Apple, M. W. (1984). The political economy of text publishing. Forthcoming in *Educational Theory*.

Arnold, M. (1962). *Democratic education: The complete prose works of Matthew Arnold*. R. H. Super (Ed.). Ann Arbor: University of Michigan Press.

Bettelheim, B., & Zelan, K. (1981). "Why children don't like to read." *Atlantic Monthly*, November 1981, 25 – 31.

Bobbitt, F. (1918). *The curriculum*. Boston: Houghton Mifflin.

Bourdieu, P. (1977). The economics of linguistic exchange. *Social Science Information, 6*, 645 - 68.

Bowles, S., & Gintis, H. (1977). Capitalism and education in the United States. In M. F. D. Young and G. Whitty (Eds.), *Society, state, and schooling* (pp. 192 - 227). Guildford, Surrey: Falmer Press.

Callahan, R. (1962). *Education and the cult of efficiency*. Chicago: University of Chicago Press.

Chaytor, H. J. (1966). *From script to print: An introduction to modern vernacular literature*. London: Sidgwick and Jackson.

Clymer, R., Meyers Stein, R., Gates, D., & McCullough, C. M. (1980). *Tell me how the sun rose*. New York: Ginn and Co.

Covell, H. M. (1961). The past in reading: Prologue to the future, *Journal of the Faculty of Education of the University of British Columbia, 1*(6), 13 - 18.

Cremin, L. (1961). *The transformation of the school*. New York: Random House.

de Castell, S., & Luke, A. (1983). *Literacy instruction: Technology and technique*. Paper of the International Conference on Language Policy and Social Problems, Curacao. A revised version of this paper is forthcoming (1986) in the *American Journal of Education*.

Dewey, J. (1915). *Democracy and education*. New York: Macmillan.

Dewey, J. (1929). *The sources of a science of education*. New York: Liveright Co.

Eisenstein, E. (1979). *The printing press as an agent of change: Communications and cultural transformations in early modern Europe*. Cambridge: Cambridge University Press.

Fitzgerald, F. (1980). *America revised: History schoolbooks in the twentieth century*. New York: Vintage.

Ginn 720 (1980). New York: Ginn and Co. Canadian version, Toronto: Ginn and Co.

Goodenough, F. (1949). *Mental testing: Its history, principles, and applications*. New York: Rinehart.

Goody, J. (1977). *The Domestication of the savage mind*. Cambridge: Cambridge University Press.

Gould, S. J. (1981). *The mismeasure of man*. New York: Norton.

Graff, H. (1979). *The literacy myth: Literacy and social structure in the nineteenth century city*. New York: Academic Press.

Graff, H. (1982). The legacies of literacy. *Journal of Communication, 32*(1), 12 - 26.

Gray, W. S. (1925). *The twenty-fourth yearbook of the national society for the study of education*. Bloomington, Ind.: Public School Publishing Co.

Habermas, J. (1974). *Communication and the evolution of society*. Boston: Beacon.

Havelock, E. (1976). *Origins of Western literacy*. Toronto: Ontario Institute for Studies in Education Press.

Heath, S. B. (1980). The functions and uses of literacy. *Journal of Communication, 30*(1).

Hoggart, R. (1958). *The uses of literacy*. Harmondsworth: Pelican.

Huey, E. B. (1909). *The psychology and pedagogy of reading*. New York: Macmillan.

James, W. (1899). *Talks to teachers on psychology*. New York: Henry Holt and Co.

Johnson, H. (1964). *A history of public education in British Columbia*. Vancouver: University of British Columbia Publications Press.

Joncich, G. (1968). *The sane positivist: A biography of Edward L. Thorndike*. Middletown, Conn.: Wesleyan University Press.

Kirsch, I., & Guthrie, J. (1977). The concept and measurement of functional literacy. *Reading Research Quarterly, 4*, 487–507.

Lockridge, K. A. (1974). *Literacy in Colonial New England*. New York: Norton.

MacCallum, A. (1975). Compulsory education. In A. Prentice & S. Houston (Eds.), *Family, school and society in nineteenth century Canada*. Toronto: Oxford University Press.

McGuffey, W. H. (1879, 1962). *McGuffey's Fifth Eclectic Reader*. New York: New American Library.

May, H. F. (1959). *The end of American innocence*. New York: Knopf.

Mead, G. H. (1934). *Mind, self, and society from the standpoint of a social behaviorist*. Chicago: University of Chicago Press.

Neatby, H. (1953). *So little for the mind*. Toronto: Clark, Irwin.

Olson, D. R. (1977). From utterance to text: The bias of language in speech and writing. *Harvard Educational Review, 47*(3), 257–86.

Olson, D. R. (1980). On the language and authority of textbooks. *Journal of Communication, 30*(1), 186–96.

Peters, R. S. (1965). Education as initiation. In R. D. Archambault (Ed.), *Philosophical analysis and education*. London: Routledge and Kegan Paul.

Pratt, D. (1975). The social role of school textbooks in Canada. In R. Pike & E. Zureik (Eds.), *Socialization and values in Canadian society*. Toronto: McClelland and Stewart.

Prentice, A. (1977). *The school promotors: Education and social class in mid-nineteenth century upper Canada*. Toronto: McClelland and Stewart.

Putnam, J., & Weir, G. M. (1925). *Survey of the Schools*. Victoria: King's Printer.

Repo, S. (1974). From pilgrim's progress to Sesame Street: 125 years of colonial readers. In G. Martell (Ed.), *The politics of the Canadian public school*. Toronto: James Lewis and Samuel.

Sharon, A. T. (1973). What do adults read? *Reading Research Quarterly, 3*, 148–69.

Smith, N. B. (1965). *American reading instruction*. Nevark: International Reading Association.

Soltow, L., & Stevens, E. (1981). *The rise of literacy and the common school in the United States: A socioeconomic analysis to 1870*. Chicago: University of Chicago Press.

Stubbs, M. (1980). *Language and literacy: The sociolinguistics of reading and writing*. London: Routledge and Kegan Paul.

Taxel, J. (1981). Outsiders of the American Revolution: The selective tradition in children's fiction. *Interchange, 12* (2–3), 206–28.

Taylor, F. W. (1911). *Principles of scientific management*. New York: Harper and Bros.

Thorndike, E. L. (1906). *Principles of teaching*. New York: A. G. Seiler.

Thorndike, E. L. (1917). Reading as reasoning: A study of mistakes in paragraph reading. *Journal of Educational Psychology, 8*, 323–32.

Tyack, D. (1967). Bureaucracy and the common school: The example of Portland, Oregon, 1851 – 1913. *The American Quarterly, 19*(3), 475–98.

Webster, N. (1873, 1962). *American Spelling Book*. New York: Teachers College.

Wilden, A. (1981). *The Imaginary Canadian*. Vancouver: Pulp Press.

Williams, R. (1976). *Communications*. London: Oxford University Press.

Wittgenstein, L. (1953). *Philosophical Investigations*, (trans. G. E. M. Anscomb). Oxford: Blackwell and Mott.

7   A sociohistorical approach to remediation

Michael Cole and Peg Griffin

For the past several years, members of the Laboratory of Comparative Human Cognition have been engaged in a variety of explorations of literacy acquisition among Americans of different walks of life. A major goal of this work was to see if insights obtained in earlier work by members of the laboratory (Cole et al., 1971; Griffin, 1977a; Griffin and Mehan, 1980; Hall et al., 1977; Scribner and Cole, 1980) could be used to gain insight into the relationship between the cultural organization of experience and educational performance among subpopulations within the United States.

In this paper we discuss that thread of the work which led us into the study of specific learning disabilities, especially difficulties in learning to read.[1] The framework that we apply in this work is derived from many sources, but we find it particularly fruitful to think and talk in the idiom of the sociohistorical school of psychology associated with the names of Lev Vygotsky (1962, 1978), Alexander Luria (1932, 1978), and Alexei Leont'ev (1981). Because interpretations of what a "sociohistorical" psychology means are quite variable, even within the USSR, we will proceed by example (Wertsch, 1981).

We begin with a broad conception of literacy. Our goal is to arrive at an understanding of the basic structure of remedial reading instruction and to see how it has been shaped by its sociohistorical context. As a part of this process, we undertook experimental programs of remediation based upon our reading of the Soviet literature as well as the current theorizing of American cognitive scientists. This research has provided us deeper insight into the nature of literacy and the circumstances that limit its acquisition by various subgroups within the population of elementary school children.

A sociohistorical psychology

Let us back up, then, and describe what it means to adopt a sociohistorical approach to literacy. First, this approach emphasizes that we are talking about uniquely human characteristics of human behavior, ones that are not likely to have been invented spontaneously by individuals or to be related directly to our near animal neighbors. Whatever else there is about reading and writing, if you grew up and lived for a long time on an island with no reading or writing and no one had ever heard of it, and you were there by yourself, it is extremely unlikely that you would invent the alphabet. It took about ten thousand years from the earliest signs of writing to the invention of the alphabet, and one individual is not likely to get it done in a lifetime.

Aspects of human behavior with a long social history constitute what Vygotsky (1978) called higher psychological functions. They arose a long time ago, they were there in some form at the dawning of *Homo sapiens*, and they have been transformed in social interaction as a part of historically accumulated experience.

The unique form in which *Homo sapiens* learns from the experience of prior generations is heavily emphasized by the sociohistorical psychologist; hence, the heavy emphasis on human language as the basic medium of specifically human development.

At the core of human nature is the language-using capacity, so there had to be an intimate link between higher psychological functions and language. As closely as we can figure the precise relationship, it is roughly in the form proposed by Mikhail Bakhtin in *Marxism and the Philosophy of Language*.[2] The precise nature of this link is a deep mystery that we may never know fully, but certain basic structural universals are discernible – in particular, the insight that language gives us the world twice. As Alexander Luria (1981, p. 35) put it:

The enormous advantage is that their world doubles. In the absence of words, humans would have to deal only with those things which they could perceive and manipulate directly. With the help of language, they can deal with things which they have not perceived even indirectly and with things which were part of the experience of earlier generations. Thus, the word adds another dimension to the world of humans . . . Animals have one world, the world of objects and situations which can be perceived by the senses. Humans have a double world. . . . humans not only can regulate their perception, they can also regulate their memory by using images. They can control their actions. That is to say, words give rise not only to a duplicate world, but also to a form of *voluntary action* which could not exist without language.

Now, let us apply that idea to the notion of reading and writing. When did reading and writing begin? You can argue that the existence of writing as a function is about 2,500 to 3,000 years old, depending upon how you measure it. Even if we set the date back, it has been around for a very short part of *Homo sapiens'* existence (see Graff, this volume). Writing is definitely a "new" human acquisition; as A. R. Luria liked to emphasize, we would not expect to find a constant, unique, and localized area of the brain to be damaged whenever writing impairment followed head injury.

The sociohistorical approach pushes deeper into the past, looking for the starting point, so as to trace the basis of literacy all the way back to the beginning. We will choose Austrolopithecus, perhaps 300,000 to 400,000 years ago, as a useful beginning point. In sites where Austrolopithecus are found we find evidence that people who can be credited with being *Homo sapiens* regulated their interactions with the world and each other by modifying and using pieces of the world external to themselves. Beginning at the beginning of *Homo sapiens*, one finds the basic property that we believe underlies modern reading and writing. This property is embodied in the basic act of mediation, which requires that one interacts with the world indirectly through objects that are artificial (that is, made by human hands). The initial product of mediated activity may be as simple as a mark on stone that regulates when one person meets another; it may be a mark on a stick to remind you that you've done something before. In each case, the simple mark reorganizes your coordination with the world by virtue of its properties as a mediator.[3]

There are many remnants of this early manifestation of pre-writing. The caves of Lascaux, Alexander Marschak's work on Ice Age people – much is available to show that the activity of mediation through external signs is as old as *Homo sapiens*. Stonehenge is a particularly impressive example of a mediated system of interaction: Begin to ponder about the fact that very big rocks were carried a very long way by people with no trucks or trains. Those were people who *really* cared. They were not carrying those rocks for their own sake. They were carrying them because they were told that if they arranged those rocks in a certain way they could discover regularities in the universe that would allow them to predict what was going to happen next, and roughly when it would happen (Chippendale, 1983).

In the desert south of San Diego there are remarkable places that have this same property. On the winter solstice, and only on that day, the sun rises over a particular hill. Its light slices through a particular slit in a rock where there are drawings of humans on rocks. One human has a dagger raised in his hand, and just at sunrise on that day, the sun creeps across the rock and hits the dagger, then bounces off and hits the other man. An enormous amount of human ingenuity went into figuring that out. Those rock pictures, like Stonehenge, regulated people's interactions with the world and with each other. The burgeoning field of ethnoastronomy is turning up many such examples (Averi & Urton, 1982).

To repeat, the basic character of literacy is that we create objects to regulate our interactions with the physical world, with our social world, and with our inner worlds. Literacy then makes possible new forms of coordination in time and space. Writing systems, embodied as cultural objects mediating our interactions with the world, make available the potential for new forms of higher psychological processes.

Technologies of mediation

What is remediation all about from the perspective of the sociohistorical school? In its root meaning, "remediation" means a *shift in the way that mediating devices regulate coordination with the environment.* A very interesting early example of such a shift occurred historically when syllabaries were replaced by an alphabet. A shift from a syllabary to an alphabet creates a representation of language at a level of analysis that is qualitatively new (Gelb, 1963). Alphabets make possible activities that can have a powerful potentiating affect on people's ability to regulate their activities with each other and, as we say, to create common knowledge. (See bibliographic notes in Graff for relevant references.)

In a sociohistorical approach, it is important to remember that the beginning of the symbol systems that eventuate in the alphabet goes back to the initial forms of exchange using money (Sohn-Rethel, 1978). From the beginning, writing and reading were embedded in socioeconomic practices, in activities that had a complex, higher-level goal. From the simple token systems in the Middle East, to the Bronze Age, with the evolution of multiple tokens scratched in clay, and then to the Phoenician syllabary (Schmandt-Besserat, 1978), we can trace the history and development of various technologies of mediation. When the Greeks tried to trade through the syllabary they ran into difficulties, which forced them to do some analysis on what the syllabary was about (Gelb, 1963).

These difficulties led eventually to the fundamental breakthrough that is now the bane of many children in our society: the breakthrough from representing language at the level of directly communicable sound elements (syllables) to communicating through a medium in which you cannot explicitly make clear what it is that you are doing (the alphabet).

In order to make this difference clear, let's look at how we might talk about reading the word *cat*. In societies where "cat" is written as a syllable, it is represented by one sign that is supposed to evoke that sound image so that people think or can say "cat" when they see the symbol and thereby interpret a bit of the world.

In an alphabetic system, "cat" isn't simply made up of a single character. In an alphabetic system there are three parts to the word: *c*, *a*, and *t*. But we quickly have to retract our statement. The letters *c*, *a*, and *t* are not really the parts of the word; it is really the three sounds /k/, /*/, and /t/ that are the parts.[4] But, then again, a retraction: The sounds are not parts in the same way that letters would be – they are not really separable. You cannot say a /k/ or a /t/ by itself, as a separate part. You can only say them in combination with something else – namely, a vowel like /*/. If you try to say them alone, some unstressed vowel comes out, even if you repress a full vowel like /*/. The question then is what the letters *c* and *t* separately represent if the sounds /k/ and /t/ are not separable. What the alphabet represented was an abstraction, a kind of analysis that allowed the languages spoken in that area of the world to be represented with an extreme degree of economy (Havelock, 1976; Gleitman and Rozin, 1977).

Our alphabet is a more elegant system than is a syllabary. In an alphabetic system, the answer for how to represent a word is very constrained: We must use some combination of the 26 available letters. (Repetitions are allowed and order differences count as meaningful variants.) With such a closed inventory, the system "grows" mediating conventions for linking the word in oral language to the word in written language; these conventions develop over time and often lose any initial transparency they may initially have exhibited. Literates accept these conventions; for example, they act "as if" the letter *c* in isolation represents a sound in isolation, but in demonstrating the simple direct correspondence that they believe in, they invariably produce a syllable instead of a consonant sound. Conventional orthographies provide another mediating layer – defeating bi-unique letter – sound mapping (O'Neil, 1980), reflecting morphological relations among words at the expense of sound transparency (Vaughn-Cooke, 1977), encoding historical pronunciations and reflecting prestige dialects of a language (Shaklee, 1980; Brice Heath, 1980). A single alphabet can be used for writing many different languages, but (like a syllabary) it is not very good as a "stand-alone device," to borrow a phrase from the more recent computer technology. That is, knowing the alphabet and having some ability to write is not "enough" for us to be able to read a language we do not know. The alphabet is a *mediating* device, requiring more of the user than just the knowledge and skills narrowly related to it. We must know something of its context of use – the systems related to it, its function and its historicity.

Consider the problem of how to explain to children what it is that happens when you go from /k/, /*/, /t/ to /k*t/. All we can do to explain is to illustrate what we mean by a process that we call blending. We *simulate* the process of reading. We have a procedure. We start out slowly pronouncing an approximation of /k/, /*/, and /t/ in the correct sequence; then we do the same routine faster and faster until we are saying /k*t/. But blending does not really work. No matter how fast we say the parts in sequence, we don't say the whole. Blending is not what happens in the mature act of reading the alphabetic representation of "cat." What happens is that there's a qualitative reorganization of the sounds that the alphabet models. You can think of the blending strategy as analogous to a bird trying to get off the ground. The theory of blending tries to give a start, like a mother bird urging along a fledgling. You give the fledgling a push, and if it can just get off the ground, the right dynamic properties will take over. Applied to children and the alphabet, we suppose that by blending, kids will "automatically" begin to do the synthesis. The icy fact is that to make use of the alphabet, you can't just do analysis; that's how history arrived at it. You have to have both analysis and synthesis to use an alphabet. There's the hub of the teaching problem. Both sides of the process are required to induce reading, yet we can't communicate directly about the real nature of this two-sided process.

Consequences of the alphabet

As summarized by several contributors to this symposium, the alphabet made possible really new forms of organization of knowledge (Havelock, 1976; Goody, 1977; see Graff for many more references). In the Middle Ages and late Middle Ages, it allowed the reclamation of vast sums of scientific work from an earlier era. When combined with the ability to smelt iron and make papers in certain ways, the alphabet made possible the printing of bibles. It supported an incredible notion for the time: You no longer had to mediate your interactions with God through Rome (which, if you were German peasants, didn't seem like a particularly reasonable thing to do under the circumstances). You could reach God, as they say, through the book. You could get directly to Him through His word – the Bible (Eisenstein, 1979).

Alphabets and the reduction of people to numbers

It seems that what we were buying in the alphabet was an analytic device that enabled a new mode of cultural interaction and metaphors for living eventuating in the creation of the industrial mode of production. If Havelock and Goody are correct, the alphabet made possible modern science and modern states. Thus, mankind's recent achievements – the ability to send astronauts into space, to see the other side of Venus, to look into little pieces of your body too small to imagine – all owe a lot to the analytic power of the alphabet.

The kind of science that we developed through the analytic principles of the alphabet allows us to be explicit in particular ways, and to create models of reality that operate on high-speed machines. As psychologists we use it to quantify our descriptions of psychological process, contrast groups of subjects within highly constrained contexts, and make statistical predictions to other contexts (Cole and Means, 1981). This analytic strategy has created computers that simulate aspects of human thought and which have proved themselves useful in the workplace. Education for a more scientific world is a very general, social demand. But this way of knowing the world comes at a great cost.

Let us concentrate on the cost that has to do with education. Three countries – Japan, the Soviet Union, and the United States – suggest what these costs might be. In each country the outcome of current psychological methodology applied to the organization of education is to reduce people to a single number. This number is scaled as a value on a dimension that defines the "main effect" in experimental studies of learning and instruction. The ultimate embodiment of this academic reductionism in Japan is the score you get when you graduate from high school on a national examination. We tell our Japanese colleagues that "We Americans don't know how to subordinate ourselves as well as you; we have two numbers, verbal and quantitative," but an SAT total score and an IQ are very powerful single numbers. Our Soviet colleagues would deny that they had one number, and they would say that human values are distributed in a lot of ways. That's certainly their ideology. But clearly one of the driving concerns behind the Soviet education system today is the alienation of labor from the university. In response to the dominant need for efficiency in a modern industrial world, they have reintroduced the use of IQ-like achievement tests in industry and schooling, re-creating classes based on educational attainment.

What we seem to find in the educational systems of this "information age" is that high scores on a single dimension of human capacities more and more determine your ability to get access to, and to be skilled in the uses of, systems for coding information. We have a very powerful system for reducing nature as a mode of exploiting it. But this system neglects the fact that we are *in* nature and it does not have a metatheory of its own limitations.

Japan, the United States, and Russia each wrestle with this fact in their education system. The Japanese worry about producing educational automatons and about the alienation of family life that modernization has brought to their country. Russians are deeply concerned about the low educational achievement of their heterogeneous population and the alienation of education and work. We in the United States share the Russians' concern in many ways. We are especially concerned that as many as 20% of our adult population cannot read and write at a level which is needed to support bureaucracy and industry.

Three different countries, three different recapitulations of one-dimensional man. Culturally and politically the metaphors of analytic science are contrary to long-standing traditions for the Russians and Japanese. But that doesn't seem to help them much. All three countries have the same problems: massive school failure, runaway bureaucracies, and centralized control over many, many forms of individual life.

Reduction and reading

From a sociohistorical point of view, research on the teaching of reading must start with an understanding of this historical backdrop; we have had to understand how contemporary social and historical contexts arose to appreciate how they shape the nature of instruction and the production of school failure to produce the problem of re-mediation.

Educational failure is done in the classroom, it is done at home, it is done on the way from the classroom to the home, it is done in the workplace, it is done everywhere. It is *systematic*. If you're going to make a change in the level of literacy characteristic of society you cannot restrict your focus to a single context, such as school. You're going to have to be able to create changes at many different levels of the system (Scribner and Cole, 1981). However, at some point you must consider the central role of the curriculum as embodied by the classroom teacher in the process of changing the system. You must also consider the existing reading curriculum to see how underlying scientific assumptions are converted into social practice.

In the remainder of this paper we will concentrate on the standard curriculum for teaching reading. More particularly, we will concentrate on practices for repairing the damage when standard practices fail. In their efforts to re-mediate reading failure, educators reveal with particular clarity the basic assumptions of their efforts.

Standard remedial practices

The standard remedial program reflects the analytic strategy that we have associated with alphabetic literacy; it analyzes the system of reading into a set of elements that are ordered from simple to complex and from small to large. Reading is taught as a "bottom – up" process. First one begins with letters of the alphabet and letter – sound correspondence; then one learns words; then words are combined into sentences and sentences are grouped into essays or stories. Observers of the operation of reading instruction in the early grades have commented that children who succeed must come to school with some idea of what adults really mean by "reading" because they rarely glimpse it in school (Anderson & Stokes, 1984; Moll and Diaz, 1983).

Curricula for alphabetic literacy routinely institutionalize this "bottom – up" strategy by invoking a sequence of two major subprocesses into which the full act of reading can be divided: decoding and comprehension. These two component processes are taught in a sequence that follows the simple-to-complex rule by declaring decoding to be at the simple end of the process. Many of the failing children we have studied were "stuck" at (or put back again into) the decoding stage even though they had been in school for five or six years and even though decoding instruction had not been particularly useful to them.

Whether or not a young child's introduction to literacy actually occurs according to the "decode first" dominant pattern, there is little doubt that should children find themselves in a remedial reading curriculum (whatever the diagnosis of the child's difficulty), the instruction they encounter is very likely to be an intensified version of a strategy that might be called "Go back to the beginning and start over." The children are drilled on letter – sound correspondences and the physical skills of letter creation. Children are drilled on these "lower-order skills" on the assumption that automaticity will lead them up the ladder of complexity.

We questioned, in principle, this bottom – up approach to reading. A review of recent literature on computer and mathematical models of reading demonstrates that reading is widely understood to be an interactive process, wherein levels of the system always and only exist as interactions of neighboring levels, above and below. In the terminology of this literature, reading, even once it is mastered, requires that both "top – down" and "bottom – up" factors be present and coordinated to make reading possible (McClelland & Rumelhart, 1981). Consequently, any curriculum that requires children to work resolutely on one level at a time would be minimizing the possibilities of producing adequate reading. The results of such school instruction have a good chance of becoming self-contained; the conditions for transfer of training to the full act of reading do not appear to be available.

Reading as a whole activity

An alternative system, which we set up to do our research, was designed to ensure that several levels of the hypothetical process of reading were simultaneously present as much of the time as possible, so that students would virtually never be working at a single level of the task in isolation. Adopting Vygotsky's idea of the zone of proximal development (1978) and the basic principle that development can occur only within the framework of the whole (Hamburger, 1957), we created settings wherein the whole task of reading was organizing the activity. This methodology, of course, committed us to stating what we believed the whole task of reading to be, and what it means for that whole task to be organizing activity.[5]

We started from the assumption that reading is an extension via print of the basic human ability to mediate activity through language. We could assume that all the children possessed this basic ability, because the children were perfectly competent in most culturally organized settings. They are not retarded. Rather, they experience difficulty reading in a particular medium – scholastic, alphabetic literacy. (Cf. Wolf, 1977 for a history of this older and broader notion of "reading.")

In our formulation, the children have an incorrect conception of the process of reading; instead of using print to help them mediate future activity, they conform as closely as possible to the precise level of the system that their educational experience encourages them to concentrate on. The very tenacity with which they subordinate themselves to instruction fatally cuts them off from the insight that reading means comprehending. They become "text-bound," parroting the sounds of letters and words.

A case in point

Deanna typifies one outcome of the ordinary school approach to reading. Deanna was in fifth grade. She had been working in our experimental setting for a few months and knew that we encouraged joint activity and knew how to get help if it did not happen to be immediately available. She had also been in school for many years and knew how to take reading tests.

The following incident took place as we were pretesting the children for our reading experiment. We had our video cameras recording while half a dozen youngsters were given a three-paragraph story, adapted from a newspaper article, and a 10 question quiz about the story. The children were told to read the story, and then to answer the questions. They were told that if they needed help there was a group of teachers and UCSD undergraduates that they could call on to get it. Ms. G. was one of the adults; in a previous type of reading training carried on with Deanna, she had sometimes taught Deanna.

Deanna read the three-paragraph story, evidently with little trouble; at least, she looked at the paper for some period of time and she did not request assistance. The story was about a 10-year-old in a nearby community who was in a coma after having hung himself while trying to demonstrate to a friend what he had seen on TV. We chose this passage for a variety of reasons that we will not go into here. As Deanna read it, no one observed any special reaction. She turned to the quiz. For the first two questions, the only help she wanted was some help with handwriting, but she formulated the answers herself.

The first question asked about what had happened to the boy victim, Jared Stockham. She answered that he had accidentally hung himself. This was an adequate answer, as was her answer to the second question.

Then she asked Ms. G. for help with the third question. She claimed it was unfair. The question asked who Eric Burton was. He was the child who had been playing with the victim and who told the adults what had happened. Deanna insisted that the question was unfair. When Ms. G. failed to understand how she could help or what was unfair, Deanna pointed out that the name Eric Burton appeared three times and that you couldn't answer that kind of question. Ms. G. could not understand what was wrong with the name appearing three times or how that related to the question being a kind of question that could not be answered.

Ms. G. was still in the dark about the unfairness, but started to read the paragraph in question with Deanna. The conversation that followed was a collaborative, two-party act of reading, with the teacher asking questions that reading the sentences would help Deanna to answer, and helping Deanna to figure out some words, to paraphrase some ideas, and to make up questions and answers about some connections among the phrases and sentences.

After a few minutes, and unexpectedly, Deanna became quite agitated. She exclaimed in surprise, asking, "He hung himself?"

Recall that Deanna had provided, as an answer to the *first* question, exactly what she was now asking for verification about. Now, several minutes later, it was new information, worthy of exclamation, question, comment, and emotion.

Deanna had a way to answer reading test questions, but it had very little to do with comprehending what she had read. "Word barkers" is a phrase used to describe people who can read words without knowing what they mean. Deanna's performance suggests that more than words can be barked, and that the barking can be in writing as well as through oral language. Her "answer" to the first question and the "unfairness" of the third question reveal a part of what reading instruction has given her as a way to understand reading. We call it *copy matching*, and we find more children than Deanna doing it.

Under the copy-match analysis of reading, the question about Eric is unfair because the use of the name three times leaves this kind of reader without a unique thing to copy for the answer. The question about Jared can be answered by taking the phrase next to his name in the opening paragraph and making a copy match in the answer slot on the quiz paper. Deanna has a quite sophisticated copy-match reading procedure: She transforms nouns into pronouns and adjusts verb tense and aspect appropriately, but otherwise gives a verbatim copy of the text in her answer, including spelling and punctuation marks.

Interpersonally, in synthesis with the adult, Deanna can substitute the adult analysis of reading (that includes synthesis of abstract representations of sounds into words and comprehension of whole stories) for her analysis of reading as copy matching. Unless special care is taken to engineer the interactions, this "passing" (Goffman, 1959, 1969) goes unnoticed.

An alternative practice for researchers and teachers

The big challenge in our alternative research strategy is to engineer it so that children participate in "higher" levels of the system before they are really capable of doing so. In particular, for children who do not engage with print in ways that adults consider reading (i.e., to mediate their activity in productive ways), the experimentalist's first task is to create a setting where the children "comprehend before they can comprehend." We wanted to institutionalize the kind of help that the teacher was able to give

Deanna and to make it a matter of routine rather than just a lucky accident.

Our response to this challenge was to move to what Vygotsky called the "interpsychological plane." Since the children could not comprehend and, left to their own devices, responded to reading tasks with something that we could not identify as reading, we decided to add to their "intrapsychological" resources by making reading an interpersonal activity. Vygotsky's theory motivates this treatment of higher psychological functions when he claims that the same function occurs on two planes, sometimes intrapsychologically and sometimes interpsychologically. Given what we had observed about Deanna and her peers, the interpsychological plane was what we needed to give our notion of reading a fair chance of appearing.

It is important to note that our approach is quite different from the notion of "starting where the child is" that guides much pedagogical practice. We were particularly fearful of starting where Deanna and her friends were, lest it lead her, them, and us to some activity that we might no longer recognize as the sociohistorical entity we call reading. We wanted to be *with* her, but not where she was. We did not want her to get better at copy matching but rather to adopt a different idea of what reading was all about.

We made explicit the interpersonal nature of reading in structured "dramas" wherein the whole task of reading was divided between participants in theoretically motivated ways. The children and the adults all had roles to play in the reading drama. An example will show how this was accomplished.

First, we elaborated a basic "script for reading." Like the script used in more traditional dramatic performances, this script spelled out roles and even set lines for the players.[6] We called our script "Question-Asking Reading." It has four acts: Goal talk, Paragraph reading, Test, and Critique.

Goal talk. The first part of the script called for conversation about the goals of the activity. Here the definition of reading as mediating future activity in productive ways), the experimentalist's first task is to create a set- a more powerful, independent, and effective adult. "Reading is a part of growing up, so you need it to help you grow up." This very general goal was made concrete in a variety of ways: by having the children read about the world of work; by arranging for them to engage in "grown-up activities" (such as a school fund-raising event), and through their pairing with

UCSD undergraduate "older siblings" who read a lot themselves and could act as admired role models. Other parts of "goal talk" describe how asking questions is related to why adults read and to how they read so well. Still other parts deal with more immediate goals related to tests and changing statuses in the setting in which we worked with the children.[7]

Paragraph reading. Once the conversation about the goals of reading was completed, the first paragraph of the reading text for the day was introduced and the roles in the drama that the participants were to play for that paragraph were distributed. As props for this part of the activity there were the text; five cards, upon each of which was printed a role-appropriate activity; a timer; note pads; and pencils.

Following the script, the role cards were shuffled and distributed to the participants. Then the timer was set and the first paragraph was to be read silently, while people took notes if they wanted to. Everyone had the same scripted role at this point. When the timer rang, it was time for the individual roles to be fulfilled by the people holding each role card. These cards said:

- Ask about words that are hard to say. (You do not have to admit that they are hard for you to read.)
- Ask about the words whose meanings are hard to figure out.
- Pick the answerers.
- Ask about the main idea.
- Ask about what is going to happen next.

Each of these roles had to be fulfilled with respect to the text that the children and adults had read in common. As this phase of the script drew to a close, someone chosen as a scribe for the group had to write down the group's consensus on a good question to ask about the text. This question was then written down on a list to be used by the children in a test that they, themselves, would take at the end of the reading period.

The children did not have to carry out all of these scripted activities by themselves. The experimenter/group leader and one or more undergraduate "big siblings" were always coparticipants. All participants accepted roles, so it might be that the researcher or one of the undergraduates would have to supply a word that is hard to say or one of those adults might have to ask (or answer) a question about what comes next in the text. In cases where there were extra players, the college students would team up with their younger "siblings" to help them play their role.

Through these stategems, the children were repeatedly pulled into the full drama of "question-asking reading" even though not one of them could read the assigned texts and answer questions about it in the manner that would be called adequate independent reading. Difficult words were discussed, compelling suggestions for what the main idea might be were argued over, and finally the consensus was written down in the form of a good question that the text could help a grown-up reader to answer. The procedure was repeated twice for two paragraphs of the text, and then the children moved on to the third act of Question-Asking Reading.

Test. It was so arranged that the quiz consisted of three paragraphs on the same topic, two of which the children had read within the group reading drama. The questions on the quiz were a combination of questions the children had constructed themselves, questions constructed by other reading groups, and questions thought up ahead of time by the adults.

Critique. After the test, the children scored their answers and criticized the various questions. This was a time for discussing what it meant to pose a good question about something written. The talk here fed into the discussions of grown-up reading during the goal talk in subsequent performances of the Question-Asking Reading drama.

Typical performance. The crucial feature in these activity settings is that the adults, coordinated around the reading script and a shared knowledge of what reading is, create a medium in which individual children can participate at the outer reaches of their ability. Almost from the beginning the children were able to get the overall idea of question-asking reading, setting the stage for crucial developmental encounters between the adult's conception and the child's conception of reading.

The role of picking the person who has to answer questions that arise as a part of other roles was, of course, the children's favorite. They could call on friends to answer (or enemies, if they were trying to be mean). They could call on the adult participants if they thought the answer was going to be difficult, or themselves, if they knew the answer and wanted to show off. After a while, the cards about individual words became favorites, too, and the children would try "marking the deck" to get their favorites as the role cards were distributed. They would even beg for a chance to have more than one card, if they didn't get their favorite on the first try. We went along, whenever we could, since children doing more and more reading-related activities was something we were in favor of!

These scripted rules and roles helped create a dynamic group activity organized around making sense of a text by coming up with good questions about it. It was a noisy affair (except during the silent reading time), with a good deal of improvisation (as might be expected, since the text was constantly changing) and byplay. As time went on, more and more of the scripted procedures were executed without comment or were even built into the presuppositions of the group, so that shortcut procedures could be adopted.

However, one crucial juncture in the script, the activity surrounding the main idea, did not, in general, run smoothly. The card which read "Ask a question about the main idea" was poison at first. In fact, the main idea card was not so bad: You could simply ask, "What is the main idea?" and thereby pass the responsibility off on someone else. The children found this out two times each day, but continued to try to deviate from this part of the script rather than deal routinely with anything having to do with a "main idea." Main ideas require interpretation, and interpretation was what these children were not doing.

However, we could maintain their participation by relying on the script and the roles and engaging with them in interpsychological acts of comprehension. At exactly those moments when the child is actively trying to read (in the adult meaning of the term "read"), it becomes possible to diagnose very precisely the nature of the child's disabled system of mediation. At the same time, since the child's activities are carefully structured to conform with the adult definition of reading, optimal conditions are created for a developmental reorganization, a remediation, to occur.

The way in which close coordination around the interpersonal production of reading can lead to fine-grained analysis and crucial developmental episodes is illustrated by the incident with Deanna described above. In the process of our Question-Asking Reading training, we have been able to identify both children who "copy match" and children with other patterns of reading activity that interfere with comprehension (cf. Griffin, Cole, Diaz, and King, in press). In the course of our work, we have seen changes in the children on three levels:[8]

1. During group reading sessions, children who start out not understanding or misunderstanding the specific passage end up understanding it and being able to formulate and answer interesting and important questions about it.
2. In the course of the training, the children begin to anticipate and presuppose the supporting and main reading acts that the Question-Asking Reading script embodies. More independence on the children's part can be seen as time passes.
3. Over time, the children begin to display different behaviors indicative of a change in their idea of reading – that is, they begin to treat reading as mediating activity in the world.

Contrast with ordinary practice

In a standard remedial reading curriculum, focused on decoding, Deanna and her peers learn some procedures associated with reading and invent some others on their own. But taught or invented, their procedures are unconstrained by the framework of the whole of adult reading. (We met one fifth-grader who knew how to find the main idea – it is in the second sentence of a paragraph!!) The inventiveness and creativity of the children are not the problem; their orientation to the school work of reading is the problem.

Without a doubt, these children sometimes appear to be dull and uncreative and to lack attentiveness. However, they have learned and augmented the procedure for reading to which they have been exposed. Our procedures provide one way to see what the children are doing, because they provide a framework embodying the whole of adult reading that allows the children to develop an analysis of reading text that is more serviceable to their futures out of school.

The key to the children's misunderstanding is that to them reading means "Read the individual words so that they sound right." Reading as it is most often encountered in the classrooms of elementary school children *is* reading aloud. But the fundamental nature of reading, from a sociohistorical perspective, is that reading includes looking at the sign, knowing what is coming, knowing where you have been, and knowing where somebody else is (Luria, 1981). These crucial facets of reading are absent for these children. Reading as a process of interpreting the world beyond the information given at the moment is left out of their information-processing theory altogether, and left out of systems of remedial reading instruction.

Reading, as Freire (1970) has said, is a way of theorizing about the world. The children we work with have a different notion. Their notion is this: Reading is a system of mediation restricted to them, the teacher, and text. In a particular question-and-answer frame wherein the questions are always given to them ahead of time, they only have to follow the learned grammatical and phonetic script.

This situation is typical of systems of mediation for poor readers. They are truncated, artificially truncated, and the children can get incredibly good at operating within them. They can get so good at it that you actually think they can read. You believe simply that they read very badly, but you do not get to question whether they are doing what you think they are doing or doing something totally different and somewhat bizarre.

Most of our children do not have the slightest notion of what the system of mediation *we* call reading is about. The system of remediation most commonly used does not re-mediate the overall understanding of what reading is or is for. Instead, it instantiates the reductionist theory and the analytic strategy that grew up with the alphabet: Start with the small, the simple, and proceed to the complex. Insofar as the child completely follows the procedures that the remedial programs specify (for example, sounding out *c – a – t* as /k/, /*/, /t/), there can be no progress. In contrast, we argue that the procedures need to be taught as cultural vehicles to help children experience that emergent activity that will allow them to understand what we adults are talking about when we say reading.

The future for nonreductionism in reading and research

The reductionist approach violates the fundamental principle that development always occurs within the framework of the whole (Hamburger, 1957). And, following reductionism, psychologists and educators rarely teach reading as a whole activity embedded in a communicative system. Our theories of reading acquisition are weak. One difficulty arises because theory testing at the level of real teaching – learning interactions cannot yet be conducted as simulations on a computer or with mathematical models. But these methods are closely associated with what we can recognize as serious scientific work upon which to base pedagogy and theory.

The activity of reading (and its acquisition) happens to have a social element in it, and that is the problem for our current methods and theories. It is for this reason that a sociohistorical analysis of reading is so important to understanding what it means to remediate this activity for some children; it is also a good guide to the necessary conditions for acquisition of reading in the first place.

What a sociohistorical point of view shows us is that we should be trying to instantiate a basic *activity* when teaching reading and not get blinded by the basic *skills*. Skills are always part of activities and settings, but they only take on meaning in terms of how they are organized. So instead of basic skills, a sociohistorical approach talks about basic activities and instantiates those that are necessary and sufficient to carry out the whole process of reading, given the general conditions for learning.

When we create such lesson contexts we find that the kids who cannot read in other contexts can, in fact, in our special conditions! Are they all reading perfectly, and independently of adult help? Is this a miracle? Of course not; they have problems, and a number of them have serious problems. For some children, you see immediate, dynamic improvement. Teachers report that "a miracle has happened." Other children are worse behaved in the classroom than before. For many there are significant but limited areas of improvement. Some children may have gained a deeper insight into just how deep a hole they are standing in. When one child sees another leap out and begin to experience success, the first begins to have a better understanding of what a deep hole he or she is in and goes further down. That might also be development; we know that development is not always achievement of a fixed criterion. Rather, development implies *systems reorganization*. Remedial reading instruction requires a social system's reorganization. When this perspective is properly applied, you can teach children to read who otherwise could not be taught. When it is misapplied, it can make a bad situation worse.

There are a great many scientific problems to be addressed when endorsing this sociohistorical approach to understanding literacy development. First, when you have "people acting in a setting" as the unit of analysis in psychological research, educational, experimental, and child psychologists alike all experience difficulties assessing the scientific validity of the work. It is also difficult to develop the insights of this approach so that our insistence that cognition is a social activity among human beings becomes practically useful. In our research we worry a lot about how to establish credible evidence, how to be scientific. We are currently wrestling with the problems of turning videotape evidence from what appears at first blush to be a demonstration of total chaos into something that is analyzable, and practical for classroom teaching activities. We are also experimenting with new "activity centers" that implement sociohistorical principles (Griffin and Cole, 1984). If we have succeeded in convincing the reader that this perspective is worth further explanation, we will have achieved our immediate goals in contributing to this symposium.

Notes

The work on which this paper is based was supported by the U.S. Department of Education and the Carnegie Corporation. An earlier version appeared in the *Quarterly Newsletter of the Laboratory of Comparative Human Cognition* 5:3, 1983. We thank our colleagues and students at the University of California, San Diego, for helping to make our work possible.

1. Other aspects of the LCHC research program are described in Anderson, Diaz, Moll (1984), Moll and Diaz (1984), and Newman, Griffin, and Cole (1984).

2. Published in English as Voloshinov (1973), the Russian original was published in 1929. Bakhtin used the names of various Russian colleagues for publishing his work (Holquist, 1983).
3. The lexicon of English obscures the relation between saying language is a mediator and saying that language is indirect. Consider these word pairs: direct/indirect, direct/immediate, indirect/mediated.
4. We are enclosing sounds in slashes; the * symbol is used for the vowel sound usually represented by the close juxtaposition of the letters *a* and *e*.
5. See *Laboratory of Comparative Human Cognition* (1982) for an early account of this work.
6. The script was elaborated on the basis of a reciprocal questioning procedure reported in Brown, Palincsar, and Armbruster (1982). In the Brown et al. experiments, an instructor and an individual child took turns leading a discussion and asking questions about the main ideas of paragraphs of text. Considerable improvement in comprehension was demonstrated for their subjects, seventh-graders who were classified as good decoders but poor comprehenders. Brown and J. Campione assisted us in the adaptation of the procedures so that we could use the idea with our subjects, who would be in groups and whose ages and classifications were quite diverse.
7. The setting "Field Growing Up College" is described in detail in other reports (*Laboratory of Comparative Human Cognition*, 1982; Griffin, Cole, Diaz, and King, in press). Suffice it to say that it is an after-school school (in Japanese, a "juku") which the children attend voluntarily for two hours twice a week and where they engage in a mix of literacy and computer activities. In this setting, children who demonstrated certain competencies (such as doing well at reading like a grown-up), could change status and become assistants to the adults.
8. Some of these changes were reflected in tests and in reports from the school they concurrently attended, and other evidence can be found in microanalysis of the taped training situations (Griffin, Cole, Diaz, and King, in press).

References

Anderson, A. B.; Diaz, E.; & Moll, L. C. (1984, July). Community Educational Resource and Research Center. *The Quarterly Newsletter of the Laboratory of Comparative Human Cognition, 6* (3), 70–71 (work in progress).

Anderson, A. B., & Stokes, S. J. (1984). Social and institutional influences on the development and practice of literacy. In F. Smith, H. Goelman, & A. Obers (Eds.), *Awakening to literacy*. New York: Heineman.

Averi, A. F., & Urton, G. (1982). *Ethnoastronomy and archeoastronomy in the American tropics.* New York: New York Academy of Sciences.

Brice Heath, S. (1980). Standard English: Biography of a symbol. In T. Shopen & J. M. Williams (Eds.), *Standards and Dialects in English*. Cambridge, Ma: Winthrop.

Brown, A. L., Palincsar, A. S., & Armbruster, B. B. (1982). Inducing comprehension-fostering activities in interactive learning situations. In H. Mandl, W. Stein, & T. Trabasso (Eds.), *Learning from texts*. Hillsdale, N.J.: Lawrence Erlbaum Associates.

Chippendale, C. (1983). *Stonehenge Complete*. Ithaca, N.Y.: Cornell University Press.

Cole, M.; Gay, J.; Glick, J.A.; & Sharp, D. W. (1971). *The cultural context of learning and thinking.* New York: Basic Books.

Cole, M., & Means, B. (1981). *Comparative studies of how people think.* Cambridge, Ma.: Harvard University Press.

Eisenstein, E. I. (1979). *The printing press as an agent of change* (2 vols.). Cambridge, Ma: Cambridge University Press.

Freire, P. (1970). *Cultural action for freedom* (Monograph No. 1). Cambridge, Ma.: Harvard Educational Review.

Gelb, I. J. (1963). *A study of writing* (Rev. ed.). Chicago: University of Chicago Press.

Gleitman, L. R., & Rozin, P. (1977). The structure and acquisition of reading I: Relations between orthographies and the structure of language. In A. Reber & D. Scarborough (Eds.), *Toward a psychology of reading*. Hillsdale, N.J.: Lawrence Erlbaum Associates.

Goffman, E. (1959). *The presentation of self in everyday life*. New York: Doubleday-Anchor.

Goffman, E. (1969). *Strategic interaction*. Philadelphia, Pa.: University of Pennsylvania Press.

Goody, J. (1977). *The domestication of the savage mind*. Cambridge: Cambridge University Press.

Graff, H. J. (1975b). *The literacy myth*. New York: Academic Press.

Griffin, P. (1977a, December). How and when does reading occur in the classroom? *Theory into Practice, 16*, 376–83.

Griffin, P., & Cole, M. (1984). Current activity for the future: The Zoped. In B. Rosoff & J. V. Wertsch (Eds.), *Children's learning in the "zone of proximal development." New directions for child development* (No. 2, pp. 45–63). San Francisco, Ca.: Jossey–Bass.

Griffin, P., Cole, M.; Diaz, S.; & King, C. (in press). Re-mediation, diagnosis and remediation. In R. Glaser (Ed.), *Advances in instructional psychology* (Vol. 3). Hillsdale, N. J.: Lawrence Erlbaum Associates.

Griffin, P., & Mehan, H. (1980). Sense and ritual in classroom discourse. Conversational routine: Explorations in standardized communication. In F. Coulmas (Ed.), *Systems and prepatterned speech*. The Hague: Mouton Janua Linguarum.

Hall, W. S.; Cole, M.; Reder, S.; & Dowley, G. (1977). Variations in young children's use of language: Some effects of setting and dialect. In R. Freedle (Ed.), *Discourse production and comprehension*. Norwood, N.J.: Ablex.

Hamburger, D. (1957). The concept of development in biology. In D. D. Harris (Ed.), *The concept of development* (pp. 49–58). Minneapolis: University of Minnesota Press.

Havelock, E. A. (1976). *Origins of Western literacy*. Toronto: The Ontario Institute for Studies in Education.

Holquist, M. (1983). The politics of representation. *The Quarterly Newsletter of the Laboratory of Comparative Human Cognition, 5* (1), 2–9. Laboratory of Comparative Human Cognition (1982, July). A model system for the study of learning difficulties. *The Quarterly Newsletter of the Laboratory of Comparative Human Cognition, 4* (3), 39–66.

Leont'ev, A. N. (1981). *Problems of the Development of Mind*. Moscow: Progress Publishers.

Luria, A. R. (1932). *The nature of human conflicts; or, emotion, conflict and will*. New York: Liveright.

Luria, A. R. (1978). The development of writing in the child. In M. Cole (Ed.), *The selected writings of A. R. Luria*. New York: Sharpe.

Luria, A. R. (1981). Cited in J. Wertsch, N. Minick, & F. Arns, *The creation of context in joint problem solving action: A cross cultural study*. Paper presented at the sessions of the SRCD Study Group "The Social Context of the Development of Everyday Skills," March 18–20, Laguna Beach, California.

Luria, A. R. (1981). *Language and consciousness*, New York: Plenum.

McClelland, J. L., & Rumelhart, D. E. (1981). An interactive activation model of context effects in letter perception: Part 1. An account of basic findings. *Psychological Review, 88* (5), 375–407.

Moll, L. C., & Diaz, S. (1983). *Towards an interactional pedagogical psychology: A bilingual case study*. Center for Human Information Processing, University of California, San Diego.

Moll, L. C., & Diaz, S. (1984). *Bilingual communication and reading: The importance of Spanish in learning to read in English*. Manuscript submitted for publication.

Newman, D.; Griffin, P.; & Cole, M. (1984). Social constraints in laboratory and classroom tasks. In B. Rogoff & J. Lave (Eds.), *Everyday cognition: Its development in social context*. Cambridge, Ma.: Harvard University Press.

O'Neil, W. (1980). English Orthography. In T. Shopen & J. Williams (Eds.), *Standards and Dialects in English*. Cambridge, Ma.: Winthrop.

Schmandt-Besserat, D. (1978). The earliest precursor of writing. *Scientific American, 238* (6), 50–59.

Scribner, S., & Cole, M. (1980). *Consequences of literacy*, Cambridge, Ma.: Harvard University Press.

Scribner, S., & Cole, M. (1981). *The psychology of literacy*. Cambridge, Ma.: Harvard University Press.

Shaklee, M. (1980). The rise of standard English. In T. Shopen & J. M. Williams (Eds.), *Standards and dialects in English*. Cambridge, Ma.: Winthrop.

Sohn-Rethel, A. (1978). *Intellectual and manual labor: A critique of epistemology*. London: Macmillan.

Vaughn-Cooke, A. F. (1977). Phonological rules and reading. In R. Shuy (Ed.), *Linguistic theory: What can it say about reading?* Newark, Del: International Reading Association.

Voloshinov, V. N. (1973). *Marxism and the philosophy of language*. New York: Academic Press.

Vygotsky, L. S. (1962). *Thought and language*. Cambridge; Ma.: MIT Press.

Vygotsky, L. S. (1978). *Mind in society; The development of higher psychological processes* (Eds., M. Cole, V. John-Steiner, S. Scribner, & E. Souberman). Cambridge, Ma.: Harvard University Press.

Wertsch, J. V. (Ed.). (1981). *The concept of activity in Soviet psychology*. White Plains, N.Y.: Sharpe.

Wolf, T. (1977). Reading reconsidered. *Harvard Educational Review, 47*(3), pp. 411–29.

8 The business of literacy:
the making of the educational textbook

Rowland Lorimer

Introduction: the commoditization of learning materials

With division of labor and hence specialization, individuals and now business institutions have become oriented to satisfying the needs of others. As business comes to play a larger role in satisfying these needs, the needy themselves cease to participate directly in that activity. As a result, business attains a position that allows it to redefine what is necessary to satisfy a particular set of needs and, in fact, to generate new needs. In so doing, it "commoditizes." With their product in mind, corporations elaborate a need in such a way that only their product is capable of satisfying it.

The acquisition of literacy is a good example of such a process. Over a considerable period in history, people learned to read and write by reading and copying from available texts, which in Western societies typically meant the Bible. In due course, books were designed first to capture the interests of children and secondly to cater to their developing skills. Today, it would be difficult to find a child reading literature that was not specifically designed for children. In spite of the fact that children can learn to read without the benefit of "purpose built" materials, the needs of children have been elaborated and redefined by professionals and businesses to such an extent that few consider it appropriate for children to learn to read by using material not specially designed for that purpose. In other words, the acquisition of literacy skills has been commoditized.

This commoditization has led to the development of a literature that supposedly appeals to children on the basis of its dramatic force. Unfortunately, that dramatic force focuses around the psychological or individual dynamics of the mainstream of society, omitting, among other things, cultural dynamics and diversity. It does not reflect the full richness of the lives that children lead. Nor does it reflect the psychology of nondominant groups. Instead, it is a workable formula sufficient to be moderately successful in allowing children to acquire some literacy skills. Having said that, it is important to remember that the Bible was able to do the same.

The responsibility for this content, arising as it does through commoditization, cannot be said to rest solely with publishers. Rather elaborate evaluation and selection procedures have been developed by educators in their role as consumers to ensure that educational quality is a priority in determining what reaches the classroom. However, these procedures have, in (unintended) consequence, restricted the participation of publishers in the market. The publishers financially best suited to cope with these procedures have turned out to be the large multinationals, the very groups most prone to commoditizing.

It is my intention in this paper to describe the characteristics of the content of literacy acquisition materials and the control processes that contribute to the presence of those characteristics. My purpose is to show how influential business dynamics have become in defining and satisfying the needs of both children and the educational establishment in the area of literacy training.

An overview of literacy materials

Cultures are shaped by the collective images that their members share. At this point in history those images emerge in large part through the printed word, although the electronic media are well on their way to asserting dominance. The study of language arts is regarded by many educators as an exercise in skill acquisition which involves exposure to writing of the best aesthetic quality. However, it is also very much an introduction to a particular ideational content. Even in the early acquisition of reading skills and aesthetic taste, the place given to specific, culturally based visions and realities, as well as to indigenous literature, reflects the importance Canadians and other nationals place on our own community and culture.

The commoditization of materials to teach literacy and the capture of the market by large multinational companies have led to the promotion of a content and literature which places the individual in a massified or generic world. It erases distinctive qualities, whether they be based on class, ethnicity, or geography. Moreover, it silences the distinctive features of indigenous national cultures.

A contemporary example

Starting Points in Reading (Moore & Hooper, 1973), a reading series published by Ginn, a subsidiary of Xerox, is a good example of the commoditization process extending into the selection of content. In *Starting Points in Reading*, the world is portrayed as filled with clumsy institutions in a society that proceeds along according to a momentum of its own. Society is arbitrary at best, often wrong-headed, uncomprehending, unappreciative, and something against which one must struggle to survive. The realism of such a portrayal derives from its inherent "explanation" of individual ineffectiveness and frustration. What makes living tolerable is the imposition of the wills of individuals on events. In this reading series, peace, harmony, growth, and so on are the results of individuals acting alone against the mass (Lorimer & Long, 1979–80).

In such a simplified, adversarial world, where individuals are pitted against society, concrete references to specific social institutions are an embarrassment – they would identify the culprits. Because social institutions are foils for exploring the strength of will of individuals, they are reduced to a generic form and not singled out for specific prejudice. The world is not presented as composed of a number of differentiated communities but rather as a boundless, homogeneous conglomeration of individuals, each striving to make his or her own way. Cultural distinctions are blurred; specific national cultures barely exist. The social order is portrayed as the "fallout" resulting from everyone competing with each other to make out as best they know how. Cooperative groupings are rearguard actions, ways of coping with the imposed order.

The apparent arbitrariness of the social process, together with its implied homogeneity, generates a single basic set of rules of behavior, valid across all situations. That is to say, the arbitrary social momentum of the portrayed world demands individual initiative and persistence – *individual* initiative, because social groups are portrayed as cumbersome and conflict-ridden; persistence, because a considerable will is required to affect the ongoing momentum of society. Individuals cope with such demands in two basic styles. Main characters use cleverness and trickery. These often inherited traits are methods by which main characters resist the social order, assert their individuality, and thereby command a following. Secondary characters have a separate set of traits which cluster around obedience, humility, loyalty, and acquiescence. In outline, we are exposed to people portrayed in binary opposition: the rulers and the ruled.

In short, human beings are presented as embodying the character traits of "successes" or "failures." The world is presented as separate, as something quite distinct from the intentions and abilities of the individuals of which it is composed. In the final analysis, the world emerges as one without concrete realities and therefore without a cultural significance.

For example, one story used at the grade five level tells of a boy who has become known as "the bully of Barkham Street." It emphasizes the psychological and family dynamics involved and the usual storybook-type cast: nosy old man, disciplining principal, and complaining neighbors. The boy is portrayed as being in a real dilemma, partially because both of his parents work. There are no positive portrayals of social groupings such as the neighborhood, parents, the school, the community center, or peer groups – even in this situation, where it would be quite apt. The boy is presented as having no social support. He is left alone to cope with his own personal misfortune in his own individual way (Moore & Hooper, 1973, pp. 32–49).

Other reading programs, however, offer a contrast to this value orientation. For instance, a Nelson program called the *Language Development Reading Series* (McInnes & Hearn, 1971) presents cultural content and thereby develops a cultural perspective. As quality literature, it places on view a world with recognizable particularities. Places, events, individuals, opinions, and so forth are recognizable in their specificity. National culture and physical setting, in this case Canadian, become the backdrop for the entire series, not as a geographical or attitudinal boundary, but as a concrete locus from which the student reaches toward ever broader understanding and appreciations.

Other characteristics of literacy materials

Other attributes of reading series besides their story content are also commoditized. For instance, working with very large start-up costs but with potentially huge sales, expensive technological production processes become not only feasible but also defined as intrinsic to "high-quality" learning materials. In the case of elementary reading series, illustrators are presently paid more per story than are authors, and such cosmetics as four-color printing have become a minimal requirement for the illustration of every "good" textbook. These aspects of commoditization, which serve to restrict competition from publishers oriented to smaller markets and with less access to capital, are further legitimized through social scientific investigations designed to show that such cosmetics motivate children to learn more than do less expensive production modes (Lorimer & Long, 1979–80).

Endorsements play a significant role in educational publishing. Whereas originally only persons who made major contributions to educational materials were listed at the beginning of the book, now notable consultants and editors are often named solely to enhance sales. Such individuals are paid for the use of their names as consultants, not for their contribution to the materials. Educational products are also "piggybacked" and sold on the basis of brand loyalty. Piggybacking involves the introduction of one product riding on the back of the success of the first. Supplementary library collections, workbooks, and teachers' guides are all piggybacked onto a successful series. Brand loyalty is encouraged by naming a series embracing various subject areas after a successful first volume – thus, *Starting Points in Reading* (Moore & Hooper, 1973) spawns *Starting Points in Mathematics* (Barnhold, 1973) and *Starting Points in Language* (Moore & Hooper, 1973).

The pinnacle of commoditization is achieved when the educational product asserts primacy over the educational process. This comes about with the full acceptance of such products and explanatory concepts as elaborate management systems (i.e., fancy teachers' guides) and the popularity of "teacher-proof" materials. The latter refers to a "product warranty" that no matter how generally inept the teacher, the product, which is designed with an explicit rule system that constrains teacher behavior, is guaranteed to ensure that the child will learn. The teacher is thereby an adjunct to the textbook rather than *vice versa*. (See de Castell & Luke in this volume.)

In search of educational value in a structurally rigid market

Whatever the excesses of commoditization, there is no doubt that a learning materials market has been carved out of general publishing. This market has attracted a number of specialty producers, who in recent years have clearly identified their consumers. These consumers are not children but those who are making decisions to purchase or not to purchase books on behalf of children and on behalf of their school, district, or province. How has this market emerged?

In the purchasing of learning materials, educational value must take first priority. Good purchases are intended to ensure the highest quality of education. Educators, such as curriculum consultants, administrators, and department heads, who participate in such purchasing are, by virtue of their responsibilities, an identifiable consumer group. For the sophisticated market and profit-oriented multinational publishers, these consumers become the audience whose needs must be met and whose wants must be catered to.

Let us consider the procedures of selection and adoption that education ministries – those who have constitutional responsibility for education – have devised to bring order to their purchasing decisions.

Selection and adoption procedures in Canada

The four major procedures by which Canadian educators attempt to bring order to their purchasing of learning materials at the provincial level are as follows: limited prescriptions or authorizations, multiple listings, contract development, and provincial self-publishing. Such procedures are common to many other countries. The first and most commonly used method is limited prescriptions or authorizations. This method involves an elaborate process of curriculum review, curriculum revision, solicitation of materials, further review, and final authorization of materials. The provincial committees formed to undertake these tasks are composed of subject-area experts along with representatives of various administrative levels of the educational system. In no case are there committee members whose direct and sole responsibility is to attend to the cultural, subcultural, national, or regional significance of the materials being considered. That is to say, no one assesses how the materials fit into the general task of introducing the child to his or her culture and society, either from the point of view of the curriculum as a whole or from the point of view of regional cultures. This applies not only to language arts and literature but also to all other subjects.

The second method of selection/adoption involves multiple listings; in Canada this method is used by the Province of Ontario. Here materials are submitted to a committee of the provincial Ministry of Education which scrutinizes them on the basis of a number of fairly technical criteria, such as reading level or, in other subject areas, subject matter covered. Once they have been so evaluated, if they are deemed to be "suitable educational materials" – that is, not offensive to general and specific societal, moral, and educational values – they are placed on a master list, in this case called Circular 14. This list is circulated to schools and districts. In addition, Ontario purchases several hundreds of copies of the list for circulation to selected schools in the province, so that those in a position to choose materials (teachers, principals, district employees, etc.) can have a view of the product they are selecting.

Selection is further constrained by a provincial law stating that to be approved for use in schools, materials must be written, published, and manufactured in Canada.

The third method of selection/adoption is contract development. This method is used in cases where no satisfactory materials can be found from existing publishers' lists. Publishers are given an outline of the curriculum and requested to submit a proposal and a budget, which are then reviewed by the Ministry of Education.

A fourth method used to control both development and implementation of classroom materials is self-publishing by the province. While a certain amount of self-publishing has been engaged in by various provinces, this method has come to be viewed as something to be undertaken only in quite unusual circumstances. Publishers have come to feel that they have certain rights to the market and are rather unhappy to be excluded when a province takes on the publishing function itself.

In short, the Ministry of Education acting by itself, with one of its adjunct departments, or in conjunction with another department in the province, may undertake the development and distribution of materials. Almost all 12 Canadian educational jurisdictions have undertaken such development on a small scale at one time or other. Usually the materials have a distinct regional focus and are unlikely to be marketable in great numbers elsewhere. In addition, every province involves itself to some degree in the creation and distribution of audio-visual materials.

To provide some perspective on the importance of each of the above methods, it should be noted that about 95% of all print materials used in Canadian schools are selected by the first two methods: limited prescriptions or authorizations and multiple listings. In contrast to the latter two methods, the former two demand that the material exist fully published before it can be considered for authorization. This means that maximum risk is placed on the publisher. In the case of material sufficient for a single grade, a minimum investment of $50,000 is required. For an integrated language arts and reading series spanning grades 1 to 6, the required investment is somewhere in the region of $4 million (Lee, 1980).

The development and marketing strategies of educational publishers

Faced with the first three selection procedures, the educational publishing industry has arrived at several different strategies to maximize profitable participation at minimal financial risk. These strategies vary with the size of the market represented by the province and the predominant selection procedures used.

First and foremost, small companies have bowed out of the market. The remaining large (multinational) companies use six main strategies to ensure survival. They are as follows:

1. "Codevelopment" is the undertaking of a major effort with extensive cooperation by all levels of the educational hierarchy within the province. This method is common in provinces outside of Ontario. Done well, it provides early promotion for the product and elicits an initially favorable response from materials selection committees.
2. "Grassroots development" means undertaking development with a small group of teachers within one or several provinces. This method is widely used in Ontario and to a limited extent elsewhere. In Ontario it is used sometimes in combination with codevelopment in other provinces. Marketing these materials demands a combination of commercial marketing and promotion through educational review channels.
3. "Transplanting" consists of the importation of a product from one province and its sale in another. This is really a second phase of strategies 1 or 2. It relies for sales and/or provincial adoption primarily on formal and informal educational review channels augmented by commercial marketing.
4. "Importing" refers to the importation of a product from a foreign market and its adaptation for use in the Canadian markets. Like codevelopment, this method is also common outside Ontario. (Its unpopularity in Ontario is attributable to the provincial statute mentioned earlier.) This second-phase publishing from a foreign market demands fairly clear-cut commercial marketing procedures.
5. "Importing high-profile American government-inspired programs" constitutes a special case involving the importation (and usually the adaptation) of a program based on a major American government-sponsored effort. This second-phase method is used in all provinces and relies on both commercial marketing and educational review channels.
6. "Contract development" refers to the development of a product under contract with a province. (See above.) This method is used in all provinces. It requires very little marketing.

The implications of publisher/educator interaction

The major implication of this publishing/selection interface is that it is biased toward the investment of a great deal of money before a decision on selection is made. As a result, it favors large multinational companies whose vast borrowing power allows them to spread their risk as widely as possible by publishing materials intended for more than one provincial market. Thus, any one provincial or state decision becomes a small matter rather than something that might make or break the company.

What are the implications of this bias? The multinationals have gained market hegemony. In consequence, most textbook series, especially those first produced in the United States, are essentially identical in their primary function. They succeed in teaching reading to approximately the same extent and induce roughly the same set of mainstream, dominant values (e.g., Clymer, 1978, 1972). They do, however, differ in their identities as commodities (See Lorimer, Harkley, Long & Tourell, 1978). Some take the phonetic approach; some sight-words methods; some are high-interest, low-vocabulary; some are inner city – oriented; and so forth. But the literature and the cultural values that they put forward are not significantly different from one series to the next. They are different versions of the same story, one which fails to reflect a genuine cultural diversity (Robinson, 1981). In addition, the features put forward to potential consumers to encourage purchase, such as the teacher resource book, library supplements and workbooks, and indeed the "management systems," have only marginal educational value. More significant is their function as marketing devices: They are the bucket seats, the rear defrosters, and the power steering options of the textbook world. The thematic organization, featured authors, and theoretical foundations of today's textbooks are like the ad man's attempt to associate his product with the power to attract beautiful people, be in beautiful places, and live a beautiful life. The commoditized text offers guaranteed success rates, student receptivity, measurability of progress, and effortless teaching methods.

Although the market is dominated by such processes, other types of materials are allowed to develop on the fringes, in 5% or perhaps even 10% of the market. Contract development refocuses the bias away from already published materials toward the local submission of proposals, thus making possible the participation of smaller companies. Contract development appears to favor companies that have secured the services of educators who enjoy good local reputations and connections. Unfortunately, such qualifications usually arise from prior participation in the American professional educational establishment (Lorimer, 1984).

Similarly, grassroots development allows smaller publishers to participate in the market. However, even grassroots development unduly strains the resources of small publishing companies, since $50,000 of working capital is required for the development of a single text. This contrasts with approximately $10,000 for a single trade book. The only compensatory attraction of the market is a large, multiprovince sales potential.

This bias toward one type of company, the large multinational corporation, contrasts dramatically with the state of trade publishing in Canada today. There, a heterogeneous mix of firms exists, capable of responding to a wide variety of audiences and authors (MacSkimming, 1980). Trade publications run the gamut from the profit-oriented mass paperback industry to university presses to the culturally and politically oriented medium-sized and small presses. For virtually all of these companies, arguably companies that publish the culturally most significant Canadian materials, any but peripheral participation in the educational market is highly restricted. Education, for its part, is cut off from a divergent industrial infrastructure capable of a flexible response to intellectual, vocational, and cultural demands.

The point is that somewhat accidentally, in trying to bring order to their decisions, educators have constituted themselves as the focal audience and have created a set of financial constraints which have enabled multinationals to attain a position of overwhelming predominance in the educational market. Assured of their position, these corporations have been able to commoditize the market in such a way that variables wholly external to the educational and cultural value of curricular materials have become the primary determinants of market shares. As a consequence, all a company must do in order to secure an acceptable market share is expend sufficient marketing effort in all possible areas. In the process of gearing up for such an effort, publishers signal to one another their intentions, so that competition never becomes cutthroat. Instead, the large corporations, capable of the fanciest marketing efforts, over the long-term merely become larger, swallowing their brethren; the dislocation they cause in the process is barely noticeable (the swallowing of Macmillan Canada by Gage is a case in point). The majority of workers, managers, educators, and especially shareholders go away happy. None of this, however, has anything whatsoever to do with maximizing educational value.

References

Barnhold, D. L. (1973). *Starting Points in Mathematics*. Toronto: Ginn Canada.
Clymer, T., et. al. (Eds.), (1972). *Reading 360*. Toronto: Ginn Canada.
Clymer, T., et al. (Eds.) (1978). *Reading 720*. Toronto: Ginn Canada.

Lee, R. (1980). Book Production: Ramifications and Problems, in Bevan, G. H., *1980 Publishers' Conference Proceedings*, Calgary, June 1980, Edmonton: Curriculum Branch, Alberta Education.

Lorimer, R. (1984). *The Nation in the Schools: Wanted, a Canadian Education*. Toronto: OISE Press.

Lorimer, R., Harkley, J., Long, M., and Tourell, D., (1978). Your Canadian Reader, *Lighthouse*, pp. 6–15.6.

Lorimer, R., & Long, M. (1979–80), Sex-role Stereotyping in Elementary Readers, *Interchange*, 10(2), 25–45.

Macskimming, R. (1981, April). Trade Publishing in English Canada. Paper presented to *Book Publishing and Public Policy Conference*, Ottawa. Toronto: Association of Canadian Publishers.

McInnes, J., & Hearn, E. (Eds.) (1971). *The Nelson Language Development Reading Program*. Toronto: Thos. Nelson & Sons.

Moore, B., & Hooper, H. (Eds.) (1973). *Starting Points in Language*. Toronto: Ginn Canada.

Moore, B., & Hooper, H. (Eds.) (1973). *Starting Points in Reading*. Toronto: Ginn Canada.

Robinson, P. (Ed.) (1981). *Publishing for Canadian Classrooms*. Halifax: Canadian Learning Materials Centre.

Part III

Matters empirical

9   Learning to mean what you say: toward a psychology of literacy

David R. Olson

One of the most conspicuous properties of language is that it serves as an expression of meaning. Language consists of a sequence of sounds or a string of marks on paper which express the meanings or intentions of a speaker or writer. We use language to express our intentions, and we interpret the utterances of others to recover their intentions, ideas, and feelings. That much, it seems, is obvious.

Yet this shared meaning, this intentionality, has proven to be the most obscure and the most difficult strand of language to unravel theoretically. Meaning remains one of the most recalcitrant problems in philosophy and psychology. Behavioristic psychologists and linguists avoided the problem altogether in the hope that an explanation of speech, thought, and action might be developed without addressing that problem. The attempt failed conspicuously. There seems no alternative but to address it directly. Indeed, as Ryle (1956, p. 8) pointed out, "The story of twentieth century philosophy is very largely the story of this notion of sense or meaning."

What is meaning? More importantly, what is meaning to children who are learning to read and write? Is it I as a speaker who has meaning? Or is it my sentences that have meaning? Do words have meanings? What does it mean to understand me as opposed to my sentences? More importantly, how are the two, what I mean and what my words or sentences mean, related?

Before we address that question, it is important to see that with reading and writing, the "meaning" tends to be dislocated from the intentions of speakers – what *you* mean – to the surface structures of language – what *it* means. School talk is largely about what words, sentences, and texts mean and only secondarily about what I mean, you mean, or they mean. Hence, the solution to the problem of the relation between what sentences mean and what we mean by them differs somewhat depending on whether we

145

are discussing speech or writing. Consequently, when children learn to read, they are not reading to recover the intentions of a speaker as they do when listening to talk, but rather trying to recover the meanings of words, sentences, and texts. We shall later consider the importance of that dislocation for a theory of comprehension.

For now, we may note that the psychology and pedagogy of reading is blessed (one might almost equally say cursed) with theories that insistently pursue only one side or the other of these poles. Some theories are particularly oriented to the meaning in the language and hence emphasize processes of decoding, word and letter recognition, and word meaning – processes involved in recovering a linguistic form from written symbols. The opposite view of meaning is taken by theories that are concerned with the recovery of speakers' and writers' meanings and intentions. This emphasis gives rise to theories of comprehension, interpretation, and the like. Theories of the first sort handle intended meanings poorly, whereas theories of the latter sort tend to underestimate the importance of linguistic forms and the meaning of those forms.

Some attempts have been made to reconcile these differences by talking of reading as an interactive process between "top–down" and "bottom–up" processes. While this is a step in the right direction, it is problematic in that the so-called bottom – up processes involve knowledge and expectancies in much the same way as the so-called top – down ones. The primary difference between these processes is that the former involve the analysis of subordinate structures, such as letters or words, whereas the latter involves the superordinate structures of meanings and intentions.

But that distinction seems not to capture the critical problem in reading: namely, working out an explicit understanding of the relations between the two systems I have been contrasting above – the meanings familiar to the child (that is, the intended meanings in the speaker's mind) and the new level of meanings that he or she is expected to come to deal with, the meanings of the linguistic forms. That distinction I have marked as one between what sentences mean and what we mean by them. In other contexts, I have described this distinction as one between what we say and what we mean by it. It is that distinction that, I shall urge, is closely tied to literacy. Children who make the distinction, I suggest, will find learning to read relatively easier than those who do not. Furthermore, it is a conceptual distinction that, itself is a by-product of literacy, not merely the inevitable consequence of maturity.

Although Ogden and Richards (1923) early in the century sorted out the differences in forms of meaning, it was relatively recently that Grice (1957) showed that a theory of language must differentiate between what he called "sentence meaning" and "speaker's meaning." That is the distinction I am drawing here. By "sentence meaning" – or, equivalently, "what is said" – I refer to the linguistic form of an expression, the very words employed and their syntactic relations, along with the conventionalized meanings expressed by those structures. Together they make up a semantic structure. The sentence "I'm bigger than you" has a semantic structure even if we do not yet know who the "I" refers to or who the "you" refers to. That is its sentence meaning.

By "speaker's meaning" – or, equivalently, "what is meant" – I, following Grice, refer to the meaning intended by the speaker who uttered the sentence. The speaker's meaning includes values for who the "I" and the "you" are in the above sentence. That meaning is a claim about the relative sizes of two particular people.

Now, how are the two, sentence meaning and speaker's meaning, related? Some theorists have suggested that we can go from one to the other by pragmatic rules that map sentence meanings onto intended meanings. But we need not go far before we are forced to recognize that recovery of intended meanings goes well beyond the conventions of language and appeals rather to bodies of knowledge only loosely if at all related to the linguistic rules. Winograd (1980, p. 210) provides one example. Suppose a child is reading the following text: "Tommy had just been given a new set of blocks. He was opening the box when he saw Jimmy coming in." Winograd continues: "There is no mention of what is in the box – no clue as to what box it is at all. But the person reading the text makes the immediate assumption that it is the box which contains the set of blocks. We can do this not because of any property of the sentence but because we know that new items often come in boxes, and that opening the box is the usual thing to do. We derive an intention, in other words, not merely from sentences but from prior knowledge of the world."

To handle such problems, theorists have differentiated what a sentence says, its semantic structure, from what it means, the intention it expresses or conveys. The means for going from sentences to intentions is a context – a situation or a possible world. That is, in order to explain how our sentences are related to our intentions, we must have at least three constituents: sentences (*S*), possible worlds (*PW*), and intended meanings (*M*). Figure 9-1 shows this relationship and provides some synonymous expressions for these terms.

As to the semantic structure of a linguistic form, the *S* column of Figure 9-1, a great deal of progress has been made by linguists in analyzing these structures and their acquisition by children (see Brown, 1973; and de Villiers and de Villiers, 1978, for summaries of this work). In speech, this

S	+	PW	=	M
"Said" semantic structure		knowledge of the world		"Meant" intended meaning
or		or		or
linguistic meaning		knowledge of context		speaker's meaning
or		or		or
sentence meaning		possible world		utterance meaning
"I hear talking"		in school		Be quiet
"Where's the salt?"		at table		Pass the salt
"You have more than me"		in dispute over shared goods		Give me some

Varieties of M

Casual meaning.
(PW is invariant.)

S S'
$S' + PW = M$

Piaget: S : Are there more ducks or animals?
             S' : Are there more ducks or rabbits?

Literal meaning.
(S is invariant.)

PW PW'
$S + PW' = M$

Are there more ducks or animals?
PW ducks/rabbits PW' ducks/animals

Indirect speech act and
    metaphor.
(S and PW are invariant.)

M M'
$S + W = M'$

You have more than me.
I hear talking.

Figure 9-1. Some relations of sentences and contexts in the determination of meaning

knowledge of linguistic form or semantic structure remains largely implicit; in reading and writing, these very structures become the object of study and learning. In learning to read, children come to possess explicit knowledge about letters, sounds, words, and even meanings of words, as we shall see later. For now, note only that much of what has remained implicit in speech is made explicit in writing.

As to possible worlds, the PW column on our chart – what for purposes of this paper we may think of as a way of discussing contexts or situations

– we may note that a sentence expresses an intention only in some world. A possible world is simply that world. The real world, the world we are physically present in, is the most important of such worlds. But it is not the only world in which sentences may receive interpretations. Consider the world of literature, the world of imaginative fiction, the classical worlds of antiquity. Much of our language is used in such worlds. We may say (or think), for example, "If only I hadn't bought a Pinto" or "I wish it were Friday." These are common uses of such possible worlds. More relevant to literacy are those worlds the knowledge of which we possess only by virtue of written texts – the world of the ancient Greeks, for example. Possible worlds are basically like the real world except in the specified aspects (Kripke, 1972). Unless otherwise told, we assume that ancient Greeks, like us, walk rather than fly, and so on. But, when specified, the possible world deviates in systematic directions from the ordinary or common world. Sentences are the means of stipulating possible worlds. It is the text which specifies how the possible world is to be taken. Sentences, in these contexts, may be considered as recipes for building possible worlds.

Notice how the context of an utterance has been dislocated. In most ordinary oral language, sentences are assimilated to their contexts; in stipulating possible worlds, it is the context that is assimilated to the sentences. Language and reality, we may say, are reordered. For language to serve the purpose of stipulating possible worlds with sufficient precision that another may reconstruct such a world – whether that world is a theoretical claim in science or an imaginative world in fiction – requires that the sentence meanings, the S's, be more conventionalized and elaborated than they would have to be to talk only of the more immediate world.

The knowledge of practical contexts, the PWs in terms of which most ordinary language is assimilated in the process of arriving at an interpretation, has been discussed in cognitive science in terms of schemata, scripts, and frames. These frameworks provide a mental representation of the contexts used to interpret sentences. Indeed, a good deal of research has gone into showing that if these structures of knowledge are not in place, comprehension of language will not occur (Rumelhart and Ortony, 1977; Spiro, 1980). But we should note that the use of such schemata in comprehending language may be quite different from constructing those schemata on the basis of written texts. A large part of reading and study consists of building up schemata for imaginative, possible worlds on the basis of texts. Again, such construction throws a heavy burden on the linguistic form in constructing an interpretation, whereas ordinary comprehension is made easy by putting the conceptual load on the prior knowledge of schemata already possessed by the listener or reader and only a minimal burden on the lexical and syntactic features of the language.

But it is the meaning, the M, that requires most analysis and consideration. What do we mean by "meaning" and by "reading for meaning"? By understanding? We have a relatively clear intuition of understanding and of failing to understand, but we lack a clear and explicit concept of understanding. Studies of children's judgments of their own comprehension (Markman, 1977) have shown that children frequently claim to have understood something although subsequent questioning of the understanding shows that they have not "monitored" their comprehension as an adult would have. Part of the problem, it appears, is that children do not have a clear concept of what it is to understand. In view of the difficulty we have in formulating a clear concept, children's difficulties are not all that surprising.

"Understand," like "mean," is a basic or undefined term. If we were to read a story to a child, we would look for signs of pleasure, fear, or excitement as indications of understanding. If the story were greeted by puzzled looks or questions such as "What?" we would assume that the child did not understand. We judge understanding through what the child says or does; it cannot be assessed directly. Even worse, we cannot explain the concept by appeal to simpler concepts; "to make sense of" is no clearer than "to understand." "To know what I'm talking about" may help, but it is not equivalent.

The expressions "mean," "understand," "believe," "remember," "notice," "think," "perceive," and "forget" are members of a class of verbs that are sometimes referred to as "intentional predicates" (Dennett, 1978; Fodor, 1979; Searle, 1983). They are verbs which express an attitude or psychological orientation toward propositions. Together, they make up a commonsensical or folk theory of the mind. It is concepts like these which insert mental states between the stimuli presented by the world and humans' and animals' responses to the world. As I mentioned earlier, behaviorists argued that these "mentalistic" terms were fictions that were better forgotten; to quote Bloomfield: "Scientific description requires none of the mentalistic terms" (1939, p. 13). Stich (1983) has recently attacked the explanatory usefulness of these mentalistic concepts from a cognitive science point of view as well.

Intentions, I shall argue, are not only important in understanding language – they are what sentences express in particular contexts – but they are the basic concepts for the intentional management of our minds. To the extent that these concepts are absent or fuzzy, to that extent children or adults are not in a position to manage voluntarily their mental activities of knowing, believing, thinking, or guessing, let alone understanding, interpreting, inferring, concluding, and the like. Even worse, because these are concepts in ordinary language it is assumed that every child will already know these distinctions. The assumption is either that such distinctions are innate, natural to the species, or at worst that children will pick them up in the course of learning to talk. Hence, they are not the focus of explicit instruction in the school. One consequence may be that children don't have a clear notion of what it is to understand something, let alone to describe it or explain it and so on.

Although the processes represented by these concepts are crucial to understanding both speaking and reading, they have not received the attention they deserve, either by theorists or by the parents and teachers who are responsible for passing them on to children. Venezky (1982) has pointed out that, historically, the teaching of reading laid very little emphasis on comprehension. The McGuffey Readers, for example were primarily designed to teach children to read orally for an audience. Whether the reader understood was not emphasized, presumably because it was assumed that if you got the words, you got the meaning.

Let us consider somewhat more fully the structure of speakers' intended meaning and its relation to sentence meanings, and some of the ways that this relation is altered in written language. These relations are displayed in Figure 9-1. Notice first that there is no direct mapping between what is said and what is meant. That relation is established only through a third term – namely, a possible world or context. As an aside, I would point out that the central question as to the relation between language and thought, like the question of the relation between sentences and intended meanings, has proven insoluble for just this reason. There *is* no direct relation between language and thought. All language is related to thought or meaning only through an agreed-upon – that is, a presupposed – context, or through a stipulated one.

How then are the things said, S, related to the things meant by them, M? A sentence meaning (S), together with a context or possible world (PW), specifies an intended meaning (M). Some of the implications of a three-term theory of the relation between what is said and what is meant by it are also indicated in Figure 9-1. In most cases of the expression of meaning, what in Figure 9-1 is referred to as casual meaning, it is the context or possible world, including people's scripts for representing that world, that is taken as invariant. A semantic structure will be glossed or otherwise interpreted to fit that invariant possible world. Piaget's discovery that a young child will gloss the question "Are there more ducks or animals?" into the simpler question "Are there more ducks or rabbits?" is an example of this process. My suggestion is that in ordinary oral language, the meaning in the language is subordinated to the intentions of the speaker and the context in which the utterance occurs. For much oral language, not much need be said: "A wink is as good as a nod."

For written language, the relation between the meanings in the language and the meaning intentions of the speaker or writer is reversed. When the meaning in the language, S, is superordinate – that is, when the semantic structure is taken as invariant – we have what is usually called literal meaning. In this case it is the possible world and the intentions of the reader that have to give way to the meaning in the language. We (Hildyard and Olson, 1982; Olson and Torrance, 1983) have presented some evidence to show that children readily compute a casual meaning rather than a literal meaning for sentences and that the latter, as the name implies, is associated with literacy. It is the literal meaning of the questions that requires children in Piaget's task to reorganize their understanding of the class-inclusion relation between ducks and animals.

Thirdly, Figure 9-1 shows that to compute a metaphorical meaning, the comprehender must preserve both the linguistic form and the stored prior knowledge of a possible world. It is for this reason that metaphor, as opposed to casual or literal meaning, is difficult for children to comprehend.

We may now use the analysis of the ways in which sentences relate to contexts and intentions to examine changes in children's comprehension of language that occur in the early school years – changes which, I shall argue later, are prompted by literacy.

Clearly, children have some knowledge of the relation between sayings and meanings. Even very young children appear to have intentions (but see Shotter, 1984, for an interesting alternative view of the relation between speech and intentionality), and they express them through language, gesture, and action. Furthermore, there is little doubt that children recover the intended meanings of others, often with minimal attention to the expression used. Two examples are shown in Figure 9-1. Children hearing the sentence "I hear talking" spoken in the classroom know that the teacher means "Stop talking" (Sinclair and Coulthard, 1975). Similarly, when two children argue over the sharing of goods, and one child says, "You have more than me," both know that he or she means "Give me some." It is apparently not the case that they first derive a literal meaning for the sentence and then infer an intention. Rather, given the context and their knowledge of the interlocutor and some knowledge of the language, they arrive at the putative intentions of the speaker. The meaning arrived at is the casual, contextually, and interpersonally expected one.

It is also the case that preschool children know something about the terms expressing these constituents. They understand and use the predicates "say" and "mean" from a very early age (Limber, 1973; Bretherton and Beeghly, 1982; Wellman and Estes, 1984). They appear to be able to use these verbs to express their own mental states earlier than they can comprehend these verbs well enough to use them to understand the mental states of another person. In one study, Angela Hildyard, Elaine Minsky, and I asked Kindergarten, Grade 1, and Grade 2 children the questions "What did he say?" or "What did he mean?" following statements in a story which had either a direct, literal meaning or an indirect, sarcastic meaning. The "say" questions were answered appropriately with a verbatim answer for both direct and indirect statements more than 65% of the time by the Kindergarten children and over 90% of the time by the Grade 2 children. The "mean" questions, on the other hand, were answered by giving an intention by only 39% of the Kindergarten children and only 56% of the Grade 2 children. The Grade 1 children fell in between. But most children gave different answers to the two questions, suggesting that they made some distinction between "say" and "mean." However, most of the children appeared to have difficulty computing the intended meaning when it was not congruent with what was said. The youngest children either failed to answer the "mean" question or gave a literal interpretation of sentences that in context should have been interpreted sarcastically. That is, children's working assumption seems to be that what is said and what is meant are not two things, but one; people mean what they say. But only the oldest children could explicate that relation; those who could say, "She meant what she said," the assumption held by the younger children, could also say, "She didn't mean what she said" for the sarcastic items. The younger children rarely used these terms contrastively.

Children's understanding of the relation between the meaning of sentences and the intended meaning has been pursued in another way in a study by Elizabeth Robinson in Bristol and Hillel Goelman and myself in Toronto. In some of her earlier studies, Elizabeth Robinson (Robinson and Robinson, 1977a, 1977b) discovered that in cases of communication failure in which responsibility could be logically traced to the speaker and his or her inadequate message, children invariably "blamed the listener." To illustrate, an example is provided in Figure 9-2. If the child in a communication game intends to say "blue flower" and inappropriately says just "flower," and the listener picks a red flower, the child blames the listener for not picking the blue one. Furthermore, the child blames the listener whether the listener is a child or whether the listener is an adult. As Robinson points out, it seems not to occur to the child that the speaker or his message may be at fault. This tendency disappears in the first year or two of schooling.

Our collaborative study (Robinson, Goelman, and Olson, 1983) was designed to determine if the pattern of "blaming the listener" was the result of the inability to differentiate what was said from the intentions of the speaker – what we may call a conflation of the said/meant distinction – or more precisely, a conflation of the sentence meaning/speaker meaning distinction. To this end we repeated the game, but this time, on each occasion that the child inappropriately blamed the listener, we asked the child what the speaker (whether child or adult) had said. This question was asked only when, by looking (on the sly) at the object in the speaker's hand – or, when the adult was speaker, at his or her own hand – it was clear what the actual intended object had been. Hence, we had independent evidence both of what the speaker had said and of what the speaker had meant by it.

Our hypothesis was that the listener blamers are not aware of the difference between what the speaker said and what the speaker meant and hence not aware of the possible discrepancy. Children who conflate what

A child and an adult, separated by a screen, each have in front of them a collection of objects. The task is to tell the other what to pick up.

Blue flower	Red flower
Blue hat	Red hat
Blue lollipop	Red lollipop

Child:	(Holding a blue flower): Pick up the flower!
Adult:	(Picks up the red flower): This one?
Child:	No, you got the wrong one.
	You made a mistake. You didn't try hard enough.
	[Listener – blamer]
Adult:	Did you say the blue flower?
Child:	Yes. [Conflation of said/meant]

Figure 9-2.

was said with what was meant, we predicted, would answer the "say" question with a correct description of the intended object rather than with a repetition of the original sentence. If children differentiate the two, they have the option of saying something like, "I said 'flower' but I meant to say 'blue flower.' " To this end, we looked at cases in which there was a discrepancy between what was said and what was meant. Figure 9-2 shows the course of one of these exchanges. If the child says "flower" while holding (and intending) a blue flower, and then was asked "What did you say?" the child replied that he had said "blue flower." Symmetrically, if the child was listener and in fact heard "flower" but knew that the adult had intended to say "blue flower" (by virtue of the fact that the adult held a blue flower in her hand), the child still replied that the adult had said "blue flower." That is, the child does not differentiate what was actually said from the intention held by the speaker. After children have been in school for a year or two (some children work this out at an earlier age), the majority of them make the differentiation in their thinking, and they use that distinction in blaming the speaker for his inadequate message.

A recent study by Beal and Flavell (1985) has taken this finding one step further. As long as children had not assigned an intention to an utterance, they appeared to recognize its ambiguity. As soon as they had assigned that utterance an intention, however, the ambiguity of the sentence was lost on the children.

It seems clear enough that children in the early school years work out a distinction between what sentences, and words, and the like mean and what speakers and writers mean by those words and sentences. Now let us consider the possibility that this distinction is a by-product of literacy and acquired as children become literate.

The problem these children are attempting to sort out – the relation between what is said, the intentions of the speaker in producing it, and the interpretations that a listener can assign to it – is a problem that is implicit in all language but that becomes central in dealing with written texts. The childlike assumption that a speaker means what he says, is entirely appropriate for oral language. What a speaker's sentence means is what he or she meant by it; the process of interpretation is simply that of recovering speaker's intentions. The sentence has no inherent meaning that is subject to interpretation in its own right. But with written text, the relation changes. In his discussion of this point, Kebler (1983, p. 92) writes:

The text as a linguistic artifact . . . is separated from its own writer and open to an infinite range of readers and interpretations. In writing the author loses control over the process of interpretation.

In ordinary oral language, as Kebler notes, speakers do have control over interpretation. If someone misinterprets, the speaker can repair the utterance or deny that they meant it. Speakers have means for tuning interpretations to intentions, and the only proper interpretation is to recover the intentions of the speaker. This is the relation, Kebler says, that is lost in writing.

But such control is also lost in speech on some occasions. In his remarkable work on witchcraft and oracles of the Azande, Evans-Pritchard (1937, p. 133) described how the speech of someone suspected of witchcraft was interpreted: "Anything that a suspected witch may say is interpreted in a different sense from the one he intended to give to his words." Even in oral language contexts, intentions, and interpretations diverge on occasion. The important point, however, is that for the Azande, as Evans-Pritchard notes, these interpretations were directly attributed back to the speaker and used to prove his guilt. Hence, we may conclude that the problem is not whether or not the speaker can control interpretation but the more fundamental issue of whether or not a distinction is made between the intentions of the speaker – or, if that is lost, the semantic structure of the text – and the interpretations assigned to that language by the reader or listener. The mark of nonliteracy is the absence of the distinction. This is just the problem that children have in dealing with the language of our experiment. They do not acknowledge the possibility of ambiguity of language; they assume that their interpretation is exactly what the speaker said. Having arrived at an interpretation, they are convinced that the sentence could not be interpreted in any other way.

How does literacy bring this about? Literacy changed language from an ephemeral means of communication to a permanent, visible object, the written word. Once the written word is seen as an object, the spoken word can also be "seen" as an object. Generalizing, language becomes an object. Writing preserves the wording, what was said, but it does not preseve the meaning, if we take the meaning to be the intentions of the speaker or writer. Thus, writing creates a meaning problem. Preserving language as an object brings into awareness the latent ambiguity of language, and invites attempts to solve the meaning problem through various attempts at interpretation. It is in the attempts at solving the problem of interpretation that one is led to distinguish intended meaning, sentence meaning, and interpreted meaning. These attempts also bring into high relief such distinctions as whether one was actually asserting or merely suggesting or conjecturing, and so on. To note these distinctions requires an elaboration of concepts and the growth of a lexicon to distinguish these meanings, including the concepts just mentioned as well as the larger set of speech act and mental state verbs central to contemporary analyses of language and thought.

The development of a literate tradition involves the invention and the systematic application of these concepts. To be literate today is to have these conceptual distinctions at hand and to be able to apply them to problems of interpreting language – primarily written language, but also, to a lesser extent, speech. Equipped with such distinctions, a person is in a position to break down any utterance read or heard into two parts, what was said and the interpretation he or she assigns to it. The preferred interpretation is the speaker's intention, if it can be recovered. Once this distinction is made, listeners are much less likely to identify their interpretations with what the speaker actually said. They will recognize the residual ambiguity of language.

But becoming literate involves not merely coming to make this distinction but also learning to refine "what is said" so as to make it an explicit and precise expression of "what is meant." This is a long-term undertaking, only the first step of which children have made when they begin to distinguish what they said from what they meant by it. To read with understanding, on the one hand, and to write with precision, on the other, require not only the attempt to make what is said a reliable indication of what is meant, but also a knowledge of the language and its meaning sufficiently rich and precise that it can serve the higher-order goal of representing the intentions of the writer. A fuller understanding of literacy will require some analysis of just how language was specialized to serve those literate purposes.

Note

Preparation of this paper was supported by grants from Spencer Foundation and from the Social Sciences and Humanities Research Council of Canada. An earlier version of this paper appeared as "What is said and what is meant in speech and writing" in *Visible Language, 16,* (1982), 151–161.

References

Beal, C., & Flavell, J. (1985). Development of the ability to distinguish communicative intention and literal meaning message. *Child Development,* 1985.

Bloomfield, L. (1939). Linguistic aspects of science. *Foundations of the Unity of Science, 1* (4), 1–59.

Bretherton, I., & Beeghly, M. (1982). Talking about internal states: The acquisition of an explicit theory of mind. *Developmental Psychology, 6,* 906–921.

Brown, R. (1973). *A first language: The early stages.* Cambridge, Ma.: Harvard University Press, 1973.

Dennett, D. (1978). *Brainstorms.* Montgomery, Vt.: Bradford Books, 1978.

de Villiers, P., & de Villiers, J. (1978). *Language acquisition.* Cambridge, Ma.: Harvard University Press.

Evans-Pritchard, E. (1937). *Witchcraft, oracles, and magic among the Azande.* Oxford: Clarendon Press.

Fodor, J. (1979). Three cheers for propositional attitudes. In W. E. Cooper and E. Walker (Eds.), *Sentence processing: Psycholinguistic studies presented to Merrill Garrett.* Hillsdale, N. J.: Lawrence Erlbaum Associates.

Grice, H. (1957). Meaning. *Philosophical Review, 66,* 377–88.

Hildyard, A., & Olson, D. (1982). On the structure and meaning of prose texts. In W. Otto and S. White (Eds.), *Reading expository material.* New York: Academic Press.

Kebler, W. (1983). *The oral and the written gospel.* Philadelphia: Fortress Press.

Kripke, S. (1972). Naming and necessity. In D. Davidson and G. Harman (Eds.), *Semantics of natural language.* Boston: Reidel, 1972.

Limber, J. (1973). The genesis of complex sentences. In T. Moore (Ed.), *Cognitive development and the acquisition of language.* New York: Academic Press.

Markman, E. (1977). Realizing that you don't understand. *Child Development, 48,* 986–92.

Ogden, C., & Richards, I. (1923). *The meaning of meaning.* New York: Harcourt, Brace & World.

Olson, D., & Torrance, N. (1983). Literacy and cognitive development: A conceptual transformation in the early school years. In S. Meadows (Ed.), *Issues in childhood cognitive development.* London: Methuen.

Robinson, E., & Robinson, W. (1977a). Children's explanations of failure and the inadequacy of the misunderstood message. *Developmental Psychology, 13,* 151–61.

Robinson, E., & Robinson, W. (1977b). The young child's explanation of communication failure: A reinterpretation of results. *Perception and Motor Skills, 44,* 363–66.

Robinson, E., Goelman, H., & Olson, D. (1983). Children's understanding of the relationship between expressions (what was said) and intentions (what was meant). *British Journal of Developmental Psychology, 1,* 75–86.

Rumelhart, D., & Ortony, A. (1977). The representation of knowledge in memory. In R. C. Anderson, R. J. Spiro, and W. E. Montague (Eds.), *Schooling and the acquisition of knowledge.* Hillsdale, N. J.: Lawrence Erlbaum Associates.

Ryle, G. (1956). Introduction. In F. Ayer et al. (Eds.), *The revolution in philosophy.* London: Macmillan.

Searle, J. (1983). *Intentionality: An essay in the philosophy of mind.* Cambridge: Cambridge University Press.

Shotter, J. (1984). *Social accountability and selfhood.* Oxford: Blackwell.

Sinclair, J., & Coulthard, R. (1975). *Towards an analysis of discourse: The English used by teachers and pupils.* London: Oxford University Press.

Spiro, R. (1980). Constructive processes in prose comprehension and recall. In R. Spiro, B. Bruce, and B. Brewer (Eds.), *Theoretical issues in reading comprehension.* Hillsdale N. J.: Lawrence Erlbaum Associates.

Stich, S. (1983). *From folk psychology to cognitive science: The case against belief.* Cambridge, Ma.: MIT Press.

Venezky, R. (1982). The origins of the present-day chasm between adult literacy needs and school literacy instruction. *Visible Language, XVI* (2), 113–26.

Wellman, H., & Estes, D. (1984). *Children's early use of mental verbs and what they mean.* Ann Arbor: Center for Human Growth and Development, University of Michigan, Mimeo.

Winograd, T. (1980). What does it mean to understand language? *Cognitive Science, 4,* 209–41.

10 Metalinguistic awareness and the growth of literacy

Michael L. Herriman

In this paper it is proposed that encouragement of children's awareness of language structure and function will contribute to the emergence of literacy. Within existing educational structures it is possible to give more attention to these aspects of language. Preceding papers have looked at the theoretical questions regarding literacy, so little attempt at further theorizing is proposed.

A major problem facing a discussion of literacy is one of definition. This is not just because the term is used to cover many activities and identify many perceived inadequacies in present education; it has rather to do with the lack of clarity surrounding the whole area of language and its development. Put simply, we do not have a clear idea of the nature of language – either from the point of view of what phenomena are covered by the term, or from the perspective of its growth in humans. We can define language so broadly as to include any kind of signaling behavior in organisms or so narrowly as to confine it to the domain of humans reflecting on the process of language itself. The concept of literacy is similarly elastic, with some people using it to refer to a narrow range of activities having to do with correct spelling, reading, and grammar and others broadening the notion to include ideas of communication generally.

Perhaps some attention to the etymology of "literacy" is in order. The relationship of that etymology to the traditional study of letters is significant, suggesting as it does the development and skilled uses of a written language. It is from this context that we derive terms such as preliterate, illiterate, and, of course, literature. This derivation suggests that literacy is an elaboration of spoken language, leading to the question of whether language exemplified in writing is significantly different from that of speech.

That question is addressed by David Olson in the article "From Utterance to Text: The Bias of Language in Speech and Writing" (Olson, 1977). I shall refer to Olson's view as the dichotomy view, since it supports

159

the claim that there is a "specialized form" of language exhibited in writing. Olson does not claim that the latter is necessarily superior to the language embodied in utterance; it is, rather, "specialized" in that it permits activities perhaps not possible in a spoken language. It is indeed mastery of written language which Olson equates with literacy – a claim not explicitly stated but clearly implied in his article. The particular power of a written language is seen to derive from its alphabetic character (related to what linguists call "arbitrariness") and its explicitness of reference (as opposed to the poetic and polysemous character of spoken language). These features permit theorizing as an aid to both personal and objective knowledge. (Olson enlists the ideas of Piaget, Ricoeur, and Popper in support of these claims.) Literacy attains its highest art in logic and hypothetical reasoning – "the deduction of counter-intuitive models of reality," in Olson's words. He seems to be saying that it is an historical rather than a logical fact of language that it has evolved to this formal level. It would be difficult to claim that the limitations of preliterate language were of a logical kind – that is, that its expressive power would have been necessarily diminished.

The argument of this paper is that there may be a close relationship between literacy as described above and an awareness of the form and function of language. It is this latter awareness that has been called metalinguistic awareness (Cazden, 1975). Metalinguistic awareness refers to a conscious awareness, on the part of the language user, of language as an object in itself. The person who is linguistically aware will recognize that language is more than transparent. He or she will see it as a manipulative system. In its highest forms it is indeed a creative medium: That is, it is more than a means by which we see the world; it is a means for creating a world – the world of our experience and imagination. The realization of this creative power of language seems to begin in middle childhood, its most obvious manifestation being the use of puns and jokes involving various transformations of sounds and meaning. The phenomenon is much more than that however, being recognizable at most levels of language structure, – in particular, at the phonological, lexical, syntactical, semantic, and pragmatic levels (Tunmer, Pratt, & Herriman, 1984).

Many commentators have referred to the ability of children to step aside and take note of the language they use. Mattingly, in reference to learning to read, says, "Speaking and listening are primary linguistic activities; reading is a secondary and rather special sort of activity that relies critically upon the reader's awareness of these primary activities" (1972, p. 133). Mattingly calls this awareness of the primary activities "linguistic awareness," arguing that it varies considerably among speakers. He also observes that "this variation contrasts markedly with the relative consistency from person to person with which primary linguistic activity is performed" (1972, p. 140). Cazden (1975) defines metalinguistic awareness as "the ability to make language forms opaque and attend to them in and for themselves," and argues that this is a "special kind of language performance, one which makes special cognitive demands and seems to be less easily and less universally acquired than the language performances of speaking and listening" (p. 603). Reference to "cognitive demands" links the notion of metalinguistic awareness with that of "metacognition" (see Flavell, 1977, 1978, 1981). Flavell defines metacognition as "knowledge or cognition that takes as its object or regulates any aspect of cognitive endeavor" (1981, p. 37). Hakes (1980) talks about "linguistic developments that might parallel the cognitive developments characterizing the emergence of concrete operational cognitive functioning." He suggests that "the parallel is to be found in the emergence of a new set of ways of dealing with language, ways that are different from and require cognitive abilities going beyond those involved in understanding and producing utterances" (p. 97). He calls these "metalinguistic abilities," noting that they emerge in middle childhood.

A significant interest in the phenomenon is also evident in Russian psychology. Downing (1979) traces its development back to Vygotsky's emphasis on the importance of the child's capacity to step aside from the word and think about it as an object. He also sees Luria's elaboration of this idea in what is termed the glass theory, according to which at some stage the child realizes that language is a "glass" through which the world is seen and which has its own existence and structural features.

To take a developmental view of language and incorporate metalinguistic awareness within it, it could be said that three stages of development are detectable up to middle childhood. The first is the stage of single- and two-word utterances (approximately 8 months to 3 years); then follows the stage of complete sentence production, characterized generally by a simple Subject-Verb-Object construction (3 to 5 years); then normally follows the development of the awareness to reflect on language structure and function (6 to 8 years), along with the production and comprehension of more complex syntactic constructions.

The key features mentioned in the analysis of metalinguistic awareness so far are: that it is a different activity from normal language use, that it occurs in middle childhood, that it may be related to an emerging set of cognitive activities, and that it is a conscious process. Not all writers on the topic would accept these generalizations. For example, one view holds that children are "aware of language, its forms and functions, throughout the acquisition process" (Clark and Anderson, 1979; p. 11). According to this view, which is based on study of spontaneous speech repairs, metalinguistic awareness develops with language acquisition and can be found as early as 18 months (Clark, 1978). To analyze this view it is necessary to look at possible models of error correction. Marshall and Morton (1978) claim that error-detecting devices can be part of an information-processing model of language production and comprehension. According to such a model, the language system has a monitor which compares both input and output with semantic and phonological representations. Marshall and Morton also allow a weaker interpretation of error correction in which no monitoring occurs (the adult often performing that role), but in which an altered sequence "should be regarded as the recirculation of the original content through a system of unstable rules" (p. 236). This latter interpretation, they believe, may apply to early speech correction. In such cases, "error [is] due to noise in the system and not due to the systematic mischaracterization of language in the expressor" (p. 236). In Marshall and Morton's view, metalinguistic awareness occurs only when the speaker is conscious of the monitoring system – that is, conscious of the process of error correction. This would seem to preclude the repairs characteristic of early childhood.

Another way of treating early error correction is to make the distinction between awareness of failure and awareness of linguistic structure, only the latter of which is probably associated with knowledge or awareness of the process of error correction. It is the latter kind of awareness that is said to be metalinguistic. However, this is not to claim that the child (or the adult) is aware of the physical processes involved in language comprehension or production (Tunmer and Herriman, 1984).

Another view of language awareness sees it as part of the *effect* of early education (Donaldson, 1978). Donaldson argues that formal schooling, in particular learning to read, brings about an increase in language awareness and general cognitive abilities – specifically, the ability to "disembed" thought. It may well be that metalinguistic ability will increase as a result of reading instruction, but research so far indicates that metalinguistic ability can be found in pre-readers. Ehri (1979) reviews a number of studies which indicate that many preschool children who have not been exposed to reading instruction and who cannot read perform well on tests of metalinguistic ability that correlate highly with reading achievement. If we take the task of learning to read to be the discovery of the way to map the printed text onto the existing speech and speech-knowledge of the learner, then a basic requirement is the ability to deal explicitly with the structural features of the spoken language (Foss and Hakes, 1978). For example, some kind of awareness of phonological structure would seem to be required to enable the child to undertake phoneme-grapheme decoding. It is fairly certain that the physical signal, the continuous stream of speech, contains no indication of the segmentable features we identify as phonemes and words.

Ehri's own view is that there is probably an interaction between metalinguistic awareness and the process of learning to read. If this means a joint cause-and-effect relationship, however, it might be difficult to separate the concepts logically. Rather more to the point, in some of the studies reviewed by Ehri (1979) and in others (Tunmer and Fletcher, 1981), a relationship, if not a linear one, is found to exist between kinds of metalinguistic abilities, particularly phonemic segmentation, and processes associated with reading abilities (e.g., as tested by the Synthetic Word Test and the Wide Range Achievement Test). In the studies quoted, few readers exhibited no metalinguistic abilities, whereas many who did exhibit these abilities had not yet learned to read. There are not sufficient research data yet to allow us to resolve the main question of the language acquisition, reading attainment, and metalinguistic awareness nexus. Present evidence, though, suggests that the development of metalinguistic awareness should be seen as separate from language acquisition and as a necessary though not sufficient condition of reading attainment.

What has been said about metalinguistic awareness so far is not meant to establish incontrovertibly the existence of the phenomenon, though the construct is no more resistant to empirical verification than a majority of others in child development studies. The intention here is to draw attention to the topic as one of increasing interest in studies of language and cognition in middle childhood. For the present study its relationship to the acquisition of reading is most pertinent, since reading is the means whereby one attains that knowledge of letters (in the Renaissance sense) we call literacy.

The concept of metalinguistic awareness as described can be seen to fit into a general framework of Piagetian thought, since it is usually related to cognitive change of a qualitative kind in middle childhood – the period of concrete operations. It is from the Piagetian framework that Donaldson seems to take her departure in discussing language awareness.

In relation to literacy, the conceptual connections made so far suggest the posing of two hypotheses. The first is that metalinguistic awareness can play a role, directly or otherwise, in the attainment of literacy. The second is that metalinguistic awareness is part of a set of emerging cognitive abilities of which the child becomes conscious, and that these abilities play a role in literacy. Before examining these hypotheses in detail, it should be recognized that they necessarily commit one to the view that language is a cognitive activity involving much more than a phenomenon describable at the level of the physical signal (the printed word or the utterance). To fully appreciate this distinction it is important to look at the alternative view of language. This view, that language is describable at the level of the physical signal alone, has been the dominant one in recent anthropology, psychology, and education.

The general form taken by this alternative view is that language is simply an aspect of communication. Communication is a behavior typical of most species, and what characterizes human language is just that it deals with human experiences. In this view language is learned in an aggregational way, mainly as a reinforced response. This, with appropriate modifications, is the view of Skinner, Osgood, and Bloomfield, to name some of its prominent proponents.

The question of language acquisition is determined by this initial view of language itself. Since language is a behavior, it is learned incrementally as a response to specifiable features of the environment, very often the language environment itself – that is, another piece of language. This view is typified in much of the contemporary reporting of primate language research (Premack, 1971; Linden, 1976). The counterpart of this view in education is that language-related activities, such as writing and spelling, are learned as behaviors. The techniques of teaching and assessment, and the identification of problems in language, all proceed from a behavioral analysis. In other words, the initial conception of language as a behavior imposes a conceptual framework on consequent activities related to it.

I do not propose to offer a critique of behaviorist theories of language, but rather to point to the difficulties of defining literacy within an conceptual scheme as restricted as the behaviorist one. The task is not impossible, however. The well-known *Distar* programs of Bereiter and Engelmann could be seen as dealing with literacy as a behavior. *Distar Language (I & II)* is based on the idea that language ability is learned as a behavior. The programs concentrate on "drilling," and on "reinforcement" in the group situation. They have, it is claimed, worked especially well with "culturally disadvantaged" children whose assumed-to-be-deprived linguistic repertoire would otherwise mark them for failure in the kinds of formal tasks characteristic of school learning. Part of *Distar Language*, for example, involves learning the use of prepositions; in this case, the preposition or prepositional phrase is spoken in conjunction with the action it signifies, suggesting the interpretation that what has to be learned is a behavior – an utterance in response to another utterance, or in this case, an action. *Distar Reading* deals with the problems of initial reading by teaching "shaping" (the physical positioning of the mouth in response to a grapheme) and "blending" (the merging of phonemic units to make a syllable or morpheme). This view of the reading process is mechanist-behaviorist, conforming clearly to the language-as-behavior view.

An even more rudimentary application of behaviorist techniques is found in the teaching of reading via word recognition. The use of "flash cards," though much superseded now, was seen by many as the best method of reading instruction some years ago. If it had any merit, it might be said to have been its relationship to what could be seen as one *part* of metalinguistic awareness – namely, lexical awareness – and as such it could be said to be related to one part of the reading process. Only in a naive stimulus – response framework could the flash card method be said to bear any relationship to the whole of reading. Such a framework rules out any conception of reading as involving cognitive processes.

The problem with relating literacy to behaviorist views of language learning or reading is that these views do not provide the scope for describing it as more than just a behavior; that is, literacy is seen as a behavior. Spelling can be drilled fairly successfully; but if we see reading as primarily a learned behavior, then the scope of the literacy emerging as a result of this emphasis is narrow. Perhaps the most telling argument against this identification of literacy is that it concentrates on a limited aspect of language. Its attraction is that it is recognizable by its absence: It is very easy to say that because children cannot write and spell as well as their predecessors (parents, a previous generation, etc.) may have been able to, the standard of literacy has declined. Poor spelling and writing, and reading problems, may be necessary conditions for identifying poverty of literacy, but they are not sufficient conditions.

I now wish to turn to the main argument – the claim that literacy can be more usefully related to a view of language that is not as restrictive as the behaviorist one, and that this wider interpretation allows for the introduction of the concept of metalinguistic awareness.

The wide view of language to which I refer is the view that equates language with communication generally and gives particular emphasis to the expressive power of written language or text. Olson's view of text allows it the formal power to codify reasoning – to represent the wide range of human conjecture. It would be difficult to deny that speech can now have that power too, but it would have to be allowed that such a specialized power is an artefact of the alphabetic system (in Olson's view). One cannot argue this position formally, for no system of logic adequately characterizes the variety of either written or spoken language (though some systems, such as that of Montague, point the way). The most convincing demonstration of Olson's claim can be made by comparing samples of spoken and written language. The ability to transcribe speech is a product of recent technology, and no more telling a demonstration of the differences between utterance and text can be had than by examining transcripts of any proceedings recorded verbatim. With some exceptions, transcripts generally show speech to be plagued by incomplete grammatical constructions, false starts, hesitancy phenomena, anacolouthia (change of construction in mid-sentence), and general vagueness resulting from the loss of the interaction and gesture that would have accompanied the original utterance. To anyone who had studied speech, this kind of corruption would have been obvious. In everyday situations we overlook the medium in favor of the message, allowing context to fill in the literal inadequacies of speech. Can we admit, then, of a double standard when the two forms of expression are to be evaluated? If so, does the claim for literacy become a hollow one? The answer to both these questions is preempted by the recognition of the need for a precise language for just the kinds of activities that Olson identified with text and the kinds of activities typical of the classroom.

This still has not answered the question about the expressive power of text, however much it recognizes its distinctiveness from speech. The power of text is related to its means of production. The choice of words, constructions, tone (style), emphasis, etc., is conscious and planned ahead, unlike speech, which is mostly spontaneous. The process of planning in writing is basically one of reflecting on language and the suitability of its forms for the expression of the ideas intended. In speech, the checking process is the almost automatic one that can be described in information-processing terms, where the output is compared with semantic and syntactic models for the type of expression in question. Although the initial process in writing may be of this kind, the subsequent transference of the piece of language to an assayable form on paper makes it more the object of direct linguistic (grammatical) inquiry than is speech. The writing of a lecture or address will involve large multiples of the time its delivery will take, ignoring the time taken by the literal process (i.e., the writing itself). Much of the time in question is devoted to checking the suitability of the language. This checking process is a metalinguistic one: It relies on that awareness of language earlier referred to as metalinguistic awareness.

The earlier discussion of metalinguistic awareness tied it to the context of middle childhood. There it was said to be part of an ability that seems to emerge in conjunction with a number of other cognitive properties, all of which are characterized by the direction of the child's attention to the (cognitive) task being undertaken (Flavell, 1981).

This recognition permits us to return to the two hypotheses posed previously: The first is that metalinguistic awareness may be related to the attainment of literacy, via its emphasis on the kind of attention that can be given to the construction and comprehension of written language. The process of expository prose writing involves constantly attending to the syntax and semantics of language. The choice of words and grammatical constructions, especially in relation to details such as tense, mood, and aspect of the verb, is important to conveying the precise intention of the writer. The claim here is that the ability to become aware of and analyze language in this way is a consequence of the initial metalinguistic abilities that emerge in middle childhood. Unlike the earlier linguistic processes – the comprehension and production of the complex patterns of sound we call speech – which occur relatively effortlessly in most humans, the attainment of metalinguistic awareness is by no means as successful or universal. Without wishing necessarily to subscribe to an innatist view, we note that the learning of speech has an automaticity to it that seems to mark it as an evolutionary trait. By comparison, the acquisition of the skills of reading and writing is much more difficult. It is not merely a coincidence that most literate societies have developed formal institutions (schools) devoting some three years initially to this task.

Yet even after the first years of schooling a spread, or range, of reading and writing abilities becomes apparent, and it increases with subsequent years. It is this fact that is central to the view of literacy taken here. In identifying literacy closely with reading comprehension and written production, we are forced to recognize significant differences in these abilities. The crucial question, therefore, is whether anything can be done to improve the ability of those who don't measure up to the standard some can attain. Psychologists have a variety of answers to this question, citing individual differences, intellectual differences, environmental differences (the earlier Bernstein), or disagreeing with the basic claim. The tentative proposal here is that literacy can be learned through emphasizing children's awareness of the processes of reading comprehension and writing, following their initial encounter with these processes. Tunmer and Bowey (1984) have provided a model of stages of reading acquisition in relation to emerging subskills of a metalinguistic kind. Their model, based on research findings, suggests that more attention needs to be given to monitoring the process at its various stages. On this view one could trace subsequent failure in reading to failure at the underlying metalinguistic level.

The argument so far is that the emergence of metalinguistic awareness marks the emergence of literacy generally. The child's recognition of the literate properties of text depends upon metalinguistic abilities. It was seen, too, that some children have difficulties here that are not found in the initial experience of learning to speak. To establish an empirical relationship between metalinguistic awareness and literacy, however, would require large-scale longitudinal studies of children or elaborate cross-sectional ones. What has been suggested is that there is a conceptual relationship between literacy and metalinguistic awareness, that the concepts are tied together.

We should then ask the question of how we might look at the practical issue: the role of education in relation to changing metalinguistic awareness into literacy. Some researchers in this area speculate that metalinguistic abilities, if not continually used, may decrease. Mattingly, for example (1979, p. 6), argues that

if grammatical knowledge is not directly used in linguistic performance, it is to be expected that after language acquisition has ceased to be a major preoccupation grammatical knowledge should tend to become less accessible.

It must be emphasized that this is speculation. However, we are aware of the fact that after the first few years of reading instruction, in most educational programs there is a tendency for much less attention to be given to it – not unreasonably in most cases, because most children have achieved an acceptable proficiency. We are equally aware of the fact that a large gap begins to show between good and poor readers, poor readers being measured as equivalent to years behind their peers who read well. This suggests that there may be a group who never really achieve any level of metalinguistic skills. It can be presumed that students lacking such skills will not achieve any significant sensitivity to the subtleties of text, either as readers or as writers.

The argument, then, is circumstantial. If metalinguistic awareness is the basis of literacy and if it can be seen that attention to formal aspects of language (Mattingly's second linguistic activity), as in the reading process, will encourage metalinguistic development, then it is reasonable to suspect that continued attention to the formal or structural aspects of language will further develop and exercise metalinguistic awareness and, with it, literacy. I wish to claim that teachers and curriculum planners are too little sensitive to this point. Attention is rightly given at the early level, but in general it is not followed up; after about the third grade, most attention is given to the comprehension aspect of reading. Many kits are used to promote individual progress in reading comprehension, but this very use of individualized programs overlooks the important role that the teacher can play in the learning process at this point. Normally, if a child is not progressing well in comprehension, he or she will work at a lower level, the presumption being that the accumulation of experience is an aggregational and not necessarily a qualitative one. Instead, however, the teacher should intervene to discuss the difficulty with the child. Failure at comprehension may indicate a variety of difficulties: For example, the method of making logical inferences from text which comprehension requires not only depends on clearly stated information being in the text, but may also require a familiarity with syllogistic reasoning. Such reasoning can be contained in a set of propositions or sentences, but the argument structure may not be clear if the child fails to grasp key lexical or syntactic elements of the propositions. The meaning of logical constants (*unless, therefore, if, but,* etc.) may not be fully understood. On the other hand, the pragmatic structure of discourse generally might not be appreciated.

Unless the teacher is aware of the possible problems here and can talk with the student about them (using the metalanguage: terms such as *word, sentence, proposition*), then it is unlikely that much progress will be made. The competent reader, however, by his or her very grasp of the metalinguistic aspects, will comprehend and further learn from the success of the activity. In other words, an important element in the early learning about language is the recognition by teacher and student that language can be the object of thought and discussion, and as such an object, can be exploited and manipulated to fit precise needs – specifically, the clear expression of intended meanings.

The second hypothesis was that metalinguistic abilities may be part of a more general set of cognitive abilities that emerge around middle childhood, and that these cognitive abilities can play a role in developing literacy. As mentioned above, this hypothesis is built upon the claims of researchers who have either seen correlations between metalinguistic abilities and cognitive operations (in particular, Hakes, 1980) or described metacognition in terms that clearly emphasize the cognitive control aspect of it – that is, the ability of the cognitively aware child as expressed in his or her direction of attention to the task in question (Flavell, 1981). The hypothesis proposed is that this cognitive control (called meta-attention) can be directed toward language, via control of the structuring of language production. This suggests that the development of metalinguistic awareness may be a by-product of the ability to attend to details of one's own cognition, which includes language production. At the earliest stages it seems that metalinguistic awareness is turned toward phonological properties of language; the clear aid that such realization would give to reading (where the initial task is realizing phoneme – grapheme encoding) should be obvious. Successful reading, furthermore, would reinforce the ability to recognize the lexical, syntactic, and logicosentential aspects of language. The suggestion of the hypothesis is more than that, however; it is that the process of coping with language as an object of control or attention is itself a logical one. "Logic" in this case refers to the fact that language is or can be a manifestation of controlled process of thought – a description that fits one of our notions of logic, anyway.

The use of the term "logic" is sometimes masked by its more formal application to the canons of deductive inference. But before a person can even appreciate the power that formal logic can confer on thought (if indeed that recognition is ever achieved), it is necessary that some recognition be given to consistency or otherwise of thought and expression. Such consistency is the product of controlled thought processes; it is sometimes referred to as informal logic. Written language (Olson's "text") is the prime medium for making judgments about consistency, because written language can be separated from context, which often confuses, or adds more to, the message.

Under this view, literacy can be seen as an extension of the logical process of controlled cognition. The clue to this identification can be derived from the fact that most formal problems are solved on paper. Mathematicians and logicians provide the best examples, but many less formal examples can be found. In this way, written language can be seen almost as a physical extension of the brain. In Olson's view, it is the logical capability of text that is its most significant attribute. Literacy is fully manifested when a person is able to realize this power of text, to exercise it to both convey and extend his or her capability for logical thought. Again I emphasize that this applies to both informal (loosely consistent) and formal (strictly deductive) logic.

The connection between thought, logic, and language has not only been explored by psychologists and psycholinguists, but has been a recurrent theme of philosophy since Plato, and of grammarians (e.g., the Ramists and the Port Royal grammarians). The exploration has not progressed beyond the conceptual level, however, and even though it is possible to indicate some significant correlations between logical operations and metalinguistic abilities (Hakes, 1981), the subsequent connection with language-using ability, particularly the ability to write clear expository prose, is not established yet. At present the possibility of the connection allows the wider interpretation or definition of literacy proposed above; as such it has heuristic value.

Finally, as a practical question, it might be asked: What can be done to build upon the sense of language gained by the child who develops metalinguistic awareness around the age of entry to school? It has been suggested already that there is a problem with the group of children who fail to accomplish anything above the minimal ability to read. As well, it is often the case that, following two or three years of attention to reading, children are left to their own devices for building on the initial skills. The use of individualized reading kits was seen as concentrating on comprehension, at the same time precluding the important interaction between the child and the teacher for diagnostic purposes. It can be said, then, that after the first few years of schooling there is never again the same attention given to language, even in the case of foreign language teaching, which some students might encounter in high school. Smith, Goodman, and Meredith (1976) note as well the importance of the child's exposure to higher levels of language usage (called speech-thought). They claim that "the child often has no one to talk with except his unsophisticated peers" (p. 209). As well, they observe that

only in social environments where the young are included in the talk and have opportunities to ask questions and participate in the dialogue of inquiry with adults can they develop their speech-thoughts adequately. Otherwise, thinking as well as speech becomes retarded. The conceptualizing process never develops sufficiently. The grammar of reasoning is never heard. [p. 210]

Smith, Goodman, and Meredith believe that much language activity is actively discouraged in the classroom. Their work is an important contribution to the recognition of what can be done with language in schools – its emphasis being on the development of language to exhibit thought. Their selection of activities and practical advice for teachers is probably unmatched, and it is not my purpose to add to their contribution. In fact, their range of activities and teaching strategies for developing language sensitivity indicates that a vast potential is yet untapped. There are many other texts or programs claiming to deal with language learning, enrichment, or sensitivity, particularly in elementary schooling; in assessing their usefulness to the development of literacy as described here, it is important to distinguish between those programs that simply involve language use and those that encourage thought about language. In the latter category, probably, are those that involve language across subject areas – for example, relating language to elements of drama, music, and mathematics. The key programs are those that will build upon the abilities that first become identified when the child is able to direct his or her attention and control to language. Such programs must treat language awareness and literacy as part of a continuity, rather in the way that mathematics is both perceived and taught. The metastatus of mathematics in relation to language is clearly recognized by mathematics educators (I take it as a presupposition of the "new" mathematics), and hence one could expect a similar recognition of the metastatus of metalinguistic awareness.

In the earlier discussion of text, particular recognition was given to the logical or expository potential of the written word. This is not to suggest that the paradigm of literate expression should be the kind of language found in the best scientific texts. Although a clear and objective use of language is desirable in many situations, children should be equally aware of the expressive potential of the language of literature and be able to distinguish the genuinely creative use of language from the cliché-ridden and linguistically impoverished language of the "pulp" press and most of television.

Finally, I wish to claim that the language of text can probably instruct the language of utterance and refine it in such a way as to increase its expressive power. Speech, being mostly spontaneous, is seldom subject to the kinds of checks that text is. The production of text provides a rare occasion for one to check one's own language forms and, through enlightened analysis, improve those forms in a way that might be reflected in later speech. One of the objects of early language teaching in schools should be the control of spoken language through the analysis of written forms. Debating and speechwriting are suitable activities for such language refinement.

In summary, I have proposed a view of literacy that places it in a continuity which begins not so much with initial language acquisition, but with the child's realization of language as an object in itself. This realization, called "metalinguistic awareness," begins for most children around the time they enter school. Teachers take advantage of this development to teach reading, but after a few years it is left aside, and further language development is generally left to take its own course. Because literacy, the awareness of the power of letters, is best related to just that process of concentrating attention on the structure and function of language, including one's own, I have argued for a continuation of the kind of attention to language that is given in early reading instruction throughout the school curriculum. Without taking sides in the controversy over declining standards of literacy, it is possible to recognize nonetheless a potential for much greater language involvement in education and, through metalinguistic awareness, a higher general standard of literacy.

Note

The author wishes to thank colleagues at the Max Planck Institut fur Psycholinguistik, and the Max Planck Gesellschaft, for their support during completion of the present article.

References

Cazden, C. B. (1975). Play with language and metalinguistic awareness: One dimension of language experience. In C. B. Winsor (Ed.), *Dimensions of language experience*. New York: Agathon Press.

Clark, E. V. (1978). Awareness of language: Some evidence from what children say and do. In A. Sinclair, R. J. Jarvella, and W. J. M. Levelt (Eds.), *The child's conception of language*. Berlin: Springer Verlag, pp. 18–43.

Clark, E. V., and Andersen, E. S. (March, 1979). Spontaneous repairs: Awareness in the process of acquiring language. Paper presented at Symposium on Reflections on Metacognition, Society for Research in Child Development, San Francisco.

Donaldson, M. (1978). *Children's minds*. Glasgow: Collins.

Downing, J. (1969). How children think about reading. *The Reading Teacher, 23,* 217–230.

Ehri, L. C. (1981). Linguistic insight: Threshold of reading acquisition. In T. G. Waller & G. E. MacKinnon (Eds.), *Reading research: Advances in theory and practice* (Vol. 3). Orlando Fla.: Academic Press.

Flavell, J. H. (1977). *Cognitive development*. Englewood Cliffs, N. J.: Prentice-Hall.

Flavell, J. H. (1978). Metacognitive development. In J. M. Scandura and C. J. Brainerd (Eds.), *Structural process theories of complex human behaviour*. Leyden, The Netherlands: Sijthoff and Noordhoff.

Flavell, J. H. (1981). Cognitive Monitoring. In W. P. Dickson, *Children's oral communication skills*. New York: Academic Press.

Foss, D. J., and Hakes, D. T. (1978). *Psycholinguistics: An introduction to the psychology of language*. Englewood Cliffs, N. J.: Prentice Hall.

Hakes, D. T. (1981). *The development of metalinguistic abilities in children*, Berlin: Springer-Verlag.

Linden, E. (1976). *Apes, men, and language*, New York: Penguin Books.

Marshall, J. C., and Morton, J. (1978). On the mechanics of EMMA. In A. Sinclair, R. J. Jarvella, and W. J. M. Levelt (Eds.), *The child's conception of language*. Berlin: Springer-Verlag, pp. 225–39.

Mattingly, I. G. (1972). Reading, the linguistic process, and linguistic awareness. In J. F. Kavanagh and I. G. Mattingly (Eds.), *Language by ear and by eye*. Cambridge, Mass.: M. I. T. Press, pp. 133–47.

Olson, D. R. (1977). From utterance to text: The bias of language in speech and writing. *Harvard Educational Review, 47,* 257–81.

Premack, D. (1971). Language in the Chimpanzee, *Science, 172,* 808–22.

Smith, E. B., Goodman, K. S., and Meredith, R. (1976). *Language and thinking in schools*. New York: Holt, Rinehart and Winston.

Tunmer, W. E., and Bowey, J. A. (1984). Metalinguistic awareness and reading acquisition. In W. E. Tunmer et al. (Eds.), *Metalinguistic awareness in children: Theory, research, and implications*. Berlin: Springer-Verlag, pp. 144–68.

Tunmer, W. E., and Fletcher, C. M. (1981). The relationship between conceptual tempo, phonological awareness and word recognition in beginning readers. *Journal of Reading Behaviour*, XIII (2), 173–85.

Tunmer, W. E., and Herriman, M. L. (1984). The development of metalinguistic awareness: A conceptual overview. In W. E. Tunmer et al. (Eds.), *Metalinguistic awareness in children: Theory, research, and implications*. Berlin: Springer-Verlag, pp. 12–35.

Tunmer, W. E., Pratt, C. J.; and Herriman, M. L. (1984). *Metalinguistic awareness in children: Theory, research, and implications*. Berlin: Springer-Verlag.

11 On modeling comprehension

Walter Kintsch

There is a considerable interest today in the processes that are involved in comprehension, particularly reading comprehension. Historically, research on reading has focused on the decoding aspects of the process, and we have seen some real achievements in this area. Some very knowledgeable persons maintain that we now have enough knowledge about the decoding aspects of reading, at least for such practical purposes as the design of programs for beginning reading instruction. None, I think, would dare to make a similar claim for reading comprehension.

But the time has come when progress can be made in the study of comprehension processes. Efforts in this direction are currently being undertaken by many groups, and it would be interesting to catalogue the various approaches taken and discuss what they have achieved so far. But instead of such a state-of-the-art paper, I shall restrict myself to our own work, in which we are trying to work out certain aspects of a psychological model of comprehension processes (Kintsch & van Dijk, 1978; Kintsch & Vipond, 1979; Miller & Kintsch, 1980; van Dijk & Kintsch, 1983). I shall outline this project and point out its implications for a problem that has been of continuing interest to educational researchers – namely, readability.

The terms "comprehension" and "readability" are not easily defined. At one point in the history of psychology, psychologists talked about the faculties that the mind possesses, such as the "will," "imagination," "memory," or "moral taste." Some remnants of this view are still with us today. We say "Jenny has an IQ of 112," as if intelligence were an inalienable personal possession. Similarly, we might say about a text that "it has a Flesch score of 56." Readability is considered here a property of the text. A number of reading researchers have objected to this practice and have proclaimed an interactionist view, in which readability is considered to be the outcome of a reader – text interaction. Most texts are easy for some

175

people to read but hard for other people to read, or they are easy to read for some purposes but not for other purposes.

Stated in these terms, this interactionist position is no more than a truism. For it to become fruitful, some precise ideas about the nature of the reader – text interaction are required. In other words, we need a theory of comprehension: not just miniature models of certain components of comprehension processes, but a model of how the system as a whole works. It would be nice if we could avoid the obvious risks that are involved in modeling a system of such complexity. But the response of a complex system cannot always be predicted from the component responses; in order to intervene successfully, we need some idea about how the system as a whole behaves. In general, a text with long sentences is hard to read, but everyone knows by now that this is not always so. Likewise, short sentences do not necessarily make a text easy to comprehend. In general, a certain amount of repetition supports comprehension, but quite absurd texts are created by taking this principle too literally. Shuy and Larkin (1978) have recently discussed some informative examples of this kind. Similar examples occur in our own work.

Our model focuses on the inferences that a reader must make in comprehending a text. We have proposed the working hypothesis that the more inferences a text requires, the harder it becomes to read. But, as several authors have noted (e. g., Meyer, 1975; Shuy & Larkin, 1978), it is easy to make a text too explicit. Indeed, we observed some time ago (Keenan & Kintsch, 1974) that stating explicitly in a text what every reader would quite readily infer on his or her own merely confuses the reader. The overly explicit phrase is falsely considered by the reader as an indication of some complexity in the text that is not actually there, and this starts a train of useless and confusing inferences. In such a case, the reader tries to figure out what subtle meaning the author had intended by saying what was obvious anyway – except, of course, that the author had not intended anything in particular but was merely trying to improve readability.

What we need, then, is a complete model that tells us under what conditions and why a long sentence might be better than several short ones; when repetition is helpful, and when it is simply distracting; when something is better left implicit in a text, and how overexplicitness confuses the reader. We have been trying to develop such a model, relying primarily on two sets of empirical observations: the time it takes people to read texts, and what they can recall later. Our plan is to design a model so that it predicts reading time and recall data as well as possible, and then to see what this model implies with respect to other interesting issues.

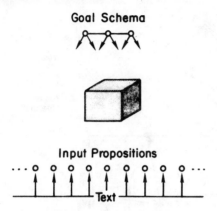

Figure 11-1. The starting point for a model of text comprehension: the text, its propositional representation, and the reader's goal schema are considered as given; the black box is to be filled in.

To model "comprehension" in all its complexity is either impossible or very hard to do. But one can decompose the problem into a set of reasonably independent components that can be studied in isolation and that then can be combined to evaluate their interactions. Thus, we are treating "comprehension" as a partially decomposable system, in the terminology of Simon (1974). I shall outline what the components of this system are and how we think they work. I shall be brief and informal; the theory is described in more detail in Kintsch and van Dijk (1978) and van Dijk & Kintsch (1983). I shall then present some readability and recall data that test one component of the model. Finally, I shall indicate some further developments of the model that are now in progress and mention another application of the model to a problem of practical educational interest.

The primary goal of the theory is to account for what people remember when they read a text and to tell what makes a text easy or hard to read. Figure 11-1 illustrates the situation we are dealing with. There are two givens: the text, and the reader's goals and purposes. Actually, we are not really dealing with the text at all. Instead, we simplify our task considerably by accepting as an input to the model a semantic representation of the text rather than the real thing. One can hand-code the text into a set of propositions or conceptual structures that represent the meaning of the text. This is done in a nonarbitrary, codified, but nonalgorithmic manner

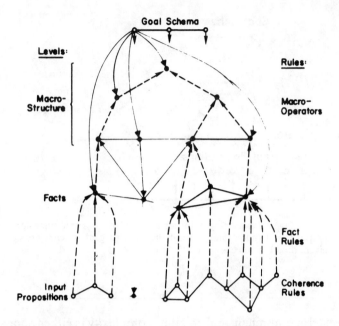

Figure 11-2. An outline for a psychological model of text comprehension distinguishing three levels of processing and indicating the nature of the rules relating these levels. The information flow is both bottom–up and top–down.

(Kintsch, 1974). In a sense, this step is outside the model: We need it, but we don't as yet know how to model it explicitly, so we bypass it. This is a weakness of the theory, but I am confident that in a few years the work on semantic parsers that is being done today at several institutions will be so far advanced that we shall be able to borrow their results for our purposes and to incorporate them into this theory.

Note at the top of the figure the reader's goals, which are represented here in terms of a schema. Without such a schema to control processing the model could not work at all. If we are dealing with an unspecified reader, we have no way of predicting what he or she will get out of a text. Both the reader and the text need to be specified in a model; otherwise, comprehension processes are not sufficiently constrained to be theoretically explainable.

Between the input propositions and the control schema, there is a big black box in Figure 11-1. The goal of the model is to account for what happens inside that black box. We hypothesize three levels of processing, as shown in Figure 11-2. The input propositions are arranged in a network called a coherence graph. This is done on the basis of some simple coherence rules: Connections are formed whenever two propositions share an argument. That is, coherence is defined here in terms of referential coherence alone. At the same time as the coherence graph is formed, the propositions are grouped together whenever they belong to the same fact. We might, for instance, know that the driver of an old VW lost control on the ice and smashed into a parked pink Cadillac. A lot of propositions are involved, but they all belong to the same fact: an accident, with various participants, circumstances, and modalities. Not all of the facts related in a text, however, are relevant. Consequently, we need to distinguish further levels of representation – namely, the macrostructure of the text. The macrostructure results from the operation of the macro-operators, which are a set of abstraction or summarization rules. Indeed, the macrostructure itself may have several levels – corresponding, say, to a long abstract of the text and to ever more concise summarizations. Eventually, merely a title is left.

One might question whether the theory really needs to be so complicated; are all these levels really needed? In order to predict which portion of the input people recall, the lowest level is needed. In order to predict the summaries that people make of a text, the hierarchical macrostructure is needed. One can think of the fact level as the lowest level of the macrostructure, and I shall demonstrate later the important role that facts play in the theory.

Indeed, instead of making the model simpler, we need to make it more complex. In order to make the model work, direction from above is required. One cannot arrive at a summary merely by working upwards from the data level, because there is no way of knowing what in the data is or is not relevant and what, therefore, can be deleted or generalized. A schema is required that determines what is relevant, that sets up expectations, and that calls for certain facts, inferring them if they are not directly represented in the input set. I have indicated this in the figure by the downward-pointing arrows.

The part of the model that is fully developed at present and from which the readability predictions are derived is the one that contains the coherence rules depicted at the bottom of the figure. It takes as its input a set of propositions, ordered as they appear in the text, and from this input constructs a coherence network, identifying places where inferences are required in order to obtain coherence. I shall illustrate this construction of a coherence graph with a simple example. I shall suppress the propositions in the example (see Figure 11–3) and use English text in which

Coherence Analysis – Cycle I:

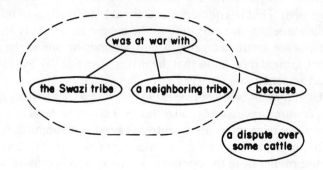

Figure 11-3. The construction of the coherence graph for the first sentence.

word groups that roughly correspond to underlying propositions are bracketed.

Thus, consider the sentence: "[The Swazi tribe] [was at war with] [a neighboring tribe] [because of] [a dispute over some cattle]." This sentence constitutes the input to the first processing cycle, where a coherent network is constructed with five input propositions as nodes, as shown in Figure 11-3. The "being at war" proposition is selected as the superordinate of the net (the question how the superordinate is selected belongs to another component of the system with which the coherence rules interact), and the other propositions are annexed to it by a very simple rule: Connect all propositions which share a common argument. Since propositions are not shown in Figure 11-3, the way this rule operates is not obvious, but it is an objective, algorithmic rule. Once the graph is constructed, the process goes on to the next cycle.

But now the question arises as to which portion of the coherence graph just constructed should be retained in short-term memory so that the graph constructed on the next cycle can be integrated with it. A separate network cannot be constructed each time one reads a sentence. The information from all the sentences in a text must be interrelated. Ideally, the whole tree could be retained and the propositions simply could be added when another sentence is read. But people's processing capacities are limited; people cannot keep arbitrarily large amounts of information active in short-term memory. Hence, a few propositions must be selected on each cycle and kept in a short-term memory buffer while all the other,

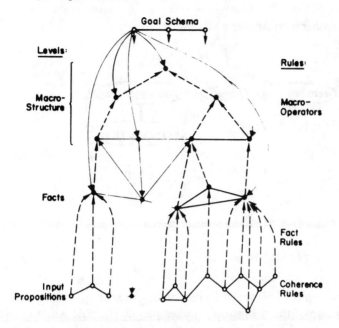

Figure 11–4. The construction of the coherence graph for the second sentence.

nonselected propositions are relegated to inactive status in long-term memory. A rule or strategy is needed that indicates which of the propositions are to be kept in the short-term memory buffer. Such a strategy has been described in Kintsch & van Dijk (1978), and when used here it would select the three propositions encircled by the broken line. The principle behind the strategy is a preference for propositions high up in the graph (which tend to be important ones) combined with a recency bias.

Now consider the next sentence. There are now three old propositions in short-term memory plus a new input which reads in English: "[Among the warriors] [were two [unmarried] men] [named] [Kakra and [his younger brother] Gum]." The task of the comprehender in this model is to connect these six new propositions with the three old ones still in short-term memory (Figure 11–4). This fails in an interesting way. There are no concepts shared by the propositions in the buffer and the new input that would serve to connect the two sets. So the model says: "Well, maybe I kept the wrong propositions in my buffer. I'll go back and look at everything I have in my long-term memory; maybe there is something there that relates

Coherence Analysis – Cycle 3:

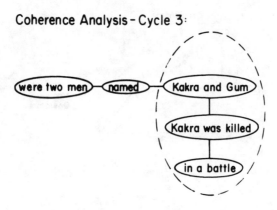

Figure 11-5. The construction of the coherence graph for the third sentence.

to the new input." This we call a reinstatement search, and we hypothesize that it is one of the things that makes people stumble when they read a text. If a text and a reader interact in such a way that the reader must perform frequent reinstatement searches, then we have a text that is hard to read. In our example the reinstatement search fails: There simply are no common concepts in the first two cycles. So the model builds a new graph, this time selecting "were two men" as its starting proposition and annexing the rest via the concept repetition rule. It may also perform an inference at this point to interrelate the two graphs: namely, that "the warriors belonged to the Swazi tribe," or that "the people who fight in a war are warriors." This is the kind of bridging inference that Clark and his colleagues have studied quite extensively (e. g., Haviland & Clark, 1974).

Again we select three propositions for our short-term memory buffer, and we go to the next sentence: "[Kakra was killed] [in battle]." This time there is no problem (Figure 11-5). We still have "Kakra" in short-term memory, and the new sentence repeats that concept. Therefore, we can add it to our graph, select a buffer set, and continue reading. But that is enough of this example for the present. Its purpose was merely to show intuitively how this part of the model works.

What does the model do for us? First of all, it permits us to make some readability predictions. If the model has to make a large number of reinstatement searches and a large number of inferences, then we predict that readers will have a correspondingly hard time with the text. Of course, the frequency with which the model has to backtrack and go rummaging

Kakra Text:
Data and Predictions

PROP	RECALL (100 Ss)	PRED S=3	PRED S=2
1	45	+	
2	80	+	+
3	78	+	+
4	46		
5	39		
6	42		
7	82	+	+
8	47		
9	79	+	+
10	81	+ +	+
11	45		
12	84	+	+
13	17	+	

Figure 11–6. Predictions of the model of the pattern of recall for two values of short-term buffer capacity. The data are fictitious.

through its long-term memory depends crucially on the amount of short-term memory we give it. In the example used here I have assumed a buffer size of 3. Obviously, if the size had been 1 or 2, there would have been more reinstatement searches. In general, the larger the short-term memory, the less trouble the model has with a text. Thus, we need to know what the model's parameters are before we can make any specific readability predictions.

By making some simple assumptions about memory, one can use recall data to estimate the model parameters. Fitting the model to recall data has another advantage: It permits one to evaluate how well the model accords with standard statistical procedures. The logic of this argument is shown in Figure 11–6. In the first column we have the 13 propositions from the three sentences discussed above. The second column shows how many subjects (out of 100) recalled each proposition on an immediate free-recall test (the data are fictitious). As is typical, there is quite a bit of variability. Now consider the model's predictions. It is assumed that every time a proposition is processed, it is stored in long-term memory with some probability p (which is another parameter of the model). All propositions are processed at least once (we assume a careful reader here, but this is not necessary). Some propositions, however, are processed more than once. For instance, Propositions 1, 2, and 3 were processed again in the second cycle because they were held over in short-term memory. Proposition 10 in fact, had two extra chances to be stored in long-term memory: It was first processed in the second cycle, held over for the third, and then held over once more for the fourth cycle. These extra processing chances are indicated by plus signs in column three of Figure 11–6, but in the actual model these would be a set of stochastic prediction equations.

From here on the testing procedures are straightforward: One finds the value of p (the probability of long-term memory storage) that generates the "best" predictions, where "best" means the minimum chi-square on a goodness-of-fit test. This procedure yields a minimum chi-square value of 36.35 in the present case. For 12 df (degrees of freedom), this is not impressive and indicates that the model predicts a pattern of recall that just was not there in the data. But that is no reason to despair: Maybe the model was right, and our guess about the size of the short-term memory buffer was merely wrong! So we try the same thing again, deriving predictions as before except that this time we restrict short-term memory so that it holds only two propositions. The resulting predictions are shown in the last column of Figure 11–6. Now the plus signs seem to correspond to the high values in the data column, as they should. This is borne out by the corresponding minimum chi-square of 19.34.

This is still not perfect, however, and if the table is examined a little more closely it is apparent that most of the trouble is caused by Proposition 13 (Kakra was killed "in battle"), which only 17 people recalled. The model predicts 46, and this discrepancy greatly inflates the minimum chi-square. Proposition 13 is essentially redundant. We know that there was a war and that Kakra was killed, and most people simply do not bother to write down in their recall protocol the redundant information that this happened "in a battle." The Kintsch and van Dijk model actually has a component that deals with this kind of recall suppression: There are production rules that prevent redundant statements from being expressed under certain conditions. Thus, the low recall of Proposition 13 is not really an embarrassment to the model. It is simply irrelevant to the evaluation of the coherence component of the model. If we delete this proposition and recompute the chi-square, we obtain a value of 2.81 for 11 df. This is a more valid indication of the fact that, except for small random deviations, the model predicts the pattern of recall remarkably well.

We have followed this strategy to test the model in a large experiment in which 20 paragraphs from various sources were used as the text material (Miller & Kintsch, 1980). The paragraphs, each about 80 words long, were selected so that they would span a wide range of readability. In other words, some of them were pretty awful. Reading time and recall data for these texts were obtained from 120 subjects. So far, we have analyzed the data from half of the paragraphs.

The recall data were analyzed as shown above. That is, only reproductive propositional recall was scored; all errors and constructions were ignored. (However, immediate recall with such short texts is known to be almost wholly reproductive.) The reliability of the proposition scoring was .91 in this experiment.

A question arises, however, when we come to the operational definition of readability. The measure preferred here is an efficiency statistic: reading time per proposition recalled. Intuitively, this measure appears to be more satisfactory than either reading time or amount recalled alone.

A little bit more technical detail about the model itself now needs to be added, specifically about the model parameters that were estimated. One of these has already been introduced in the example above: the capacity of the short-term memory buffer. In previous work, we have estimated this capacity to be 4 propositions (Kintsch & van Dijk, 1978). Spilich, Vesonder, Chiesi, and Voss (1979) have obtained an estimate of 2, but their buffer contained some macropropositions, so that the two estimates are not incompatible. Another parameter of the model which must be considered is the maximum input size per cycle – i.e., the number of propositions accepted each time. In the present version of the model, input size is determined by the sentence boundaries in the text. When a sentence is too long, a cycle is limited to I propositions, where I is to be estimated from the data. The third and final parameter of the model estimated from the data is p, the probability that when a proposition is processed it will be stored in long-term memory and will be recalled subsequently.

Quite crucial to the model is the strategy that selects the propositions to be retained in the short-term memory buffer from one processing cycle to the next. Such a strategy was described in Kintsch and van Dijk (1978). In the present work we have basically retained this strategy, although it has been modified in some ways (for details, see Miller & Kintsch, 1980). The model, with these small changes, is formalized as a computer program (written in LISP) that accepts as input a proposition list derived from a text with indications of sentence boundaries. The program processes this input list in the manner hypothesized by the model, utilizing fixed values of the short-term memory and maximum input size parameters. This generates recall as well as readability predictions. The recall predictions thus obtained are then fitted to the actual data by means of a minimum chi-square procedure that yields the third model parameter (the learning probability p) as well as a measure of goodness of fit.

Overall, for the 10 paragraphs so far analyzed, these goodness-of-fit measures are quite satisfactory. The average minimum chi-square per text is 60 for 24 df. Although that deviation from the data is highly significant, the absolute size of the deviation rather than its significance level is more important in goodness-of-fit tests, and that is fairly good here. Our best-fitted text yielded a nonsignificant chi-square of 28. Most of the texts were in the 40–60 range. Only one paragraph was fitted really poorly (a minimum chi-square of 122 was obtained). It was the most difficult text of the set, and the model – with only the coherence mechanism at its disposal – simply could not handle it. There was, indeed, a general relationship between the goodness-of-fit values and the difficulty of the texts: The easier the text, the better the fit of the model. When comprehension involves a lot of inferences and top – down processing, then the coherence rules alone are simply insufficient and need help and guidance from other aspects of the model, to which I shall turn presently.

The best estimates of short-term memory capacity were in the range of 3 to 5 propositions, with a mean of 3.88. Maximum input sizes ranged from 5 to 8 propositions, with a mean of 6.2. The mean learning probability was rather high for these short texts: $p = .64$.

But the most interesting results of this study are the readability predictions. The small variations in the estimates of the short-term memory capacity for the ten different texts appear to be unrelated to readability. The same is true for the learning probability, p, which appears to be determined mostly by the proposition density of the text. The third parameter of the model is more interesting: Input size correlates .67 with readability. More propositions are accepted per cycle for the easy texts than for the hard texts. Input size is also a factor in how long subjects take to read a text, as would be expected.

The most important factor in the model related to readability is, however, the number of reinstatement searches that are made in processing each text. Reinstatement searches are instances of backtracking: The present input is not related to the propositions that were retained in the short-term memory buffer, and the system has to go back and search its long-term memory for a possible relationship that would establish the coherence of the text. The three easiest texts in our sample did not require any reinstatement searches, and the three medium texts required an average of .5 reinstatements; but for the three hardest texts this number increased to 1.67. Overall, reinstatements correlated -.62 with readability and about equally with total recall (-.59).

On the other hand, the number of inferences that have to be made in reading a text in order to make it coherent correlates much less highly with the readability statistics. Bridging inferences occur when a concept is not repeated from cycle to cycle – as, for instance, in the example above, where "war" was mentioned in the first sentence and "warriors" in the second. We know from the work of Clark and others (e. g., Havil and Clark, 1974) that such inferences require extra processing time, but apparently this effect is relatively weak compared with the extra effort involved in reinstatement searches. There is an important qualification here: Many of the bridging inferences in our material were very easy and obvious, as in the example just mentioned. If things are arranged so that the reader does not have the necessary knowledge base to make the inferences that the text requires, inferences could be just as resource-consuming as reinstatement searches and perhaps even more so. Such a case, in fact, occurs in one of our texts, where you have to know that Sloan was one of the witnesses who appeared before Judge Sirica in the Watergate trials – information that does not appear to be current among Colorado graduates.

I do not want to suggest a new readability formula, but the equation below is an easy way to summarize our results. In our limited set of data, the multiple correlation between six predictor variables and reading difficulty (defined here as the number of seconds of reading time per proposition recalled on an immediate test) is an impressive .97.

Reading Difficulty = 2.83 + .48RS - .69WF + 51PD +.23INF + .21C - .10ARG, where RS is the number of reinstatement searches made by the model in processing the paragraph, WF is the average word frequency, PD the proposition density, INF the number of inferences, C the number of processing cycles, and ARG the number of different arguments in the proposition list.

Most of the variance is accounted for by the first two factors – the number of reinstatements, as just discussed, and the traditional word frequency. Two other factors make smaller contributions: proposition density (that is, the number of words in the text divided by the number of propositions in its base) and the number of inferences. The number of processing cycles (which is obviously related to the traditional sentence length variable as well as to maximum input size in the present model) and the number of different arguments make negligible contributions. That word frequency and sentence length are related to reading difficulty

Coherence Analysis – Cycle 4:

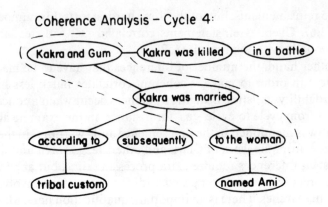

Figure 11-7. The construction of the coherence graph for the fourth sentence.

is no news. That proposition density and number of different arguments are so related replicates some of our earlier work. We have learned about reinstatement searches, number of inferences, and number of processing cycles from the present model. I think they are important and interesting factors that deserve a lot more scrutiny in the future.

The Flesch formula, by the way, does not predict readability (as defined here) for this particular set of paragraphs. It does predict raw reading times, however, and is also related to ratings of subjective readability, just to complicate the picture a bit further.

Let me recapitulate what has been talked about so far. I first outlined a very complex model with several interacting components. One of these components – the coherence rules – was then discussed in some detail. I have pointed out the implications that this part of the model has for recall data and for readability and then described an experiment that tested these predictions. Things seemed to be going quite well with this rather simple component of the model. So why, then, do we need a more complex model, with facts, macrostructures, and all that?

The basic problem is that at the level we have operated so far the model is simply too stupid. Let us go back to that example of the tribesmen Kakra and Gum. In the last sentence Kakra was killed, and that fact was still held in the active memory buffer. Suppose the story is now continued with: "[According to] [tribal custom], [Kakra was married] [subsequently] [to the woman] [Ami]." Everything is fine with the model (Figure 11-7): The "Kakra" in the buffer reappears in the input sentence, and a nice coherent graph structure is obtained. The computer does not scream, the model

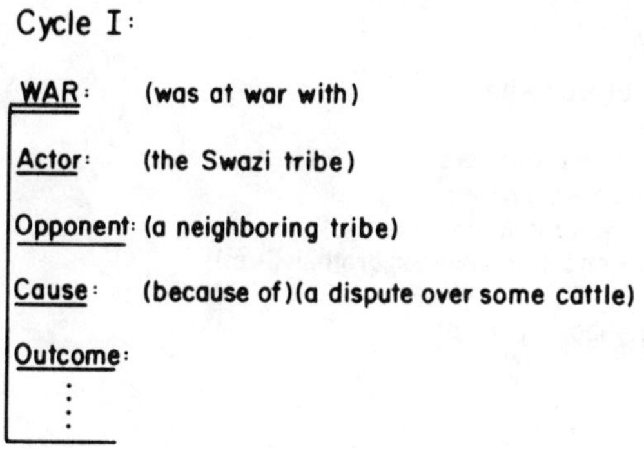

Cycle I:

WAR: (was at war with)

Actor: (the Swazi tribe)

Opponent: (a neighboring tribe)

Cause: (because of)(a dispute over some cattle)

Outcome:
⋮

Figure 11-8. The fact analysis of the first sentence.

does not blink an eyelid when a dead man is being married; whereas readers at this point experience considerable puzzlement with the text. That is why the model is stupid. It is concerned only with the coherence of the text and does not care at all what is said. A real reader will reject this text as nonsensical; or if he or she is very imaginative, invent some appropriate tribal custom; or if they know about ghostmarriages, recognize Kakra's marriage as an instance of ghostmarriage. In fact, my example comes from a study by Caccamise (1979), who was concerned with the effect of knowledge on understanding. She gave her subjects anthropology lessons in which they learned, among other things, about the custom of ghostmarriages. In a ghostmarriage, if the oldest son of a family dies without an heir, he is legally married, but his younger brother takes his place until an offspring is produced.

Comprehension requires knowledge, and the way knowledge enters into the present model is through the grouping of propositions in terms of the facts to which they belong. A fact, once established, generates expectations about other related information in the text as well as about other facts. The way a fact is established in the model is that an appropriate knowledge structure is pulled out of the reader's knowledge store, and the text propositions are related to that knowledge structure.

Let us return to the earlier example. In the first sentence we were told that the Swazi tribe was at war with a neighboring tribe. This activates the "war" framework. The Swazi tribe is inserted as the actor in this war, the neighboring tribe becomes the opponent, and there is also a cause (Figure 11-8). Many other things that we expect when we hear about a war are unspecified at this point, but the system is ready for other information related to this war. Therefore, the next sentence (Figure 11-9) comes as no

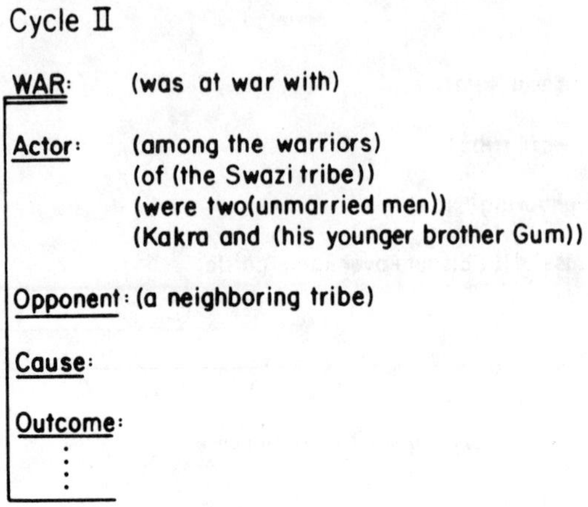

Cycle II

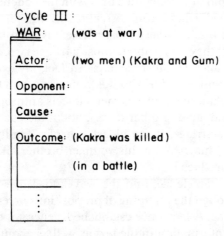

Figure 11-9. The fact analysis of the second sentence.

Cycle III :

Figure 11-10. The fact analysis of the third sentence.

surprise. What we have here is a further specification of the actor in the "war" framework. The third sentence (Figure 11-10) adds an outcome. Note that what is being shown here are exactly the same propositions as those in the coherence analysis; the only difference is that we are now grouping these propositions in terms of their fact relations. In Cycle IV (Figure 11-11), something interesting finally happens. We are no longer talking about war but about marriage. So the "marriage" framework becomes the basis for an organization of the input propositions, but it fails: A dead Kakra does not make a good husband. If the system knows

Cycle Ⅳ:

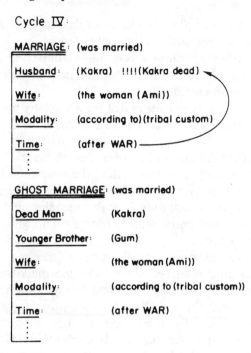

Figure 11-11. The fact analysis of the fourth sentence.

about ghostmarriage, however, that framework is called up. Now there are no difficulties. All of the information in the text fits into the slots of the "ghostmarriage" framework, and no contradictions arise.

What has been gained by this additional analysis? First, consider the readability predictions again. In the coherence analysis we predicted trouble with the transition from the first to the second sentence, because there was no direct conceptual overlap between them. A bridging inference was required – something like "the warriors belonged to the tribe at war." As our data have shown, such bridging inferences do not necessarily make a text harder to read as long as the reader has available the background knowledge from which to derive the inferences. The reanalysis of this text in terms of its underlying fact structure provides a somewhat different picture. The bridging inference is still there, but since the appropriate knowledge structure (the "war" framework) is already activated, it should be an easy inference. On the other hand, a major problem arises when the text shifts from war to marriage. Realizing that we are talking now about ghostmarriage is no trivial feat. Readers as well as the model are very likely to experience comprehension problems here. A second advantage of our reanalysis is that the facts provide a basis for dealing with inferences. Although the inference mechanisms themselves are not the focus of our work at present, clearly they will be a very important part of a complete comprehension model. Finally, fact analysis permits an easy transition to the topic of macrostructures.

Macrostructures, in this theory, are generated from a text by the reader and correspond to what one usually calls its "gist," as might be expressed by a summary or abstract. By their very nature, macrostructures are hierarchical, corresponding to more and more concise abstracts. It is useful to think of fact representation as constituting the lowest level of the macrostructure, containing everything that was in the text. The macro-operators pick out from all these facts only those that are relevant. In order to do this, of course, they must know what is relevant. This guidance is provided by the control schema.

I can only illustrate this point with a brief example. Once more we go back to Kakra and his ghostmarriage to see how the macrostructure gradually evolves during the processing of the text. In Cycle I, when only the first sentence is processed, the hypothesized macrostructure is a simple generalization of the input – "Two tribes were at war" – with everything that appears to be irrelevant at the time deleted. In Cycles II and III an additional macroproposition is added each time: "Kakra and Gum were warriors" and "Kakra was killed." In Cycle IV, however, a complete reorganization is required. Because of the ghostmarriage, different facts now appear to be relevant. The fact that Kakra was unmarried when he died and that he had a younger brother now appear as the presuppositions for the ghostmarriage, and a new macrostructure is generated by the model at this point: "Kakra and his younger brother Gum were unmarried; Kakra was killed; he ghostmarried Ami." Thus, if we asked subjects to summarize our text after the third sentence, they would write something about the war. But if we asked them to summarize after they had read the whole story, a rather different summary would be obtained – namely, one that referred to the marriage.

But what has all this to do with education? First of all, there is the importance of having available a general framework for the understanding of comprehension processes. Educators deal with problems involving comprehension on a day-to-day basis, and they often have to make complex decisions on the spot. Their best guide has been common sense. We are all experienced comprehenders, and we all have had our comprehension problems and have developed reasonably good intuitions about them. But common sense will help us only so far. A scientific, theoretical understanding of comprehension processes could be of great help – not because the theory will solve every one of the educator's problems, but because it can provide educators with another set of intuitions about comprehension processes that may sharpen their perception and help to make them more efficient problem solvers.

In addition, of course, there are the specific results that are produced by work such as this. I have stressed here the implications of the model with respect to the concept of readability. The model provides a more refined notion of what is involved in readability, and this may eventually have some practical consequences. But that was just one example. Several other potential areas could be identified to which this theory could be applied. Not surprisingly, a general theory of comprehension seems to have strong consequences for numerous educational questions.

I shall merely mention one of these. Mathemagenic behaviors (in particular, asking people questions about what they are reading) have been investigated extensively by educational psychologists. These investigations seemed to hold a lot of promise for improving learning from text, but when all the research was in the results were a little bit disappointing. It was hard to get really spectacular effects, and there were lots of inconsistencies in the data. Now from my point of view, and the advantage of hindsight, this is not surprising if you look at the nature of that research effort. A good review of that work was written in 1975 by Anderson and Biddle. Their main section contained a discussion of the following factors that determine the effectiveness of adjunct questions: nature of test items, positioning and timing of questions, response mode, feedback, overt response, motivation, and finally, just before "other factors," the "nature of the questions." Only four studies were included in that section, from a combined reference list of 3 1/2 pages! But the kind of question that is asked ought to be the most important factor of all. The problem is, of course, that in order to investigate this factor one needs to have some kind of theory regarding comprehension and the possible roles that adjunct questions might play.

Consider, once more, Kakra and his ghostmarriage. Suppose that after the sentence "Kakra was killed in a battle," someone has asked the reader, "How does the tribe provide for the inheritance of family property and status when an older son dies without an heir?" In the knowledgeable reader, this question would have primed the ghostmarriage framework and hence ensured correct comprehension of the remainder of the passage. Such a question might facilitate retention of new material in the text. On the other hand, suppose someone had asked instead, "What was the cause of Kakra's death?" This question does not engage the reader in processing that will help him or her later on; the answer is merely computed from an already initiated framework. Therefore, such a question would have very little effect beyond the better retention of the immediately queried item. As a third possibility, imagine a question that would be harmful because it prompts the reader to set up the wrong expectations. For instance, suppose that after the first sentence in our text (which says that there was a war because of a dispute over some cattle), someone had asked the reader, "What do you think happened to the cattle?" The reader now would focus inappropriately on the dispute over the cattle and organize the input propositions in terms of a "dispute" fact that would have to be replaced by a "war" fact in the second processing cycle.

Thus, adjunct questions may have positive, negative, or neutral effects depending upon how the process of question answering meshes with the comprehension process. If it is known that at a certain point in the text the reader needs a concept that, according to the model, is no longer available in working memory, reinstating that concept via a suitable question ought to help. But asking about something that is in working memory anyway will do little good. And a really inappropriate question can confuse the reader.

Anderson and Biddle (1975) complain that we do not need another demonstration that adjunct questions "work." Instead, we need to know why they work and under what conditions. A model like the present one will let us find out why and when. Even an incomplete model and one that is undoubtedly wrong in many of its details is better in this respect than no framework at all, as long as it permits the researcher to ask the right kind of questions.

Note

References

Anderson, R. C., & Biddle, W. B. (1975). On asking people questions about the way they are reading. In G. H. Bower (Ed.), *The psychology of learning and motivation* (Vol. 9). New York: Academic Press.

Caccamise, D. J. (1970). The effect of knowledge on the ability to make inferences. Unpublished Master's Thesis, University of Colorado.

Haviland, S. E., & Clark, H. H. (1974). What's new? Acquiring new information as a process in comprehension. *Journal of Verbal Learning and Verbal Behavior, 13*, 515–21.

Keenan, J. M., & Kintsch, W. (1974). The identification of explicitly and implicitly presented information. In W. Kintsch, *The representation of meaning in memory*. Hilldale, N. J.: Lawrence Erlbaum Associates.

Kintsch, W. (1974). *The representation of meaning in memory*. Hillsdale, N. J.: Lawrence Erlbaum Associates.

Kintsch, W., & van Dijk, T. A. (1978). Towards a model of text comprehension and production. *Psychological Review, 85*, 363–94.

Kintsch, W., & Vipond, D. (1979). Reading comprehension and readability in educational practice and psychological theory. In L. G. Nilsson (Ed.), *Perspectives on memory research*. Hillsdale, N. J.: Lawrence Erlbaum Associates.

Meyer, B. J. F. (1975). *The organization of prose and its effects on memory*. Amsterdam: North Holland.

Miller, J. R., & Kintsch, W. (1980). Readability and recall of short prose passages: A theoretical analysis. *Journal of Experimental Psychology: Human Learning and Memory, 6*, 335–54.

Shuy, R. W., and Larkin, D. L. (1978). Linguistic consideration in the simplification/clarification of insurance policy language. *Discourse Processes, 1*, 305–21.

Simon, H. A. (1974). How big is a chunk? *Science, 183*, 482–88.

Spilich, G. J., Vesonder, G. T., Chiesi, H. L., & Voss, J. F. (1979). Text processing of domain-related information for individuals with high and low domain-knowledge. *Journal of Verbal Learning and Verbal Behavior, 18*, 275–90.

van Dijk, T. A., & Kintsch, W. (1983). *Strategies of discourse comprehension*. New York: Academic Press.

12   Reading is recognition
when reading is not reasoning

J. Jaap Tuinman

> Meaning, as I think of the term, is the result of the application of prior
> codings of the organism to the present decoding (i.e., reading) task.
> – Wendell W. Weaver, 1977.

When someone reads a story these questions can be asked:

- What must the reader comprehend?
- What does the reader comprehend?
- What can the reader comprehend?

By and large, efforts to conceptualize the measurement of comprehension have concentrated on the last of these questions at the neglect of the first two. In the final section of this paper it will be argued that as a result we have mistakenly come to believe that "reading is reasoning," whereas, in fact, much comprehension activity can best be characterized as recognition.

Those persons concerned with the improvement of practices in the measurement of reading comprehension face two immediate challenges. First, criterion-referenced measurement of comprehension skills is in a chaotic state. Tests proliferate in the absence of either theoretical justification or adequate psychometric undergirding. One cannot fault practitioners for their actions; neither can one avoid the need for such action. Nevertheless, the large array of criterion-referenced tests marketed and used rests on very shaky assumptions, indeed. Second, cognitive psychology's rather recent preoccupation with both learning and reading has resulted in a number of insights that require assimilation in the conceptualization of the measurement of reading comprehension.

Criterion-referenced measurement of comprehension

The first part of this paper will briefly elaborate on some of the problems with criterion-reference measurement of reading comprehension skills.

196

Some of the modifications of current thinking about measurement of comprehension suggested by recent formulations in cognitive psychology will subsequently be discussed.

Lumsden (1976) argues that educational measurement per se is at an impasse. When viewing its application in reading comprehension I must agree, in spite of increasing mathematical sophistication in establishing indices of reliability, validity, etc. The problem, unfortunately, is not with the algebra but with the thinking behind it. This, of course, is not a new problem. Throughout the yet brief history of educational measurement influential writers such as Richardson (1936) and Buros (1948) have cautioned against the mistake of confusing the proliferation of mathematical superstructures with genuine progress in laying solid foundations.

The point, unfortunately, is well illustrated by current work on technical concerns in criterion-referenced measurement (CRM). Illustrative of the problematic nature of much of the activity is a recent paper by Berk (1978). Specifying a 95% confidence interval, he is able to show that one needs 58 items to test the comprehension of a population of 1,000 sentences if one uses 80% mastery as the criterion score. This sounds very precise and helpful until one realizes that Berk's calculations are based on Bormuth's unproductive conceptualization of the measurement of comprehension (Mehrens, 1970; Tuinman, 1970).

That the development of new indices does not necessarily even reflect progress on the technical side is demonstrated by Downing and Mehrens (1978). When these authors compared six single-administration reliability coefficients for CRMs, they found that only one measured a test characteristic that was different from the classical Kuder – Richardson formulas.[1] More disturbingly, when Smith (1978) compared five popular item-selection methods he found that none of the methods was consistently superior. Indeed, random selection of items worked just as well as any other method.

The general point that the elaboration of mathematical techniques can obscure basic conceptual problems is yet more clearly demonstrated when one reviews recent work on establishing adequate criterion, mastery, or pass scores. The intent of such work is, of course, to formulate techniques that will validly classify individuals as masters or nonmasters. Two of the more interesting papers, by Huynh (1977) and Faggan (1978), illustrate current attempts to deal with the issue and the inadequacy of these techniques.

The procedures for establishing mastery scores are elegant and appear effective. Nevertheless, both papers share a very fundamental problem.

Whether or not a student is validly classified as a master on test *I* is judged by his or her performance on test *J*. Presumable, test *J* is more complex, more general, or higher in some skills hierarchy than test *I*. Granted, adequate tests of accuracy of classification are needed. The bulk of the unresolved issues, however, relates precisely to the specification of the relationship between tests *I* and *J* and to the adequacy of test *J* as a criterion.

This is far from being an issue for idle contemplation; rather, it raises its head in every reading management system currently in use. As test constructors, we are saved by the fact that most tests, whatever their label, format, or content, include a strong verbal factor. Were it not for that fact, teachers would be confronted with many more puzzling patterns of performance on series of tests in their "management" batteries than they already face.

Seldom are relationships among tests made explicit. Implicitly, however, hierarchical connections and the transfer of acquired skills to other, more complex, ones are routinely assumed. Criterion-referenced comprehension tests fail, however, precisely because either they cannot satisfy these assumptions or, in the event they do, there are precious few ways to demonstrate the fact empirically.

An early optimism about the possibility of isolating and describing learning hierarchies is not tempered by the realization that even in the case of simple behaviors, empirical verification of hierarchical relationships is difficult. Two recent papers demonstrate the paucity of effective techniques. Guay and McCabe (1978) point out serious shortcomings in existing tests of hierarchical dependency. They then present a test that, they claim, remedies these problems. However, their test, too, being restricted to a pair-wise comparison of skills, is very limited in scope. The state of the art is best illustrated by Griffiths and Cornish (1978). They extended White and Clark's test of inclusion to more than three items per skill. The relationships among seven skills, representing the development of an introductory chemistry concept, were then analyzed. In all, some 10 possible hierarchies result from the analysis – hardly a comforting thought, considering the relatively simple nature of the skills involved. The prospect of extracting ourselves from the measurement muddle through specifying skills hierarchies in the comprehension domain is dim indeed.

Even if more powerful statistical techniques were available and practical, there is still grave doubt regarding the applicability of the hierarchy concept to the comprehension domain. Every teacher knows that it is possible to ask a very easy "higher-order" question and a very difficult "lower-order" question. If skills hierarchies are to be studied at all, this should be done within a given level of language, within a defined lexicon. We will never understand the contribution of, for instance, "being able to use context" to "being able to draw inferences" unless we first systematically study the relationships among such skills for a particular set of lexical elements, syntactic patterns, and semantic domains.

Comprehension and context

It is perhaps important to admit that "skill" may be an inappropriate metaphor for much of what readers do with language. In the distinction between "skill in" and "knowledge of" language, reading educators have tended to emphasize the former. It is possible, however, to view "drawing an inference" as "knowing an inference" under certain conditions. Pace (1978) studied children's comprehension of stories with familiar and unfamiliar content. In discussing her results, she makes the following comment:

Even kindergarten students can answer questions about the implicit forms for familiar stories. Thus, they look like they are making inferences because they go beyond the information given. However, since these same kindergarten children fail similar questions about unfamiliar situations, they are not likely to be using deliberate inferential processes. Once they recognize that a story concerns something that they know, they may simply use their own knowledge – their own "scripts" – to supply effortlessly information that was omitted from the story itself. [p. 12]

Pace provides a clear example of a reading behavior that looks like reasoning but is in fact an instance of recognition.

In 1917, Thorndike made his well-known claim that reading is reasoning. At the same time he initiated a measurement tradition that made his claim virtually unfalsifiable. Had Thorndike been a rhetorician concerned with the structure of narratives, he might have made the leap to questioning how structure variables would relate to comprehension. But he was not, and those questions did not arise in full force till some 60 years later. Instead of stories, Thorndike chose brief paragraphs to study and measure comprehension. This, in the author's opinion, has had some most unfortunate consequences for the teaching and testing of reading comprehension.

Thorndike set a measurement tradition that has saddled us with a vexing conflict: Many test items ask questions, often very clever ones, about story information that tends to be totally neglected, overlooked as of no interest, when reading anything except reading tests. There are pragmatic reasons why reading tests exploit trivial information. Tests must be limited in bulk for "obvious" reasons. Therefore, most tests use a large number of exceedingly brief paragraphs or a lesser number of somewhat larger passages. In either case, to achieve respectable reliability, relatively large numbers of items are written. The combination of many questions asked of limited textual material frequently leads to a near exhaustion of the available information.

There is a second practical consideration for test writers in this regard. Often items must be of a specific kind, such as "inference questions." Many passages provide very restricted opportunities to ask such questions. Hence, item writers frequently are forced to pounce on trivial information if it provides an opening for a question requiring inferencing. The problem is not only that unimportant information forms the basis for questions but also that so much of the content of the passage is used in this fashion. The text is milked dry; the reader is forced to process it in a manner atypical of much natural reading.

One can conceivably argue that such tests are useful in revealing potential limits of a reader's comprehension, even though under many reading conditions he may not pay attention to most of the details tested, either for the purpose of remembering them or as take-off points for elaboration.

Notice that this argument acknowledges that these tests, then, emphasize what the reader *can* comprehend at the price of ignoring what he *does* comprehend. The argument, moreover, has merit only as long as one acknowledges that the shift from actual to potential comprehension may, and the author will argue does, entail a qualitative difference in the product of the comprehending.

Flavell (1976) crystallizes much of the perspective of current cognitive psychology on intellectual functions when he remarks:

In any kind of cognitive transaction with the human or nonhuman environment, a variety of information processing activities may go on. Metacognition refers, among other things, to the active monitoring and consequent regulation and orchestration of these processes in relation to the cognitive objects or data on which they bear, usually in the service of some concrete goal or objective. [p. 232]

The notion that the reader is an active processor of text, monitoring the information encountered and interactively assigning and reassigning meaning, is central to the cognitive psychologist's view of reading. An important question, therefore, is how effectively a particular reader regulates his understanding of what is being read; how sensitive is the reader to multiple interpretations; how efficient is he in selecting appropriate ones; how attuned is he to relative loss of meaningfulness of the larger message when inappropriate meanings are assigned to its components. When, in tests, we ask questions of readers we subject internal monitoring to an external force. The fact that the reader when prompted externally can find a fitting answer, can detect a semantic incongruity, can be made aware of a contradiction, tells us little about what happens to the reader's comprehension when the only prompt is internal.

Cognitive psychologists have added the terms "intention" and "goal" to the lexicon of motivation and purpose. Intentions and goals shape the interaction between reader and text, codetermining level and speed of processing. Intention and goal are part of and arise from the larger pragmatic context of the communicative act. Too often, the author believes, has measurement of comprehension been conceptualized without reference to this context.

To elaborate this claim, let me introduce three, somewhat arbitrary, contexts for comprehending reading.

1. Private comprehension: the reading of materials without further demands on the information contained in the text.
2. Communicative comprehension: the reading of materials containing information likely to be informally shared with others.
3. Formal comprehension: the reading of materials containing information to be formally shared with others.

Private comprehension

A few moments before starting the writing of this section of the paper, the author finished the hurried reading of yet another best-seller, Gerald Seymour's *Kingfisher.* The narrative is fast and packed with action, both physical and psychological. The story has a strong forward pull; it is difficult to put down and, under time constraints, invites a fair amount of skipping of marginal paragraphs. (I was also experiencing guilt, arising from giving priority to Seymour's writing over my own writing.)

If anyone were to query me as to specific events, gestures, clothes, etc., in the novel, I might not know appropriate answers, as I did not attend to many of those details. I did not find them important; they were not relevant to the kind of comprehension required for enjoying the novel. Moreover, I read the book not expecting to have to share that kind of information with others. I did not "milk" the story, did not have a pragmatic (in a discourse sense) or aesthetic (as in the case of reading Shakespeare) reason to do so. The essential characteristic of private comprehension is that it both results from and satisfies inner needs for information.

It must be emphasized that the focus of my argument is not on the distinction between product and process of comprehension. The point is that typical tests of the product of comprehension zero in on products that are atypical rather than typical of certain types of reading frequently engaged in.

A by-product of Thorndike type measurement, however, is indeed the neglect of the study of comprehension processes in naturalistic settings. How do readers, for instance, differ in their processing of story information, in their selection of salient information; in their need to understand, in their tolerance for ambiguity and redundancy, and so forth? How do readers grow as private comprehenders?

Communicative comprehension

A good example of what I have in mind here is the reading of an account of a sports event. There is an unspoken expectation that I may share some of the information. The probability that the event will come up in exchanges with fellow enthusiasts is high. Moreover, I may be already partly informed. I hear a newscast; I read a "preview of the event" – type analysis; I discuss the upcoming event with friends.

I suspect that reading in this context differs from private reading in at least two dimensions: (a) the amount and detail of pre-reading information available, and (b) the expectation that the information read will be shared in communication. Note that I use the term "pre-reading information," not script, frame, schema, etc. Private comprehension, too, presupposes scripts. The kind of pre-reading information involved in communicative comprehension is specific, factual knowledge rather than general, abstract, structural knowledge.

If my distinction has merit, materials that ordinarily are read in the pragmatic context of informal communication tend to be more known. As a consequence, we may expect a different kind of processing than takes place in either private or formal comprehension.

Though certain types of writing may be more frequently associated with one type of context, the distinction is far from absolute. When working with colleagues who are all avid readers of "best sellers," I may develop an informal communicative comprehension mind-set when reading novels. I may discuss characters and events before reading about them. I may expect to contribute to staff room talk.

The expectation that information read for communicative comprehension will be shared at a later date is not formal, well-defined, or deliberate. Yet, who has not come across an odd bit of information about a well-known public figure and decided to remember it to tell later? "Did you know that Reagan...," for example. This behavior, this processing strategy, does not tend to exist during private comprehension. "Did you know that Elg Schwartz (the hero in Schweig's best-seller, *Come in the Rain*) dyed his hair?" is just not a statement readers are likely to make.

Formal comprehension

This category is probably most suited to present testing practices. The reading of a social studies chapter in a textbook is a good example. Here the reader's orientation and the external prompts in the form of questions are probably not too far apart. The test duplicates the process the reader has already gone through. The reader is aware that he has to "understand" every detail and "relate" it to the other information presented. Specifics are important; generalizations must be recognized; summaries are prepared physically (or merely in the mind) to be presented later. Fine discriminations among facts, events, motives, and abstractions may be crucial.

One of the most curious developments in the measurement of reading comprehension is that concepts and techniques suitable for the measurement of formal compehensions have come to be used for the measurement of all comprehension. The typical set of test items presented below demonstrates that contention unequivocally.

Janet and Jim went for a short walk. They went for about ten minutes. Janet wore boots, but Jim was wearing sneakers. Mother did not go along. She was cooking dinner.

1. The children went for a short: ride   walk   flight
2. Janet wore: a skirt   sneakers   boots
3. Who did not go for a walk?   Mother   Janet   Jim
4. The children couldn't stay out because they had to: go to bed   clean up their room   eat

To repeat, the issue is not whether these questions measure what a young reader can understand. Rather, our concerns with a measurement tradition exemplified by these kinds of items can be summarized as follows:

- neglect of what the reader does comprehend as he reads in various types of contexts, versus what he can be made to understand when faced with external prompts in the forms of questions

- neglect of research on techniques for measurement of typical products of comprehension in a variety of natural reading contexts
- as a corollary, neglect of the study of the psychological processes associated with obtaining such typical comprehension products and of the instructional interventions required to further their attainment

Reading as reasoning and recognition

We remarked earlier that Thorndike's claim that reading is reasoning was made nearly unfalsifiable in the context of the measurement tradition that developed in the years following his pronouncement. Elsewhere (Tuinman, 1971), this author has argued that Thorndike's view of reasoning, typically associationistic, probably was narrower than ours. Nevertheless, once test constructors included inferential comprehension items in test batteries it naturally became increasingly impossible by any technique of statistical reduction to show anything other than that reading was indeed reasoning. The work of Davis (1944, 1968, 1972) nicely illustrates the premises, the procedures, and the unavoidable outcomes. This point is well known and well argued. There are two further facets to the issue, however.

One direct consequence of the short paragraph–many questions paradigm, coupled with the necessity for many levels of questions (in a taxonomic sense), is the concentration on ever finer discriminations. Anyone who has written comprehension test items knows the tortuous process of "having to find one more angle," so that one more question may be asked of a specific paragraph or passage. Conceptual distinctions are made for the sake of asking a question, and perspectives on the information contained are pursued that would not normally occur to any reader as a reader (as opposed to a test taker). The question, therefore, is whether reading is reasoning because it is reasoning or because we invest so much of our reasoning as testers into its measurement.

Neisser (1976) develops a somewhat analogous argument in the case of intelligence testing. He holds that psychometric intelligence tests basically measure academic intelligence per se. Test constructors, by definition, are people who were good students, academically successful. As Neisser puts it: "Tests are devices for finding other people who resemble their creators."

To what degree is reading reasoning because of the clever minds of those who construct reading comprehension tests? To what extent have decades of cross-validation of tests also been decades of conceptual in-breeding: decades of an unconscious process of boosting the reasoning factor and minimizing other aspects of the task?

Thorndike's first reading test questions have long been the prime vehicle for measuring comprehensions (as opposed to, e.g., summaries, paraphrases, or retellings), and this practice has naturally led to the use of multiple choice items in comprehension tests. This convention, I believe, has seriously exacerbated the "imposed reading" problem. Multiple choice tests require response alternatives that are credible and yet not true or correct. Consequently, each alternative shares certain conceptual features but not others with the correct responses. The process of deciding among alternatives has a name: reasoning. Once more the measure used colors the intellectual operation of interest. To what extent is reading reasoning because of the reasoning processes built into the creation of clever distracters?

Traub and Fisher (1977) analyzed the equivalence of constructed-response and multiple-choice tests across two sets of mathematical reasoning and two sets of verbal comprehension items. The specifics of their study, which sought to identify format differences – other than those due to different errors of measurement, units of measurement, and arbitrary origins of measurement – are not particularly relevant to the purpose of this discussion. Their conclusion, however, is important.

The tests of mathematical reasoning that were employed were equivalent regardless of format, but the tests of verbal comprehension were not. In particular the free-response test of verbal comprehension seemed to measure something different than standard multiple-choice and Coombs tests of this ability.... [p. 367]

It would be interesting, indeed, to apply the methodology employed by Traub and Fisher to current comprehension tests to ascertain whether such format differences could be replicated and whether they would be interpretable in terms of an "added on" reasoning feature.

Comprehending reading is (a) a recognition of propositions stating a fact about the world – including facts that are statements of relations among facts; (b) a "reasoning out," an inferring of such facts; or (c) a mixture of both (a) and (b). In most cases of reading, (c) is operative. Facts about the world can be either known or inferred from what is known. If reading is the mechanism to call such facts to the reader's attention, it is a process of recognition in the former case and a process of reasoning in the latter. All conceivable inferences can be either inferred, if they are not "known," or recognized, if they are.

A view of reading comprehension that invokes schemata, scripts, or frames must of necessity curb the role of reasoning in certain contexts. Consider the conclusions Rumelhart and Ortony (1977) draw about the relationship between cognitive schema theory and comprehension:

Providing information in a structured form most closely resembling the structure of the schema which will be required for its interpretation ... minimizes the processing required. [p. 131]

In other words, under conditions in which the schema is very complete or in which the text contains little new information, processing is minimal. Under those conditions reading becomes less reasoning and more recognition. The reverse is true when the gulf between existing schemata and information presented in and implied by a text widens. The reading becomes less recognition and more reasoning.

Pace (1978) has concretized this view in the study referred to above. Consider further the following illustration to reinforce the point.

John is 6 feet 6 inches tall, a giant basketball player. Mary, standing 5 feet tall, watches him in awe. So does Ken, who knows that Mary never again will look up to him as she used to.

The reader of this paragraph can infer the fact that Ken is taller than Mary either from general knowledge (i.e., the probability of a person named Ken being shorter than 5 feet low) or from the linquistic cue "never again will look up to him as she used to." Reading is reasoning!

Or is it? Imagine that the narrator stands in a television studio with John, Mary, and Ken. They all look at the story, projected on the wall in an effort to facilitate editing for a human-interest public broadcasting story. What if someone would ask how tall Ken is? Would any reasoning or inferring take place?

The example is extreme. Rarely does a narrative mirror a known reality so closely. Yet, when a reader reads about realities with which he is familiar he can either infer unstated aspects of that reality from the text or, with far less effort, supply them from his memory. Then, reading is not reasoning and neither is there any reason it should be.

I have argued that current mechanical problems in the measurement of comprehension cannot be resolved until we reexamine our view of comprehension as skill, rather than knowledge. I have tried to elaborate the view that our perspective on comprehension has been narrow, unduly circumscribed by our preoccupation with the assessment of what can be comprehended using the vehicle of information-exhausting questions on passages void of genuine content. Those arbitrary contexts for comprehending were proposed in an effort to illustrate that different information-processing needs direct different processing strategies and conceivably result in different products of comprehension, inaccessible through the use of questions as external prompts. It was argued that reading has come to be viewed as reasoning in part because we have inadequately separated the product measured from the process of measuring. Finally, it was contended that a more appropriate view of reading characterizes comprehension as a process that involves both recognition and inferences about facts stated and unstated. Reading requires reasoning either when the linguistic code is complex or when the reader's schemata are inadequate to accommodate the text's information structure. When the message is coded in known linguistic structures (phonetic, syntactical, or semantic), and the text's information structure matches the reader's schemata, reading is merely recognition.

Notes

This article previously appeared in *Research on Comprehension*, J. Harste (Ed.), 1979, Bloomington: University of Indiana Educational Press.

1. This study did not include Brennan and Kane's (1977) index. However, see Lumsden (1976) for a critical evaluation of the signal-to-noise ratio indices.

References

Berk, R. A. (1978, March). Item sampling from finite domains of written discourse. Paper presented at the annual meeting of the American Educational Research Association, Toronto.

Brennan, R. L., & Kane, M. T. (1977, 1978). Signal/noise ratios for domain-referenced tests. *Psychometrika, 42* (4), 606–25; *43* (2), 289.

Buros, O. K. (1948). Criticisms of commonly used methods of validating achievement test items. *Proceedings of the 1948 Invitational Conference on Testing Problems.* 18–20. Princeton, N. J.: Educational Testing Service.

Davis, F. B. (1944). Fundamental factors of comprehension in reading. *Psychometrika, 9,* 195–97.

Davis, F. B. (1968). Research on comprehension in reading. *Reading Research Quarterly, 3,* 499–545.

Davis, F. B. (1972). *The literature in reading with emphasis on models.* New Brunswick, N. J.: Rutgers University Press.

Downing, S. M., & Mehrens, W. A. (1978, March). Six single-administration reliability coefficients for criterion reference tests: A comparative study. Paper presented at the annual meeting of the American Educational Research Association, Toronto.

Faggan, J. (1978, March). Decision reliability and classification validity for decision-oriented criterion referenced tests. Paper presented at the annual meeting of the American Educational Research Association, Toronto.

Flavell, J. H. (1976). Metacognition aspects of problem solving. In L. B. Resnick (Ed.), *The nature of intelligence.* Hillsdale, N. J.: Lawrence Erlbaum Associates.

Griffiths, A. K. & Cornish, A. G. (1978, March). An analysis of three methods for the identification and validation of learning hierarchies. Paper presented at the annual meeting
of the American Educational Research Association, Toronto.

Guay, R. B. & McCabe, G. P. (1978, March). A chi-square test for hierarchical dependency.
Paper presented at the annual meeting of the American Educational Research Association, Toronto.

Huynh, H. (1977). Two simple classes of mastery scores based on the beta-binomial model.
Psychometrika, *42* (4), 601–08.

Lumsden, D. (1976). Test theory. *Annual Review of Psychology*, 223–58.

Mehrens, W. A. (1970). Scientific test construction–Pure and sterile. Review in *Contemporary
Psychology*, *15* (11), 666–67.

Neisser, U. (1976). *Cognition and reality*. San Francisco: Freeman.

Pace, A. J. (1978, March). The influence of world knowledge on children's comprehension of
short narrative passages. Paper presented at the annual meeting of the American
Educational Research Association, Toronto.

Richardson, M. W. (1936). Notes on the rationale of item analysis. *Psychometrica*, *1*, 69–78.

Rumelhart, D. E. & Ortony, A. (1977). The representation of knowledge in memory. In R.
Anderson, R. Spiro, & W. Montague (Eds.), *Schooling and the acquisition of knowledge*.
Hillsdale, N. J.: Lawrence Erlbaum Associates.

Smith, D. U. (1978, March). The effects of various item selection methods on the classification accuracy and classification consistency of criterion-referenced instruments.
Paper presented at the annual meeting of the American Educational Research Association, Toronto.

Traub, R. E., & Fisher, C. W. (1977). On the equivalence of constructed response and
multiple-choice tests. *Applied Psychological Measurement*, *1* (3), 355–69.

Tuinman, J. J. (1970, December). Bormuth's views on the theory of achievement items: Some
questioning comments. Paper presented at the annual meeting of the National Reading
Conference, St. Petersburg, Fla.

Tuinman, J. J. (1971). Thorndike revisited-some facts. *Reading Research Quarterly, 7* (1), 195–
202.

13   Critical factors in literacy development

Shirley Brice Heath

In the past two decades, scholars have detailed the historical courses of literacy in the contexts of modernization and nation building in Western societies. Today's students who are curious about the foundations of the literacy habits upon which their success in higher education now depends may trace the underpinnings of these habits back to ancient Greece (e.g., Havelock, 1982) and follow their linkage with scholasticism in the Middle Ages (e. g., Parkes, 1973; Bauml, 1980). In the early modern era, print culture spread first to the elites; its subsequent gradual diffusion to the middle class through schooling (e.g., Eisenstein, 1979; Maynes, 1980) came with industrialization and urbanization in nations such as England and France, and the United States.

The relatively recent field of the history of literacy in the Western world contains numerous critical evaluations of the impact of print on the spread of knowledge, achievements in socioeconomic mobility, and links between individuals and controlling bureaucratic institutions of modern societies. Common underlying themes within studies of the social development of literacy since the 16th century are: the state as the primary unit of political identification, socioeconomic conditions bringing an increasing percentage of the population into industrial and professional work forces, and promotion of a standard/national language through institutions of formal schooling. Numerous studies examine the role of literacy in the building of nationhood as individuals and groups shifted their primary identification from ethnic or local community to the nation. Corollary to this shift is the spread of print and formal schooling, which together promote a standard linguistic norm – that is, a language form identified with the state's internal administration and communications with other nations. Linked to acquisition of literacy and use of this standard language is the possibility of improved socioeconomic standing through entry into or mobility within the industrial work force.

Yet in spite of the many common themes in these studies of literacy in modern Western nations, scholars have also demonstrated the different roles literacy has played for individuals and groups at different times and places in the Western world. Currently, historians search for new and more effective methods of describing the social, economic, and political conditions which coincided with different rates, types, and effects of reading, writing, and extending print (see Graff, this volume). Increasingly, philosophers and literacy critics suggest the need for new ways of determining the cognitive and cultural changes literacy brings to the society (see Wilson's and Solomon's chapters in this volume). Two such features previously accepted as beneficial but now appropriate for re-evaluation and critical assessment are the submersion of creative approaches to problem solving and the widespread insistence upon linear thinking (Calhoun, 1973; Foucault, 1977; Illich, 1981).

This paper suggests that a foil is needed for these studies of "modern" literacy or the societal development of literacy in the contexts of modernization and nation building. With the exception of the classic collection edited by Goody (1968), scholars have given little attention to literacies among nonindustrial peoples or groups within modern nations that are marginal to the mainstream of the formally schooled work force. Goody and Watt (1968) posited a continuum of literacy, ranging from nonliterate to "fully literate" (with some groups having "restricted" literacy), and suggested the need for detailed studies of the social, cognitive, and linguistic habits of groups at points along the continuum. Such a continuum and its connotation of a single dimension of variation, with oral societies at one end and literate societies at the other, has left scholars with a dilemma: What are the "middle" groups, and how do we study them? Some scholars, such as rural sociologists and teachers of literacy or standard language, have written about the middle groups in the context of their success or failure in acquiring literacy and using it as a tool for obtaining goals often established by agents external to the group.

The modernization paradigm, or the view of the "modern" person as the "literate" person, underlies much of this work, and the majority of such studies examine these groups' reception of primers, literacy programs, and adult education brought in by outsiders. Numerous aspects of modern literacy, ranging from the use of illustrations in printed texts to modes of instruction, come with this externally imposed literacy, and agents of literacy measure the abilities of new literates along a scale of cognitive skills established for use with formally schooled populations. Thus, many such studies seem to accept the continuum and describe these groups in terms of an implicit value judgment of where they are on the path toward "full" literacy, and to what extent they are following the patterns often implied as universal for modern literate groups.

An increasing number of social scientists wish, however, to study these middle groups without value judgments or implicit denunciations of their failure to become modern literates. There are few guidelines for such work. If these middle groups are described within their own societal contexts, to what extent are the findings generalizable? If such groups are not measured by standards used for groups formally schooled in literacy, what descriptions can be used?

The study of the indigenous literacy of the Vai of Liberia by Scribner and Cole (1981) represents a major breakthrough with respect to the dilemma of studying the middle groups of Goody's continuum. These psychologists, by detailed descriptions of the contexts of uses of literacy and adaptations of standard tests of cognitive abilities, demonstrated the importance of situations for uses of literacy and the institutional and social networks for which literacy served critical purposes. Moreover, they demonstrated that the purposes, effects, and types of literacy among this group were distinct from those previously described for schooled populations, and their research methods enabled them to separate literacy effects from schooling effects. The case study of the Vai suggests the value of detailed individual case studies of literacies within the middle groups – that is, among those who have literacy, but not in terms of the forms, situations, or functions of modern literates.

The accumulation of studies that detail the sociocultural settings in which different forms of literacy emerge and develop promises to give us contrasts that may enable us to recognize some of the previously submerged or unnoticed aspects of modern literacy and to identify a wider range of social and psychological principles for framing concepts and transmitting knowledge. Two of these precursors or concomitants of literacy discussed here are the ability of a group (a) to take language apart for analysis and (b) to create institutional settings in which knowledge gained from written materials can be repeatedly talked about, interpreted, and extended. A question that is as yet unanswerable is: Did these features or the potential for their development previously exist in groups that adopted modern literacy, or did the adoption and spread of literacy bring these features? We need much more cross-societal data before we can know if these features are prior conditions or consequences of literacy.

Other precursors or concomitant conditions of the literacy of these middle groups are sometimes noted in studies of these groups. For example, it seems that in all of these communities the usual channel of communication is a language or dialect that is not standard; and if formal institutions of schooling exist for community members, pedagogues do not value the nonstandard language form for reading, writing, or speaking. Moreover, members of these communities do not have a primary identification with a group beyond their own locale, and though existence as part of a state may be acknowledged, self-identification is through primary, face-to-face interactions. Within these communities, members do not link literacy skills to work habits or opportunities for shifts in subsistence patterns. For the majority of such groups, some members are tied in some way to either agricultural production or other forms of labor that are not dependent on complex modern technology. Thus, though some members of these groups may depend upon work in industrial settings as a major means of livelihood, other group members maintain some involvement in agricultural, handicraft, or medicinal practices that are not dependent upon access to modern technology.

Taking language apart

Underlying all studies of modern literacy are implicit notions about how one can talk about language by identifying its parts and talking about how they work in systematic relationships in speaking, reading, and writing. Language arts classes and "grammar" courses in formal schooling depend upon the analysis of language into letters and sounds, parts of words and their interrelationships, and sentences and their combinations. Moreover, an early emphasis in reading and language arts classes is interpretation of two-dimensional representations of three dimensional objects. Through the artwork of early reading materials, the child learns to respond to illustrations in the text "by assigning a privileged, autonomous status to pictures as visual objects" (Ninio and Bruner, 1978). This same type of autonomous status is assigned to language, when students learn to name and describe letters, to recognize consonants, vowels, nouns, and verbs, and to analyze the structure of sentences apart from their communicative messages. These underlying notions about forms of art and language in printed texts carry over into primers and other materials for literacy teaching and reflect the following basic expectations.

1. Printed materials symbolize meaning through both their illustrations and uses of language.
2. Fundamental to comprehension and composition in writing is the ability to analyze language as a system of bits and pieces in patterns. This

analysis requires the use of a metalanguage used to dissect language as an artifact (Olson, 1984).

Critical to these basic tenets is segmenting, isolation, labeling, and describing bits of language apart from their communicative context. To become literate is to be able not only to recognize patterns in print and link these patterns in oral language, but also to talk about how one knows vowels, consonants, words, sentences, etc. (See Herriman's and Tuinman's chapters in this volume.) Yet some cultures do not appear to conceptualize either their art forms or their language by abstracting their parts or features and developing a terminology for talking about these.

Anthropologists and psychologists report on groups that have intricate and detailed forms of pictorial art, carrying complex and symbolic meanings. Many members of these groups can recognize "good" and "bad" art and instruct the young on the production of art forms in which almost imperceptible differences carry serious meaning. Yet it is not necessarily the case that these teachers or masters of art forms can identify specific parts or name the features characterizing such differences (e.g., Childs and Greenfield, 1980). Moreover, individuals who excel in such artistic production may not transfer the skills of visual perception used in their indigenous art forms to seeing letters or words in written texts. Discriminating among shapes of letters or words requires recognition of whole shapes and also parts of shapes, and ways of distinguishing these (e.g., right – left or up – down orientation, or by the initial and final letters of words). However, these means of taking apart either illustrations or print in written texts may not be at all compatible with the ways in which some groups distinguish aspects of the design of their own art forms.

Gudschinsky (1969, reprinted 1979) pointed out that even in communities where there are elaborately developed art forms, teaching people to recognize simple illustrations as portrayed in primers could take more effort than that required to teach them to read. She reported that a group of European children from 6 to 12 years of age recognized geometric forms fastest, words next most rapidly, nonsense syllables more slowly, and pictures of familiar objects most slowly. Recent research on mainstream school-children in the United States indicates that pictures do not necessarily aid them in comprehending text, and that the interpretation of pictorial illustrations is as rule-bound and in many ways as complex as decoding and comprehending printed texts (Samuels, 1970; Concannon, 1975; Schallert, 1980).

Olson (1984) has pointed out that "highly literate parents may teach their children a distinctive orientation to language in the very process of teaching them to talk" (p. 186). He has pointed out that parents who "pre-school" their young children in literacy skills have the view that language is an artifact that can be examined in bits and pieces and named and analyzed apart from the representational or expressive meaning it carries. Ways in which this view is expressed by mainstream parents have been described in detail by Ninio and Bruner (1978), Scollon and Scollon (1981), Cochran-Smith (1984), and Heath (1982, 1983a). All of these studies illustrate the ways in which adults "model" language for their pre-literates and teach them to talk about language by using a metalanguage that refers to the structure and properties of language. These children learn to name and recognize parts and wholes in language and to describe the features of letters, words, stories, titles, and so on. They learn that the written text is autonomous, capable of standing alone without belonging to a specific individual or situation.

Thus, there is increasing psychological and cultural evidence that the view of language "as such" is basic to the literate or literacy development of individuals, and that this view underlies materials, methods, and motivations for teaching literacy in societies around the world. Though reports about other views of language are rare in the scholarly literature, there are some descriptions that indicate the ways in which these views affect the degree of readiness with which certain groups accept literacy.

Hollenbach (1979), reporting on the Copala Trique in Mexico, observed that this group considered language "as a vehicle of communication . . . not . . . as an object to be dissected, nor a toy to be played with." Within this group, speakers do not simplify their speech in the ways some linguists have discussed as universal processes of simplification (Ferguson, 1978, 1982). They neither slow down their speech nor break it into small chunks; they "usually cannot answer any question that focuses on the linguistic form of an utterance, as opposed to its content" (Hollenbach, 1979). They do not engage in language play. Single Trique words do not constitute utterances; a two-word sequence is the smallest natural utterance. Moreover, the structure of Trique is such that any one clause-level constituent may permute to a position in front of the predicate. However, any permutations that do not follow the normal order of predicate first have a special focus that is determined partly on the basis of the preceding sentence. It is not difficult to imagine the consequences of these features of language use for the teaching of literacy. The usual initial reading materials depend on pulling apart language into letters, syllables, and words, in order to enable the new reader to understand how combinations of units provide meaning. In this group, such techniques could not be used and had to be abandoned in favor of using short connected narratives based on Trique daily life. Moreover, the usual habit of using permutations to give practice in using new words in different contexts created problems, since such permutations in oral language were used only to give special focus in context. Thus, isolated permuted sentences led the Trique to question the larger context in which such sentences would naturally fit if they were to make sense. An advantage of their approach to language was that they did not have to be taught that written materials are supposed to communicate meaning; they transferred their view of oral language as a vehicle of communication to written language, and in the early stages of reading, they searched for meaning.

Such reports of oral language uses that seem inconceivable in modern literate societies occur with surprising frequency in the research literature that describes functional literacy programs or the initial school experiences of children in developing countries. Some communities, for example, do not, except under very special circumstances, repeat verbatim something that has been said either by them or by another speaker (Haviland, 1980). It should go without saying that children in these communities grow up acquiring not only the structures of these languages, but also their uses. Thus, when these children enter a formal schooling setting, such commonplace approaches to teaching as examining discrete features of written language in isolation, rearranging combinations of words, and repeating sentences or isolated words for practice in both decoding and explaining what oɲe comprehends from the printed word are unexpected requirements that may be diametrically opposed to customary habits. Moreover, though detailed and extensive ethnographic evidence on ways in which adults talk to children in their communities is not available, it is reasonably safe to assume that if processes such as simplification and verbatim repetition of language segments are not exhibited among adults, these processes have not been employed by adults interacting with children learning their mother tongue. Schieffelin's work (1979) among the Kaluli of Papua, New Guinea, and Ochs's work (1982) in Samoan communities suggest that the labeling and sentence-extending practices portrayed as universally common in a majority of child language-acquisition research do not occur in these communities. These groups also do not use the simplifying and attention-focusing strategies (such as the use of "teaching questions") upon which early reading instruction in formal schooling for both children and adults usually depends (Ochs and Schieffelin, 1984). Summarized elsewhere is research (Heath, 1983b) in a black working-class community of the Southeastern United States in which adults neither simplify their language to children nor read to them following the labeling and attention-focusing strategies Ninio and Bruner (1978) have suggested are universal.

As yet, there is relatively little research that gives us detailed insights on ways in which speakers in different communities talk about their language and how their views relate to their acquisition and retention of literacy skills. In particular, we need studies of what happens to basic literacy skills once a formerly nonliterate group attains such skills: How are they extended and interrelated with social needs and functions so that they can be retained? It is particularly important that scholars of what we have termed here "middle groups" attend to the question of whether features of talk about language implicit in formal-schooling approaches to language were indigenous – that is, existed prior to the introduction of literacy – or whether they developed with literacy skills. With such information, we can then begin to judge the influence of these features on whether or not members of these groups (a) learn to read and write only with excessive effort; (b) come to see written uses of language as unrelated to oral uses and consequently give literacy an unnecessarily marginal cultural position; or (c) reject literacy as having no relevance to the ways in which one makes sense of the world.

Institutional reinforcements for literacy

Institutional reinforcements represent a second important factor for examining literacy in nonindustrialized communities or in communities marginal to the mainstream of a highly formally schooled work force. Is it necessary to have social and technical supports for literacy beyond the family or others in a primary, face-to-face network? Does the retention of literacy depend on the decontextualizing and depersonalizing of the content of written materials? To what extent does oral debate on the possibilities of turning literacy information into new values and behaviors facilitate the retention of literacy habits? Paulo Freire and liberation theologists in Latin America strongly suggest that literacy planners establish institutional contexts that foster talk among new literates about the meaning of written materials for new ways of thinking and acting in their own lives (Freire, 1970). Are there indigenous developments with respect to such uses of literacy, and do these make the retention and extension of literacy possible in communities that are not centrally engaged with formal schooling and do not constitute an urban industrial work force?

Studies of a modern peasant-organized literacy movement in the village of Ayou in Southern Benin (formerly Dahomey) illustrate what can happen when a grassroots self-help movement links literacy to an institution that provides extended opportunities for talk about written technical and sociopolitical information (Elwert, 1979; Giesecke and Elwert, 1982; Tchitchi, 1982). Among an adult population with a literacy rate of less than 1%, a self-help group decided to produce their own literacy materials to exist side by side with oral and graphic forms indigenous to the society. For centuries the people of Ayou had handed down elements of knowledge in proverbs, songs, and stories, summarized in a proverbial sentence, the *loo*. This sentence could also be symbolized through a drawing that represented its essence in symbols, forming a *loo-wema*. The self-help literacy group produced leaflets containing the proverbs in both drawn and written forms. All members of the group had copies, thus making the leaflets "public." Traditionally, certain types of information had been controlled through a hierarchical organization, such as the religious vodun groups, and most recently through formal schools. Talk in a nonhierarchical institutional setting enabled new learners to overcome their earlier fears that learning from books brought power for doing harm to others.

Extended oral discussion about written knowledge became an integral part of a web of supports that the peasants created to maintain their literacy. In Ayou, some of the materials for reading were leaflets and posters on herbalist medicine, an area of knowledge previously limited to a small group of specialists. The self-help group chose to distribute copies of the leaflets to 11 members, and to make public their information both through this distribution and through open discussion of their contents as well as of plans for producing more literacy materials. The self-help group thus made a conscious decision to use "collective sociopolitical discussion" (Giesecke and Elwert, 1982) among equals as an integral part of their literacy program. Talk surrounded the production of texts (leaflets with proverbs and tables of words for study), and in this talk, group members linked the written proverbs to traditional knowledge and to new, extended sociopolitical meanings.

The pattern of development of this indigenous out-of-school literacy movement was such that institutional membership and group support of literacy became necessary to provide a stable and ordered or somewhat predictable background of experience for the interpretation of written materials. The opportunities for talk about written materials that such institutional membership provided increased the amount of shared background brought to the interpretation of autonomous texts and thus made a common basis of comprehension possible. Giesecke and Elwert (1982) suggest that institutions provide "an ordered space" and "define rules and meanings and guarantee their transmission to the new learners" (p. 31). These authors further note that often these institutions use control and sanctions as part of the learning and ordering process. These characteristics are similar to those of such powerful institutions as the state, the church, the school, and the industrial workplace; the key differences in the Ayou project were its indigenous initiation and the cooperative nature of the interpretive group of literates. Their grassroots organization provided opportunity for repetitive, overlapping, and multiply reinforcing talk about reading and writing.

The need for a network of such stabilizing and ordering institutions is perhaps most obvious when new literates come from different dialects to texts that reflect some standardization of several dialects. In these cases, the institution's resources include some form of codification of the language or an expert in the codification principle behind the production of written materials. Moreover, the coming together in the network of institutions provides opportunities for talk about the text which helps new learners understand the meanings of words and develop "rules of correspondence between the established standard text and the new realms of life" (Giesecke and Elwert, 1982, p. 31).

Is there evidence that the kinds of institutions that support literacy make a difference? Does it matter whether these institutions are indigenous or imposed by outside change agents? Though sparse, some evidence from both historical sources and modern economic and social change programs suggests that not only does the source of institutions matter, but the extent of interdependence of literacy-supporting institutions and economic and political conditions will vary markedly from one community to the next and across cultural and national boundaries.

Examining the methods of reading and writing propagated by Valentin Ickelsamer in southern Germany in the early 16th century, Giesecke (1975) provides a case study of literacy program initiated before formal schooling. Ickelsamer based his grassroots movement on the then revolutionary notion that to "judge for oneself" requires literacy; thus the common people had to learn to read in order to be able to learn about and judge technical innovations. The spread of literacy within this movement was accomplished without schools, although it was dependent on the use of Ickelsamer's literacy manuals and the help of a literate person. However, literacy learning by Ickelsamer's methods was banned after 1545, and subsequently adult literacy was linked with formal schooling. The rate of illiteracy increased following this shift from deschooled methods to formal schooling (Giesecke and Elwert, 1982, p. 27). A similar decrease in literacy retention and in the spread of literacy to new learners accompanied the shift from the peasant-initiated literacy movement in Benin to formal schooling (Tchitchi, 1982). Thomas (1974) suggests also that in terms of both individual retention of literacy and cost-benefit ratios in adult programs, providing some literates with materials and institutional settings for information exchange and group membership may do more to spread literacy and technical information than extensive formal schooling efforts.

Other studies suggest that neither formal schooling nor externally imposed adult literacy programs ensure the spread of technical information and the adoption by individuals of changed behaviors which planners argue could lead to improved socioeconomic status. For example, Fliegel (1966) examined the relationships between literacy and exposure to information about agriculture among farmers in Southern Brazil and demonstrated that literacy did not enhance receptivity to information about technical development among these farmers. Moreover, contact with agricultural technicians was not influenced by either literacy or level of education, and exposure to other nonprint sources of agricultural information was only moderately influenced by these factors. His study suggests that the failure of agricultural demonstration, discussion, and extension of knowledge from print and nonprint sources left the farmers without the necessary forum through which they could build and expand upon their new common base of knowledge regarding technical development.

Detailed studies of variations in institutional networks at the community level are rare. Missing are detailed ethnographic studies that would provide community-level evidence to help answer critical questions raised in studies of continental and national groupings. For example, Schramm and Ruggels (1967) divided 82 developing countries into Latin American, Middle Eastern, and Asian areas and correlated literacy with GNP, mass media consumption, and urbanization. There were vast differences: the correlation of literacy with urbanization was .04 for Latin American nations and .64 for Asian countries. Why is urbanization apparently a prime mover in some situations, GNP and mass media consumption in others? Why does literacy develop ahead of urbanization and income in some places, behind them in others? There is growing evidence to suggest that institutions that can develop and sustain a role for literacy at the local level may make a considerable difference in how new information enters nonindustrialized communities or those communities in developed nations that are marginal to the mainstream schooled population. The development and maintenance of such institutions seems to depend, however, on cultural factors that operate at the community level – factors such as the previous role of hierarchical control of knowledge, the availability of leisure time in which to debate information gained from literacy, and the motivation to carry new information into action.

A comparative case study

Illustration of the powerful role that different types of institutional networks and varying perceptions of language play in the acquisition and retention of literacy can be gained only by comparison of carefully detailed studies of communities. I summarize here data from a longitudinal study of two working-class communities in the Southeastern United States (Heath, 1983b). Both were marginal to the mainstream schooled communities that surrounded them, though members of both communities depended upon work in textile mills as their major source of income. Within both communities, some members of families kept gardens or worked cooperatively on a part-time basis with relatives who still owned farms. Roadville is a white working-class community of families steeped for four generations in the life of the textile mill; earlier generations had lived in the Southern Appalachian mountains and had come to the Piedmont Carolinas in the 1920s to find work in the rapidly developing textile industry. Trackton is a black working-class community whose older generations have been brought up on the land or working for other landowners; only since the 1960s have they found work in the textile mills. Children of both communities are judged unsuccessful in school, and school authorities have traditionally blamed the failure of these students on the fact that the school-related skills of reading and writing are not reinforced or promoted in their homes by their parents. The data reported here are based on ethnographic fieldwork carried out in the two communities (and in the adults' workplaces and children's schools) from 1969 to 1977 (Heath, 1983b).

Both Trackton and Roadville are literate communities, in the sense that the residents of each are able to read printed and written materials encountered in their daily lives and can on occasion produce written messages as part of the total pattern of communication in the community. In both communities, children go to school with certain expectancies of print, and in Trackton especially, children have a keen sense that reading is something one does to learn something one needs to know (see Heath, this volume). In both groups, residents turn from spoken to written uses of language and vice versa as the occasion demands, and the two modes of language expression seem to supplement and reinforce each other. Yet there are vast differences between the two communities – located only a few miles apart, and both speaking a nonstandard communicative norm – in the ways in which children and adults interact in the preschool years (Heath, 1982). Trackton and Roadville view children's learning of lan-

Instrumental	Reading to gain information for practical needs of daily life (telephone dials, clocks, bills and checks, labels on products, reminder notes, school messages, patterns for dressmaking).
News-related	Reading to gain information about third parties or distant events (newspaper items, church denominational magazines, memos from the mill on the union, health and safety, etc.).
Confirmational	Reading to check, confirm, or learn facts or beliefs (the Bible, Sunday School materials, camper or sports magazines, newspaper stories, appliance warranties and directions).
Social/interactional (primarily women and children)	Reading to gain information pertinent to social linkages and forthcoming activities (church newsletters; greeting cards; letters; newspaper features, especially on sports page).
Recreational/educational	Reading for temporary entertainment or for planning a recreational event; (comics in newspapers; brochures on campgrounds; advertisements for movies or musical programs; ball game schedules, scores, and line-ups; bedtime stories to preschoolers).

Figure 13-1. Types of uses of reading in Roadville (listed in relative order of frequency of occasions when time on these types of tasks exceeded five minutes per day).

guage from radically different perspectives: In Trackton children "learn to talk," whereas in Roadville, adults "teach them how to talk."

Figures 13-1 through 13-4 illustrate the differences in the ways in which reading and writing are used in Trackton and Roadville homes. In Roadville, reading is viewed as "a useful habit and a good one besides." People often talk positively about the importance of reading, but they do little actual reading. Thus, in Figure 13-1, one should note that some of the uses of reading occurred only rarely for most individuals, though the reading materials and the belief in their value existed in every Roadville home. I classify the uses of reading as instrumental, news-related, confirmational, social/interactional, and recreational/educational.

There are relatively few links between Roadville's reading materials and outside institutions. The external links to the instrumental uses of reading are primarily numeracy based and come from local businesses and schools; news-related uses come from the church and the mill; and confirmational and recreational from the mill, the church, and community recreation workers. Social/interactional links come from the church and secondary, television-reinforced sports events. In a sample of 72 days

Memory aids	Writing to serve as a memory aid for both the writer and others (grocery lists, labels in baby books, outlines of the sequence and content of circle meetings, frequently called telephone numbers jotted in front of phone book).
Substitutes for or reaffirmations of oral messages	Writing used when direct oral communication was not possible or to follow up on oral exchanges (notes for tardiness or absence from school, assignments following class discussions, messages left by adults for children coming home before parent arrived home).
Financial	Writing to record numerals and to write out amounts and purposes of expenditures and signatures (writing checks; signing forms; filling out church, school, and mail-order forms).
Social/interactional	Writing to give information and extend courtesies and greetings pertinent to maintaining social linkages (letters, notes on commercial greeting cards, thank-you notes).

Figure 13–2. Types of uses of writing in Roadville (listed in relative order of frequency of occasions when time on these types of tasks exceeded five minutes per day).

selected over eight years, Roadville adults did not average more than sixteen minutes of reading per day. On the sample days, they exchanged or solicited information from others in institutional settings outside the home on the average of eight minutes per day. The method for determining the amount of time during which Roadville adults exchanged or solicited information that was either directly or indirectly related to topics read was to identify topics from reading material and relate these to conversations individuals held during their daily activities outside the home. The only topic excluded from this analysis was the weather, since the topic material usually read on the weather was the "report," a brief blurb that averaged only 33 words at the top corner of the morning paper. However, if individuals discussed materials gathered from a newspaper feature story on a football game (which included information not covered in the television broadcast), this topic and these minutes were counted. In essence, reading for Roadville residents did not serve the purpose of introducing new information and that created the desire for information exchange with others.

Writing followed a similar pattern, in that, as Figure 13–2 indicates, most writing was done strictly for individual purposes and was highly restricted in scope. I classify the uses of writing as memory aids, substitutes for or reaffirmations of oral messages, financial, and social/interactional. Roadville parents did not like to write notes to the school, for example;

Memory aids (primarily used by women)	Writing to serve as a reminder for the writer and, only occasionally, for others (telephone numbers, notes on calendars).
Substitutes for oral messages (primarily used by women)	Writing used when direct oral communication was not possible or would prove embarrassing (notes for tardiness or absence from school, greeting cards, letters).
Financial	Writing to record numerals and to write out amounts and accompanying notes (signatures on checks and public forms, figures and notes for income tax preparation).
Public records (church only)	Writing to announce the order of the church services and forthcoming events and to record financial and policy decisions (church bulletins, reports of the church building fund committee).

Figure 13-3. Types and uses of writing in Trackton (listed in relative order of frequency of occasions when time on these types of tasks exceeded five minutes per day).

Instrumental	Reading to accomplish practical tasks of daily life (telephone dials, clocks, bills and checks, price tags, street signs, house numbers).
Social/interactional/ recreational	Reading to maintain social relationships, make plans, and introduce topics for discussion and storytelling (greeting cards, cartoons, letters, newspaper features, political flyers, announcements of community meetings).
News-related	Reading to learn about third parties or distant events (local news items, circulars from the community center or school). school).
Confirmational	Reading to gain support for attitudes or beliefs already held (Bible, brochures on cars, loan notes, bills).

Figure 13-4. Types of uses of reading in Trackton (listed in relative order of frequency of occasions when time on these types of tasks exceeded five minutes per day).

they preferred to send oral messages with their children. With the exception of church materials, there were few materials they wrote that were subsequently expanded in oral form. The program outline for a circle meeting at church or the tentative agenda of a meeting were the usual limits of the writing Roadville adults engaged in that was followed up in any way by oral communication. In Roadville churches, the pastor kept the church records with the help of the superintendent of the Sunday School; thus it was not customary for a millworker to be called on to record minutes or prepare, say, building fund reports.

In Trackton churches, on the other hand, laymen carried most of the responsibility for recording and reporting orally the business of the church. Thus, many of the members were called upon for help in these tasks, and many members in a group association carried them out. Figure 13–3 indicates the writing for the public record done in Trackton. This type of writing followed business meetings and building fund sessions and preceded preaching Sundays, which came only twice a month in the churches attended by Trackton residents. There was also considerable group reading (see Figure 13–4) on the open porches of the community, in which individuals shared letters received and discussions of newspaper features and brochures on political office-seekers. The pattern for these oral reading-aloud sessions was for one individual to read the piece and then for members of the group to contribute related experiences. For example, the reading of an obituary would call forth recollections of the individual's life, assessments of the merits of past deeds, and the future of the remaining family. Following this discussion of the written text, which could take an hour or more, group members would usually give a summary-type series of statements about the individual or the larger relevance of either the course of the individual's life or the fate of the family (cf. the *loo-wema* used by the Ayou self-help group).

In Trackton churches, both sermons and hymns are written and are extended orally from the written text. Once again, the extension is joint, in that numerous members share in its creation. The same is true of discussions of materials provided by the mill or by politicians who visit the community. One person reads, and others join in the negotiation of the meaning of the text according to the contextual experiences of Trackton residents. New games at Christmas, new gadgets for automobiles, and directions for repairing broken wiring produce about the same type of shared negotiation of the meaning of written materials. In short, written material in Trackton never stands alone. Members write little and almost never read alone unless they wish to be designated social misfits. Reading is a group activity. Women shop together, discussing advertisements and prices; men discuss the brochures on new cars. Adults expect very young children to be aware of price differences and to recognize different brand names, but these expectations of reading are functionally related to daily living.

There are few occasions in Trackton for the reading or writing of extended texts by an individual. Thus, individuals have limited opportunities to practice decoding; reading aloud is usually a public performance and the weaker readers need not expose themselves, since they can pass the letter or newspaper feature on to someone who reads and performs better than they. Moreover, everyone is equally eligible to contribute to the interpretation of the text at the level of shared experiences, and to debate the meaning and relevance of the words for the individuals or groups he or she knows. Yet almost all texts read aloud are synthesized and assessed in some way unless there are several intervening events. Thus, the Trackton residents as a group manage to retain their literacy habits, on the average, for a much higher percentage of their time than do Roadville residents. In a selection of 72 days made over eight years, Trackton residents spent an average of 46 minutes per day in oral interactions as follow-ups from reading or writing. Their primary institutional link for reading and writing was the church, but this institution followed the same patterns of group composition and interpretation of written materials as those followed elsewhere in the community. Detailed historical analysis of church records by Bethel (1979) indicate that this is a long-established practice, and written church records strongly reflect community familiarity both with the format and formulaic expressions of written materials and with the group negotiation process of the church meetings that surround building funds, worship committees, and the like.

In both Trackton and Roadville, the patterns of uses of literacy and the presumed benefits of literacy do not match those predicted from the general literature. The children of both Roadville and Trackton do not fare well in formal schooling, and neither group has the receptive and productive skills and values surrounding reading and writing that fit those described for "modern" communities. Written materials are not a major source of new information for either community, and neither group writes to distribute ideas beyond their own primary group. In neither community does literacy bear any direct relationship to job status or chances for upward mobility. The members of these communities make an income greater than that of beginning school teachers in their region. Though work may be seasonal, wages compare favorably with those of many other occupations in their regions.

Of the two critical factors for literacy discussed in this chapter, each of these communities has only one. In Roadville, adults regard language as an artifact and introduce their children to talk about talk at an early age; however, Roadville residents do not carry their knowledge from written sources into debate in institutions beyond their family. In Trackton, adults do not assign an autonomous status to language by taking it apart, identifying its parts, and asking children to name and describe letters, words, two-dimensional drawings, or passages of text. Trackton children, unlike Roadville youngsters, are not "preschooled" to know language as an artifact that can be examined in bits and pieces and analyzed outside its representational or expressive meaning. However, Trackton adults do debate knowledge from written sources which originate outside the community, and the church and its related social groups demand oral negotiation of written materials. Trackton adults add new information to their repertoire of knowledge by drawing from written sources and debating this information orally to determine its relevance for their actions.

Children in Trackton come to school knowing how to read many of the instrumental pieces of information around them, because they have been given roles of responsibility that depend on such reading (see Heath, this volume). Yet they cannot respond appropriately to the ways in which primary grade-level teachers expect them to analyze and talk about language as such (see de Castell & Luke and Herriman, this volume). Thus Trackton children fail in language arts classes in the early years of school, unable to acquire the school's reading and writing habits. By the upper elementary grades, when teachers expect students to read to learn, the students have a record of failure that many cannot overcome by reinstating for school use their "preschooled" success in reading information for instrumental purposes. Neither do they see the possibility of transforming their community's ways of public negotiation of the meaning of texts to the school's demands that meaning be private and reading and writing a task for individuals working alone.

Roadville children come to school well versed in the decontextualization of reading and in school-approved approaches to written texts as artifacts. They have had extensive experiences with bedtime stories, workbooks, and Sunday School activities related in form and function to school practices. They are successful in their early language arts experiences, but their skills fail them by the end of the primary grades, when they are asked to move beyond the text to interpretation based on their own experiences and generalizable evidence (Heath, 1983). In their communities, literacy has not served them or their parents beyond the routines of practicing literacy skills. They have not seen their parents incorporate information from written materials into their value or behavioral systems; they have not known their parents' literacy skills to affect their participation in institutions beyond their primary group.

Conclusions

We are left with questions about the importance of both institutional supports for literacy and talk about language as prerequisites or consequences of literacy. In Trackton and Roadville, examples of Goody's "middle groups," different ways of talking about language and linking literacy to institutions coincided with very different patterns of using reading and writing. In addition, the research of Giesecke on an indigenous 16th-century literacy movement, and of Elwert and Tchitchi on a modern-day self-help movement, gives further evidence that in very different cultures, places, and times, views of language and the establishment of institutions in which talk about written sources takes place are important for retaining and expanding literacy. From the literacy teaching and rural sociology literature, scattered reports also suggest the importance of viewing language as an artifact and of providing institutional settings for oral exchange of knowledge gained from literate sources. Formal schooling and adult literacy programs based on assumptions drawn from traditional language arts curricula carry little influence on the transmission and adoption of new information in communities that do not have institutions that can sustain both oral debate and new sources of written materials.

Community studies that detail practices of using and producing written materials are needed to provide data on the range of types of social and cultural environments that facilitate or restrict the development of factors such as talk about language and institutional supports for literacy. However, we suggest that such detailed studies will demonstrate that in any society the following two factors play critical roles in the acquisition, retention, and extension of reading and writing habits.

1. Fundamental to comprehension in reading and composition in writing is the ability to analyze language as a system of bits and pieces in patterns. This analysis requires the learning of a metalanguage used to dissect language as an artifact by segmenting, isolating, labeling, and describing bits of language apart from their communicative contexts. To become literate is to be able not only to recognize patterns in print and to link these patterns in oral language but also to talk about how one knows vowels, words, sentences, etc. Some language groups may carry within their habits of talking about language the precursors of the development of a metalanguage; other groups may have to acquire, along with literacy, new ways of viewing language and new occasions for interpreting what it is that written language signifies.
2. Where there are written texts, there must be voluntary groups to study

them if literacy is to be retained. Textual communities must be developed to allow opportunities for talk about knowledge gained through reading and transmitted in writing. The process of learning from written materials includes reflecting on the meaning of such knowledge for changed values and behaviors. For literacy as a habit to be sustained, interaction must take place around the ultimate goal of determining an agreed-upon meaning for the text. Thus the maintenance and extension of functions and types of literacy within a society depend upon opportunities for participation in multiple and reinforcing occasions for oral construction of the shared background needed to interpret written materials.

References

Bauml, F. (1980). Varieties and consequences of medieval literacy and illiteracy. *Speculum, 55,* 237–65.

Bethel, E. (1979). *Social and linguistic trends in a black community.* Unpublished manuscript, Department of Sociology, Lander College.

Calhoun, D. (1973). *The intelligence of a people.* Princeton, N.J.: Princeton University Press.

Childs, C. P., and Greenfield, P. M. (1980). Informal modes of learning and teaching: The case of Zinacanteco weaving. In N. Warren (Ed.), *Studies in cross-cultural psychology* (Vol. 2). London: Academic Press.

Cochran-Smith, M. (1984). *The making of a reader.* Norwood, N. J.: Ablex.

Concannon, S. J. (1975). Illustrations in books for children: Review of research. *Reading Teacher, 29,* 254–56.

Eisenstein, E. (1979). *The printing press as an agent of change.* Cambridge: Cambridge University Press.

Elwert, G. (1979). *Alphabetisation in Ayou.* Untersuchung einer Bauerlichen Selbsthilfe – Bewegung. In Osnabrucker Beitrage zur Sprachtheorie.

Ferguson, C. A. (1978). Talking to children: A search for universals. In J. H. Greenberg (Ed.), *Universals of human language: Method and theory* (Vol. 1). Stanford, Ca.: Stanford University Press.

Ferguson, C. A. (1982). Simplified registers and linguistic theory. In Loraine K. Obler and Lisa Menn (Eds.), *Exceptional language and linguistics.* New York: Academic Press.

Fliegel, E. (1966). Literacy and exposure to instrumental information among farmers in Southern Brazil. *Rural Sociology, 31* (1), 15–28.

Foucault, M. (1977). *Language, counter-memory, and practice.* Ithaca, N.Y.: Cornell University Press.

Freire, P. (1970). Cultural action for freedom. In *Harvard Educational Review,* Monograph Series, No. 1, Cambridge, Ma.

Giesecke, M. (1975). *Lesen und Schreiben in der deutschen Screibescule des ausgehenden 15 und beginnenden 16, Jahrhunderts,* Unveroffentl Examsarbeit, Universitat Hamburg.

Giesecke, M., and Elwert, G. (1982). Adult literacy in a context of cultural revolution: Structural parallels of the literacy process in sixteenth century Germany and present-day Benin. Paper presented at X World Congress of Sociology, Subsection 9.

Goody, J. (Ed.). (1968). *Literacy in traditional societies.* Cambridge: Cambridge University Press.

Goody, J., and Watt, I. (1968). The consequences of literacy. In Jack Goody (Ed.), *Literacy in Traditional Societies.* Cambridge: Cambridge University Press.

Gudschinsky, S. (1979). Pre-reading: Some misperceptions about prereading. *Notes on literacy. Selected Articles, Issues 1–19.* Dallas, Te.: Summer Institute of Linguistics.

Havelock, E. (1982). *The literate revolution in ancient Greece and its consequences.* Princeton, N. J.: Princeton University Press.

Haviland, J. (1980). *What happens when there is no food from heaven?* Working papers in Anthropology. Australian National University, Canberra.

Heath, S. B. (1982). What no bedtime story means: Narrative skills at home and school. *Language in Society, 11* (2), 49–75.

Heath, S. B. (1983a). A lot of talk about nothing. *Language Arts, 60,* 999–1007.

Heath, S. B. (1983b). *Ways with words: Language, life, and work in communities and classrooms.* Cambridge: Cambridge University Press.

Hollenbach, B. (1979). The importance of naturalness in literacy materials. *Notes on literacy. Selected Articles, Issues 1–19.* Dallas, Tex.: Summer Institute of Linguistics.

Illich, I. (1981). *Shadow work.* Boston: M. Boyars.

Maynes, M. B. (1980). Work or school in the making of Frenchmen. *Historical Reflections, 7* 1–15.

Ninio, A., and Bruner, J. (1978). The achievement and antecedents of labelling. *Journal of Child Language, 5,* 1–15.

Ochs, E. (1982). Talking to children in Western Samoa. *Language in Society, 11,* 77–104.

Ochs, E., and Schieffelin, B. (1984). Language acquisition and socialization: Three developmental stories and their implications. In R. Shweder and R. LeVine (Eds.), *Culture and its acquisition.* Cambridge: Cambridge University Press.

Olson, D. B. (1984). "See! Jumping!" The antecedents of literacy. In H. Goelman, A. Oberg, and F. Smith (Eds.), *Awakening to literacy.* Exeter, N. H.: Heinemann Educational Books.

Parkes, M. B. (1973). The literacy of the laity. In D. Daiches and A. Thorlby (Eds.), *The medieval world.* New York: Aldous.

Samuels, S. J. (1970). Effects of pictures on learning to read, comprehension, and attitudes. *Review of Educational Research, 40,* 397–407.

Schallert, D. I. (1980). The role of illustrations in reading comprehension. In R. J. Spiro, B. C. Bruce, and W. F. Brewer (Eds.), *Theoretical issues in reading comprehension.* Hillsdale, N. J.: Lawrence Erlbaum Associates.

Schieffelin, B. (1979). Getting it together: An ethnographic approach to the study of the development of communicative competence. In E. Ochs and B. Schieffelin (Eds.), *Developmental pragmatics.* New York: Academic Press.

Schramm, R., & Ruggels, D. (1967). Cross-national surveys in literacy. *World Politics, 13* (2), 64–75.

Scollon, R., and Scollon, S. (1981). *Narrative, literacy, and face in interethnic communication.* Norwood, N. J.: Ablex.

Scribner, S., and Cole, M. (1981). *The psychology of literacy.* Cambridge, Ma.: Harvard University Press.

Taylor, D. (1983). *Family literacy: Young children learning to read and write.* Exeter, N. H.: Heinemann Educational Books.

Tchitchi, T. (1982). *L'ecriture comme condition du developpement de la culture: Le cas de quelques societes d'Afrique noire.* Paper presented at X World Congress of Sociology, Subsection 9.

Thomas, H. (1974). Literacy without formal education: A case study in Pakistan. *Economic Development and Cultural Change, 22,* 489–95.

Part IV

Matters practical

14   Foundations for literacy:
pre-reading development and instruction

Jana Mason

Parents often ask, "Should we teach our child to read?" or "Will it harm our child if we teach her to read?" Even "How should we teach?" has been difficult to answer because not only have parents' roles in instructing their children never been clearly defined but until recently, reading instruction of any sort before the first grade was considered inappropriate.

Preparation for reading in the home has centered instead on the whole child, involving drawing, exploration of concepts, and language. Reading was often tied to religion and to reciting, if not interpreting, the Bible or other sacred writings. Indeed, until the 20th century, preparation for reading was seldom distinguished from its function as an occupational or religious tool (see de Castell & Luke, this volume; Gammage, 1979; Graff, this volume).

In the first half of this century, when the predominant occupation was farming, preparation for reading was called "reading readiness." In 1925, William S. Gray listed six prerequisites to reading: facility in the use of ideas, wide experience, sufficient command of English, wide vocabulary, accurate enunciation, and a desire to read. The issue of when to teach young children to read was raised then but dismissed. A review by Colthart (1979) documents how beliefs against early reading were supported despite contrary empirical evidence. For example, Gesell (1940), in his widely read guide to the study of preschool children, decried early reading instruction:

The attempt to force reading by the age of six frequently leads to temporary or permanent maladjustment and more or less serious disturbance in the course of normal school achievement.[p. 208]

Because of similar pronouncements by many, it was common practice to discourage parental reading instruction. School reading books were (and still are) unavailable in bookstores and were seldom allowed out of school buildings. Arguments for this practice are that parents might interfere

233

with teachers' instruction, that children might "read ahead" at home (and be bored at school), or that a younger sibling might see or read the next year's reading book. In other words, books for children to read in school have been treated as sacrosanct. Ironically, there are a large number of books for children to listen to and many materials for them to read once they have learned. Only the materials to lead children across the threshold of literacy are scarce. It is as though there is a conspiracy to keep parents from helping their children to read.

Today, in keeping with the general loosening of social restrictions, parents are not criticized for providing reading instruction. Still, they are not clearly advised about what they can do. Benjamin Spock's popular book on child care contained no information about reading. White (1975) issued this warning:

> ... reading simple, entertaining stories to your child, particularly at night before he goes to bed, seems to be a good idea. On the other hand, if you insist on story reading during the waking hours when the child wants to be doing something else, out of some sort of notion that it is an absolute essential or very desirable, I think both you and your child will pay for it. [pp. 171–72]

Current books on the subject (e.g., Dodson, 1981) are a confusing mixture of reading readiness games, first-grade-level phonics activities, and word drills. Since clear advice has not been forthcoming, many parents and teachers do not understand that literacy truly begins at home. Teachers assume they are responsible for most instruction in reading, and parents continue to be unsure about whether or how they should prepare their children. Yet, as is noted by many of the contributors to this volume, literacy encompasses far more than reading school books. Contexts for literacy go beyond the classroom setting, placing parents in a better position than teachers to offer varying kinds of reading experiences and to help children realize how and why reading is important.

Problems with the traditional view of reading

A traditional view of how children begin to read places teachers in a prominent position. It is supposed that parents prepare children to *want* to read but then children do not begin learning until teachers provide formal instruction in letter identification, letter sounds, word reading, and story reading.

There are two problems with this view. The first is that school reading instruction is not necessarily successful. Some children learn to read easily while others do not, regardless of the amount of instruction. To avoid blaming the teacher or educational materials for the children's failure, the traditional view is supplemented by the notion of maturation differences among children. That is, those who learn to read easily are termed "more mature" while those who do not are called "less mature" and may be held back for another year of kindergarten or first-grade instruction, on the assumption that they will later be "ready to learn." Alternately, they are removed from the classroom and given remedial instruction. These approaches, however, assume that there is something wrong with the children rather that with the instruction. They must either be brain-damaged (having a nonspecific learning disability) or mentally retarded. Labeled as dyslexic or retarded, they can be placed in special classes and removed from an accountability system, so they need not be expected to become good readers. Thus, the traditional view that schooling is successful at producing readers is upheld at the expense of some children. Those children who fail to read are disabled, disturbed, dyslexic, or dumb, not inadequately taught.

There is a second problem with the traditional view. The focus in schools is on the product – say, a test score outcome – rather than on the *process* of learning, and the role of the student in trying to understand, learn, and remember. Though it is often taken for granted that if teaching occurs then learning is taking place, we know that instruction need not necessarily lead to learning. For example, I might be teaching a class by lecturing, but I do not know whether my students are learning. To learn requires action by them – whether reading, rephrasing, summarizing, or discussing. To assess their learning I must lead a discussion, have them present their views, or give them a test. Those who can discuss, present, or answer questions may have learned because of my lecture or may have known quite a bit about the subject before entering the class. Some who failed might have learned from me but could not demonstrate it because certain terms or concepts could not yet be articulated. Hence, we cannot be sure that our instruction really "takes," nor can we be confident about why students do well or poorly on a test. All we know is their relative ranking and whether they have responded to our questions.

Focusing on instructional results, the product-oriented view of learning led educators to assume that learning is a function only of the amount and quality of presented information. Like sponges taking in liquid, children were supposed to learn by absorbing new information and, through practice, forming permanent memory bonds about the information and collecting new skills. Because laying down the right memory bonds was important, teachers rather than parents were supposed to supervise instruction. The error here was an overemphasis on behavioral objectives and skill learning and an underemphasis on interpretation, problem solving, background knowledge, and the use of learning strategies.

Children do not mindlessly learn only as they are told. They learn by extending, interpreting, and evaluating. They test new concepts against their own store of knowledge; accept, reject, or modify information to fit their perspective; and embed learning in a purposeful search. Learning about reading, for example, occurs in and out of school, through incidental and direct attempts to read words and messages on billboards and food packages, in joke books and television programs, and in books and magazines. Printed information is learned when children notice it, and it exists beyond the classroom, in most homes and communities – where it is intrusive and has meaning.

Because children do acquire knowledge at home and through their own pursuits as well as at school and because literacy at home can be functional while school literacy is more likely to emphasize its abstracted quality, the traditional view of teachers as the single conduit through which children learn is unacceptable.

An alternative view of school reading instruction

At the turn of the century, Maria Montessori (1909 – 64) was determined that very poor Italian children should be schooled. She established a program, the heart of which was sensory training through active involvement by the children with learning materials. She trained adults to *direct* rather than teach children and to organize the learning setting so that children could use more materials correctly and learn through mastering increasingly more complicated materials and tasks. Language, reading, and writing activities were similarly constructed. Versions of this approach are popular in Montessori schools today.

In 1959, MacKinnon published a book called *How Do Children Learn to Read?* He worked with several groups of first-grade children, contrasting three types of instruction. The most successful procedure had children in small groups use a very easy book that contained only a few words on each page along with an accompanying picture. The children were asked to take turns reading sentences aloud; they were allowed to help each other while the adult listened. The adult did not give help unless asked, and when asked did not give answers or correct children's errors but helped children figure out what information they needed to read or interpret a line of print. After 10 lessons, the children were looking at print as a problem-solving venture, one that they could cope with. They were using letter information, comparing similarly spelled words, and paying attention to meaning. They did very well on a subsequent achievement test even though they had been introduced to a smaller number of words than had other groups of children.

Similar results have been obtained by a research team in Hawaii that has been experimenting with ways to help native Hawaiian children become better readers. The approach that has been most successful is reported by Tharp (1982). Reading lessons from first grade on emphasize children's comprehension of the story. Children talk about how the topic fits their experiences, figure out how events in the story are related, and try to predict outcomes of the story. It is the adult's job to keep everyone in the group thinking about the written text and trying to solve problems by reading the text without telling them what or how to learn. It is the children's job to figure out how to understand the text.

Finally in a study by Anderson, Mason, and Shirley (1983), a way to improve third- and fourth-grade children's comprehension of written materials was tested. We found that, after children read a sentence, if we asked them to "tell what might happen next," they remembered what they had read or what they had heard other children in the group read aloud better than if we asked them to read or reread until they made no oral reading errors. This work suggests that if adults orient children to pay close attention to text meaning and give them opportunities to expand on and interpret text information, they are likely to remember what they read.

These four examples of instructional approaches indicate two key elements for ensuring that children are learning a subject or acquiring a skill from instruction. One is to give children tasks that engage their attention and allow them to construct or reconstruct information. They should play an active role: figure out solutions, classify words and meanings, explain ideas in their own words, and relate information to their own experience. As Olson (this volume) and I (Mason, McCormick, & Bhavnagri, in press) have reported elsewhere, children need to know how to know, think, and remember. If children are discouraged or do not understand a task, adults have made an error. They have ignored the learner's rights or assigned the wrong task, or they did not explain it well enough.

The other key element for ensuring learning is for adults to serve as advisors. Adults can decide in what environment a task is easily learned. They can set forth learning tasks whose concepts and purposes are clear.

Furthermore, they can watch and listen to children's responses to tasks to determine whether the tasks are appropriate and, from the errors that are made, whether children are making progress in understanding a concept or acquiring a skill.

A role for parents

Giving up the traditional view of reading means that instruction is not the sole prerogative of the teacher. Parents and community members can play important roles of support and guidance, as indeed they used to do prior to universal public schooling, or as they did in Sweden in the 17th century (Graff, this volume). Moreover, it means that learning is not a passive accomplishment but an active working out by the learner of the task concepts. Therefore, the learner must know why something is to be learned or accomplished. Reading must have a purpose.

What parents ought to do to prepare their child for reading instruction has not been clarified, in part because researchers do not yet agree about what ought to be taught, and in part because school instructional materials are still restricted or not easily purchased by parents. Thus, clear, unambiguous advice and high-quality materials are hard for parents to find. Moreover, since today's parents were raised in an era of social disapproval for home reading instruction, few have useful memories (or models) of parental guidance for reading and writing beyond that of reading bedtime stories and alphabet books or giving children chalkboards and coloring books. Finally, there is a tendency by parents and teachers alike to limit reading instruction to stories and to disregard, ignore, or underestimate the importance of writing activities, and of the reference, recreation, and reading activities routinely carried out by adults in the home and community.

A proposed solution

The relationship of reading to one's needs and interests is central to the development of literacy. To that end I have two recommendations. First, I recommend that parents look more carefully at what their preschool children understand about reading and how they change in that understanding as a result of paying attention to printed letters, words, and stories (Mason, 1980). I assume that most children will begin to pay attention to print long before they start school if the parents support such interest. Parents can support reading interest by providing picture, story, and alphabet books, by helping children point out and name common printed signs, posters, and packages, and by fostering reading and writing in games and home activities. With older children they can support independent reading, learning from reference materials, and creative writing.

Studies of successful young readers show that learning how to read can occur through children's use of books and reading materials, when it is supported or fostered by parents. Bissex (1980) documented the steps her son took to learn to write and read. The child started by writing words and messages, using an invented spelling system. He then became interested in reading. All this occurred without direct instruction but with parental encouragement to write, and the provision of parental help whenever requested. Soderberg (1977) described how her 3-year-old daughter learned to read by being taught separate words and then reading the same words in simple made-up stories. Mason (1980) worked for a school year with 4-year-old children, providing many informal opportunities for children to hear and then read simple stories, to see and print their own names and other familiar words, and to recognize and print alphabet letters. By the end of the year all of these children were reading signs and labels; some were reading books by themselves. Mason and McCormick (1981) set up a 2-week introduction to reading that led 4-year-old children to seek out printed information and to begin writing and reading signs and labels. Mason, McCormick, and Bhavnagri (in press) documented how children in a Headstart classroom could be encouraged to begin learning to read by being given simple-to-read stories.

These studies suggest that a very effective way to help children begin to learn to read is through meaning-laden but easy-to-learn stories, signs and labels, games, and activities that encourage them to read, reread, spell, and print. They learn that familiar, meaningful words have printed counterparts, and how reading and writing are useful to them. For example, they learn that the word "STOP" on a stop sign or in a book has the same meaning as the lower case word "stop" and the spoken word "stop." They begin to communicate with written notes and keep written records. They notice that words beginning with the same letter resemble one another in sound. They try to anticipate how words are spelled and what words mean. And so they begin to look at print more carefully and to ask questions of adults about meaning, spelling, and pronunciation.

A classification of reading and writing

My second recommendation is that parents expand their view of reading. I have prepared a chart that indicates typical activities in our daily lives that involve reading or writing (see Table 14 – 1). There are nine categories, only one of which encompasses "schooled" reading (information for learning in an instructional setting), yet all nine represent common uses or examples of print.

Across the top of the table are three ways in which printed information is typically presented: as *Labels & Lists*, as *Directives*, as *Narratives & Informational Texts*. The left margin distinguishes three settings – routine, recreational, and self-educational – for the use of print. In the first column are examples of print that labels, locates, or orders objects, events, or ideas. Such information can serve as restaurant menus and calendars do, to supply us with memorable or useful data for our day-to-day activities; as crossword puzzles do, to amuse us; or as diagrams, maps, or stock market reports do, to instruct us. Next are instrumental and directive statements about what to do or how to do something. Directives supply routine information in the form of traffic signs or warnings on medicines; offer recreation through games (e.g., "Do not pass GO. Do not collect $200") and social experiences (invitations, letters); and provide self-educational reading opportunities to learn how to build a computer, operate a car, or plant a garden. In the last column, texts can involve routine descriptions of daily affairs or social events or can occur in the form of books, magazines, and journals that are read for narrative or informational purposes or, in the case of younger children, to learn how to read text. Recreational materials can be joke books, songs, poems, and stories; instructional materials are used for schooling and self-education.

The examples of activities in the table are meant to describe each category; they do not constitute an exhaustive list and exhibit some overlap, particularly as between labels and directives. The point to make is that eight of these nine categories represent activities that are seldom utilized by the schools in reading instruction, but could be fostered at home by parents. Reading and writing are deeply integrated into most of our lives and, in this wider framework, should be shared with children. Printed information encompasses far more than narrative and exposition and is utilized for more purposes than self-education. Parents and communities can acquaint children with this broader outlook.

Now our initial question, about how parents can help children learn to read, will be answered. The first part of the answer is that parents ought to find out what children already know about reading by asking them questions about their knowledge of signs and labels, of letters and letter sounds. Listen to their answers and figure out what their mistakes mean. Provide tasks, materials, and activities that fit their interest and level of understanding. Think broadly of activities that use reading or writing, not

Table 14-1. *Reading and writing*

	Labels & Lists	Directives	Narratives and Informational Texts
Routine, and business, and record keeping	food labels clothing labels street names building labels grocery lists billboards expense accounts restaurant menus telephone directories want ads calendars inoculation records	traffic signs warnings directions advertisements work assignments tax statements credit applications job applications	daily records business letters

Recreational & social	clothing labels
	crossword puzzles
	greeting cards
		invitations
		board games
		video games
		TV and other
		  schedules
			news of sports and
			  social affairs
			comics
			novels, poems,
			  plays
			letters
			diaries
			songs

Self-educational/ Instructional	categorized labels maps & diagrams stock market reports dictionaries price tags	arts & craft guides gardening guides manuals recipes	workbooks textbooks encyclopedias newspapers magazines scientific reports religious texts

narrowly of only books and magazines. The second part of the answer is that parents should make sure that children have opportunities to figure out reading tasks, constructing solutions and not just choosing between restricted alternatives provided by adults. Rather, adults should encourage children to construct their own *interpretation* of what they read rather than just fill in blanks or circle right answers. Moreover, they should help children verbalize their own reading concepts rather than simply listen to or parrot what an adult says and understands. In short, they should foster learning to read through child-initiated reading, writing, and explaining: trying out, using, and talking about print. Then children can develop a sense of what it *means* to read and gradually construct a more complete understanding of *how* to read.

References

Anderson, R., Mason, J., & Shirley, L. (1983, February). *The reading group: An experimental investigation of a labyrinth* (Tech. Rep. No. 271). Urbana: University of Illinois, Center for the Study of Reading.

Bissex, G. (1980). *GYNS AT WRK: A child learns to write and read.* Cambridge, Ma.: Harvard University Press.

Colthart, M. (1979). When can children learn to read – and when should they be taught? In T. G. Waller & G. E. MacKinnon (Eds.), *Reading research: Advances in theory and practice.* New York: Academic Press, 1979.

Dodson, F. (1981). *Give your child a head start in reading.* New York: Simon and Schuster.

Gammage, P. (1979). *Children and schooling.* Boston: George Allen & Unwin.

Gesell, A. (1940). *The first five years of life: A guide to the study of the preschool child.* New York: Harper & Bros.

Gray, W. (1925). *The twenty-fourth yearbook of the National Society for the Study of Education: Part 1.* Bloomington, Ill.: Public School Publishing.

MacKinnon, A. (1959). *How do children learn to read?* Vancouver, B.C.: Copp Clark.

Mason, J. (1980). When *do* children begin to read: An exploration of four year old children's letter and word reading competencies. *Reading Research Quarterly, 15,* 203–37.

Mason, J., McCormick, C., & Bhavnagri, N. (forthcoming). How are you going to help me learn? Lesson negotiations between a teacher and preschool children. In D. Yaden & W. Templeton (Ed.), *Metalinguistic awareness and beginning literacy: Conceptualizing what it means to read and write.* Exeter, N. H.: Heinemann Educational books.

McCormick, C., & Mason, J. (1981). *Intervention procedures for increasing preschool children's interest in and knowledge about reading* (Tech. Rep. No. 312). Urbana: University of Illinois, Center for the Study of Reading.

Montessori, M. (1964). *The Montessori method: Scientific pedagogy as applied to child education in "the children's houses"* (Translation from 1909). New York: Schocken Books.

Soderberg, R. (1977). *Reading in early childhood: A linguistic study of a preschool child's gradual acquisition of reading ability.* Washington, D.C.: Georgetown University Press.

Tharp, R. (1982). The effective instruction of comprehension: Results and description of the Kamehameha Early Education Program. *Reading Research Quarterly, 17,* 503–27.

White, B. (1975). *The first three years of life.* Englewood Cliffs, N.J.: Prentice-Hall.

Kieran Egan

It has been confidently asserted that speech is biologically determined whereas literacy is not (e.g., Havelock, 1976). Thus learning to speak is easy and, given no relevant biological subnormality, is achieved universally, whereas literacy is relatively difficult and is achieved with ease and fluency by a relatively small proportion of the population, the proportion varying with the criterion of literacy used. This assertion is taken as a premise in arguments that go on to make claims about education and society. And yet the assertion seems at least very implausible. Children are brought up in oral language environments. They receive constant vocal stimulation in contexts in which continual efforts are made to associate the sounds with things, people, and events of significance to them. Similarly, the sounds they make are constantly shaped to fit the conventions of the language group they are being initiated into.

If children were brought up in a silent world we would hardly expect some biological determining mechanism to produce articulate speech. And if children were subjected to the same intensity of stimulation to read and write from birth to age 5, we would reasonably expect universal and fluent literacy. So to argue that speech is biologically determined whereas literacy is not as an explanation of difficulties in stimulating and sustaining the development of literacy is surely misguided. One might say that biologically we have the capacity for speech, and speech may be evoked and developed by appropriate interactions with an oral language environment. Equally one might suppose that biologically we have the capacity for literacy, and literacy may be evoked and developed by appropriate interactions with an environment in which reading and writing matter.

The focus for this essay is on the kind of environments that evoke, stimulate, and sustain the development of literacy. I don't mean the social environments. That middle-class children from homes in which there is much pleasure gained from reading and writing tend to learn and to read

243

and write better than children from homes where none of this goes on is now a commonplace observation. Nor do I mean the kind of immediate "environment" created by certain reading curriculum packages. There is a danger, evident in such packages and in some of the writing and research on literacy, of treating the achievement and development of literacy as narrowly technical problems toward whose solution technical tools are paramount. This is a danger not because techniques of teaching reading and writing are not important, but because such a focus tends to disguise the much more important matter of more general environments in which the things read or written about are made meaningful and accessible. Thinking in terms of decoding and encoding may make us feel in command of a more scientific approach to our problem, but it can do so at the expense of a sense of proportion. We say, for economy's sake, that our aim is to teach children to read and write. We might try to remember that "read" and "write" are primarily transitive verbs and that our aim is to teach children to read *something* or to write *something* (as de Castell and Luke have stressed earlier in this volume). The difference between the intransitive and transitive senses of these words leads to a subtle but potentially important matter of focus. By focusing on teaching to read and write, to decode and encode, we tend toward contentless techniques. By focusing on the things we want to teach children *to* read or write, our focus tends toward what makes the achievement worthwhile, toward the appropriate environments for stimulating reading and writing.

A related observation is that in certain circumstances children tend to find some things more accessible, engaging, and meaningful, and they can more readily learn and remember such things in such circumstances. R. C. Anderson shows how what he calls "schemata" determine what is seen as meaningful, what is learned most easily and remembered longest, and so on (Anderson, 1977). If we can design reading and writing materials to fit children's dominant schemata, it would seem to follow, we will be better able to aid their learning to read and write and to improve their continued development of literacy.

A schema, in Anderson's usage, seems to refer to a property of the mind. If one has schema x, then a, b, and c content would seem to be more readily accessible. Such a usage is apparently akin to Piaget's. His logico-mathematical structures are seen as properties of the mind whose possession or absence determine whether or not a child will be able to understand a particular concept or perform a particular task which exhibits a corresponding logico-mathematical structure.

Attempts to characterize such schemata or structures are of considerable interest to educators. One of the more obvious things about children is that when they are engaged by something their learning power is prodigious. We want some general theory about what, as it were, turns on that power.

Clearly some particular facts about, say, Roman history might be of no interest to a particular child at age 5, but become quite fascinating at age 15, while they remain of no interest to some other 15-year-old. What makes the facts meaningful and interesting is affected by age and what has already been learned and by the particular child's attachment to some more general context within which these particular facts "fit." To a child whose past learning, temperament, and so on, have produced a romantic engagement with heroes and the struggle for freedom, the revolt of Spartacus will likely be engaging. That child will want to learn about these events, will be "motivated" to do so, will exhibit the kind of interest we find desirable as both a stimulus to learning and a part of what we mean by the process of education. What we could well use in education, then, is a theory characterizing the general contexts of meaning that seem to determine what particular things children will find first accessible and meaningful and then engaging and stimulating at different ages or stages in their educational development. I will in what follows make an attempt to sketch such a theory.

So my concern with environments here is with the environments of meaning within which children and students make sense of things. An assumption in what follows is that what most matters in teaching children to read and write things and in teaching them to become increasingly sophisticated readers and writers is that the things one wants them to learn need to be embedded in contexts or environments that are rich in meaning for them. I will characterize four distinct contexts of meaning, or – perhaps because one needs to identify one's own scheme by a distinct term – paradigmatic forms of understanding. These four paradigmatic forms of understanding are age-conditioned and environmentally influenced. I call them mythic, romantic, philosophic, and ironic.

These are necessarily unlike the kinds of stages one finds in psychological theories such as Piaget's. The psychologist is concerned to establish what is the case with respect to psychological development. The educator is concerned to prescribe what ought to be done to bring about some ideal. Clearly the educator's prescriptions must not contravene whatever the psychologist securely establishes is the case.

The relationship between psychological theories and educational prescriptions, however, is a problematic one. Psychology is a relatively young field of study, and perhaps for that reason has securely established very little about significant features of human behavior and development. How far should the educator feel constrained by insecure psychological theories? Of course each educator has to deal with particular theories as seems most sensible. But many of the educator's prescriptions apply to areas that are rather remote from the kinds of questions psychologists deal with. For example, in his seminal essay on "The Rhythms of Education" (1922), Alfred North Whitehead argues for the importance of romance in education. Neither a study of the nature or structure of knowledge nor psychological research would lend credence to such a concept; it is not a part of knowledge nor a necessary stage of psychological development. It is, rather, a quality of thought that can come about when we use knowledge for particular human purposes.

Though we may reasonably argue with Whitehead's Hegelian scheme – romance/precision/generalization – we cannot reject his categories as invalid. There is a logical progression that underlies his developmental scheme; it rests on the empirical basis of common, uncontentious observations; and the categories refer to matters of considerable educational importance.

What follows, then, has similar characteristics. It deals with what seem to me important and general matters that are central to education; it focuses on phenomena that are on the whole remote from areas where psychological theories provide either support or constraints; it prescribes what seems to me a desirable educational scheme; it embodies a complex logical progression; and it is supported empirically by a wide range of uncontentious observations.

The mythic paradigm of understanding

The first, mythic stage is appropriate from earliest years to about age 6, 7, or 8. If the scheme is to be empirically based on uncontentious observations, where might we begin looking for descriptive data? We might reasonably begin with those things that seem to engage typical children most – games and stories. Given that our topic is literacy, I'll focus on stories here. For purposes of theory building we will need not only descriptive data but also some attempt at an explanation of what we find.

Two things are immediately evident about those stories whose appeal to young children seems most powerful. First, concerning their content, they are full of weird creatures like talking middle-class bears, monsters with human motives and emotions, ghosts, and so on; they also tend to be set in exotic times and places – or no-times and no-places. Second, concerning their form, they seem to involve powerful and pure emotions and forces in conflicts that are clearly resolved: That is, they follow the pattern of the basic story form.

We have, then, two sets of questions to answer: First, what are stories, why are children so engaged by them, and what are they for? Second, why are young children's stories full of middle-class talking bears and other weird creatures?

Take the incident, "He took the book." We know in some vague sense what it means, but the sense is very vague because we don't know who "he" is or what the book contains, or whether taking it is good or bad, or anything else about it. It has no significance for us by itself. By adding a context, a time and place and circumstances in which "he" is a clean-cut young man who is taking the book to help his grandmother, we add meaning to the incident. Most significantly, we begin to orient our feelings about his taking the book. But we might extend the context further, so that he and his grandmother are drug pushers and the book contains information about where to make their next drop. This widened context of meaning will cause us to reorient our feelings about the incident. Where we were, mildly, glad before, we may now feel sorry that he was able to take the book. The story writer can play with our affective responses by adding to the context that determines the meaning of the incident. The only unit in language that can ultimately fix the meaning of incidents is the story. We know we have reached the end of a story, not when it says "and they lived happily ever after," because it often doesn't, but when we know how to feel about all the incidents that make up the story. Similarly, we know when we have reached the end of a well-formed sentence when each of the morphemes has only one meaning. The general organizing function, whether syntax or plot, reduces the huge number of possible meanings of the smaller elements to one for each element, and they thus agglomerate into an unambiguous larger unit with a precise but complex meaning.

So a story is the linguistic unit that can determine the affective meaning of incidents. In history, for example, we do not know ultimately how to feel about an event. Horrible events sometimes lead to wonderful conclusions. Because history has not ended we can only provisionally feel glad or sorry about any event. Those who become certain of how they feel about particular events do so by converting history into a story in which they assert an end. In a sophisticated way this is what Marxists do. They can feel confident about the meaning of certain events because they have imposed a plot on history which asserts a particular end to the process. We have the same general problem with our lives. Until the end, we cannot be sure abut the meaning of any part of them. We can falsify this experience, in the way

Marxists falsify history, by imposing a plot on our lives that determines the meaning of particular experiences. The commonest way of doing this is by asserting a more general religious story whose context can fix the meaning of the events of our lives.

If a story is the machine we have for fixing the affective meaning of events, we may be approaching a reason why young children find them so engaging. In a world where the meaning of events and incidents must be quite puzzling, the story offers a haven of clarity. But why the middle-class talking bears?

If, as we have been told by many educators, we should seek reading material that is "relevant" to children's own situations, we should notice that children tend to seek quite the opposite. A common impulse is to move toward the most exotic content. Early developmental theorists stressed that children could deal only with the most simple matters in their immediate experience. John Dewey suggested that we should move children only gradually outward from their daily social experience. Piagetians have told us that children lack the concepts that enable them to handle abstraction, most logical connections, causality, geographical space, and historical time, and that only very slowly are these mastered. How, one must wonder, do children so easily have access to Darth Vadar, witches, talking dragons, and space warriors?

Consider how children develop the conceptual apparatus that enables them to articulate what they know about the temperature continuum. First they learn the concepts "hot" and "cold." They start, that is, with binary opposites. Next they mediate between these poles by learning the concept "warm." Then they mediate between cold and warm – perhaps with "cool" or "quite cold" – and between warm and hot ("pretty hot"). After elaborating this continuum by mediating between poles they develop an abstract concept of a temperature continuum, on which meaning is established by acceptance of an arbitrary numbering convention.

And middle-class talking bears? What are the most basic, prominent, and powerful polar opposites in our environment? Surely nature and culture. So basic, indeed, that we tend to forget about it. The guinea pig does nothing to make himself a table or chairs. The cat resolutely refuses to talk back. If we mediate between natural and cultural objects, what do we get? Talking bears, for one thing. A feature of the mythic paradigm of understanding is its attempts to mediate between polar opposites, and its energetic attempts to generate mediating categories between poles that we later learn do not have such mediating categories. That other great evident division, between life and death, also absorbs endless mythic energy in attempted mediation. In the shadow between life and death, worlds of gods, spirits, and ghosts pullulate. These are things that are both alive and dead, as warm is both hot and cold. We learn, or fail to learn, that life and death are discrete empirical categories that lack a mediating category.

So, in a preliminary way, we can say that a brief examination of some of the most obvious features in children's stories begins to sketch a possible explanation of those features. The explanation matters because, if it is valid, we can infer from it principles that can guide our teaching of literacy. Let us, then, in a similar sketchy way see roughly where we might be led with regard to teaching practice by assuming that the above sketch in the direction of an explanation is valid.

Designing early literacy programs might be seen as a task of setting up an environment comprising the mythic paradigm of understanding. We would want to use mythic-type stories, characterized by binary opposites in conflict, clear affective meaning, mediation between life and death, nature and culture, or other binary categories derived from concrete, empirical properties of the world and children's experience in families: big/little; brave/cowardly; afraid/secure; good/bad; and so on. But more importantly, we would want to borrow the story *form*. The form – as distinct from the fictional stories – seems crucial in helping children in their early years to make sense of things. The story form is a most important tool for making its contents meaningful. Thus any content we can organize in terms of young children's basic polar categories and put into a story form of binary conflict, elaboration, and resolution can be made meaningful.

It is surely not coincidental that children master the story form about the same time as they master the sentence form. Indeed, some scholars of poetics claim that the story is simply the sentence writ large; syntax and plot are the same mental function working at different levels of content (Barthes, 1966; Greimas, 1966; Todorov, 1969). Growing appreciation of the forms and conventions of stories would thus likely transfer to increased mastery of sentences. Mastery of story and sentence do appear to occur together: Nusery rhymes are incomplete, fragmented stories that appeal most strongly when children's sentences are mainly incomplete and fragmented; simple complete stories tend to be enjoyed when simple complete sentences are mastered; more sophisticated stories are appreciated when more sophisticated sentences figure in students' writing; and eventually we enjoy those exploding parodies of story and sentence in *Finnegan's Wake*.

Perhaps it should also be noted that learning to follow a story requires a sense of causality, problem solving, analyzing events and situations, forming hypotheses and reforming them in light of further content, and so on. Learning the conventions of increasingly sophisticated stories is equivalent to learning such intellectual skills. Teachers occasionally have a tendency to talk *about* a story a great deal. Better to read a second story. The one practice that seems to work almost invariably in schools is immersion. We might think of these early years as a time for immersion in stories, and in any content we can organize within the story form.

What seems to follow with respect to the promotion of literacy skills is that such exercises should as far as possible be put into the context of stories. Workbooks with lists of more or less discrete exercises will (runs an empirical claim generated by our proto-theory) be much less effective than the same exercises organized into a story having the characteristics sketched earlier.

The romantic paradigm of understanding

The romantic paradigm is appropriate from ages 6, 7, or 8 to about ages 15, 16, 17. The stories that seem most to engage children and students during this next phase of development have features significantly distinct from those of the mythic phase. They share the story form – the basic sense-making tool – but it is more sophisticated. In terms of content one new feature is paramount: The stories are realistic. They are not realistic in the sense of seeking to be literally true, but they are concerned always to be *possible* within the real world. Even in stories such as "Superman," there is considerable energy devoted to his etiology. It would be insufficient in the romantic paradigm for him to have superhuman powers by magic; there has to be some explanation or account of the magic. So we know all about his birth and escape from the dying planet Krypton.

Prominent in romantic paradigm stories are heroes and heroines, but they often have common and curious qualities. They both live an ordinary life and can in some way transcend ordinary life. Superman is also Clark Kent. These heroes and heroines are clearly figures with whom the student in the romantic phase identifies in some important way.

In a romantic story a hero or heroine (or institution, nation, or idea) with whom or which the student can identify, struggles against odds to a glory and transcendance over threatening nature (or persons, events, institutions, nations or ideas), in which glory the reader may then share. Such stories have more complex plots than mythic stories. They are concerned with realistic detail or plausibility. They have clear and powerful heroes or heroines. They often have exotic, though realistic and plausible, settings.

The content of mythic-stage stories often ignores the limits of what is possible. The crucial index of transition to the romantic stage is a concern with precisely what are the limits of what is possible. Associated with this is the beginning of a realistic mastery of concepts of historical causality, geographical space, and abstract logical relationships. These developing skills, however, do not focus immediately on the "relevant" everyday content of students' lives. Rather, they seem to focus most insistently on the extremes, the limits, of reality, on the most exotic and romantic content. No longer are students immediately engaged by the mention of giants and monsters; their stronger interest during this stage is in who was really the biggest person, the most monstrous creature, the fastest, the slowest, the smallest. *The Guinness Book of Records* ideally responds to the dominant interest of the romantic stage. Romance, in this sense, is myth confined within reality. The mythic impulses are still evident, but they are in conflict with the intellectual desire to know where reality ends and the mythic begins.

One may say, then, that this romantic stage is concerned with the discovery of an autonomous world which lacks magic and works according to its own rules, regardless of what we might wish. This autonomy is threatening to the immature ego, which begins to be aware of itself as a part of the everyday world, but also as a rather powerless part. This threatening everyday world is countered by the students forming romantic associations with those forces that most clearly transcend the everyday world. Heroes and heroines appeal most powerfully to the imagination at this stage because they embody the power to meet and overcome those forces which the student is increasingly aware that he or she is subject to and determined by. That transcendent power is expressed in qualities such as courage, ingenuity, nobility, wisdom, and all the old virtues. If we embody these in characters who face and overcome the threats that flesh is heir to, we have the kind of hero or heroine who most readily engages the romantic-stage student.

These qualities, however, need not only be embodied in fictional characters in stories. They can also be uncovered in the content of history, geography, physics, and so forth, in such a way as to engage the romantic mind (Egan, 1979).

If our concern is with expanding students' literacy, such a characterization of the romantic paradigm of understanding suggests that certain forms of literature will best engage and carry forward students' educational development at this stage. The poetry we choose, for example, should be the most "romantic" (within the bounds of simple expression) rather than that which is of the highest quality. Thus, often students are introduced to poetry which celebrates nature in its quotidian forms. However simple the language in which such sentiments are expressed, the meaning of such poetry is not within the romantic paradigm of understanding. The mountains of the moon and the valley of the shadow are more easily accessible than the daffodils by Ulswater. A strong narrative line, strong and clear rhythms appropriate to the theme, heroic actions, human qualities *in extremis,* high drama or humor, and sentiment verging on sentimentality seem the qualities of verse appropriate, because most engaging, at this stage.

Selecting such verse is not a matter of pandering to inappropriately crude interests. It is proper for the immature to be immature; there is no point in trying to treat the immature as though they were mature. Reaching maturity is a process, and selecting the appropriate kind of verse, and of stories and academic content, at each stage is intended firstly to provide what is currently most engaging and secondly to move the process along. Such verses as Macauley's *Lays of Ancient Rome* or A. E. Housman's or Kipling's more dramatic poems help students understand a little more what poetry is for; it helps extend their appreciation of rhythms in language; and it develops a little further their sentiment and emotion.

Their writing should be expected to pursue similar themes, and they should be encouraged to write similar sentiment-full verse. They should be encouraged to write a great deal. It is a mystery that some teachers seem to expect students' mastery of literate expression to improve while giving them little practice, and much of that practice in the impoverishing context of workbook exercises.

The philosophic paradigm of understanding

The philosophic stage appropriately begins, when it does begin at all, during mid to late adolescence and continues into the twenties. The crucial feature of the move from the romantic to the philosophic paradigm is the realization that the world and one's experience are made up out of complex processes of which the student is a part. The establishment of the individual's sense of identity can then no longer be achieved by romantic associations with transcendent qualities, but is to be achieved rather by understanding his or her place within the complex processes that make up the world and experience. Thus the philosophic mind is most readily engaged by knowledge that promises to tell *the truth* about these general and complex processes. In history, then, the romantic events and great deeds of heroic characters are increasingly less engaging, and the general patterns of the historical process engage students' minds with increasing insistence. By knowing *the nature* of the historical process, philosophic-stage students can establish their place in the process. Thus the Marxist may understand that the historical process is the progressive story of class conflicts leading toward a classless state. Marxist students' identities are thus in part established by such a general scheme because it fixes their place *within* the scheme and tells them what they should do as agents within it. Similarly, the liberal-humanitarian scheme of late-19th-century Western countries provided a general scheme, which was accepted by the philosophic-stage mind as expressing *the* truth about the historical process and so establishing the proper role of the individual as an historical agent within it.

Interest in this stage, then, is focused on general schemes that offer truths about history, psychology, science, sociology, and so on. Philosophic-stage individuals provide the major market for those books that reach for very general truths about the human condition. The term "philosophic" is chosen to echo Aristotle's observation that poetry is more philosophic than history, because the former is concerned with what *happens*, the latter with what *happened*. The philosophic mind is attracted toward the general, the recurrent; toward the law, the general theory – toward *the truth* about what *happens*. The philosophic mind tends toward the reductive – trying to understand the whole within the clearest and simplest scheme possible. It is the stage at which ideologies and metaphysical schemes are most attractive.

The literature that attracts at this stage is largely a literature of ideas; even heroes become ciphers for ideas. Typical of such literature is Borges's *Inquisitions* or O. Henry's stories. Human particularity, the quirks of individual character, become less engaging, and there is a tendency toward a greater interest in theory than in literature itself; in poetics rather than poetry.

The curriculum that should advance literacy to and through this stage may be inferred from the general characterization suggested above. Very general concepts begin to proliferate in students' writing and conversation: "society," "culture," "the mind," "evolution," "human nature," etc. Poetry and fiction should perhaps tend to take a somewhat less prominent place in the philosophic curriculum than matters of rhetoric. The philosophic is above all a stage of *argument*. The curriculum might be taken up with exercises in argument; the essay is probably the "cutting edge" of literacy development through this stage. Essays should be written constantly – all aimed out into the world in order to have an effect on it. The essays may be in the form of letters – to newspapers, politicians, advertisers, manufacturers, and so on. Students should learn the arts of persuasion through words. Formal debating might also further this.

The ironic paradigm of understanding

The ironic stage is the stage of maturity, and the significant index of the move into this stage from the philosophic is the individual's realization that the general schemes that were so engaging because they offered to tell the most profound truths are seen at last as not open to truth tests. Their generality ensures that they evade falsification. The ironic stage sees a return to particularity but also to seeing the necessity of general schemes for creating more general meaning out of those particulars. However, the general scheme is seen as not true or false so much as useful, beautiful, or elegant – or their opposites.

Education is a cumulative process, so these stages are not stages one leaves behind. Rather, each one contributes something to the developing understanding. Properly, the mythic stage contributes imagination; the romantic stage contributes a vivifying association with knowledge; the philosophic stage contributes the tools for searching for more general meaning, for pattern and theory construction; and the ironic stage represents the regulator of these, along with an appreciation that life and the world are made up of particulars and the coalescence of these into more general forms is the contribution of our minds. This maturity allows access to all forms of literature, along with the flexibility to express private experience in appropriate public forms.

Conclusion

Some of the above observations may seem sensible to some readers, but perhaps the scheme seems at least – shall we politely put it? – epistemologically unclear. What kind of sketch of what kind of theory for what kind of use is the above supposed to be?

It is based on, and elaborated from, observations of common qualitative changes in children's and students' interests. It is an attempt to schematize these changes, recognizing four quite distinct stages in the process of becoming most fully literate. It is indeed epistemologically unclear, because it is unclear what an educational theory should be composed of. That is, though there needs obviously to be an empirical component to educational theory, it is also clear that education is very largely a prescriptive matter. So whereas the above sketch obviously yields a variety of empirically testable claims, it is not *only* based on observations, but also involves a prescription that the scheme outlined is one that *ought* to be followed. No empirical finding is relevant to the latter claim – unless it is to show that what is prescribed is impossible – but rather it is properly open only to analysis and argument.

It is, then, a sketch of a prescription for how to become literate. Its use is as a guide to what ought to be read, what kinds of activities students ought to be engaged in in order to become literate. It embodies, in addition, a set of empirical claims. These follow the form: If you teach these kinds of things at these stages, then students (a) will be more engaged by their reading and writing and (b) will become more fully literate by maturity. It is clearly easier to test (a) than (b), and if all tests of (a) are wildly positive, still none of this establishes (b). The generality of (b) leaves it out of the realm of what we can test with any precision, but even so this does not make it other than an empirical claim, nor does it leave us helpless in making relatively imprecise judgments about the success of curriculum developed on a scheme such as is set forth here.

References

Anderson, R. C. (1977). "The notion of schemata and the educational enterprise." In R. C. Anderson, R. J. Spiro, and W. E. Montague (Eds.), *Schooling and the acquisition of knowledge*. Hillsdale, N. J.: Lawrence Erlbaum Associates.

Barthes, R. (1966). "Introduction à l'analyse structurale des recits," *Communications 8*.

Egan, K. (1979). *Educational Development*. New York: Oxford University Press.

Greimas, A. J. (1966). Elements pour une theorie de l'interpretation du recits mythique. *Communications 8*.

Havelock, E. (1976). *Origins of Western literacy*. Toronto: Ontario Institute for Studies in Education.

Todorov, T. (1969). *Grammaire du Decameron*. The Hague: Mouton.

Whitehead, A. N. (1922). "The Rhythm of Education." In *The Aims of Education*, New York: The Free Press.

16 Teaching students not to read

Walter H. MacGinitie and Ruth K. MacGinitie

There has been considerable controversy over whether the reading abilities of North American children have been declining or improving (see e.g., Layton, 1981). Actually, there has been less real disagreement than there seems. Those who claim that reading ability has been improving usually cite studies which seem to show that skills involving the mechanics of reading and simple comprehension in younger children are better now than they were a decade or two ago. Those who contend that reading ability has been decreasing usually cite studies which seem to show that the comprehension abilities, particularly with respect to inferential comprehension of difficult material, of secondary level students have declined. There is actually very little dispute over the fact that both of these trends have occurred. There is little doubt that the average student in the primary grades today is better at decoding words and reading simple stories than was the primary student 20 years ago. Similarly, there is little doubt that senior secondary students cannot read and understand the subtleties of difficult expository material as well as senior secondary students 20 years ago.

One example of a study with such findings is the British Columbia Reading Assessment (Tuinman & Kendall, 1980). This study found that the word attack and comprehension scores of children in British Columbia at the grade 4 level increased slightly between 1976 and 1980, and the comprehension scores of children in grade 12 decreased between 1977 and 1980.

In the United States, the National Assessment of Educational Progress (1981) found that in the period 1971 to 1980, 9-year-olds improved in both easy ("literal") and difficult ("inferential") comprehension tasks; 13-year-olds improved somewhat in easy comprehension tasks but stayed about the same in difficult comprehension tasks; 17-year-olds stayed about the same in easy comprehension tasks but declined in difficult comprehension tasks.[1]

256

It is not surprising, of course, that both of these trends – improved reading ability for primary-grade students, particularly in the mechanics of reading, and declines in the ability of secondary students to read difficult materials with comprehension – should be found. There has been a great emphasis on reading and reading instruction in North America during the past several years. This emphasis has focused mainly on the primary and intermediate grades, for it is at those levels that the curriculum typically provides directly for the teaching of reading. Several factors –the *initial* influence of modern linguistics, public attitudes about what is basic in reading, and the relative ease of systematizing and incorporating the mechanics of reading into instructional programs and materials – have led to an emphasis on the *mechanics* of reading in the reading curriculum.

At the secondary level, the declines in Scholastic Aptitude Test (SAT) scores have led to concern and to studies of the possible causes. The SAT score decline is pertinent here, because the verbal section of the SAT contains a measure of reading comprehension and depends on a knowledge of vocabulary that is typically attained through extensive reading. The major study of the SAT score decline (College Entrance Examination Board, 1977) suggests several potent factors that may have led to decreased reading experience and decreased reliance on reading among secondary students. In fact, the descriptions of changes in curricula, academic requirements, and student activities lead one to wonder, not why there is a score decline, but why the decline is not greater.

It is clearly a case of the old story: Students learn what the curriculum emphasizes (Calfee & Pointkowski, 1981). When there is heavy emphasis on reading in the primary grades and the instruction and materials emphasize the mechanics of reading, children will learn the mechanics of reading. When the curriculum in the secondary school deemphasizes writing practice and the reading of literature and content-rich material, the students will do less well at logical interpretation of difficult written material.

Not only are the curricular bases for changes in reading achievement clear, but the bases for the emphasis in the curriculum of the early grades on the mechanics of reading are also clear. It is easier for teachers to help children with those things for which rules and right answers are prescribed and with those things that are systematically organized into topics and exercises. It is easier to systematize the mechanics of reading and incorporate that systematization into instructional materials than it is to systematize reading comprehension instruction. When a child makes an error in decoding, or in an exercise simulating decoding, it will be clear to the teacher that the child is wrong and which rule the child should have followed. The teacher can help the child learn the correct response to a particular situation and guide the child in generalizing to new situations by citing a rule and giving examples. However, many teachers are not able to provide effective guidance when children make errors in understanding text. They cannot explain why they themselves interpret a text in a particular way; they cannot identify and specify the language patterns that would help the child generalize an interpretation to a new situation.

The difficulty that many teachers have in helping children with reading comprehension is surely not surprising in view of the preparation and support that teachers receive. Whereas teaching the mechanics of reading (and other aspects of early reading development) are important parts of most reading methods courses in teacher training institutions, there is nothing comparable in most such courses concerning the teaching of comprehension. The same holds true of most reading instructional materials (Durkin,1981). There is almost no guidance for the teacher or student relating to comprehension. There is, of course, a great deal in both methods courses and reading instructional materials that is labeled "comprehension" instruction, but it consists mainly of simplistic and nonfunctional taxonomies for the teacher and a flood of questions for the student.

There is essentially nothing in instructional materials or in teacher training that helps the teacher learn what to do when the child does not understand. The comprehension sections in instructional materials consist almost exclusively of questions that the teacher is to ask the students or written questions for the students themselves to read. Essentially never is the child told why one answer is correct and another wrong, and essentially never is the teacher given any guidance in explaining to the students how a passage conveys a particular meaning.

There is evidence that reading comprehension is, in fact, currently not being taught. The observational studies by Durkin (1979) indicate that the teachers who were studied gave almost no comprehension instruction to their elementary school students. The teachers did ask the students many questions about the meaning of the text, probably following the general model of instruction suggested by teacher's manuals, and, like the manuals, they gave no guidance to students who did not understand the text.

Michael Cox, a graduate student at the University of Victoria, has recently completed a study of what teachers do when students cannot correctly answer a comprehension question during a reading lesson. The most common teacher response was to call on another student. Cox saw very few occasions in which the teacher asked the student to look again at the text and very few occasions in which the teacher made any effort to ascertain whether the second student's answer made any sense to the student who had not been able to answer.

An examination of teacher's manuals for any basal reading series confirms that they offer a great many comprehension questions to be asked of the students but they do not suggest to the teacher any ways of helping the student who gets the wrong answer. Of course, there may not be very many wrong answers, for a great many of the questions suggested by some of the manuals can be answered without reading the story. This is one way in which we teach students not to read. Many of the comprehension questions that the teacher's manuals list can be answered by looking at the pictures which accompany the story, by means of the prior knowledge possessed by most of the children, by simply stating an opinion, or, in the case of multiple-choice questions, by matching grammatical forms or eliminating obviously foolish answers (MacGinitie, 1979). Nearly half the questions in some instructional materials can be answered in these ways by *not* reading. It seems clear that some current instructional materials not only fail to provide instruction in comprehension but actually encourage children to develop unproductive reading strategies and to succeed by learning not to read.

Why is there so little real comprehension instruction? Why don't teachers teach reading comprehension? Why don't instructional materials include instruction in reading comprehension? There are a number of reasons for this critical deficiency. One of them is that many children, extrapolating from their knowledge of spoken language, seem to *need* very little instruction in reading comprehension. They intuit the communicative intent of written text. Most children understand written text to a considerable extent on this basis, though they may never understand well some of the special conventions of written language. Thus, it may sometimes appear that reading comprehension instruction is unnecessary. But this superficial and false impression is not the only reason for a lack of comprehension instruction. Most teachers would readily agree that instruction in reading comprehension is one of their most important tasks, and most teachers believe that they are engaging in reading comprehension instruction. So we must look for part of the answer, at least, in what teachers do not understand about reading comprehension and reading comprehension instruction. What are the misunderstandings that lead to the situation in which teachers believe that comprehension instruction is important, believe that they are providing comprehension instruction, and yet, in fact, provide almost none?

There are a number of factors that contribute to this problem. One of them is the enormous complexity of language and language processing. Without some training and considerable practice it may be difficult for the average teacher to guess just what it is that makes a particular text difficult for a particular child to understand. It is probably even more difficult for the average teacher to articulate in a helpful way the nature of that feature of the text or to provide a simpler analogue so that it can be discussed usefully with the student. Partly because written and oral language are so obviously related, it is sometimes difficult for teachers who know both written and oral language to imagine that a particular written construction will be difficult for a child.

There are, however, many important differences between written and oral language that need to be recognized by teachers who want to help children with the understanding of written language. It is important to understand these differences as a background for helping children understand written language.[2]

The speech children hear is designed especially for them. People who speak to them are usually in the same place as they are, so there is a shared nonlinguistic context, and the participants are able to interact with each other. But writers do not prepare a text with one particular reader in mind. According to Cazden (1972), "written text is the final point on the developmental dimension towards independence from non-linguistic context" (p. 199).

This lack of a shared context removes cues, such as pointing and gesture, that may be important for children. It also makes deictic terms, whose interpretation depends on the context of their use, more difficult to understand. In order to understand deictic terms in written text, such as "now" or "a week ago," or "here" or "there," a child must take account of the framework set by the text. There is evidence that young children have difficulty taking another person's point of view (Piaget & Inhelder, 1956), and there is also evidence that the perspective that the reader takes influences what the reader learns from a story (Pichert & Anderson, 1977). Therefore, failure to assume the perspective of the text would disrupt comprehension.

Another difference between much oral language and expository written text is the greater redundancy of the oral language. Speakers tend to repeat themselves and to use more words than they would use to communicate the same message in writing (Wilkinson, 1971). Thus, the oral instruction that children receive is probably more redundant than the text they read. This may be especially true of the language addressed to children by teachers. Intuitively, it seems that teachers would focus attention on new information in many ways. Repeating new information and specifically stating the importance or novelty of the new information seem likely ways of doing this.

Judith Rogers, a graduate student at the University of Victoria, has prepared an interesting demonstration of the differences between teacher explanations and textbook explanations. She asked two experienced elementary school teachers to teach lessons based on a 200-word article from a grade 5 social studies text and videotaped the two resulting lessons. Perhaps the most striking difference between the teachers' lessons and the text was in length. What a teacher would expect students to read in 3 minutes took about 10–12 minutes for each teacher to present. Other distinctive characteristics of both teachers' presentations were the way they related new information to the background knowledge they knew their students possessed, their use of gestures to clarify spatial and sequential relationships, their repeated use and definition of new terms, and their use of repetition, summaries, and various verbal and nonverbal signals to focus student attention on particular information.

When alert junior secondary students are asked how they know when their teachers are saying something that the teachers regard as especially important, the students are likely to give an interesting description of facial expressions, gestures (including chalk or pencil tapping), and changes in tone of voice. Many students do use, consciously or unconsciously, the teacher's cues regarding new or important information – information that has a relatively high probability of being tested.

Another difference between writing and speech is that writing tends to be more complex syntactically and more detailed and precise (Horowitz & Berkowitz, 1967; Wilkinson, 1971). Preliminary work by Adams (1979) indicates that children, in their own oral language, have various ways of avoiding in speech certain complexities that characterize the written materials they must read.

In written language, there is more extensive and complex use of words and patterns that signal relationships between sentences and even paragraphs, and thus hold the text together. The use in the English language of these cohesive devices has been described by Halliday and Hasan (1976), and their role in reading has been emphasized by Chapman (1983).

If teachers appreciated the nature and extent of the differences between teacher talk and textbook language, they might have a better understanding of some children's reading comprehension difficulties. They might also have clearer intuitions about how to help children overcome these difficulties.

A significant source of confusion concerning the teaching of reading comprehension is, of course, the established practices that embody poor models of comprehension teaching. Many teachers rely on the procedures described in the teacher's manuals for basal reader series, and they find those procedures reasonably effective in teaching the mechanics of reading. They naturally assume that the procedures labeled "comprehension instruction" in those manuals will be reasonably effective in teaching comprehension. This false assumption is strengthened when the nature of reading comprehension instruction as described in their methods courses and methods textbooks coincides with the procedures they see outlined in the teacher's manuals.

Perhaps the lack of effective reading comprehension instruction would be less detrimental if the students actually engaged in a great deal of reading. Much can be learned through untutored experience. Unfortunately, both curricular and extracurricular influences seem to be encouraging less reading. At all grade levels, the emphasis on the mechanics of reading and on objectives-based instruction probably means that children spend more time doing exercises and less time actually reading. The influence of extracurricular pressures, from organized sports to television, has frequently been discussed as leading to less and less reading (College Entrance Examination Board, 1977).

Even if students were receiving effective reading comprehension instruction, it would need to be complemented and supported by a great deal of experience in reading. A daily period of reading instruction is not nearly adequate as a basis for building strong reading skills. Imagine the kind of basketball team a high school would field if practice and instruction were limited to a daily physical education period? Many years ago Arthur Gates (1947) wrote:

A mistake sometimes made is to assume that reading ability is a kind of special technique which once built up . . . will take care of itself . . . Skill in reading is like skill in singing, playing the piano, painting pictures, and doing other subtle artistic acts. To achieve high levels requires . . . spending much time in the activity. Two children of equal reading . . . abilities at the beginning of the third grade are likely to differ widely in reading ability a few years later if one does a great deal more reading than the other. No child is likely to continue to grow in reading ability or to maintain a high level of proficiency if his (or her) reading is confined to the necessary assignments in school.[p. 138]

This passage from Gates not only emphasizes the need to couple reading instruction with a great deal of practice; it makes clear that the development of reading ability is a joint responsibility of the school and the rest of society. To place exclusive responsibility on the school for the development of reading ability is irresponsible. To expect the school to compensate totally for the low reading ability of students who do little reading outside the school is nonsense. On the other hand, schools miss many opportunities to let children practice reading and, as I will now describe, they sometimes subtly encourage children to avoid books and other written school materials as sources of knowledge (especially of knowledge that will be tested).

It can be argued that students get a great deal of reading practice while doing their content area reading – while reading science and social studies, for example. Actually, it is in the content areas that we currently do the worst job of teaching reading comprehension – it is in the content areas that we most effectively teach children not to read. There is a pervasive classroom phenomenon that destroys reading comprehension instruction in the very process of helping students who don't understand a text. This phenomenon is most common in content area instruction, but it is also very common in other classroom reading situations. We have observed this phenomenon recently while giving in-service training to teachers (MacGinitie, 1984). It is a phenomenon based on the distinction between helping students understand the content of text and helping students understand the text.[3]

Most of the teachers we worked with are excellent teachers. The leading questions, analogies, and other devices they use to make the content clear to students are very effective. The problem begins when students have been assigned some reading that is related to content the teacher wants them to learn. If the teacher asks a question that some student cannot answer, or if there is any other indication that a student does not fully understand all that he or she has read, the teacher typically explains, and explains effectively. But the teacher explains the content; the teacher does not help the student understand the text.

The distinction between helping with the content and helping with the text seems difficult for teachers to comprehend in practice. When a student needs help in understanding text, it is very difficult for a concerned teacher not to step in and explain the content in his or her own way. This is particularly true, of course, in content area reading, even in the early grades.

Our observation of this phenomenon in many circumstances led Ruth to a generalization that we have dubbed *Ruth's Law*. Ruth's Law is that the more obvious or painful the student's lack of comprehension, the more likely that the teacher will explain the content rather than the text. When students cannot do the problems at the end of a section of text in a mathematics book, for example, it will be very obvious from the idle pencils, the raised hands, and the fidgeting that they have not understood the text. It will be very unlikely, however, that the teacher will, in this cirucumstance, try to help the students understand the text. Similarly, a student who does not understand the written instructions for a science experiment presents a painfully obvious problem, and the teacher is proportionally likely to give the student personal directions. After some experience, teachers learn implicitly which kinds of written materials, when not understood, will produce the most obvious classroom problems, and they often give up assigning such materials altogether. The result is that many students gain very little experience reading important types of material.

We have not found many content area teachers, even at the secondary level, rejecting the idea that they should teach reading. They readily accept the premise that one of their objectives should be for students to learn how to read material in their content area, and they are willing to devote some time to this objective. They want their students to be independent readers and learners; their training and practice simply have not incorporated that objective.

One can observe a number of teaching practices related to this tendency to explain content and ignore what the students have read. Teachers often ask students to read material in class or as homework. If the material is read in class, seldom are students allowed enough time to read it carefully. We don't seem to believe that students can be learning when we aren't telling them something. Whether material is read in class or at home, the same content is usually explained subsequently by the teacher if it is to be included in a test (Henderson, 1983). Students who have difficulty reading the material soon learn that the same content will be covered later by the teacher. Many students who *could* read and understand learn not to bother.

The obvious long-term consequence of these patterns of teacher behavior is that many students do very little reading in content areas throughout their school careers. Students who encounter difficulty with new and characteristic language forms in science or history – forms that are unfamiliar in their oral language experience – get no help in understanding those new forms. They fall farther and farther behind those other students whose backgrounds, abilities, or motivations allow them to work out an interpretation of the new forms and become familiar with them. The end result is well known: a large group of students who cannot readily learn by reading and for whom many characteristics of written language are difficult.

Although it is not possible to establish exact a priori differences in the difficulty of various text structures, contents, and questions about them, the National Assessment of Educational Progress (1982) reports that students at all three tested age levels performed less well on expository passages than on "literary" passages. Our observations clearly suggest that most students have had less help in learning to understand written expository text.

It is important to realize that good classroom teachers in the content areas have developed very effective ways of explaining the content they teach – and both students and teachers find this effective teaching satisfying. It is difficult to modify any long-established and much-practiced procedure; when that procedure is effective and satisfying, it will be even more difficult to modify. One should not expect, therefore, that teachers will find it easy to learn to occasionally help children understand the text rather than only the content. This change should be easier for primary teachers than for secondary content area specialists, partly because the habit of explaining content is less ingrained at the primary level and partly because teachers of young children are often already oriented toward watching children grow and change and toward assisting in the process. Older children are already so competent that growth in their capabilities is less obvious. With older children, it is easier to see how one has contributed new bits of knowledge to their background than to see how one has contributed to their competence in doing something on their own. It is overly simplistic to claim that teachers of young children get satisfaction from enabling while teachers of older children get satisfaction from imparting, but there is enough truth in this distinction that we must be understanding when a competent secondary teacher is reluctant to take the time to help a student understand a difficult passage.

Teachers are generally not accustomed to thinking of the particular ways in which ideas can be stated in text as content to be learned. Given the dominance of transmission teaching (se e.g., Hale & Edwards, 1981), it is not surprising that, in content area contexts, teachers fall back on explanations of content when the student seems not to have learned. The task for teacher education is to help teachers realize that written language can be content, while showing them alternatives to transmission teaching.

If there is currently very little reading comprehension instruction, and if the instruction we attempt to give is based on a faulty model, educators need to think more explicitly about what effective reading comprehension instruction would be like. We believe that effective reading comprehension instruction would be based on two fundamental principles. One of these principles is that if a student does not know something that is important, then you try to help him or her learn it. Specifically, if a student does not understand the point that an author tried to convey with a particular text, and if (a) what the student could learn about written language from understanding that text would be valuable; and (b) the student feels a need to know what the author was trying to convey; and (c) the student has the background to learn readily about the aspect of written language represented by his or her problem with that text, then it is appropriate to help the student understand that particular text. Instruction about language comprehension, as about other tasks in the school curriculum, can be appropriate, effective, and efficient. It should not be withheld.

The second basic principle is that reading comprehension instruction should be part of an ongoing reading experience that is significant and meaningful to the student (Shuy, 1981). Although we feel that reading comprehension instruction is vitally important and much neglected, we almost hesitate to promote it for fear that the form it will take will be formalized, systematized, and stultifying. Comprehension instruction should not follow the model of literary interpretation, in which each detail is analyzed to a degree that destroys both the text and the student. Nor should it follow the model of formal grammar instruction, in which the student learns names for parts but not the function of the whole. It will be inimical to growth in reading if we try to explain to a student that what he or she does not understand is simply "case *b* of the optional complementizer deletion transformation," or that the student would understand if he or she only paid attention to the emphatic contrastive adversative cohesive tie. Neither will it be helpful to provide students with an extensive set of exercises on adversative cohesive ties.[4]

Reading comprehension instruction should not consist of a set of exercises or lessons (MacGinitie, 1983). There is no single convention of language, no aspect of grammar or discourse structure, that is so important that the student must master it before moving on. Reading comprehension instruction should not be overly systematized. There is no particular sequence in which learning should take place and no value in trying to impose a sequence. Language and language use are too beautifully flexible for the understanding of one's native language to be systematized effectively. One cannot specify with precision the difficulty, function, meaning, or intent of any feature or aspect of language in isolation from others. Interaction is the rule. A text does not just exist in a context; it alters context (Ballmer, 1981).

These, then, are the basic principles of teaching reading comprehension – or anything else: (a) Find out what the student needs to know and help the student learn it; and (b) Provide this help in a context that is meaningful and significant to the student.

The teacher will continue to help students directly with content on many occasions, but will also help them work out an interpretation of the text on those occasions when the mode of expression is particularly interesting or useful to understand. If students had received such help in constructing the meanings of texts from the primary grades onward, many students in the intermediate and secondary grades would need much less help with reading and less oral instruction than they now do.

Notes

1. The significance of these differences has usually been assessed by treating the tested students as a random sample of all students at the given age level and by disregarding the fact that multiple tests were performed. In fact, the error in the comparison is not that of random selection but arises primarily in choosing samples to represent strata in a sampling plan. The effective N is smaller than assumed, and more differences have been designated significant than is warranted.
2. The list of differences that follows is based on Maria and MacGinitie (1982) and on Schallert, Kleiman, and Rubin (1977).
3. An example of this distinction is given in the appendix to MacGinitie (1984).
4. There will certainly be many studies that will report that specific instruction in cohesive ties, story grammar, transformations, or some other feature of language is helpful – that is, better in some way than no instruction or than the customary instruction. Such findings do not demonstrate, however, that the specific instruction should be included in the curriculum. What an infinitude of various possible instructional activities would be better, in some way and on the average, than no instruction or than what is customary! Most of these activities would fare badly, however, if evaluated for individual students in terms of the principles of comprehension instruction described in the closing pages of this paper. On the other hand, there will be occasions when instruction in, say, story grammar or some aspect of cohesion would be very appropriate for some students. The ability to recognize these occasions and the background and skill to help the student on these occasions are characteristics of an effective teacher.

References

Adams, M. (1979). Studies of oral conversation in relation to written texts. In B. Starr (Ed.), *Progress Report 2 on the BBN Group of the Center for the Study of Reading* (BBN Report No. 4106). Cambridge, Ma.: Bolt, Beranek, and Newman.

Ballmer, T. T. (1981). Words, sentences, texts, and all that. *Test, 1*, 163–89.

Calfee, R. D. & Pointkowski, D. C. (1981). The reading diary: Acquisition of decoding. *Reading Research Quarterly, 16*, 346–73.

Cazden, C. B. (1972). *Child language and education.* New York: Holt, Rinehart and Winston.

Chapman, L. J. (1983). *Reading development and cohesion.* Exeter, N. H.: Heinemann Educational Books.

College Entrance Examination Board (1977). *On further examination: Report of the advisory panel on the Scholastic Aptitude Test score decline.* New York: College Entrance Examination Board.

Durkin, D. (1979). What classroom observations reveal about reading comprehension instruction. *Reading Research Quarterly, 14*, 481–533.

Durkin, D. (1981). Reading comprehension instruction in five basal reader series. *Reading Research Quarterly, 16*, 515–44.

Gates, A. I. (1947). *The improvement of reading* (3rd ed.). New York: MacMillan.

Hale, A., & Edwards, A. D. (1981). Hearing children read. In J. Edwards (Ed.), *The social psychology of reading* (Vol. 1), pp. 117–30. Silver Spring, Md.: Institute of Modern Languages.

Halliday, M. A. K., & Hasan, R. (1976). *Cohesion in English.* London: Longman.

Henderson, S. (1983). *Grade twelve and university reading assignments.* Unpublished Master's Thesis, University of Victoria, British Columbia.

Horowitz, M. W., & Berkowitz, A. (1967). Listening and reading, speaking and writing: An experimental investigation of differential acquisition and reproduction of memory. *Perceptual and Motor Skills, 24*, 207–15.

Layton, R. (1981). Reading Research: The source for challenging back-to-the-basics advocates. *Contemporary Educational Psychology, 6*, 252–62.

MacGinitie, W. H. (1979). What do published reading comprehension lessons teach? In *Proceedings, Reading '79.* Toronto: York University.

MacGinitie, W. H. (1983). A critique of "What Classroom Observations Reveal about Reading Comprehension Instruction" and "Reading Comprehension Instruction in Five Basal Reader Series": Durkin's contribution to our understanding of current practice. In L. M. Gentile, M. L. Kamil, & J. S. Blanchard (Eds.), *Reading research revisited*, pp. 355–63. Columbus, Oh.: Charles E. Merrill.

MacGinitie, W. H. (1984). Readability as a solution adds to the problem. In R. C. Anderson, J. Osborn, & R. J. Tierney (Eds.), *Learning to read in American schools: Basal readers and content texts*, pp. 141–51. Hillsdale, N. J.: Lawrence Erlbaum Associates.

Maria, K., & MacGinitie, W. H. (1982).Reading comprehension disabilities: Knowledge structures and non-accommodating text processing strategies. *Annals of Dyslexia, 32*, 33–59.

National Assessment of Educational Progress, Education Commission of the States (1981). *Three national assessments of reading: Changes in performance, 1970–80* (Report No. 11-R-01).

National Assessment of Educational Progress, Education Commission of the States (1982). *Reading comprehension of American youth:do they understand what they read?* (Report No. 11-R-02).

Piaget, J., & Inhelder, B. (1956). *The child's conception of space.* London: Routledge and Kegan Paul.

Pichert, J. W., & Anderson, R. C. (1977). Taking different perspectives on a story. *Journal of Educational Psychology, 69*, 309–15.

Schallert, D. L., Kleiman, G. M., & Rubin, A. D. (1977). *Differences between oral and written language* (Tech. Rep. No. 29). Urbana: University of Illinois, Center for the Study of Reading.

Shuy, R. W. (1981). A holistic view of language. *Research in the Teaching of English, 15,* 101–11.

Tuinman, J., & Kendall, J. R. (1980, September). *The British Columbia Reading Assessment: Summary Report.* Victoria, B. C.: Learning Assessment Branch, Ministry of Education, Province of British Columbia.

Wilkinson, A. M. (1971). *The foundation of language: Talking and reading in young children.* London: Oxford University Press.

17   Teaching writing: the process approach, humanism, and the context of "crisis"

Richard M. Coe

Although it has somewhat different implications in the 1980s, the term "process approach" originated in a 1960s slogan, "Teach the process, not just the product." The second part of this article is an operational definition of a process approach to the development of writing abilities – complete with rather specific guidelines for both teaching and developing curriculum – originally drafted for a small group of classroom teachers who were remaking the high school writing curriculum in the Surrey district of British Columbia. As such, it is a pragmatic document with an explicit empirical basis.

But teachers – and those who would lead them – too often doom themselves to repeating old mistakes by losing their own history and misreading the social contexts that partially motivate curricular changes. In North America, as elsewhere, changes in the teaching of writing were intitiated within a "crisis" atmosphere, amidst charges that the quality of instruction had somehow drastically deteriorated. As Kenneth Burke enigmatically notes, "The trouble with shortcuts is that they save us from taking the long way round." The first part of this article is an attempt to take a long way round, beginning with a social analysis of literacy "crises" in general (and recent ones in particular), in order to establish not only an empirical but also a social basis for understanding current trends in composition pedagogy. This long way round will take us as far as an analysis of the recent "crisis" in China (where I taught in 1981 – 82) and as far back as the intertwined traditions of Renaissance humanism, Classical rhetoric, and the *paideia* of ancient Greece. Assuredly, the teaching practices advocated in the second part can be approached more immediately. But without this long way round, their implications are likely to be understood less fully, and that may lead to mistakes in their implementation.

270

Literacy "crises": a systemic analysis

Literacy "crises" are usually perceived as *declines* in reading, writing, and/ or associated abilities. With the exception of immediately postrevolutionary situations (e.g., Nicaragua in 1979), the problem is perceived by most people concerned as a deterioration of a previously satisfactory level of literacy (or, at least, of a previously satisfactory rate of progress toward achieving such a level). Certainly, the problem is usually so presented in both popular and professional media.

The literacy problem is often associated with a deterioration also of moral/political values and is considered one of the causes of social and economic difficulties. The problem is usually blamed on the educational practices of the immediately preceding period, and the solution is often seen, at least in part, as involving a return to previously criticized educational practices. On this level of generality, the same description fits literacy "crises" as diverse as the most recent ones in North America (mid to late 1970s) and China (late 1970s to early 1980s).

Literacy "crises" generally occur when one or more of the following conditions exist:

1. The literacy abilities developed by the educational subsystem do not adequately fit the requirements of the socioeconomic system;
2. The literacy abilities developed on one level of the educational system do not adequately fit the requirements of a higher level;
3. There are socioeconomic failures, most commonly unemployment rates rising above a previous "ceiling" of acceptability.

The function of the literacy "crisis" is to impose constraints on the educational subsystem such that it will produce socially mandated outputs (i.e., graduates who are willing and able to do what the particular society requires). It also functions to justify mandates originating from particular social classes and interest groups, making it seem that the interests of society as a whole (and especially of the students) are thus being served. And it may have a tertiary function of projecting the blame for socioeconomic failures onto the victims (e. g., for unemployment, onto the "illiterate" unemployed).

Is a "crisis" a decline?

There is good reason to doubt, however, that a decline of literacy abilities within a society is a necessary or even typical prerequisite to a literacy "crisis." Certainly, despite subjective impressions and certain misinterpreted test scores, North American literacy "crises" have generally not been responses to declining literacy abilities among the whole population.

An inadequate fit between the output of the educational subsystem and the requirements of the socioeconomic system may, of course, be created by changes in either system. To understand literacy "crises" – especially ones that occur when there is no hard evidence of declining literacy abilities – we must look at systemic relationships. Moreover, an inadequate fit may also be created by a change in the type, not the level, of literacy required. However high or low the level of literacy, it may still be of the wrong type for a particular socioeconomic context. We must, furthermore, understand literacy training as having several different relevant functions – because the process of developing literacy is inevitably also a socializing process, and the real "crisis" may have as much or more to do with the socializing as with the reading and writing aspect of the problem.

Consider, for example, the most recent North American "crisis" (the beginning of which, on a national level, is conveniently marked by a *Newsweek* magazine article published in December 1975). Roughly two decades earlier, the headlines had been "Why Johnny Can't Read"; this time, the increasing social importance of writing (especially for report writing), as well as a different level of feminist consciousness, produced headlines reading "Why Johnny and Jane Can't Write." The result of this "crisis" was a "Back to the basics" movement that presumed that the crux of the solution to allegedly declining writing abilities was a return to previously higher levels of grammar drill.

There had, indeed, been a radical shift in composition pedagogy during the "sixties" (which, in this case, refers to 1969 – 74), including, ironically enough, the beginning of a trend to devote more and higher quality resources to composition. But had writing abilities actually declined? In particular – since this was the focus of most criticism – was there a decline in the ability to produce mechanically correct writing? As it happens, we have data to answer these questions.

The evidence

The data most frequently cited by the American media were declining scores on the Scholastic Aptitude Test (SAT) of verbal abilities. This is a university entrance examination, taken by more than a million students each year. It is a combination of multiple-choice vocabulary and reading comprehension items; its function is to predict grades (i. e., it measures something that correlates significantly with success in university courses). It is not a writing test. It is not a valid measure of literacy. The "aptitude" it measures correlates with college grades, not with literacy.

The real significance of the decline in SAT scores is captured by the quest of Prof. Michael W. Kirst (Stanford). Noting that Arkansas has one of the highest mean SAT scores in the United States, he considered the possibility that California should try to emulate Arkansas. But an analysis of the data showed that in California 35% of high school students took the SAT while in Arkansas only 5% did so (Reed, 1983). In short, the best way to have good SAT scores is to depress students' aspirations so that those likely to get low scores do not take the test.

Interestingly enough, the College Entrance Examination Board, which administers the SAT, also administers a writing *achievement* test. During the same period when SAT verbal ability scores were falling, writing achievement test scores were *improving*. These data were not so frequently cited by the media, perhaps in part because the composition achievement test is taken by a smaller group of students. (But then, the students who take the SAT are also atypical of the whole population.) (College Entrance Examination Board, 1977; cf. Cooper, 1981: 4 – 7).

Meanwhile there was in progress a nationwide assessment of writing abilities. The National Assessment of Educational Progress (1980) took writing samples from 9-, 13-, and 17-year-old Americans in 1969 – 70, 1973 – 74, and 1978 – 79. These samples reveal that the incidence of mechanical errors changed little over the decade. In no age group was there a substantial decline or increase in errors. Quantitative analysis, moreover, revealed no significant change in syntactic fluency (i.e., stylistic maturity), except an improvement among the youngest group (where it was very likely the product of a popular new pedagogy, called sentence combining, that was designed to produce just such improvement). Although a minority of students (10 to 25%) demonstrated serious problems, a majority at each age could master the conventions of writing. Furthermore, black students narrowed the gap between themselves and the national norm – and on some tasks were performing at the national level in 1979. Data for disadvantaged urban pupils were more contradictory, but the oldest group did make steady gains through the three assessments.

The results of the National Assessment do reveal literacy problems. In 1973, for example, only 69 percent of 13-year-olds were able to write a minimally successful persuasive letter; by 1978; despite several years of "Back to the basics," that percentage had declined by 5 points. Responses to background questions, moreover, indicate that 13- and 17-year olds neither receive much writing instruction nor are required to do much writing in their various courses. Few have access to the type of writing instruction that is consistent with current research and recommended by leaders in the field of composition – but neither did their parents or grandparents.

Charles Cooper (1981) summarizes the data this way:

Consequently, we can say that the best data available – those derived from a nation-wide testing program designed specifically to monitor changes in achievement – show some improvements and some declines and probably on average, all the results taken together, a very slight decline. It is interesting to note that achievement over ten years in the basic skills of writing mechanics and math computation – the main concern of competency-testing advocates – has been stable, while the higher cognitive skills of composing and problem solving have declined. This result suggests that the problem may not be where some think it is: with the minimal skills of bare functional literacy; rather, the problem seems to be with the maximal skills of thinking, creating, and problem solving. [p. 6]

The contradictions between the National Assessment results and the subjective impressions of various observers (especially employers and university professors) need to be explained. To some extent, of course, this anomaly can be explained by a tendency to remember the "good old days" as better than they actually were. Certainly, there is no difficulty in finding articles written during the "good old days" that make complaints about declining literacy standards virtually identical with the ones published in the late 1970s (Greenbaum, 1969).

The "Sixties"

One of the conclusions that can be drawn from the National Assessment results suggests a more complex explanation. In the older groups, expressive writing ability improved or remained the same over the decade, but persuasive and descriptive writing abilities seemed to be declining. This is exactly what should have been expected. The years preceding the "Back to the basics" counter-revolt were characterized by a growing trend toward "creative" self-expression as the predominant genre of student writing. The false dichotomy between thinking and writing (i.e., the mistaken notion that people first think and only afterwards find words to "express" those thoughts, that language is merely a dress thought puts on) was dissolved in many quarters. The focus of research and new pedagogy was on rhetorical invention. At the same time, a growing understanding of language led to the widening realization that Standard English is in no scientific sense intrinsically superior to other dialects of English.

All of this was consistent with the general spirit of "sixties" liberalism. It was also consistent with general trends in education: a shift of emphasis from "objective" facts to learning processes, from reinforcement of conventional morality to values clarification.

In the teaching of composition, as elsewhere, the shift of emphasis sometimes became an overemphasis. Too many teachers never took students beyond the joys of "creativity," never taught them how to structure their writings to meet the needs and expectations of readers, never taught them how to do analytic as well as self-expressive writing. Student writing often remained subjective self-expression rather than becoming communicative. Too many students did not learn how to do the types of writing that are required in universities, nor the types that "make the world go round." For self-expressive writing, the pluralistic, liberal notion that all dialects are equal was adequate: As long as they were involved primarily in self-discovery, values clarification, and self-expression, students did not need to be reminded that the important business of North America is conducted in Standard English. And since self-expression cannot be evaluated objectively – as, at least in principle, communication can be – the emphasis on motivation and "positive feedback" contributed to grade inflation.

It must be emphasized that these inadequacies did not prevent the achievement of a certain type of literacy. If students who receive this type of instruction are tested on how well they can do this type of writing, the pedagogy proves to be successful. If they are tested on their ability to do other types of writing, of course, the results will be poorer. Thus the National Assessment found that, for the two older groups, persuasive and descriptive writing ability seemed to be declining between 1969 and 79, while expressive writing ability was improving or remaining stable (National Assessment of Educational Progress, 1980).

As the Story Workshop technique has demonstrated – in the ghettos of Chicago, for example – expressive writing can be very useful and liberating; it can help people discover their identities, individually and sometimes even as social groups, and it can be a stepping stone toward other kinds of writing competency. Certainly such writing is consistent with the goals of humanistic education. But it must also be admitted that one of the social obligations of an educational subsystem is to develop in students those abilities required by the existing job structure, as well as by other social structures. The question that matters is whether North Americans are literate enough and *in the right ways* to function effectively and humanly in today's and tomorrow's societies. The "sixties" emphasis on expressive writing abilities was more successful in encouraging humanistic development than in fostering vocational competence or even social effectiveness. (To some extent this was because the pedagogy was poorly implemented: In theory, expressive writing ability was just a starting point, but in practice it often became the curriculum.)

Although the most basic constraints that created the virtual inevitability of a literacy "crisis" were socioeconomic, within the educational system the "Back to the basics" movement was a counter-revolt against the humanistic, liberal, often unrealistic curriculum and pedagogy of the "sixties." This becomes especially clear when we look at particulars. The following case history is Canadian, demonstrating the international extent of the particular "crisis."

A Canadian case history

The literacy "crisis" in British Columbia began with the publication of Grade 12 scholarship examination results in the spring of 1974: 22.5 percent of the students had failed. Because of the way it was administered, this test was not comparable to previous Grade 12 examinations; thus there was no basis for determining whether this failure rate represented a decline (Berland and McGee, 1977: 18).

At the end of the fall semester of 1974, the English Department of the University of British Columbia (UBC) gave all first-year students what it called a "Grade 9" examination, including an essay that was graded solely for mechanics and formal organization. The failure rate was over 40% (Berland and McGee, 1977: 19). Once again there is no basis for saying whether this failure rate represented a decline.

The minutes of English Department meetings and discussions with members of the department make clear that the motives for the examination (and for publicizing its results) were twofold:

1. to pressure the high schools into modifying their curricula so as to meet UBC professors' requirements;
2. to pressure certain English professors, who had been emphasizing quality of thought and values clarification, into putting less emphasis on substantive criteria and more on mechanical correctness.

Over seven succeeding years, the failure rate on this examination remained approximately 40% despite obvious improvement in students' writing (especially in terms of mechanical correctness), despite changes (in practice) in grading criteria, and despite the fact (revealed by objective analysis done by the Ministry of Education) that the difficulty of the examinations differed radically. It seems clear, and this is confirmed by my own experience serving on both the committee that administers and the committees that mark the test (Coe, 1978: 19 – 20), that the test and its administration are neither valid, nor even reliable. The test was, however, politically effective in realizing the goals of those who instituted it.

In 1974 (and to a lesser extent, to this day), UBC English professors were, by preference and training, literary critics. In first-year English classes, however, they found it increasingly necessary to teach writing, a subject most of them had neither the inclination nor the ability to teach properly. Not surprisingly, they wished to avoid both the teaching of writing and complaints from colleagues in other departments that writing was not being taught. The solution was to make certain that entering students were already minimally competent writers. With logical consistency, therefore, the department dealt with the literacy "crisis" in part by abolishing its remedial writing courses.

It must be emphasized that there is no evidence proving that the youth of British Columbia wrote any less competently in 1974 than previously. On the contrary, literacy criteria in British Columbia have changed so radically during the 20th century that comparisons are virtually impossible (de Castell and Luke, 1983). What we do have is clear evidence that an ever larger percentage of the youth were not dropping out of the educational system soon enough to save university professors (or even senior high school teachers) from having to deal with them. In the 1920s, over 99 percent of students who entered Grade 8 in British Columbia had dropped out before Grade 11. In the 1950s the dropout rate was still over half, but by the 1970s more than 80% were continuing past Grade 10 (which had been the traditional dropout point) (*Composition 11*, 1982: 3). This is consistent with the general Canadian pattern: During the 1960s the university population increased more than 10 times as fast as "the nation's university-aged population" (Lockhard, cited in Berland and McGee, 1977: 24). Thus at UBC, as elsewhere in North America, university professors and high school teachers perceived declining abilities in their classrooms because the poorer students had ceased dropping out. The average 17-year-old British Columbian of 1974 almost undoubtedly wrote better than the average 17-year-old British Columbian of 1924 or 1954; the difference was that in 1974 the average 17-year-old was still in the educational system. (Similarly, as noted above, the average 17-year-old black American wrote better in 1979 than in 1969 – but because she or he was also a lot more likely to enter university, professors were a lot more likely to notice whether she or he had mastered Standard English.)

But professors and high school teachers were not the only ones upset. The "Back to the basics" movement in British Columbia was headed by a parents' organization called the Genuine Education Movement (GEM). GEM members were middle- and upper-class, predominantly professionals, with 1974 incomes over $20,000. A contrast with two Gallup polls showed them to be also more conservative than a representative sample of the population. Overwhelmingly, they – 92 percent of them – felt that discipline in the schools was not strict enough (Morgan and Robinson, cited in Berland and McGee, 1977: 18).

Three GEM candidates were elected to the Vancouver School Board, which in 1976 proposed the establishment of "value schools" that would be "more structured," put more emphasis on "basic skills," adhere closely to prescribed texts and provincial curricula, and emphasize "punctuality, attendance, class rank, and the "Judeo – Christian ethic." These schools were proposed despite a task force report showing that, although their scores were declining somewhat, Vancouver students at all grade levels still were performing on standardized tests at levels higher than the norms set by the companies that devised those tests (Berland and McGee, 1977: 20).

The social function of literacy

What we see here, as so often in literacy "crises," is that those who complain about declining literacy are often concerned about changing social values (i.e., about issues that must be described as moral or political, not just academic). Similarly, in the United States, complaints about low academic standards have evolved into attacks on humanistic education and demands that schools inculcate Christian values. In China, where for millenia Confucian education was built around a moral core (Needham, 1962: 6), and where it is still assumed that education should be overtly both moral/political and academic (i. e., both "red and expert," with "red" being presumed to exclude "decadent" immorality), the criticism of those educated during the Cultural Revolution includes charges that they are undisciplined, unmotivated, and selfish, as well as unskilled. In Nicaragua, the Sandinista literacy campaign was also overtly value-laden, introducing both concepts related to hygiene, nutrition, disease prevention, and so forth and also political positions, such as calls for the liberation of women and the expropriation of Noranda's gold mines (DeBresson, 1981: 6 – 8).

The point here is not to condemn this mixing of academic and moral/political education, but to understand and evaluate it.

Any educational system contributes to reproducing the social and economic system which generates it. Industrial capitalism did not promote public education without very private interests in seeing its workforce able to work its machines. The educational system we work in daily reproduces the biases of the society we live in. Today, for example, efforts are being made in B. C. to orient this education towards the supply of an ever increasing need for computer terminal operators and programmers. Conversely, we cannot expect the Sandinistas' educational effort to be free of social intentions. [DeBresson, 1981: 7 – 8]

The relationship between the social function of literacy and the type of literacy encouraged (or allowed) is interestingly evoked by an historical example: the Reformation in 16th-century Germany. The wider dissemination of literacy abilities was, of course, a key point in the Reformers' program to break the power of the Catholic Church. It is not so well known that the orthodox Reform curriculum emphasized "learning the catechism by heart, while regarding reading and writing as a secondary matter." Nor is it so well known that, while the orthodox Reformers emphasized the religious function of literacy, the "Schwarmer" wing of the German Reformation (epitomized by Valentin Ickelsamer of Augsburg) applied the notion of *selbs verteilen* (to judge for oneself) beyond religion to questions of politics and ideology, science and technology.

One remarkably radical implication (for the time) of this tendency was that scientific and technical knowledge should be public and published – thus undercutting the guilds' monopology of craft knowledge (and, in some cases, leading to book burnings by guild members trying to protect their secrets). Another radical implication was an emphasis on writing: The Schwarmer literacy movement created its own reading materials, which represented an effort of the movement's members both "to make their ideas publicly known and (to) create teaching materials for the newcomers." As a consequence of these "empowering" goals, Ickelsamer developed a pedagogy based on (a) "sounding out" (*lautieren*), (b) allowing learners to overgeneralize at first and correct later, (c) deemphasizing spelling and penmanship, (d) starting with the known and understandable, (e) using pictures and words in tandem (thus teaching literacy as the interpretation of symbolic language), (f) demystifying expertise, and (g) encouraging self-reliance – in short, for the 16th century, a remarkably "direct," Freirean approach (Giesecke and Elwert, 1982).

Literacy courses based on Ickelsamer's method were banned after 1545. And the mainstream of the Reformation was correct in this banning: The Schwarmers' methods encouraged a type of literacy inappropriate to the sociopolitical goals of the more reformist Reformers. Had they prevailed, the Schwarmers could have created a peculiar literacy "crisis" (which would probably have been described by pointing out that students didn't know "the basics" of the catechism).

What is basic?

There are two anomalies the resolution of which helps to clarify these relationships between literacy and society. The first lies behind the slogan "Back to the basics" – "the basics" being understood to mean usage, grammar, spelling, and punctuation. In what sense are these basic? From a writer's point of view, having something significant to say, getting that something organized and developed, and presenting it coherently so that readers can grasp the pattern of meaning – these are basic. Editing skills, although important in many contexts, are definitely superficial. Indeed, many executives relegate such matters to their secretaries. Nor is it pedagogically true that editing skills should be learned first; on the contrary, having something to say is the best motivation for learning these "finer points."

Why, then, is "grammar" the bottom line? Why, on the UBC minimal literacy test, must an essay fail if it contains serious subject – verb disagreement even if it is in every other respect clear, coherent, and even brilliant? The answer is to be found, among other places, in *Pygmalion*, which ironically enough was taught in that same UBC English program. One of Shaw's main themes in that play is that a large part of traditional education is devoted not to the real basics, but to trivia – the trivia that signify social status. What Shaw says in that play about the ridiculousness of judging people by their accents and their ability to follow the rules of etiquette is similarly applicable to judging them by their ability to use the grammatical patterns of the dominant dialect of the English language. Nonetheless, people are so judged in North America, and those immigrant or oppressed minority students who aspire to "white collar" and professional jobs are not in error when they desire to learn this particular trivium. So we can see, on one level, what is basic about "grammar": People without it are likely to end up in more oppressive jobs.

There is, of course, a point at which failure to follow the rules of Standard English grammar interferes with communication. The English language was standardized in the 18th century along with other means of production, in part because standardization led to increased productivity. But the "Back to the basics" movement advocated returning to grammar drills despite "70 years of research which demonstrate overwhelmingly that isolated teaching of grammatical skills has little or no transfer to use in actual writing" (Kinneavy, 1979: 1; see also O'Hare, 1971, and Wilkinson, 1971: 32–34). Although the case against grammar drill is sometimes overstated, there is general evidence that skills taught out of context are not well applied. (See, for example, Carry and Weaver, 1969, esp., Chapter 6 and Appendices B and D; and Brievik, 1975.)

If teaching "grammar" is not actually an efficient way of producing writers capable of mechanical correctness, what is its virtue? The answer to this question is related to a second anomaly: Even where the need for skilled workers has not increased, employers' preference for educated workers has.

Employers can now demand a bachelor's degree for jobs which once required a high school diploma ... Employers can demand that potential employees have certificates of high school or college graduation, not because a diploma indicates marketable or useful skills, but because educational certification promises maximum productivity in terms of *motivation* and *behavior* ... Bowles and Gintis in *Schooling in Capitalist America* cite a number of studies which show that the personal qualities that bring a student higher grades are similar to those that bring a worker a better position on the job ... Upwardly mobile middle class kids have internalized school values to the extent that they are usually willing to perform unquestioningly any task assigned. [Berland and McGee, 1977: p. 30]

Whatever their lack of effectiveness in teaching composition, grammar drills have a clear function in the hidden curriculum of socialization. The "Back to the basics" movement was correct to focus on them – because they are the precise contrary of the "creative" values-clarification composition curriculum.

Social status and power

One of the functions of the educational subsystem in many societies is to provide the rationale and/or basis for deciding who will have which social status and do which work. In China today, the return to using academic tests to decide who will have access to higher education and better jobs will raise the level of expertise in decision-making positions; since the children of today's cadres seem to do better than most on those tests (various personal communications; see also Tang, 1981), it will also provide a rationale for their receiving social status comparable to their parents' status.

When the Georgia Board of Regents responded to the 1975 literacy "crisis" by taking an old test of usage and (after revising it slightly) mandating that no student be exempted from or allowed to exit remedial English courses without passing it, they made it that much more difficult for students who speak Black English to obtain college degrees (Crew, 1978). Neither Black English nor Chinese has any pattern analogous to the English S-inflection. In both Georgia and British Columbia, mastery of this pattern became an important criterion for minimal competency, thereby reducing the upward mobility of blacks in Georgia and Chinese in British Columbia.

Thus a literacy "crisis" can function so as to readjust the constraints within which social status and power are distributed, perhaps to put an upwardly mobile group back in its place (or require members of that group to adopt "established" values before rising). It can also function to "blame the victim": The unemployed may be told that if they were better educated they would have jobs. In both China and North America, it is presently argued that a better educated work force would be more productive – an assertion that blames low productivity on the workers while encouraging them to transfer the blame to the educational subsystem. In North America, at least, it is clear that levels of productivity have much more to do with levels of capital investment than with anything workers can control, and the high level of underemployment also tends to negate the argument.

The socioeconomic context of literacy

This brings us to the crux of the matter: What type of literacy education will most adequately fit the requirements of a given socioeconomic system? In China, during the Cultural Revolution, the primary social goal was to prevent the consolidation of a bureaucracy comparable to the old Confucian one or the one existing in the USSR. The most crucial type of literacy was political: the ability to read and interpret the political texts that functioned as guidelines for political analysis and the ability to "read" and interpret the social signifiers of class loyalties.[1] In fact, it can be argued that the Cultural Revolution failed (and, in particular, failed to be a truly cultural revolution) precisely because the level of this type of literacy was inadequate. In any event, after the Cultural Revolution was ended, the primary social goal became the modernization of China, which required a different type of literacy.

In language teaching, for example, the importance of English and Japanese rose, of course, because these languages are instrumental in commerce and technology. More interestingly, the approach to teaching foreign languages changed. Before the Cultural Revolution the predominant technique was "intensive reading" (i.e., word-by-word translation and sentence-by-sentence grammatical analysis), a technique appropriate to philological and literary-historical study; now, however, there is a shift toward "extensive reading" (i.e., reading for comprehension, with more emphasis on speed and overall understanding than on being able to translate every word) and oral comprehension – because language is no longer studied for its own sake, but rather as a "tool." Marx is widely quoted as saying that knowledge of a foreign language is a "weapon." There is the beginning of a trend toward teaching "English for special purposes" (i.e., scientific English to scientists, commercial English to managers, and so on).

One can see a similar pattern in 19th century "crises" in the United States. The "Committee of Ten," representing the major universities, imposed curricular changes on the schools in order to facilitate a shift from classical to modern subjects (including, at Harvard, the first freshman composition course) because the educational subsystem had to produce proportionally fewer preachers and more scientists and managers (Wright, 1977; Douglas, 1966; Resnick and Resnick, 1977).

The most recent North American "crisis" provides a particularly elegant example of a literacy "crisis" grounded in a changing economic system. Various other constraints that helped create this "crisis" have already been discussed; the point here is not to negate them, but to show how those educational, political, and social factors served a basic economic function. Whatever the intentions of the "Back to the basics" movement, its effect was to adjust the educational subsystem to new economic realities. Although superficially there was a return to certain old pedagogies, the basic result was a kind of education quite unlike the "good old days." It can be argued that, although the innovations appeared radical, the "sixties" represented the logical development of traditional educational values (traceable at least back to Dewey, and in a sense back to the classical Greek *paideia*), and that what we are seeing now in North America is a radical shift operating under the cover of a return to traditional "Judeo – Christian" values.

Since World War II, a steadily increasing percentage of North Americans have been attending institutions of higher learning. Economically and vocationally, this makes sense only if one assumes that more and more professional jobs have been becoming available. It is clear that people have been coming to college in large part because, relative to total population, blue-collar jobs and small business opportunities have been decreasing. And a widely shared assumption, sometimes called the "human capital" theory (Lockhart, 1976), asserts that as societies grow increasingly technological they will need increasingly skilled and educated workers.

The restructuring of "white-collar" work

Certainly it is true that, as an ever-larger percentage of the work force is employed in "information processing," "sales," and "service" positions, more and more workers wear white collars, and more and more jobs require college degrees. In the United States, until 1920, the percentage of those gainfully occupied who worked in goods-producing industries fluctuated between 45 and 50%; between 1930 and 1950, it was approximately 41%; by 1970, it had dropped to 33% (Braverman, 1975: 237–39). Nonetheless, at least under capitalist management and constraints, the "human capital" theory is essentially false. Since World War II, North American societies have grown increasingly technological and computer-based, but most "white-collar" jobs have grown simpler and less professional.

Especially in the lower-status professions (e.g., nursing, school teaching, accounting, lower management), where an ever larger number of college graduates end up, total work processes may grow more complex, but individual jobs grow simpler (Campbell, 1978; Berland and McGee, 1977; Coe, 1978; *Canadian Dimension*, 1979; and, especially Braverman, 1975). The division of labor is increasingly hierarchical, and – under the rubric of "decentralization" – basic decisions are increasingly centralized (see Zimbalist, 1979, especially papers by Kraft, Glenn & Feldberg, and de Kadt). This means that the individual worker needs a type of literacy distinct from the type we have traditionally associated with professionalism (and with a liberal or humanistic education) (Coe, 1981a: especially, iii – vi, xii – xv).

Even within the elite professions, certain segments are losing some of the autonomy that defines professionalism. Among professors, for instance, although an ever larger percentage have doctorates, relatively fewer are primarily scholars, who go into the classroom to profess; for better and for worse, most are primarily university teachers – and increasingly overworked and deprofessionalized, although they are allowed to retain some signifiers of professioral status (especially those that do not cost money).

At the lower end, there is an ever larger group of white-collar workers who are in no sense professional and who have even less autonomy than most blue-collar workers. They include "service" workers (e.g., telephone operators) and are typified by those clerical workers who feed data into computer terminals (Braverman, 1975; Zimbalist, 1979; Howard, 1981; Garson, 1981).

The present deprofessionalizing of professors and other white-collar workers is comparable to the earlier destruction of most crafts by the "scientific" management movement (epitomized by F. W. Taylor). The essential trend is the separation of conceptualization from implementation, which among blue-collar workers meant the separation of mental from manual labor: Artisans and mechanics were replaced by a hierarchy of managers, engineers, supervisors, and skilled, semiskilled, and unskilled workers – the so-called skilled workers being less skilled and less knowledgeable than the craftspeople they replaced (hence the need for "scientific" management).

It is important to remember that many of the artisans and mechanics, to judge (for example) by the books they bought in remarkably large numbers and by their membership in scientific societies, were more literate than many of today's college graduates. Between 1791 and 1793, Thomas Paine's *Rights of Men*, for instance, sold 200,000 copies to an English population of 10 million; in 1817, Corbett's *2nd Register* was selling 40 to 60 thousand a week (while the London Times sold 5 to 6 thousand). In 1918, the *International Molders Journal* editorialized:

The really essential element in craftsmanship is not manual skill & dexterity but something stored up in the mind of the worker . . . The gathering up of all this scattered craft knowledge, systematizing it and concentrating it in the hands of the employer and then doling it out again only in the form of minute instructions, giving to each worker only the knowledge needed for the performance of a particular relatively minute task . . . separates skill & knowledge . . . When it is completed the worker is no longer a craftsman in any sense, but is an animated tool of the management.[Cited in Braverman, 1975: 136.]

Braverman notes the high amount of scientific learning that was part of an apprenticeship and the high level of participation in scientific organizations, institutes, and libraries (pp. 133–34).

As an increasing percentage of the work force deals with information and computers (instead of with goods and machines), the principles of "scientific" management are being applied to information workers. As the division of labor becomes increasingly hierarchical, decision makers are increasingly removed from the point of production and the "raw" information. Only if they have subordinates who can write accurate reports will these decision makers have the information they need to make effective decisions. They also need subordinates who can read accurately and make decisions regarding implementation within the bounds set by written instructions and guidelines.

What this increasingly hierarchical division of labor requires is many workers who can read for information, follow instructions, and (perhaps) write occasional short reports clearly and accurately; some workers with specialized reading, writing, and thinking abilities to write longer reports and handle the "decentralized" implementation decisions (which require the ability to make low-level inferences correctly); and a few real professionals with genuinely critical reading, writing, and thinking abilities to serve in (and educate) the centralized managerial elite. The "Back to the basics" movement (and the testing movement it spawned) will assure that even the lower-status colleges develop in their students the abilities required of lower-status "white-collar" workers (who, despite their white collars, increasingly resemble assembly line workers).

Implications for education

As things now stand, most junior college and many university students will get no further in composition than the ability to write more or less "clear and correct" sentences, coherent topic sentences and first paragraphs, and accurate short reports that follow standardized formulas (comparable to the standard five-paragraph essay). In a sense, this "minimal competency" may be an advance over what some students have not been learning, but it is a peculiar type of advance. Similarly, as "general education" and "humanities" requirements are cut, these students will develop cognitive competence only within narrow bounds.

Many students will receive college and university degrees, but not the quality of literacy those degrees traditionally signified. This will be especially true for "nontraditional" students from social groups who began to attend university in significant numbers in the 1960s. To put it bluntly, these students will be (and already are being) lied to and cheated. They will receive degrees that say that they are educated when they will actually be just trained. They will end up in "professional" job categories that have been deprofessionalized. The result will be alienation and anti-intellectualism as these graduates come to realize that their "educations" have neither led to satisfying jobs nor even given them the critical ability to understand their lives or their social universe.

It is easy to see that the type of literacy required by today's increasingly hierarchical and centralized "professional" work would not be produced by the liberal composition pedagogies of the "sixties." Indeed, one factor in the campus revolts of the "sixties" and of the counterculture that paralleled them was the resistance of "middle-class" children to the types of jobs that faced them. A generation earlier, they would have opened small businesses or operated as independent professionals, but an increasingly centralized economy did not provide enough such opportunities. The students of the "seventies," not having been "promised" as much and also having more to fear, were less likely to revolt.

In this sense, the literacy "crisis" seems to have led to a successful "renormalization." Except at the higher levels, the job-structure requires a specialist's literacy, not the type traditionally associated with a liberal education. This type of literacy need not include even the type of critical reading or analytical and persuasive writing abilities one needs to function effectively as consumer and citizen in a linguistically sophisticated, media-dominated environment – let alone the type of literacy we associate with a well-developed, fulfilled, and "rounded" person.

It seems to me that the implications of this contradiction are clear: Educators certainly have an obligation to develop in their students the abilities necessary for financial survival and success in the current vocational reality; but humane educators also have an obligation to educate the whole person for a whole life, not just to train the specialized worker. This contradiction does not create an either/or choice, however. It is possible to teach specialized skills in a critical humanistic context and thus to develop broad cognitive abilities and affective sensibilities. To do so is, of course, to create "overqualified" workers and is in that sense subversive of any dehumanizing job structure. But it does not produce students incapable of functioning in that job structure. (On the contrary, it produces students who can function "too well" in that job structure.)

Both in the high schools and in post-secondary institutions, there is much more writing being taught now than 10 or 20 years ago. Some of these courses hark back to the best humanistic traditions; many more, however, are highly specialized courses that teach not composition but business writing, science writing, report writing, etc. There are increasing numbers of courses that teach students how to write for particular professions – which usually means learning the formats used in that profession rather than grasping basic principles of rhetoric and developing the ability to think for oneself about writing problems and tasks.

This reductive "professionalizing" tendency needs to be juxtaposed with the tradition of humanistic education that stretches back to the humanism of the 14th century European Renaissance and beyond that to classical Greece. One should remember why rhetorical studies began among the ancient Greeks and became the core of classical "higher education," the center of the liberal arts. What the Romans called *humanitas*, what the Greeks called *paideia* were the classical equivalent of liberal arts education (Coe, 1981: v). this meant – and means – the education of the whole person, not just the professional training of a specialist (although it may include that).

Historically, at the beginning of the end of medieval feudalism in Europe, humanism was a revolt against both intellectual and political authoritarianism. It was founded on the belief that people both can and should understand the world and control their own lives. Thus, in the context of its own time and of the social classes to which it was particularly applied (i.e., the artisans and merchants of the rising bourgeoisie), it was an exaltation of human freedom and an assertion of confidence in human abilities. That confidence was the beginning of modern science, but it was also more than that.

The humanists of the European Renaissance looked back, past the narrow interpretations of medieval scholastics, to the classical culture of Greece and Rome. Like those who study anthropology in our time, they came to appreciate how different peoples in different contexts develop distinctive modes of perception and distinct insights. Thus they discovered the basis of intellectual tolerance and empathy.

Rhetoric, too, was founded on a faith in human freedom and abilities. Rhetorical study arose in classical Greece – and nowhere else in the entire ancient world – because political democracy and a legal system based on advocacy made formal speaking abilities important. Given the diversity of ancient Greece, the practical experiences of speaking to particular audiences in particular contexts made rhetoricians intensely aware that not all people are the same or have the same responses.

Rhetoric became the core of advanced education because it was the means by which Greek students could develop and demonstrate their understanding. Writing and speaking remain central to humanistic education today for the same reason: It is only by actively using concepts they have studied that students make those concepts their own. Writing a term paper is a way of exercising one's mind, a way of developing the ability to use – not just regurgitate – what one has learned.

Not only is writing crucial to any modern humanistic education, but a humanistic approach to writing is crucial to the full and proper development of writing abilities. The most basic pedagogical principle of humanism is that students should rely primarily on their own intellectual powers, and only secondarily on authority. This coincides with the well-established educational principle that active learning is far more effective than passive learning. The human mind is neither a blank slate to be written on nor a container to be filled; the human mind is an active intelligence that develops when engaged. Any approach that pretends to be humanistic and effective must ultimately develop students' knowledge of those basic principles that will allow them to make their own critical decisions, to depend on themselves even while accepting guidance from their instructors.

In the late 1980s, test scores will almost undoubtedly show North American students of that period writing better than students of the "sixties." SAT scores seem already to have bottomed out. Improved scores will occur in part because much time and many resources previously devoted to teaching literature (a humanistic subject) will have been transferred to teaching composition, in part because some "discouraged" students will not take the tests, in part because curriculum will be developed and teachers will teach "to the test." What remains to be seen is what qualitative changes in writing abilities these improved scores will actually reflect.

There is little doubt that the educational subsystem will have been "renormalized" so that its outputs will be roughly consistent with the constraints of its socioeconomic environment (and, secondarily, with its political/moral environment), both academically and socially. The relative roles of various educational subsystems will also be "rationalized." Whatever its tertiary functions, the recent literacy "crisis" was not likely to have been declared a "crisis" unless it reflected changes outside the educational subsystems, and the schools will have to adapt to those changes.

But that adaptation can come about in several distinct ways: there is considerable flexibility in the system. It is possible – perhaps probable – that composition teaching will simply be streamlined to produce nothing much more than the hierarchy of developed abilities required to match the new job structure. But it is also possible that broad "rhetorical" approaches to composition, such as the process approach advocated in the second part of this article, will manage to give students the specialized skills required by the economic system while also developing broader intellectual abilities. This is what a humanist must hope for, even though (or perhaps, because) graduates may well then revolt against the types of jobs that seem to await them.

A note on educational politics

In the first part of this article, I have tried to offer a social and historical analysis that, together with a concrete analysis of local events, can be a basis for devising effective social strategies. In the second part, I will offer guidelines that, together with an understanding of local social and educational realities, can be a basis for (re)defining instructional goals and effective teaching practices. But the particulars of educational politics – the actual processes through which teachers and those who control educational policies are motivated to reconceive and modify what occurs in classrooms – vary too much to be dealt with in a general article like this one, which is addressed to an international audience.

This much can be said, however. The quality of teaching changes when teachers change. Experience in both Canada and the United States indicates clearly that handing teachers new curricula and materials is not nearly so effective as engaging teachers in the (re)creation of curricula and materials. In part this is because the teachers know their students, usually better than the "experts" do. Given access to information about up-to-date theories and research findings, teachers can figure out how best to apply such information with particular groups of students. And actively engaged in the process of working out this problem, teachers internalize the new principles and transform their own conceptions of what they are doing. From this transformation flows basic change – bona fide new approaches, rather than the insertion of a few new pedagogical gimmicks into an essentially unchanged conception.

This sort of change becomes likely only when teachers have decent working conditions (i.e., reasonable class sizes; time for professional reading and for thinking and collegial talking; and so forth). Decent working conditions for teachers and active teacher involvement in curriculum development become, therefore, important objectives in educational politics – preconditions for the kinds of curricular changes advocated below.

Teaching writing: the process approach

The process approach of the "sixties" is simultaneously transcended and conserved in the process approach of the "realistic" 1980s. Despite the slogan "back to the basics," a return to the composition curriculum and pedagogies of the fifties is impossible. Current socioeconomic and educational realities are such that we cannot return to approaches that worked only with the "best" students; after all, almost any approach works with the "best" students because the most educationally advantaged students are predisposed to learn – if need be, despite the teacher. The process approach is here to stay (at least for a good while) because more students need to develop more writing abilities than ever before in history, and because a process approach works even with those who are not educationally advantaged. The real struggle will be over what type of process approach: a reductive, technically efficient one that produces specialists well matched to the existing vocational hierarchy, or a humanistically valid one that develops articulate, socially competent individuals.

Changes in the job structure mean that, at any given level in the vocational hierarchy, "overqualified" or "over"-educated workers are not desired by employers. At the same time, more students need to develop writing abilities than ever before in history: Changing social realities mean not only that larger percentages of the population need and/or desire literacy, but also that to function effectively as a worker, consumer, or political and social individual in most of today's world, one needs different literacy abilities than one did in previous generations. Consequently, "nontraditional" students are staying in (or returning to) the educational system.

Traditional curricula and pedagogies are not adequate to meet these students' needs. Most traditional curricula emphasized formal essay writing – which, in the "best" students, developed those critical thinking abilities that are a keystone of any humanistic education. But most students traditionally dropped out of school before the goals of these curricula were achieved, and what evidence we have indicates that even most of the students who stayed did not transfer writing abilities developed while composing essays to other writing occasions (which generally require a much more specific sense of audience and purpose than does formal essay writing).

Even insofar as traditional pedagogies may have been adequate for the traditional curricula and the "best" students, they are not adequate for what needs to be done today. The increased importance of writing abilities for the ordinary person means we need pedagogies that will work with the students who previously dropped out or were relegated to "bonehead English" (where they often did grammar drill *instead of* learning to write). Changing curricular goals means we need pedagogies that put more emphasis on writing as a communicative ability.

That set of pedagogies that we call the process approach meets these needs and will work with all types of students (see Figure 17–1). The process approach, it should be emphasized, is not brand new. It includes methods and techniques English teachers have been using for a long time.

THE PROCESS APPROACH

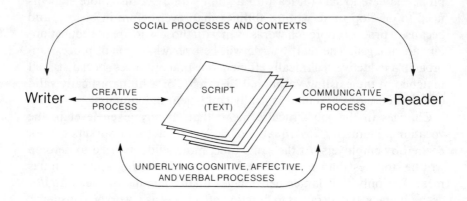

SOCIAL PROCESSES AND CONTEXTS

Writer ← CREATIVE PROCESS → SCRIPT (TEXT) COMMUNICATIVE PROCESS → Reader

UNDERLYING COGNITIVE, AFFECTIVE, AND VERBAL PROCESSES

The teaching process involves *intervening* in the various
processes surrounding and underlying the writing

Figure 17–1.

It also includes methods and techniques that will be new to many
teachers. Most important, it pulls together a variety of methods and techniques, old and new, under a unifying and coherent instructional philosophy.

The process approach, first of all, means that it is not enough to just
show students what "good" writing is, demand that they do it, and grade
them down if they fail. The process approach includes explicitly helping
students develop the cognitive, affective, and verbal abilities that underlie
effective writing and speaking.

The process approach, second of all, means treating writing and speaking as creative and communicative processes. It means guiding students
through the writing process, not just grading their written products. It
means helping them learn how to communicate effectively in various
situations.

If you were teaching a group of adolescents how to play soccer, you
might take them to a professional game in order to show them a model of
good soccer playing. You might spend some time giving them theoretical
information and explaining the rules of the game. But you would spend

more of your time putting them through exercises designed to develop their skills, allowing them to practice those skills in real or simulated game situations, and giving them encouragement, criticism, and advice.

If you were trying to help someone who was having trouble with her tennis serve, you would not repeat over and over again, "No, no! Don't hit the ball into the net." Rather, you would do a detailed analysis of her serving process. Perhaps you would even videotape her serving and look at the tape in slow motion. You might compare that tape with what you know about how professional tennis players serve. You would locate the cause of the problem – perhaps she is tossing the ball too high – and suggest how she should change her process.

If these teaching methods make sense with relatively simple skills like soccer and tennis playing, they make even more sense when you are faced with trying to develop writing abilities. It is not enough just to show students models of excellent writing, tell them to write, and mark their errors. If you understand the composing process; if you know how experienced, effective writers work and how that contrasts with what most students do; if you understand the relationship between writing process and written product, then you can do a lot more to help students learn.

1. Think of writing as a communicative process. In large part because of the traditional ways of making and evaluating assignments, students think about writing in terms of *topic* and *genre* – for example, a comparison/ contrast essay (genre) on the protagonists of *Hamlet* and *Julius Caesar* (topic). Their goal is to produce "good writing." Effective writers think not only of topic and genre but also of *purpose, audience,* and *occasion.* Their goal is to communicate, to accomplish their purposes with their intended readers. They envision the written product as a means to a communicative end. Many of their decisions – about what information to include, how to structure and verbalize it, even what format to use – are strategic, shaped to some significant extent by the communicative context.

If writing is to be understood as a communicative process, every writing assignment should stipulate not only topic and genre but also purpose, audience, and occasion (occasion = genre + situation). The assignment may even include "a soap opera," a hypothetical scenario. In most school writing, of course, this will be a fiction, the equivalent of a simulated game situation during sports practice. If this communicative context is not stipulated in the assignment, it should be generated by the students in class discussion. At any event, by the time the students sit down to write, they should have a sense of purpose, audience, and occasion.

Here are two sample assignments that meet these criteria:

Write a letter (*genre*) to the automobile insurance corporation's customer relations department (*audience*) demanding the restoration of your safe driver discount (*purpose*), which was taken away from you without notice or reason (*topic*) according to the bill you just received from them (*situation*).

Write a research paper (*genre*) on the Canadian Rebellion of 1837 (*topic*) for your history teacher (*audience*) in order to demonstrate that you understand how to reseach and present a historical event and that you therefore deserve a good grade (*purposes*) in your history class (*situation*).

Planning, peer or teacher feedback, revision, and evaluation should be based on estimates of what would be effective in the imagined communicative context. Whenever possible, the communicative context should be made real by "publication" – that is, by actually delivering the piece of writing to readers. The teacher's role is roughly equivalent to that of an editor or supervisor, who estimates the probable effectiveness of a piece of writing before allowing it to be published or otherwise distributed. This is a major change from the teacher's traditional antagonistic role as critic and judge.

2. Consider which underlying abilities are required. Insofar as students do not have the cognitive, affective, or verbal abilities necessary to perform certain writing tasks, a process approach should include activities designed to develop these abilities. A student who cannot make the distinction we call "general/particular" cannot follow instructions to "Include a topic sentence in each paragraph and support it with particulars." A student who cannot imagine the perspective of readers unlike her or himself cannot choose an effective communicative strategy or decide what information will be convincing to those readers. A student who cannot make the distinction we call "abstract/concrete" cannot follow instructions to "Use concrete language for impact."

For each assignment or type of writing, teachers should ask themselves what cognitive, affective, and verbal abilities are prerequisite to doing the writing task effectively. If students do not have some of these abilities, they should be led through activities designed to help them understand the needed concepts and develop the needed skills.

3. Guide the creative process. Like any creative process, writing is well begun by generating potentials: information, images, phrasings, and plans about how they might be used. Since the mid-1960s, the main focus of research on the composing process has been on this aspect, called *prewriting* by D. Gordon Rohman (Rohman, 1965). The tendency to emphasize rhetorical invention as the first phase of the composing process also dominated innovative pedagogy and textbooks in the early 1970s. This emphasis on discovery processes *as an aspect of writing* constituted a concrete criticism of the linear and mentalistic model that suggests that we first observe, second think (and perhaps feel), and third express our thoughts. (Cf. Richards, 1936: Chapter 1.)

But, as Richard Young has pointed out, Rohman's model – "writing consists of pre-writing, writing and re-writing" – is also "essentially linear and mentalistic" (Young, 1976: 17).[2] The implication that discovery precedes real writing remains (as does the implication that revision is something less than a reenvisioning). The underlying error, which has been cogently discussed by Kenneth Burke, is the assumption that a category which is the *logical ground* of another (and in that sense *logically prior*) must also come first in time (i.e., must also be temporally prior) (Burke, 1966: 34–36; Burke, 1950; Burke, 1945).

The writing process

Like any creative process, writing is brought to fruition by a process of critical selection and arrangement. Material must be generated, perhaps using the discovery techniques that have been emphasized by recent pedagogical innovators, and then it must be culled. Like a gardener whose seeds have sprouted and whose young fruit trees are starting to branch, a writer must cut, thin, transplant, graft, prune, and refertilize.

Of course, the two processes – generation and selection – interpenetrate: Writers do not first uncritically generate a complete set of potential meanings, words, and arrangements and then select the ones that serve their purposes. Very often it is precisely the rejection of a phrase during revision that leads to the generation of an alternative. And arrangement – which is properly conceived as an aspect of selection because it is the selection of what to put where – is often crucial, because the pattern of meaning in a piece of writing is often more important than individual propositions. The arrangement and rearrangement of material often leads to the regeneration of that material, replete with the discovery of new insights (Figure 17–2).

The process approach is based on the latest research. We learn from this research that:

1. Most experienced, effective writers do not write the way traditional composition textbooks say one ought to. (Neither do our students, except when we force them to.)

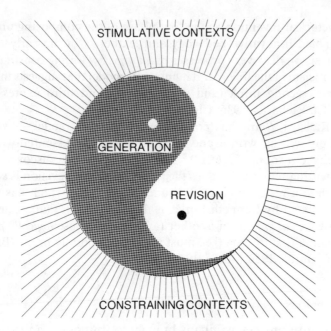

Figure 17-2. The Creative Composing Process.

2. Most experienced, effective writers do certain things that most of our
    students do *not* do.

If we teach our students to do some of the things done by experienced, effective writers, our students will presumably start to produce written products more like the ones those writers produce.

Real writers do not write the way traditional textbooks have said they
should. Often, for example, they do not know precisely what their thesis
statements are until they have finished drafting. Writers as diverse as E.
M. Forster and Erica Jong assert that they do not know what they think
until they read what they have written. Some writers work from detailed
outlines; most do not. Some delay revision until after they have finished
drafting; but most do not draft and revise in entirely distinct phases,
although they generally do revise a lot.

Not all good writers work the same way. But we can, on the basis of empirical research, make certain generalizations:

1. Experienced, effective writers are highly motivated. They usually know
    that what they write will be read. They are trying to accomplish some-
    thing, and they know that whether they succeed will depend, in large
    measure, on the quality of the writing they produce. Most productive

writers write regularly and on a schedule. They may depend on inspiration, but they have ways to encourage it. They may run into writing blocks, but they have techniques for dealing with them. They often indulge idiosyncratic habits, but only because those habits help them get started.

2. The better writers spend much more time generating material than most students do. Often they have organized techniques (e.g., heuristics) for doing so. Most of them also think a lot about purpose, audience, and occasion very early in their writing processes.

3. Experienced writers realize that writing is generative. They expect to get new ideas and insights as they write. They may work from outlines (usually *very* rough ones), but they do not feel bound by them. They know that writing is often a chaotic process and do not expect it to occur in neatly defined stages. They understand, for example, that the search for a better word may lead to the rethinking of a concept and thus to redrafting or reorganization. At best, they try to focus on certain aspects during certain phases.

4. Effective writers spend a lot more time revising than our students do. They see potentials for revision that do not occur to most of our students. Their revisions are much more substantial, and they engage in types of revision our students rarely attempt. They make major additions. They reorganize. They significantly change the substance of what they are saying. They make strategic changes to achieve their purposes more effectively with particular readers.

From these facts, we can draw certain pedagogical implications:

First, we must motivate our students, in part by giving them good reasons to write; in part by helping them perceive their successes; in part by providing opportunities for "publication." We must get them writing regularly, teach them to manage their time, and give them techniques for encouraging inspiration.

Second, we must teach them how to generate words and ideas. We must also encourage them to think of writing as a communicative act that has purposes and readers and occurs in real contexts.

Third, we must guide their writing processes without stifling them, without insisting that they work in rigid stages.

Fourth, we must help them learn how to do major revision, to reformulate as well as simply edit.

Although we know that real writers work more chaotically and recursively, for pedagogical purposes we divide the writing process into six phases:

1. *Motivation*.
2. *Generation* of material and communicative strategies.
3. Selection and composition of that material into a unified and sensible *Draft*, based on the structures of an appropriate genre.

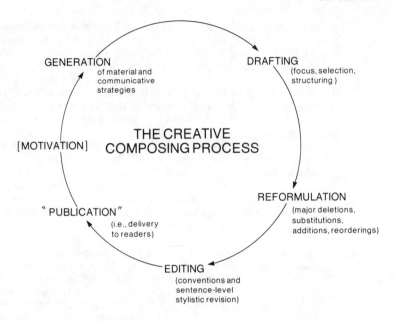

Figure 17–3.

4. *Reformulation* of that draft to make it both more true and more effective. (This should include consideration of possible reorganization and additions as well as deletions and substitutions.)
5. *Editing* for style and conformity with appropriate conventions of genre, usage, grammar, punctuation, spelling, etc.
6. *"Publication"* (i. e., delivery to readers).

Students should be guided through the various phases of the writing process; they should not just be given an assignment and then graded after they complete it. Writing assignments should be accompanied by activities designed to guide students through these phases (see Figure 17-3).

The process approach means that *students spend more time writing,* although in some cases they may actually do fewer assignments. They spend more time generating material and strategies. They are encouraged to do several drafts. They respond to each other's drafts and get advice from the teacher. On the basis of this feedback, they do major revision (if necessary).

It may also mean that *teachers spend less time grading* and more time helping students write. Problems are dealt with during the process rather than in the final product. Students learn how to give each other feedback and, in the process, sharpen their own critical abilities. A more carefully managed process with more revision means fewer errors and weaknesses. Each assignment is dealt with in depth before moving on to the next writing task, which may mean fewer assignments to grade but more learning.

Motivation

If students are to put effort into their writing processes, they must be motivated. In part this can be done via the traditional rewards and punishments – notably grades, praise, and criticism. In part it can be done through the opportunity for some sort of "publication": Just knowing that a piece of writing will be read by someone other than the teacher – even other students in the class – can be a powerful motivator. In part motivation should be intrinsic: Students' awareness of their own progress and successes are sometimes reward enough.

Somewhere toward the beginning of a writing course, however, there should be a class discussion about why anyone should want to learn to write. Such a discussion should cover both humanistic and practical motives. (See Coe, 1981a: 5 – 7).

Generation

To start with a blank page and to finish with a piece of writing is to create. We know two things about human creativity that can help us shape writing pedagogy. First, we know that human creativity typically follows a certain general pattern:

1. A period of hard work, during which information is gathered and the mind focused on the topic or problem.
2. A period of "doing nothing," of incubation.
3. Inspiration (which oftens occurs at some unexpected moment, when conscious attention is focused elsewhere).
4. Another period of hard work, during which the inspiration is developed in detail, criticized, verified, and so forth. (Ghiselin, 1952)

Inspiration cannot be scheduled, so it is important that writers learn to manage their time – and especially, to get started early. Inspiration can be encouraged by gathering information and focusing the mind. Students should be taught techniques for doing this. Such techniques include *talk then write, freewriting, brainstorming, Keeping a journal*, and various types of primary and secondary *research* (*interviewing, experimenting, reading*, etc.) (Coe, 1981a: 36 – 48).

Second, we know that human creativity is often encouraged by what Arthur Koestler (1967) calls bisociation. This means putting familiar subject matter up against a pattern, an essentially (and sometimes explicitly) metaphorical process. For the writer, this often means using a *heuristic*. Most typically, a heuristic is a set of questions for generating information. The most familiar heuristic is the journalist's five W's (*who, what, where, when,* and *why*) which generates the material needed for the lead of a news report or other narrative. Heuristics focus the mind and generate particular types of information. They are more reliable and more easily scheduled than inspiration. Distinct types of writing tasks require different heuristics. Other heuristics include Aristotle's *topoi* (for persuasion), Burke's Pentad (for analyzing human motives), and the tagmemic grid (for description and analysis).

In addition to generating subject matter, writers must also generate communicative strategies. They should ask these questions:

1. What am I trying to accomplish with this writing? (Purpose)
2. With whom am I trying to accomplish it? (Audience)
3. In what situation and using what genre am I trying to accomplish it? (Occasion)

Writing instructors might ask students to hand in a short paragraph (2 – 4 sentences) answering these questions. Here is an example of such a paragraph:

My main point is that dolphins are a wonderful and endangered species. My purpose is to convince readers to support political action to protect dolphins. Most of my readers will by British Columbians. They will read what I have written during a visit to the Vancouver Aquarium, where it will be handed to them as a leaflet.

An estimate of readers' *knowledge* about the the subject, their relevant *attitudes and beliefs*, and their vested *interests* will help students make appropriate decisions about communicative strategy.

Drafting

Creating a draft involves focusing, distinguishing relevant from irrelevant material, developing structure, and generating additional material as needed. In real writing, focus follows from purpose. Selection of which material to include and of structure also follow from consideration of the rhetorical context (i.e., purpose, audience, and occasion). In traditional school writing (which is, in a significant sense, purposeless and context-less), focus is achieved by narrowing to the point where selection is unnecessary; structure is often assigned.

Since the process approach should use assignments that stipulate rhetorical contexts, students can learn how to perceive a writing task as a communicative "problem." They can focus and select information that suits their purposes. They can choose an appropriate genre if one is not stipulated in the assignment.

It is important, therefore, to acquaint students with a variety of forms and structures. They should practice the basic patterns of organization (description, comparison/contrast, classification and division, definition, analogy and exemplification, narration, process analysis, causal explanation, logical progression); they should learn to develop an idea by giving (a) reasons, (b) examples, and (c) implications. They should also learn how to use these basic patterns and orders of development within specific genres (e.g., letters of various types, proposals, reports, essays, formal speeches). Equally important, they should learn how to choose an appropriate structure for a particular writing task.

Revision

When it comes to revision, the differences between what experienced, effective writers do and what most of our students do is stark. There is a lot that we can do to help our students with revision.

Because of the emphases of the past 15 years or so, we as a profession have an adequate complement of techniques for teaching student writers how to generate material. What we lack, partly because we have de-emphasized rhetorical arrangement, is a set of techniques for teaching students how to regenerate material by a process of critical selection and rearrangement.

For most good writers, revision means *reformulation* as well as polishing. They make significant changes in the substance of what they have written: They qualify propositions, add new arguments, etc. They make strategic changes designed to make the writing more effective in a given communicative context. And, of course, they edit: They make minor stylistic changes, correct usage, and so on. Our students usually confine themselves only to the lowest of these three types of revision: *editing*.

In principle, there are two basic types of changes writers can make on each of the three levels:

1. They can delete, substitute, or add. (In principle, deletion and addition are forms of substitution: to delete is to substitute nothing for something: to add is to substitute something for nothing.)
2. They can reorder.

But inexperienced writers rarely reorder. They also do not usually make many additions. Their revisions consist almost entirely of low-level sub-

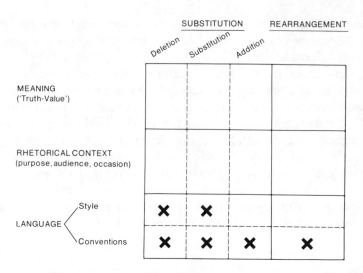

Figure 17-4. Types of revision activities.

stitutions and deletions, largely a matter of trying to avoid "wrong words," "awkward sentences," and mechanical "errors."

Figure 17-4 represents the possible levels and types of revision. The x's represent the predominant revision activities of writers. The process approach includes teaching students how to do the types of revision they presently do not know how to do.

We begin by dividing revision into two separate phases. The types of revision that most students already do we call *editing*. Major revision we call *reformulation*. Pedagogically, we ask students to postpone editing until after they have reformulated.

But they do not know how to reformulate. And most of them, having produced a draft with the number of words required by the assignment, are not motivated to do major revision. To begin with, we must motivate our students to revise more. The texts that good writers produce – the ones we use as models of "good writing" – often flow so smoothly that readers assume those texts must have flowed equally smoothly from the writers' pens or typewriters. This is generally not the case. So teachers should offer students the testimony of well-known writers. Teachers should also show them copies of manuscript pages, such as those reproduced in the Paris Review's *Writers at Work* series, bearing the visible revisions of famous authors. (For a collection of quotations and facsimiles of manuscript pages, see Coe, 1981a: 76 – 80, 82, 87, 92, and 94.) Sometimes teachers should even show their own first drafts.

If the habit of revision is to "take," students must be convinced that the work they put into revision will be rewarded; in large part, that depends on how composition teachers – and our colleagues in other subject areas – respond to their writing. What an editor or supervisor does to a clearly inadequate piece of writing is to turn it back for further revision. This bottom-line refusal is a taste of reality: A piece of writing that will not achieve its primary purpose is pointless in the real world. Students often do not put adequate effort into revision until they realize that. A low – even failing – grade lets the student avoid dealing with problems; a demand for further revision does not.

But motivation alone is not enough. Students often look at a draft and fail to see the cues that indicate revision is needed. Michael Flanigan's article in this volume describes a pedagogy for helping students to help themselves.

Students need to be given questions and techniques that will focus their attention properly. To focus their attention on the level of meaning, one could give them these questions:

1. To what extent is this true? Does it need to be qualified or modified? Have I considered important expectations?
2. What has been left out? Have I considered all relevant aspects of the subject?
3. Does each section relate to the main point(s)?
4. How do I know this is true? What are some good examples of it?
5. So what?

Note that these questions generally lead to additions (and occasionally to reordering). To focus students' attention on the communicative context – assuming that context has already been defined by the assignment or during prewriting activities – one need only ask:

will this piece of writing achieve its intended purpose(s) with its intended reader(s) in the situation(s) where it will be read?

Special emphasis should be placed on teaching students to reorder a draft. Order matters because, as I. A. Richards said in 1936,

Most words, as they pass from context to context, change their meanings; and in many different ways. . . . *It is the peculiarity of meanings that they do so mind their company*; that is in part what we mean by calling them meanings. [Richards, 1936: 10 – 11]

As the work of Francis Christensen made clear, the most important characteristic of a unified piece of writing is the proper relationship among levels of generality. What has traditionally been called unity in writing is created not only by making certain that all particulars are relevant to the general propositions with which they appear, but also by making certain that the order of sentences reflects the inductive or deductive logic of the argument (Christensen, 1965; D'Angelo, 1974; Shaughnessy, 1977: 227 – 257; Coe et al., 1986).

But most inexperienced writers do not know how to rearrange. Their revisions consist almost entirely of low-level substitutions, largely a matter of looking for a better word or phrase. They are unlikely to modify meanings or even reconsider their relationship with their prospective readers, let alone consider alternative arrangements of their material. And yet rearrangement – cutting and pasting – is often one of the quickest and easiest ways to improve a draft.

In the standard textbook rendition of the composing process – (a) find or be presented with a topic; (b) narrow and focus; (c) formulate a thesis statement; (d) collect information and arguments; (e) make a detailed outline; (f) write a draft from the outline; (g) revise for clarity, coherence, and correctness; (h) recopy; and (i) proofread – the implicit assumption is that writers know what they want to communicate, and know what they will use to support their assertions, and know how they are going to organize their material before they begin drafting. The preliminary outline here is not some rough jottings, but a developed outline.

Some writers actually work like this, at least when they are doing certain types of writing. Most do not. If assigned an outline that must be handed in, many students will write the paper first and then derive an outline from it. Such students are on the verge of a useful insight. Outlining can be not only easier but more useful somewhat later in the writing process than the traditional textbooks would have it.

The "outline later" technique is applied after the draft is complete *or* just before the conclusion is drafted *or* at any time during the drafting when the writer is blocked and does not know what to write next. At any of these points, the writer makes an outline *of what is already written*. The purpose of such an outline is to help a writer see the structure of what he or she has been saying. Instead of a messy draft, the student produces a short sentence outline, which reveals the underlying structure of the draft.

All the writer need do is to write down the main point of each section or paragraph, preferably in sentence form. Often these sentences already exist in the draft and need only be copied out. If not, they are relatively easy to compose because they are nothing more than summaries of assertions already implicit in the draft.

To translate this list of assertions into an outline, one must classify them according to level of generality. One marks the most general statements, those which seem to encompass others. The traditional way to mark them, of course, is with roman numerals; or one can follow Christensen and call them level-one generalizations. Remaining statements are then sub-classified (perhaps with capital letters, arabic numerals, lower-case letters, etc.).

The purpose of such an outline is to enable a writer to see what she has been saying. Instead of three or five or ten pages of messy draft, she now has a sentence outline of less than a page which reveals the underlying structure of the draft it represents (literally: re-presents). Since writing is a discovery process, the writer did not necessarily know quite what she was going to say before she said it; now the outline serves to help her see what she has been saying. Looking at that outline on a single sheet of paper, she can see the pattern of what she has written.

This being the purpose, it is important to keep the outline on a single sheet – perhaps by using a very large sheet. For very long writings it may be necessary to make one general outline and then detailed outlines of each chapter or section.

If the writer is blocked in mid-draft, the pattern of what has been written often suggests what else needs to be said and what logically comes next. Because the outline functions as a summary of main points, it often virtually writes a missing conclusion. In either case, it serves to get the writer writing again – serves to help the writer discover the missing part of the draft (Coe, 1981a: 91–95).

After the draft is complete, the outline functions as a basis for revision – which, it must be remembered, includes re-envisioning and thus may involve generating new material or rearranging existing material.

Certain problems can be resolved by substituting, adding, or deleting. Perhaps a more appropriate example should be substituted for one that does not quite work. Perhaps some point has been left unsupported beyond what readers will require to be convinced. Such imbalances in the development of the writing are likely to stand out like proverbial sore thumbs once the writing is outlined.

Other problems may require the rearrangement of the whole writing or of some section of it, perhaps without any substitutions, additions, or deletions at all. This potential for reordering a piece of writing is rarely considered by less experienced writers, even though it is, as noted above, often one of the quickest ways to radically improve a draft. Whole sections or paragraphs can be moved, often literally with scissors and paste or stapler or word processor; and suddenly a seemingly incoherent writing reveals its true unity. The reordered parts usually need to be recemented with new transitions (paste and staples alone will not do), but the logic that mandated the rearrangement often suggests the new transitions. (The preceding 15 paragraphs, incidentally, are not now in the order in which they were originally drafted.)

We have long known, and have recently confirmed with controlled research (Sommers, 1980), that one major distinction between good writers and ordinary writers is the amount of time spent on revision. Less competent writers look at a draft and fail to see the cues that indicate revision is needed and sometimes even suggest the nature of that revision. The outline, applied after rather than before drafting, is a technique that can help writers see those cues. It moves their attention from particular words to the structure of the whole writing. It helps them to see organization – and dis- or mis-organization.

This technique, which implicitly critiques linear models of the composing process, has two major virtues: It helps less experienced writers learn an important revision process, and it turns their attention from the superficial surface characteristics of their drafts to the underlying deep structure – and hence (since the composing process is dialectical) to the structure of their thought processes.

Publication

The final phase of the process approach is "publication." The teacher has functioned as an editor, helping the student write and insisting that the piece of writing be brought to a level of effectiveness where it would "work." Ideally, the writing should now go to some reader(s) other than the teacher/editor. This may mean no more than posting it on a bulletin board in the classroom or handing it to one particular reader for whom it is intended (perhaps a teacher in another subject area with whom a joint assignment has been worked out, perhaps a parent). It may mean submission to some school or local publication. It may mean putting the piece of writing in an envelope and mailing it.

Unfortunately, it is often not possible to arrange publication for school assignments. When publication is possible, however, it brings the writing process full circle: It turns the creative process into a communicative process and thereby provides real motivation.

Responding to students' writing

It is not enough for students to write; they will learn only if they receive useful responses. Teachers should create situations in which such feedback occurs. They also must be careful about the type of comments they write on student papers.

Simple inquiry in almost any North American writing class – including advanced composition courses for third-year university students – turns up this simple fact: After years of having their writing criticized by English teachers, most students cannot state in any precise and useful way just what their own writing problems are. They have had specific errors pointed out to them, and they have made sweeping generalizations (e.g., "I can't punctuate" or "I use 'wrong words'" or even "I can't write"). But they usually cannot say, "I don't know how to use commas with conjunctions" or "I tend to choose overly simple thesis statements."

If students could make statements like these, they would be a long way toward solving their problems. These middle-level generalizations are often the keys to devising solutions.

Consider the following piece of student writing:

The majority of the student alway major in some kinds of field that will help them in the near future. Some of them end up working in factory because of their education. Sometime I say to myself that it really don't matter whether you go to college or not because people with college degree can't even get a good job. Some countrie or manufacture will not hired them because they feel that they will only work for two month and then leaves and they company maybe just lost money.

Thirteen basic mechanical errors in an 87-word composition! This is the sort of writing that leads many teachers to throw up their hands in despair. Once the errors are circled in red, this becomes one of those "bloody" papers that leads many students to give up in despair.

When I have shown this piece of writing to English teachers, however, many of them have been able to diagnose the problem. "English is not this student's native tongue," they say. "This is a second-language problem."

Upon what is this diagnosis based? Ten of the 14 basic mechanical errors involve a single letter: *s*. Two others are common verb-form errors. In short, this student has not mastered the English *s*-inflection and has trouble with certain verb and pronoun forms. The *s*-inflection is particularly difficult for students whose first language or dialect has no analogous feature.

Note what has happened. Thirteen errors have been reduced to three problems, one of the problems has been singled out as the source of most of the errors, and we think we know why that problem exists. A teacher could now write a comment on this student's paper which said something like this:

On the level of mechanics, you have three problems. The most important one, which you should work on first, is the English *s*-inflection.

To solve the problem we need only one more thing: a set of exercises designed to help the student understand and master the English *s*-inflection.[3]

What this example suggests is a strategy for responding to student writing:

1. Locate the errors and weaknesses.
2. Decide which are most important and generalize. In short, *name the problem* for the student.
3. Form a hypothesis about why the problem occurs.
4. Find or devise a strategy for solving the problem.

In school systems that have developed writing laboratories, the solution to mechanical problems may be in the laboratory. In other systems, the solution to mechanical problems may be to refer the student to particular pages and exercises in a handbook.

But precise problem definition is not just for dealing with mechanics. This was brought home to me one September when my stepdaughter came home with a "bloodied" paper. There were about 60 red circles, several *C*'s in the margins, and a comment that read "C+, a good effort." She was upset. I looked at the paper and noted that all the circles were around contractions and first- or second-person pronouns, and that the comma splices were the sort of informal punctuation that might be acceptable in a personal letter. I said, "Oh, the English teacher you have this year wants you to write formal essays. That means no contractions, no *I*'s, *we*'s, or *you*'s, and no comma splices." Then I explained about comma splices. On her next essay, despite carelessly missing a few contractions, she received this comment: "B+, a very good effort."

Let us be clear. There was nothing wrong with what this teacher did. The problem was what he did not do, namely, write a comment that, in addition to responding substantively to the essay, said:

C+. This is supposed to be a formal essay: Don't use contractions, don't use first-or second-person pronouns, and watch out for those comma splices.

(Note that his comment is not a formal essay, so he can use contractions.)

The solutions to student's writing problems fall into five categories:

1. *Time management.* Often students' writing errors and weaknesses result from starting so late or working so slowly that they do not have time to revise properly. The teacher then wastes time marking problems that the students already understand and could have fixed. From this the students learn little or nothing. The solution is to teach them how to manage their time effectively. This is one of the quickest and easiest ways to improve students' writing because it allows them to take full advantage of the abilities they already have.

2. *Awareness.* Many writing problems go away as soon as they are defined and the student's attention is drawn to them. Certain types of problems (e.g., wordiness) are easily fixed during revision if the student just knows what they are and remembers to check for them when rereading his or her draft.

3. *Information.* Sometimes awareness is not enough; the student may also need information (e.g., the rule for using commas with conjunctions).

4. *Specific pedagogies.* Sometimes the teacher must supply a specific technique for resolving a problem (e.g., sentence combining, for a student with a choppy style.)

5. *Intervention in the process.* Often, particularly with major structural problems (e.g., unfocused topics, simplistic theses, inappropriate communicative strategies, inadequate development, lack of support), the best solution is not to teach the student how to fix the problem during revision, but rather to modify the student's writing process in such a way that the problem ceases to occur.

All five types of solutions are part of the process approach, but the fifth is the crux of it.

It should be remembered that no curriculum or approach can by itself solve the literacy problem. The process approach will be most effective in an appropriate context. Among other things, as the United States National Council of Teachers of English asserts, in a pamphlet distributed to parents, this means the following:

1. What happens at school is more effective if the right sorts of things are happening in the home and community. Parents should be informed of what they can do to help.

2. What happens in the composition class is effective if it is reinforced in other classes. If students are not being asked to write sentences, paragraphs, and essays about science, history, and other school subjects, this is not happening. All teachers, across the curriculum, have a responsibility to help children improve their writing.

3. The response to student writing, in all contexts, should be affirmative. Primary response should be to what the student is communicating and how clearly. Every piece of writing has its good points. These should be applauded before weaknesses are criticized. The mechanics of expression, although important, should be emphasized less than ideas, images, and the general effectiveness of the communication.

4. Students should write often and in a variety of forms, for a variety of pur-

poses and audiences. A wide variety of writing experiences is critical to developing effective writing abilities.

5. Watch out for the "grammar trap." Some knowledge of grammar is useful, but too much time spent on grammar steals time from writing practice. A full understanding of grammar is not needed before students start to work on compositions.

6. Encourage publication of student writing in school newspapers, literary magazines, local newspapers, etc. In a broader sense, "publication" occurs any time anyone other than the teacher reads students' writing. Publication makes writing tasks real.

The writing process is a means to an end. Once the process of creation is completed, it is the written text that must communicate. Whether the purpose is to evoke a feeling or to provoke a bureaucracy into taking action, it is the written product that must get the job done. But the quality of the written product depends on the quality of the creative process. A person who is having trouble writing or who wants to learn to write better should focus on the process.

Consciousness of writing as a process makes teachers more effective. It helps students understand why certain qualities make their writing work better and how to imbue their writing with those qualities. Thus a process approach can empower students by giving them control over their writing.

Notes

1. It matters that the boundary cannot be drawn sharply between comprehension and interpretation, between literal and metaphorical senses of "read."

2. More sophisticated recent models of the composing process, based on such notions as recursive feedback loops, are still essentially linear and reductive representations. Writing is more usefully understood as a process of adapting to a complex hierarchy of constraints of various types – a process which evolves toward meaning and communication through this hierarchy, a process of dialectical interactions and supra-linear movements.

3. This writing was a diagnostic theme written at the City University of New York by a first-year university student whose native dialect was Black English (which, like Chinese, has no feature comparable to the English s-inflection. It is published in Mina Shaughnessy's seminal *Errors and Expectations* (1977). Shaughnessy also supplies a series of exercises for teaching the s-inflection.

References

Barthes, R. (1972). *Mythologies* (trans. Annette Lavers). New York: Hill & Wang.

Bateson, G. (1972). *Steps to an ecology of mind.* New York: Ballantine.

Berland, J. and McGee D. (1977). Literacy: the atrophy of competence. *Working Teacher, I*: 1, 2.

Braverman, H. (1975). *Labor and monopoly capital: The degradation of work in the 20th century.* New York: Monthly Review.

Brievik, P. S. (1975). Effects of library-based instruction in the academic success of disadvantaged undergraduates. In H. B. Rader (Ed.), *Academic library instruction.* Ann Arbor, Mich: Pierian Press, pp. 45–55.

Burke, K. (1945). *A grammar of motives.* New York: Prentice-Hall

Burke, K. (1950). *A rhetoric of motives.* New York: Prentice-Hall.

Burke, K. (1967). *Language as symbolic action.* Berkeley: University of California.

Campbell, M. (1978). What price cost-cutting? *The Canadian Nurse, 74:* 7.

Canadian Dimension (1979). "The Labour Process." Special issue of *Canadian Dimension,* 14: 3.

Carry, L. R., and Weaver, J. F. (1969). *Patterns of mathematics achievement in grades 4, 5, and 6: X-population.* Palo Alto, Ca.: Stanford School Mathematics Study Group.

Christensen, F. (1965, October). A generative rhetoric of the paragraph. *College Composition and Communication,* 16.

Coe, R. (1974). Rhetoric 2001. *Freshman English News, 3:* 1.

Coe, R. (1978). The practicalities and politics of error. In K. Reeder and D. C. Wilson (Eds.), *Language, culture, and curriculum.* Vancouver, B. C.: UBC Centre for the Study of Curriculum and Instruction, Monograph Series No. 4.

Coe, R. (1981a). *Form and substance.* New York: Wiley.

Coe, R. (1981b). Literacy 'crises': A systemic analysis. *Humanities in society, 4,* 4.

Coe, R., et al. (1986). Toward a grammar of passages. Unpublished monograph.

Coe, R., and Gutierrez, K. (1981). Using problem-solving and process analysis to help students solve writing problems. *College Composition and Communication, 32,* 3.

College Entrance Examination Board (1977). *On further examination: Report of the advisory panel on the Scholastic Aptitude Test score decline.* New York: College Entrance Examination Board.

Composition 11: Curriculum guide and resource book for teachers. (1982). Victoria: British Columbia Ministry of Education.

Cooper, C. R. (1981). Competency testing: Issues and overview. In Cooper, (Ed.), *The nature and measurement of competency in English.* Urbana, Ill.: National Council of Teachers of English.

Crew, L. (1978). Testing in the style of the Georgia mafia. Paper delivered at the Conference on College Composition and Communication.

D'Angelo, F. (1974). A generative rhetoric of the essay. *College Composition and Communication, 25.*

DeBresson, C. (1981). B. C. Teachers observe literacy crusade: A report from Nicaragua. *Working Teacher, 3,* 3.

de Castell, S., and Luke, A. (1983). Changing paradigms of literacy instruction in North America: Socio-historical conditions and consequences. *The Journal of Curriculum Studies, 15,* 4.

de Castell, S., Luke, A. and MacLennan, D. (1981). On defining literacy. *Canadian Journal of Education, 6,* 3.

Douglas, W. (1976). Rhetoric for the meritocracy. In Richard Ohmann, *English in America.* New York: Oxford.

Fiore, K., and Elsasser, N. (1981). Through writing we transform our world: Third world women and literacy. *Humanities in Society, 4,* 4.

Foster, D. (1983). *A primer for writing teachers.* Upper Montclair, N. J.: Boynton/Cook.

Garson, B. (1981, July). The electronic sweatshop. *Mother Jones.*

Ghiselin, B., (Ed.) (1952). *The creative process.* Berkeley: University of California.

Giesecke, M., and Elwert, G. (1982). "Adult literacy in a context of cultural revolution: Structural parallels of the literacy process in sixteenth century Germany and present-day Benin." Paper presented at the World Sociology Congress.

Greenbaum, L. (1969). The tradition of complaint. *College English, 31*, 7.

Howard, R. (1981, August). Strung out at the phone company: How AT&T's workers are drugged, bugged, and coming unplugged. *Mother Jones.*

Hoyles, M., (Ed.) (1977). *The politics of literacy.* London: Writers and Readers.

Kinneavy, J. (1971). *A theory of discourse.* Englewood Cliffs, N. J.: Prentice-Hall.

Kinneavy, J. (1979). The relation of the whole to the part in interpretation. In Donald McQuade (Ed.), *Linguistics, stylistics, and the teaching of composition.* Akron, Ohio: University of Akron.

Koestler, A. (1967). *The act of creation,* New York: Dell.

Lakoff, G., and Johnson, M. (1980). *Metaphors we live by.* Chicago: University of Chicago.

Lindemann, E. (1982). *A rhetoric for writing teachers.* New York: Oxford.

Lockhart, R. A. (1976). Educational policy development in Canada. In R. A. Carleson, L. A. Colley, and N. J. MacKinnon (Eds.), *Education in a changing Canadian society.* Toronto: Gage.

Luke, A. (1980). Theory, practice, policy, research: Concepts and criteria for 'literacy' in British Columbia, 1920–1940. M. A. Thesis: Simon Fraser University.

National Assessment of Educational Progress (1980). Writing Achievement: 1969–79. *Results from the Third National Writing Assessment.* (Reports Nos. 10-W-01, 02, 03).

Needham, J. (1962). *Science and civilization in China* (Vol. 2). Cambridge: Cambridge University Press.

O'Hare, F. (1971). *Sentence combining: Improving student writing without formal grammar instruction.* Research Report No. 15. Urbana, Ill.: National Council of Teachers of English.

Reed, S. (November 13, 1983). Money and achievement: A mixed bag. *The New York Times Education Fall Survey.*

Resnick, D., and Resnick, L. (1977). The nature of literacy: An historical exploration. *Harvard Educational Review, 47*, 3.

Richards, I. A. (1936). *The philosophy of rhetoric.* London: Oxford.

Rohman, D. G. (1965, May). Pre-Writing: The stage of discovery in the writing process. *College Composition and Communication, 16.*

Shor, I. (1980). *Critical teaching and everyday life.* Boston: South End.

Shaughnessy, M. (1977). *Errors and expectations.* New York: Oxford.

Sommers, N. (1980). Revision strategies of student writers and experienced adult writers. *College Composition and Communication, 31*, 4.

Tang Li-Xing (July 1981). English teaching in chinese secondary schools with special reference to teaching methodology. Unpublished Thesis (forthcoming, under revised title, from the Shanghai Foreign Language Press).

Wilkinson, A. (1971). *The foundations of language.* New York: Oxford.

Wright, E. C. (1977). School English and social order. Dissertation.

Young, R. (1976). Invention: A topographical survey. In Gary Tate, (Ed.), *Teaching composition: 10 bibliographical essays.* Fort Worth, Tex.: Texas Christian University.

Zimbalist, A. (Ed.), (1979). *Case studies on the labor process.* New York: Monthly Review.

18   Collaborative revision: learning and self-assessment

Michael C. Flanigan

In order to revise our thinking and beliefs in any significant way, we need to understand what they are and then analyze and evaluate them in relationship to new information. The new information, of course, must be understandable, and our minds must be open to it. The same is true of writing: To revise a written piece, writers need to be able to recognize what their writing communicates, and then, in light of this information, they can analyze and evaluate it. Additional information about a piece of writing – about what others see in it, or fail to see – also needs to be understandable, openly acceptable to the writer, and therefore accessible to analysis.

Research on the revision process indicates that many students either don't know how to revise or have a very limited view of it, frequently confusing revision with matters better left to the proofreading stage. (Beach, 1976; Perl, 1979). The problem with a student's writing may have arisen at a preliminary stage, if the student's intuitive and empirical powers have not been tapped in such a way that their writing has substance or meaning for them. Ideally, the questions of how students feel, what they care about – what they value, believe in, and have experienced – and what persona (or voice) comes through in their writing already have been explored in the discovery stage of composition. Often, however, even if teachers have had students "freewrite," brainstorm, or use other, more formal heuristic procedures, their first drafts may still be simply a further stage in the act of discovery – the discovery of self, purpose, and audience.

When this happens, as it so often does with first drafts, how do we induce students to change and fully rework a paper that they thought was near completion, on the grounds that we, the teachers, believe it is still in search of an authentic language and self? I don't think we can urge students to go through more invention exercises, at least not before we treat the paper as a text worth attending to. We need to see what is in the

313

paper as represented by the language, including such concerns as its focus, speaker, and audience and the writer's unique perceptions of the world. Not to do so is to avoid the central issue of revision, which is that, in order to re-see, writers must first see what their language reveals to others about their purposes (Lloyd-Jones, 1981).

Now several paths can lead writers to see so that they can re-see. Traditionally students have been taught only to see what teachers see, to see only what we have told them is, or is not, in their writing. Teachers can point out to students that their writing reveals a self that doesn't seem to care, think, or feel sufficiently to invigorate or make vivid their language and their meaning. And so we explain and explain. Impressed by us, and perhaps with a few more ideas about how to focus their papers, students depart. Sometimes our advice takes, and the writer finds a voice. But we all know how much time our conferences consume, and we also know how seldom our comments seem to yield lasting results. It's hard enough to have conferences on final drafts without scheduling conferences on all preliminary drafts as well.

Richard Beach points out that between-draft comments by teachers do make a significant difference in students' revisions, but does such a procedure foster dependence on the teacher or does it eventually lead students to internalize the revision process (Beach, 1979)? Beach's study shows that 10th-, 11th-, and 12th-grade students who were left to evaluate their own papers without teacher support "had difficulty identifying their overall intentions, strengths and weaknesses, or necessary changes." This difficulty in knowing how to employ certain self-assessment strategies may have been due to the fact that the subjects received little prior instruction in methods of "self-assessment." But surely by the 10th or 12th grade students have received "prior instruction" and plenty of comments from teachers about their writing. Why, then, haven't they internalized strategies for revision by this time? The students in Beach's study who received teacher comments improved, and no one should be surprised that they did. But on the next paper, or on one written 6 months later, would they be able to assess their own first drafts any better than those who were left unassisted in Beach's study?

I contend that, although teacher assessment does help students improve their writing, its effectiveness will be short-term unless it is coupled with collaborative, group assessment. Through collaboration students learn strategies for self-assessment; they do so by learning to take responsibility for others' writing and therefore for their own. Revision techniques become the possession of the student, become internalized. Teacher assessment by itself creates dependence in students, further alienating them from their own voices at a point in their education when those voices ought to be emerging. Teacher assessment implies that the teacher knows the best choices to make among language alternatives (in form, content, and style). It continues an overlong tradition that has created the image of the teacher as the authority, the holder of the answers (the truth), who directs students toward a proper (standard) and appropriate language. This passive mode of instruction divorces students from responsibility for their own language; in fact, it divorces them from their language, and their writing becomes someone else's business. The result is that "most of our language choices [become] bland; one can almost say that the objective of the schools is to acquaint all students with the blandest forms of English, the forms of least commitment, the forms of superficial order" (Lloyd-Jones, 1981).

Collaborative learning differs radically from teacher-dominated learning. John Clifford's study (1981) on learning to write collaboratively shows that students learn to revise by its methods, that students gain "the necessary experience of witnessing the reader's need for precise syntactic relations and coherent organization. During the stages of this learning process, students spent time contemplating and reworking ambiguities" (p. 50). By composing collaboratively, students

> were required to give conscious, analytical attention to their own recurring patterns of confusion and to make the necessary adjustments. Vygotsky ... suggests that this kind of "deliberate analytical action" is necessary for coherent writing. The small groups provided a conducive environment for these changes by offering multiple responses soon after crucial linguistic and rhetorical choices were made. This feedback from an immediate, socially appropriate audience also seems to have provided a more compelling impetus to change than the abstract grade rewards typical of the current-traditional paradigm. It is also reasonable to assume that the collaborative composing sequence helped these writers to reduce their anxiety about when to invent, edit and reorder and when to focus on mechanics, spelling and proofreading. Writers learn to accept the inevitable confusion and banality of early drafts only after they have successfully transformed this chaos into edited prose. A holistic perspective of composing provided a reassuring map for those writers unaccustomed to backtracking and circling. By repeating the trip, again and again, they began to see that they were only temporarily stranded. It was also useful for them to understand that those seemingly remote back roads were well travelled by experienced writers. Even in planning their posttests, then, students were better able to control their composing and thus better able to relax and concentrate on crafting their work, "stage by stage." [p. 50]

Learning to write collaboratively is a model of the way most psychologists think we learn. Edwin R. Guthrie writes that "we learn only what we do" (Sahakian, 1976). We do not simply react to stimuli; we act upon them as they act upon us. We transform stimuli (words, drafts), and in doing so we, and our thinking, are transformed. For students to wait for teachers to tell them what to do is to foster dependence, passivity, and boredom and runs counter to what Piaget describes as necessary to learning:

I think... that human knowledge is essentially active. To know is to assimilate reality into systems of transformation. To know is to transform reality in order to understand how a certain state is brought about.... Knowing an object means acting upon it, constructing systems of transformations that can be carried out on or with this object. Knowing reality means constructing systems of transformations that correspond, more or less, to reality. [Sahakian, 1976, p. 333]

Thus, being told what to do with a draft is not enough. For then students learn only that the teacher will tell them what to change, and they will change it; but they themselves remain essentially unchanged. They learn to depend upon another rather than upon themselves.

I have said that in order to revise, writers need to know what they have said. Then, in light of new information (the responses of a teacher or fellow students), they can analyze and evaluate it so that revision becomes possible. I have pointed out that I think a collaborative approach to revision is more effective, and Clifford's study (1981) bears this out. Clifford says in his study that his teachers used "feedback sheets" to guide discussion. Students wrote to each other about what they had read in each other's papers, and their responses were then used by the writers to revise. Of course a good deal of discussion of each paper went on, but essential to the approach were the written "feedback sheets."

I do not want here simply to talk about how to construct revision guides or feedback sheets, because I think any competent reader/teacher can do that. What I'm most interested in is how these revision guides are used in class and how they help students improve their writing in a collaborative setting. I will try to demonstrate the approach by using a student's first draft and then showing how short, structured revision guides may serve teachers' purposes better than the sort of long, elaborate guides beginning to appear in textbooks. At least I think this is true in the beginning stages of a class.[1]

A revision guide should focus on description. To do otherwise, to begin with evaluation, often discourages students or gives information of little use to them. A "good" or "not bad" or "awful" has no point of reference beyond the reader's value system, but an outlined description of what the reader sees in the draft shows the writer what is there, and by implication what is not there. In order for writers to resee they first must understand what others see. After students have described what they see in a draft it is easier for them and the writer to analyze how all the parts of the paper work together or don't. The descriptions may show that the writer has drifted from the point or has not supported it or is still in search of a central focus. Evaluation of the paper's effectiveness will naturally grow out of the discussion that follows. The writer will see what is working and not working, and this will allow him or her to see the paper and its possibilities in new ways.

By teaching students to be first descriptive, then analytic, and finally evaluative, we teach them how to "decenter" themselves, to move outside their ego circle and into the roles of analysis and evaluation before the self is again incorporated into their writing. But by having students concentrate first on their content, rather than fussing with spelling, punctuation, and other surface concerns, we emphasize, with Perl, that what is said is much more important than how it initially appears. The closely centered self, along with its voice, its feelings, is primary to good writing. It doesn't worry about the editor that peers over its shoulder; it is intent on what it has to say and how it feels. Such writing is often the most powerful and communicates what is often the deepest and most rich in our common experiences. Analysis and evaluation must not obliterate the writer's voice; they must serve only to reinforce it.

Another point we need to consider about revision is where – at what stage in the writing process – it begins. In early drafts or "freewrites" or journal entries the writer's central task is exploratory. Writers may be searching for something to write about or trying to discover how they feel about certain experiences or events. Students' writing may go in all directions, so what we need to do in any revision guide is to help them find in their writing what seems most important to them. The following student draft, done after some initial class time spent on an early personal experience, was one from which the student thought she learned something. The teacher (in his first semester of teaching; in fact, this was his first class assignment) had discussed the assignment, had asked students to write briefly in their journals, and then had asked class members to discuss their experiences in a general way in small groups. The next assignment was to write a first draft.

Dad is running for congress. What's congress? Anyway, I just rode in the car for four hours straight and now we're stopping in a town called Silver City. Dad says it's in his district. All I know is that we are going to Joe Skeen's house which overlooks the lake here. Joe is having a Bar-be-que that dad is going to speak at.

We're at Joe's house now, from the backyard you can see the lake. The receding water has revealed the rotted pillars of the dock, which support the heavy boards as if they are nations about to fall. My eyes catch the glare of the reflectant waters, and I shield them from the troubles of the world. Then a voice calls me out of my dream, and I run back to the house, mud between my toes.

There are lots of people here. My father keeps introducing me to them and then they either pinch my face or break my hand, how disgusting.

Joe takes me away from the strangers and teaches me things I would not have known. I learn about government, and what my father is doing. My mind is clearer now, but even so, I am more confused. Why do men argue about borders and kill each other. There are no more new frontiers, we have got to make it here.

I watch my father, I watch him work. He strives to have a hand in running the world, as if something could be done to prevent the childishness of nations, causes for which many men die in vain. But he say's he can try. Maybe someday, so will I.

To keep the focus on the invention stage of writing rather than on organization or style (admittedly, it's hard to separate the three completely), a useful first-revision guide might look like this:

Revising the draft

1. Read the first paragraph. STOP. In a sentence or two write down what you think the paper is going to be about. What will be its center of concern?
2. Read the entire paper.
3. What is the paper's focus? What is it about? Does it have several focuses? What are they?
4. For each paragraph in the paper, write a sentence that tells the author what the focus of the paragraph is for you. (Letter each paragraph: A, B, C, etc.).
5. In a few sentences, tell how each paragraph in the paper furthers or does not further what you think is central to the paper. You might want to circle material that doesn't seem to belong in the paper. Give the writer advice on what could be done to improve the paper.

Additional questions about organization and style could be asked, but at this stage students might be trying to comment on features that will disappear as the writer focuses more on one or two possibilities in the draft. Early drafts, such as the one above, need focus, but in the natural way that discussions proceed, other problems will be talked about, such as its many vague references and generalizations. Students will naturally ask, "What did you mean by this?"

Using the student draft to respond to the first step on the revision guide, some students thought that the paper would be about Dad at the barbecue or about the writer's experiences at the barbecue. One said it could possibly be about something that happened at the lake while the adults were involved with political affairs. All three predictions were possible, but the relationship between the boy and his father appeared central, if not yet clearly developed.

In answering question 3, almost all students saw several possible focuses for the paper, including the boy's view of the world, the problems of government, the pointlessness of politics, how children are treated by adults, and how confusing the world is to the young. And on through the guide they went, describing the paper as really more a series of associations – some of which they wanted to read more about – than a developed, clearly purposeful, piece of writing. They did like its possibilities and noted how the draft was framed by references to Dad, but they were bothered by the voice and language of the writer (some thought it was not authentic throughout).

In the final exercise of the revision guide, almost all students advised the writer to concentrate on the relationship between the boy and his father, or on what Joe Skeen had said and its effect on the boy, or on supplying greater detail about what it was like to attend a political event as a child. Some suggested the paper should not be written in this person. Others wanted to know more about how the father looked, what he said, how he acted. In general, the comments called for richer detail and more focus.

What should be noted in the use of revision guides such as this is that they give students written reactions and descriptive material to talk about. Advice comes after the writer has been shown, from a variety of reader responses, what his writing allows others to see and feel. By responding in writing, the readers must commit themselves descriptively. This allows them to analyze and evaluate their reactions with concrete references to the draft; it also allows the writer to decenter – and to ask what is whimsical and what is purposeful in the first draft.

Many students are unsure of how to respond to revision guides, and it is important for the teacher to thoroughly demonstrate this process with the entire class participating. Each student receives the same draft and revision guide, and the teacher leads the class through it. Students then apply what they have learned as a class to their own and each other's papers in groups of three or five (it is better to begin with smaller groups until the students become more relaxed and adept and can move more easily through the processes of the revision guide). Later in the course, students can take two or three classmates' drafts outside the class, write their responses, and then discuss them in groups at the next class meeting. In addition, revision guides can focus on more and more concerns as students make progress at informal analysis and evaluation. I try to make a different guide for each writing assignment, and frequently students will use several different guides in the course of writing one paper (Flanigan & Menendez, 1980).

Students, then, need to learn that they as writers are responsible for their own language; and they need to be relieved of the paralyzing humiliation so common among young writers who have received only a teacher's authoritative and all-knowing response to their work. Collaborative work emphasizes cooperation and encourages mutual trust among students. It gives them a way to see and to resee with the help of others and moves them from a dependent role to one of active seeker. It points to the fact that authority for their own language cannot reside in another, but must reside in themselves if they are to share their views with the world in writing.

Note

1. For a fuller discussion of how to construct revision guides and the variety of ways they can be used, see Flanigan and Menendez (1980).

References

Beach, Richard. (1976). Self-evaluation strategies of extensive revisers and nonrevisers. *College Composition and Communication, 27* (2), 160–64.

Beach, Richard. (1979). The effects of between-draft teacher evaluation versus student self-evaluation on high school students' revising of rough drafts. *Research in the Teaching of English, 13* (2), 111–19.

Clifford, John. (1981). Composing in stages: The effects of collaborative pedagogy. *Research in the Teaching of English, 15* (1), 37–53.

Flanigan, Michael C., and Menendez, Diane (1980). Perception and change: teaching revision. *College English, 42* (3), 256–66.

Lloyd-Jones, Richard (1981). Rhetorical choices in writing. In Marsha Whiteman et al. (Eds.), *Writing: Nature, development, and teaching.* Hillsdale, N. J.: Lawrence Erlbaum Associates.

Perl, Sondra (1979). The composing processes of unskilled college writers. *Research in the Teaching of English, 13* (4), 317–36.

Sahakian, William S. (1976). *Introduction to the psychology of learning.* Chicago: Rand McNally College Publishing.

Notes on contributors

RICHARD M. COE has taught rhetoric and writing, "American" studies, literature, and literary criticism in Canada, China, and the United States. He has worked with teachers developing composition curricula and pedagogies for the schools and led workshops for various kinds of people, including union shop stewards, concerned with improving their writing and/or their supervision of writers. He has published an innovative composition textbook, *Form and Substance* (now distributed by Scott, Foresman), along with numerous articles on rhetoric, literacy, composition theory and pedagogy, drama, popular culture and literary criticism, including the prize-winning essay "Rhetoric 2001." He also serves as a stringer in Canada for a foreign newsweekly. He is presently an associate professor of English at Simon Fraser University.

MICHAEL COLE is Director of the Laboratory of Comparative Human Cognition and Professor of Communication and Psychology at the University of California, San Diego. Trained as an experimental psychologist at Indiana University, he has done research on culture and cognitive development in West Africa, the Yucatan, and the Soviet Union.

SUZANNE DE CASTELL is an associate professor in the Faculty of Education at Simon Fraser University. She has published a number of papers on literacy, as well as articles on educational history, philosophy, and theory, and she is presently working on a book, *Resisting Schooling*, which attempts to show how systematic deformations of classroom discourse may explain student resistance to learning.

KIERAN EGAN is a professor in the Faculty of Education, Simon Fraser University. He has published articles on education, poetics, and philosophy of history. His books include *Structural Communication* (Fearon, 1976), *Educational Development* (Oxford University Press, 1979), and *Education and Psychology* (Teachers College Press, 1983; Methuen 1984).

MICHAEL C. FLANIGAN is Brown Professor of Rhetoric and Composition at the University of Oklahoma. He has published widely in *College English, Teaching Writing, Journal of English Teaching Techniques, Theory into Practice, Journal of Writing Program Administrators, Association of English Department Bulletin* and other journals. He designed and produced a series of 17 videotapes on teaching, especially on the teaching of composition. He has conducted workshops on teaching and teaching composition at the University of Stockholm, Simon Fraser University, and Gettysburg College and has run workshops for teachers in non-formal

321

educational settings in South Africa. He has developed rhetoric and composition programs at both the undergraduate and graduate levels. His main interests are the history of the teaching of English and rhetoric, research on the revision process, and training college teachers to teach composition.

HARVEY J. GRAFF is one of the recognized international leaders in the historical study of literacy, and a comparative social historian who teaches in the History, Interdisciplinary Studies, and Graduate Arts and Humanities Programs at the University of Texas at Dallas. In addition to numerous methodological, historical, and contemporary articles, his major works on literacy include *The Literacy Myth: Literacy and Social Structure in the Nineteenth-Century City* (1979); *Literacy and Social Development in the West* (1981), also published by Cambridge University Press and forthcoming in Italian; *Literacy in History: an Interdisciplinary Research Bibliography* (1981); and *The Legacies of Literacy: Continuities and Contradictions in Western Culture and Society,* a general history of literacy in the western world, now in production for forthcoming publication. Graff is a recipient of Woodrow Wilson, CMHC, National Endowment for the Humanities, ACLS, Swedish Institute, Newberry Library, and Spencer Fellowships. His interests also include the history of education, urban studies, social structure and population, the family, and theory and method in the humanities and social sciences. He is currently co-editing with Robert Arnove a collection of original essays on *National Literacy Campaigns in Historical and Comparative Perspective* and researching a history of growing up, tentatively entitled *Conflicting Paths: The Transformations of Growing Up, 1750–1914.*

PEG GRIFFIN is a research Sociolinguist in the Laboratory of Comparative Human Cognition. Trained as a linguist at Georgetown University, she has combined extensive experience as a teacher in different cultures (the Phillipines, inner city United States) with sociolinguistic and ethnographic research on the pedagogic process.

SHIRLEY BRICE HEATH, Associate Professor, School of Education, Stanford University, is an anthropologist, linguist, social historian, and student of American literature. Since 1981, she has been a member of the faculty of the Summer Program in Writing of the Bread Loaf School of English, Middlebury, Vermont. Her first book, *Telling Tongues* (1972), traces language policies in Mexico from the colonial period to the present. Her more recent work has focused on the language situation in communities and schools of the U. S. She has taught in primary and secondary schools in bilingual and bidialectal communities, and she has done extensive collaborative work with teachers. *Ways and Words: Language, Life, and Work in Communities and Classrooms* (1983) reports nearly a decade of ethnographic fieldwork in classrooms and working-class communities of the Piedmont Carolinas. She has been awarded fellowships from the Ford Foundation, the National Endowment for the Humanities, and the Guggenheim Memorial Foundation, and she is a MacArthur Fellow.

MICHAEL L. HERRIMAN lectures in Philosophy of Education at the University of Western Australia. He holds a Ph. D. degree from Cornell University and was formerly a high school teacher. His interest in theoretical issues in the philosophy of language led to a desire to view the linguistic phenomenon from the opposite end, via the child's acquisition of language. His recent research has sought some understanding of the child's understanding of language structure and functions. A particular interest reflected in his article in the present volume is in the relationship between the child's conception of language and an ability to control language to express thought. Recent publications include joint editorship of and contributions to the book *Metalinguistic Awareness in Children* (Vol. 15) in the Springer Series in Language and Communication.

WALTER KINTSCH (Ph.D. 1960, University of Kansas) is an experimental psychologist at the University of Colorado. His original training was in the field of animal learning, which he soon abandoned for the study of mathematical psychology and, later, information processing theories of memory and language. Together with his long-time collaborator van Dijk, a linguist from the University of Amsterdam, he published in 1983 *Strategies of Discourse Comprehension* – an attempt to present a comprehensive account of language processing, and a report of some 15 years of research into this subject. Of course, such an account must remain somewhat speculative, and his more recent work has focused on filling in the theoretical detail and strengthening the experimental data base.

ROWLAND LORIMER is Associate Professor of Communication and Associate Director of Canadian Studies, Simon Fraser University. His recent book, *The Nation in the Schools*, examines the role publishing and teacher training play in producing an education system reflective of mass market rather than national cultural values. His present projects include an introductory text, *Mass Communications in Canada*, and a learning materials project describing the role of transportation and communications in Canada.

ALLAN LUKE is Lecturer in Language Education at James Cook University of North Queensland. He has written various articles on literacy and schooling. His current research areas are literacy, reading instruction, and their social contexts.

WALTER H. MACGINITIE was Professor of Psychology and Education at Teachers College, Columbia University, for 20 years, where his field of teaching and research was the psychology of language. Subsequently, he was Lansdowne Scholar and Professor of Education at the University of Victoria in British Columbia. He is now an author and consultant based in Friday Harbor, Washington. Dr. MacGinitie's earlier research included work on readability, language awareness, the predictability of language, and the written language of deaf children. His later work has been in the field of reading. He was president of the International Reading Association, and chairman of the Scientific Advisory Board of the Center for the Study of Reading, and he is the author of the *Gates-MacGinitie Reading Tests*.

RUTH K. MACGINITIE has worked closely with her husband in most of his work on reading. Their most recent studies have focused on helping children who have reading comprehension difficulties and on improving reading comprehension instruction.

DAVID MACLENNAN is a Ph. D. candidate in sociology at York University, Toronto. His dissertation examines the developing cultural authority of psychiatry and psychology in Canada in this century. Though he has devoted particular attention to the role of these disciplines in educational practice, his work addresses developments in the health and welfare systems as well. He has presented several case studies in these areas before learned societies.

JANA MASON is an associate professor in the Department of Educational Psychology and a research professor at the Center for the Study of Reading at the University of Illinois at Urbana-Champaign. She received her Ph. D. from Stanford University, where her studies focused on the reading process, beginning reading, and educational practices in reading. Her publications include *Comprehension Instruction: Perspectives and Suggestions* with G. Duffy and L. Roehler, and a forthcoming book on reading instruction with K. Au.

DAVID R. OLSON   is Professor of Applied Psychology at the Ontario Institute for Studies in Education and Director of the McLuhan Program in Culture and Technology at the University of Toronto. He received his Ph. D. in educational psychology from the University of Alberta. He is author of *Cognitive Development: The Child's Acquisition of Diagonality* and editor of *Media and Symbols: the Forms of Expression, Communication, and Education; The Social Contexts of Language and Thought: Essays in Honor of Jerome S. Bruner;* and, with Ellen Bialystok, *Spatial Cognition: The Structure and Development of Mental Representations of Spatial Relations.* His major research is on the analysis of the relation between the oral conversational language of preschool children and the formalized language of written texts, and Cambridge University Press will shortly publish a volume he edited with Nancy Torrance and Angela Hildyard, *Literacy, Language, and Learning: The Nature and Consequences of Reading and Writing.*

ROBERT C. SOLOMON   is a professor in the Department of Philosophy at the University of Texas at Austin. He is author of close to 200 articles (mainly philosophical), regular newspaper columns, a couple of songs, and numerous books. Books include *From Rationalism to Existentialism* (Harper and Row, 1972; Humanities Press, 1978); *The Passions* (Doubleday, 1976; University of Notre Dame Press, 1983); *History and Human Nature* (Harcourt, Brace, and Jovanovich, 1979; Harvester, 1980); *Love: Emotion, Myth, and Metaphor* (Doubleday, 1981); and *In the Spirit of Hegel* (Oxford University Press, 1983). He is particularly interested in the role of emotions in education and the education of the emotions, and believes that the humanities in general and literature in particular have an important role to play in this aspect of education.

J. JAAP TUINMAN   is Professor of Education at Simon Fraser University and Dean of the Faculty. His academic interest is in the area of the measurement of literacy and the pedagogy of reading. His publications include a number of reading series for elementary and secondary schools and the article on Literacy in the Canadian Encyclopedia.

JOHN WILSON   is a Fellow of Mansfield College, Oxford, and Lecturer in Educational Studies in Oxford University. His main interests are in philosophy and education. He has held various posts, including Deputy Head of a British private school, philosophy professor, professor of religion, and director of a research unit in moral education. He believes strongly that analytic or linguistic philosophy is of vital importance in all areas of inquiry having to do with concepts and language. His main publications in the field include *Preface to the Philosophy of Education* (Routledge, 1979) and *What Philosophy Can Do* (Macmillan, 1985).

Author index

Subject index

alphabet
consequences of, 17, 69–71, 73t, 115–17, 165
as technology of mediation, 113–15, 160
American Indian
Cherokee language learning, 18
languages and writing, 16
American Spelling Book, 92
Amish, 16
Aristotle, 42, 50, 253, 300
Armed Forces Qualifying Test, 64
Austrolopithecus, 112
Ayou (Benin) literacy movement, 216–18
Azande oracles, 156

basal readers, 23, 98, 102–4, 134–6, 140, 212, 257–9, 262
art work in, 213
teachers' guides, 102–3, 136, 259
see also curriculum; reading instruction, skills approaches to
Basics movement in education, 3, 274, 277, 280–3, 291
behaviorist approaches to literacy, 5, 101, 145, 165–6
Berber writing system, 18
Bible, 21, 35, 79, 91t, 93, 115, 132, 133, 233
see also religion
bisociation, 300
"Black English," 19, 282, 310n3
Brazil
literacy and agricultural development in, 219
British Columbia
literacy crisis, 276–8
Progessive curriculum, 5
British Columbia Reading Assessment, 7, 256
Burke's Pentad, 300
see also writing instruction, rhetorical approaches to

Canada
"branch plant economy," 12
cultural colonization of, 92–3, 106–7
functional literacy in, 8–13
historical criteria for literacy, 66t, 67t, 90t, 91t
illiteracy rates, 3, 13n2
schooling in nineteenth century, 80, 89, 92–5
textbook adoption policies in, 137–9
university population of, 276
vocational education in, 93
Canadian Association of Adult Education, 8
cargo cults (New Guinea and Melanesia), 17–18
Carolingian language, 73t
Catholicism, *see* Reformation
Charles XI, King of Sweden, 78, 79
see also Swedish literacy campaign
China
during Cultural Revolution, 270, 278, 282
educational policies in, 281
teaching of foreign languages in, 282–3
Chinese, 282
Chomsky, N., 10
Classical education, 73t
and definitions of literacy, 7
literacy instruction in nineteenth century and, 89, 90t, 91t, 92–5
and oral culture, 70
and rhetoric, 288
cognitive operations, 169
see also language, acquisition and cognitive development
cohesive devices, 261, 267n4
communications theory, 10
"competency examinations," 81
see also standardized testing
comprehension, 121, 310n1